Contents

Yours till Hell freezes

Sir Frederick Ponsonby
Recollections of Three Reigns (1951)

Foreword

Much of my life has been governed by the cold. After leaving the army, I looked around for a civilian job to put bread on the family table. Cold places, cold survival skills and breaking cold world records would, I hoped, do the job.

I spent the early years of my childhood in sunny South Africa, followed by a family move back to England when I was eleven, and the first time I can remember feeling cold was at Eton College, when climbing the great dome of School Hall on a dark, wet and windy November night. This was an activity which, if discovered, risked expulsion. My climbing friend and I had left his old black tailcoat flying from the lightning conductor after a difficult ascent, but on returning to ground level not long before dawn, he owned up to a shocking oversight.

'You will not believe this, Ran, but I think I forgot to remove my name tag. They will know it was me.'

'You mean . . .' I gasped.

'Yes.' He shook his head in disbelief at his own stupidity, and, looking at his watch, hissed, 'We could just about get up there again, remove the tag and be back safe before the breakfast gong.'

'We?' I was incredulous. 'You don't think I'm going back up to get your coat and risk getting chucked out of school, do you? You must be joking.'

But we both made it in time and retrieved his coat. I crept back through a rear window of my school house soon after dawn had broken, with hands numb and bleeding and shivering with cold. My teeth were still chattering in the breakfast queue an hour later.

After school and on leave from the army I dug my first snowhole and spent the night in it as part of a double wager with friends. The bet was that I would not ski up the main busy Aviemore ski run wearing only Y-fronts and ski boots, followed by a night with my girlfriend of that time in the shovelled-out snowscrape on the same piste run. That also proved a cold experience, though now just a hazy memory among a thousand and one other colder nights.

In the early 1960s I joined my late father's regiment, the Royal Scots Greys. We were stationed on the German front line during the Cold War face-off, and I began to spend my annual leaves in Norway, usually with a friend and a canoe. By our fourth visit we had come to know the rivers and fjords of central Norway fairly well. The part of Norway which interested us most was the Jostedalsbreen, which contains the largest snowfield in Europe. Many valley glaciers, forever shifting, moaning and grinding in tortured response to the stresses of gravity, descend from this great reservoir of ice and snow. From the lakes at the base of these glaciers issue raging torrents which race down the valleys to the calmer levels of the fjords and so to the sea.

In 1965 a friend and I planned to canoe from the western mountains to Oslo, starting our voyage immediately below the Jostedalsbreen (or Jostedal Glacier). This river journey proved to be a wild dash through magnificent country, but we had completed less than a third of our intended route when our canoe was dashed to pieces in a cataract and lost.

Despite this failure, Norway still lured me back. Standing at the foot of the Jostedal Glacier before the canoe journey, I had peered up at the great ice cliffs soaring above and wondered what the plateau which caused such glacial outpourings might be like. I had been told that there were routes up to the plateau if you were fit and knew where to look, and that trails existed that led right over the ice fields from the side of the sea fjords to inland eastern Jotunheimen. Once herds of cattle and the famous fjord ponies of

Jotunheimen were driven over these 'drift' trails, for they had formed vital trade links between the coast and inland Norway. I learnt that the last drift of animals was taken across the ice in 1857, but then the gently sloping edges of the glaciers leading up to the plateau began to melt and recede, so that their slopes became too steep and dangerous for the animals.

In 1967, six of us decided to explore this area by following one of the old trails right across the plateau and then canoeing down one of the rivers running east from the Jostedal Glacier. The trip was a disaster, due both to bad equipment and to the poor skiing skills of two of the team. Nonetheless it was my first real taste of ice travel, and I was determined to try other ice travels.

So I did, many times, and in 2013 I was part of a six-man team about to attempt what would be, quite literally, the coldest journey on Earth: a winter crossing of Antarctica. I had spent the previous five years organizing this endeavour. Then my left hand, already sporting five shortened fingers due to amputations a dozen years before, was further damaged by frostbite. The temperature at the time of the injury was –30°C, with a steady breeze lifting the snow around my skis. I had travelled in far colder conditions over many years without any problem, so the frostbite came as a shock, inexplicable at the time.

The journey would now prove out of the question for me, for I knew well that fingers which could not put up with –30°C would prove a major handicap on a six-month journey with temperatures likely to plummet well into the –80°Cs. Forced to return prematurely from Antarctica, I decided instead to share my fascination with the wonderful world of all things cold, and this book is the result.

Chapter One

Three years after the previous Norwegian trip, I had left the army and was planning a new Jotunheimen expedition. My personal fascination was for the hidden trails, the giant ice cliffs and the rushing rivers that issue from the Jostedal's glacial gorges, but this was not in itself enough to obtain sponsorship for a journey there. The days of sponsored exploring to discover new terrain or to achieve a purely physical goal were, by the 1960s, already numbered: most deserts had been crossed, seas navigated and mountains climbed. Even then, few expeditions could hope to get off the ground without sponsorship for finance and equipment, and this support can be hard to get without a sound scientific programme.

What did I already know about glaciers? Not very much. Glacier is a French word but has been the English term for slowly moving rivers of ice since 1744. These rivers of solid ice flow down from high mountain origins in simple response to gravity.

Glaciers are made up of densely packed snow. Beautifully constructed snowflakes, with many different shapes and exotic names, land on the surface of ice sheets as hexagonal crystals. The largest crystals, often the most delicate, fall in less windy conditions with the air only just freezing. On colder, windier days, the crystals often collide and, losing their six delicate 'arms', become mere granules. These soon become weathered, rounded and lie as layers of grains with air pockets initially trapped between them. As more snow falls, the air is expelled from these layers and the grains pack down to the point where they are impermeable and can be described as true glacier ice.

The biggest glaciated area in the world, far larger than anywhere in Norway or even Greenland, is 15 million years old and covers the continent of Antarctica. The largest glaciers are in Antarctica, and 90 per cent of the world's ice and 70 per cent of our freshwater is locked up down there. In many places glacial ice covers, and even squashes, 10,000-foot-high mountain ranges.

Whereas people who live in areas prone to tsunamis, earthquakes and floods are well aware of their vulnerability, the inhabitants of great cities in areas once covered by glaciers feel secure, even when the occasional warning of glacial advances hits the news. And yet, only 10,000 years ago all northern Europe was covered by ice, as was Canada and most of the USA, and this ice has historically advanced and retreated on a regular basis.

For three hundred years, and well into the nineteenth century, Norwegian farmers suffered from the severe conditions of the Little Ice Age. Harvest failures led to death, disease and emigration. The great-grandparents of Norwegians alive today told of mountain chalets and farms destroyed by ice surges. The resulting cold also caused the deaths of 130,000 Finns and the emigration to the New World of 2 million Swedes, one quarter of that country's population. At the same time that the British were sending ships north in 1845, under Sir John Franklin, to find an ice-free trade route from the Atlantic to the Pacific, winter sea ice extended well south of Iceland and enabled Eskimos with kayak 'sleds' to turn up in Scotland.

The slow pace of glacial advances is, of course, reassuring, but the power of glaciers to destroy natural features rivals that of great rivers, or even volcanoes. There are valleys in Greenland, tunnelled by the excavating power of moving ice, which are 8 miles wide, 50 miles long and over 2 miles deep. Although glacial advances are usually imperceptible to the eye of the visiting tourist, there are many with a creep rate of several miles a year, both in the Alps and the Rockies. Sudden spectacular surges have been measured at 300 yards per day, and they can be audible from more than a mile away.

The Jostedal Glacier consists of a high central bowl of ice, with some two dozen outlet glaciers which flow like frozen rivers down to the valleys below, where, once warm enough, the ice becomes water and heads on by way of often turbulent streams to picturesque lakes. Though huge by European standards, the Jostedal is tiny when compared with the world's largest glacier, the Lambert-Fisher in Antarctica, a body of ice nine times the size of Iceland, measuring over 1 million square kilometres. This glacier is 65 kilometres wide and 510 kilometres long, and constantly ferries a vast load of inland ice from the high Antarctic plateau towards, and eventually into, the sea. The power of the moving ice is such that rocks are often sheared off mountain sides and can end up floating out to sea embedded in icebergs.

The Jostedalsbreen, I learnt from our team's glaciologist, Norris Riley, was a small remnant of a vast block of ice that had suffocated most of Scandinavia and literally crushed the land below. Norris, who had previously worked with the British Antarctic Survey in Antarctica, told me of one ice shelf so heavy that it depressed the land underneath it to 2,500 metres below sea level.

One aim of our survey was to measure the exact outline of a valley glacier, which would enable the Norwegian authorities to compare our figures with those of previous surveys and so confirm the ongoing rate of advance or retreat of the ice front. The neighbouring glacier to the one we were to work on, the Nigardsbreen, had earlier in the century advanced into the valley below and crushed farms that were in its way, and in 1953 the Kutiah Glacier in the Himalayas surged forward at the record rate of 112 metres a day, flattening villages and forests. One cause of such events is that periodic climate warming allows the belly ice of a glacier to melt and so travel faster down its valley bedrock. Overall, however, the world's glaciers are retreating, Norris said, with their ice melting faster than new ice is forming, and this has been happening for the last thousand years.

Wanting individuals who could complete the survey and had basic parachute skills, I began to put a team together. Choosing individuals for a polar expedition (or even a simple 'cold' outing to survey a picturesque European glacier) involves a different level of selection from that needed for non-ice journeys. This is a generalization but one based on the principle that a single stupid mistake made below freezing can easily cost a life or lives. So I chose the Jotunheimen team with great care. Geoff Holder, Roger Chapman, Patrick Brook and Bob Powell were all ex-army. Peter Booth was a geologist and Henrik Forss, a Swede, was our doctor.

I made sure that additional parachute training was arranged for anyone who needed it, and top SAS parachuting instructor, Don Hughes, checked on our skills. At his final debriefing he did little to boost our confidence with the summary, 'Thank God I'm not responsible for you lot in Norway. Never in twelve years of instruction have I seen such a collective abortion as your last effort.'

With everything, including parachutes, survey gear and sledges, we drove in three Land Rovers to Newcastle to catch the ferry to Bergen on Norway's west coast.

The day before we left I had received a letter from Ginny, who was at that point my ex-fiancée, saying that she might be coming down from the north-west of Scotland to see us off. I had known her for fourteen years on and off, and we had been engaged for two years before circumstances – mainly my unfortunate addiction to wandering – had made us break things off. Now she was working for the National Trust for Scotland in faraway Torridon and aqualung diving for scallops in the sea lochs in her spare time. She arrived in Newcastle just before we caught the boat and, on seeing her after so long, I knew that there could be no other – as the saying goes – and asked her to marry me as soon as we returned from the expedition.

We drove to a lake below the Jostedalsbreen's northern flank where we unpacked all the gear and made up parachutable bundles. Don Hughes had decided to supervise the drop, which was a great relief to us all. Waiting for the plane to arrive, he summarized his policy of the day:

> You know I'll stretch a point if I can – otherwise I wouldn't be here – but it would be sheer lunacy to attempt the jump if the winds get up. If anyone gets into trouble, pulls too early, and gets blown just a few hundred yards too far, I wouldn't like to answer for the consequences. There's sheer black rock dropping away for four thousand feet, with thermal wind currents scouring the gullies. Get caught in one of those and you'll be dashed against the rock. There are downdraughts too which would deflate a canopy and you'd find yourself free-falling again. I'm not being pessimistic, you know, just realistic. If you were all experts, we might chance the conditions slightly, but you're not much better than beginners. So I'm afraid that it's a question of good weather and not much wind, or we don't jump.

The ice field where we hoped to land was at 6,000 feet above sea level. We would free-fall from 10,000 feet. ITN filmed the jump, which the *Sunday Times* subsequently described as 'The World's Toughest Jump'.

I hit the fuselage with one hand a split second after jumping off one of the Cessna's floats and, temporarily panicked, I spun away in an unstable position, cartwheeling through the air. But by the time I had counted to fifteen (to ensure that I did not activate the chute too high where the wind might whisk me well away from the only safe landing zone), I had achieved the correct spreadeagle position and pulled the red handle. Only two of the team missed the 'safe' ice field, and they narrowly escaped the dizzy drop down the cliffside abyss. Geoff hurt his ribs, bashed his eyes and lacerated his nose. All the equipment was retrieved undamaged, and we camped the night in rare good weather.

In the morning, under threatening skies, we set a compass bearing for the upper reaches of the Fåbergstølsbre, but very nearly identified the wrong glacier. Only through good luck at the last minute did we establish our actual position, and so had to make a long extra journey to the north, flanking several vicious-looking crevasse fields en route. Henrik was the only person with previous experience of ice navigation in crevassed areas.

Our camp, on a rare flat patch of ice on the high shoulder of the Fåbergstølsbre, was sheltered by a prominent group of black rocks. From that point on the next day three groups of 'surveyors' set out to three different commanding mountain tops which surrounded and overlooked our glacier. Each group took a high frequency (HF) radio, theodolite and fluorescent flags on long poles. Once all local mists lifted, the three high points would be established as inter-visible control points around the Fåbergstølsbre ice tongue, which we could then relate to the existing Norwegian charts. One control point lay on the far side of a serrated crevasse field, another atop a rocky precipice and the third on the far side of a deep valley. I went with this last party to help carry their gear, and did not return to the ice field camp for two days.

The climb from the valley back to the camp took me eight hours, and although it felt cold, the rain in the valley did not change to snow higher up. Twice in the blinding rain I took a wrong route up the final rocky buttress below our campsite. The weight of water pouring over the buttress made it difficult to see a reasonable route, and my heavy rucksack did not help matters. Being no glaciologist, I could not understand why, when it was so cold, the sleet and rain did not turn to snow, nor why it did not freeze solid on contact with the ice. True, it was August and the hottest period of the year, but the temperature appeared to me to be below freezing. I could only presume, as I watched the torrents of water gushing from the ice plateau, that the air above the ice was affected by warmer currents from the valley below and that there was just too great a volume of water racing down too quickly for it to freeze.

Worried, for exposure can set in unexpectedly in such conditions, I climbed across to the southern edge of the buttress where it met the ice tongue (though separated from it by a formidable gap) and ascended a steep but firm ramp, hauling the rucksack up after me with a 100-foot length of nylon rope. The thought of a warm tent and dry sleeping bag kept my legs moving, but cautiously, for visibility was low and I was lost.

After visiting numerous possible outcrops leading on to the ice, desperation was in the offing – as no doubt was pneumonia – when I stumbled on our Union Jack lying in a pool. I picked it up and climbed into the wind over a jumble of metamorphic rock. Suddenly the ice rim and the tents were before me, but my relief was tempered by anxiety for the others. I did not call out, for it was painfully obvious that they were absent.

Everywhere lay sodden equipment. The tents were on their sides in pools of meltwater, and sleeping bags, radios, skis and ration packs were strewn about as though abandoned in a hurry. Clothes and ski boots lay quite far from the tents, perhaps blown there by the gale before they became waterlogged. The level snow patch was now just a sloping grey layer of mush.

The faraway group, led by the injured Geoff, would be all right, for there was little or no ice where I had left them that morning and they could easily find their way back down to the gully. But what of Roger and Peter, some six kilometres over the ice on the Fåbergstølsnøse? And Henrik's group on the far side of the ice tongue and crevasse field? For some unfathomable reason they had taken none of the tents, nor any sleeping bags or rations. Even a day-tourist visiting these parts is well advised to carry gear giving full protection from the elements. Both Henrik and Roger were experienced enough to know better than to venture into the ice fields carrying no survival kit. The temperature was now well below freezing point and, together with the strong wind, made for ideal hypothermic conditions.

There was a single strip of damp snow at the uppermost lip of the ice field, and I moved the tents there one by one, cursing as they persistently blew away from my numbed grasp. Grabbing sleeping bags and clothes, I passed them through the entrance holes, knowing this to be of little use, for they were thoroughly drenched. I could see perhaps five yards into the gloom and shouted hoarsely, but my voice was carried away like a jinking feather in the gale. I found the emergency flares and fired some into the mist. There was no reply as I listened intently. I could hear nothing save the chattering of my own teeth, the hiss of moving meltwater and the wind. I called the groups on the walkie-talkie, but again there was no reply. The blizzard intensified outside the soaking wet tent.

We were by no means the first expedition to make such a basic error. On his first Antarctic trip, Captain Scott's diary recorded on 12 October 1903 that there was a need to be less 'careless in leaving our things outside the tent ... Our sleeping bags, with socks ... and other garments, lay scattered about on the ice whilst we were having breakfast when suddenly the wind swept down on us: before we could move, everything was skidding away over the surface.' But in spite of this warning, caution still appeared to be in short supply, for a few days later another series of strong gusts robbed them of a critical item.

The events of that night in Norway might well have proved tragic, due to wet-cold-induced hypothermia. As it was, the six men experienced a night they would never forget and the blind fear which comes from being lost in a dark, frozen world of roaring, yet unseen, water chutes and yawning fissures. Roger's and Peter's diaries later recorded:

> As we dismantled our theodolite at dusk, the mists closed in along with sleet and driving rain. Only then did the stupid mistake we had made begin to dawn on us. The golden rule in such mountains when a mist descends is to stay where you are, erect a tent, and crawl into your sleeping bag until the mist lifts. As the weather had been glorious when we left ice camp that morning and the weight of the survey kit, theodolite and radio had been back-breaking, we had dispensed with both tent and sleeping bags. How stupid we were! There was naught for it but to attempt to reach the safety and warmth of ice camp, but there was one large snag. Between us and the camp, on the direct route we had come by, lay a 600-foot-deep gorge. There was, however, an 8-kilometre ice traverse which flanked this gorge. It was worth a go, for even if we huddled together under a rock for warmth, we would only have a small chance of survival in this bitter howling wind.

The surface of the glacier itself was melting at an unbelievable rate. Where the ice was level, we walked through slush and rotten ice with water well above our ankles. Where there was a slope, black streams had formed which rushed past at torrential speeds. One such temporary hazard was especially impressive, not for its size, but for the velocity of the water hurtling down it. Although only a yard across and about two feet deep, it moved so fast that to have slipped and fallen in would have meant being shot down into the unseen valley below.

We slithered and fell on the ice, sometimes disappearing up to our thighs in glacial streams which flowed across the ice field. No, it was far from pleasant. Peter noticed a couple of drowned lemmings in the centre of an ice field which he felt was significant. I tried not to share his view.

According to my calculations, we should have reached ice camp by about 2015 hours, but as this hour came up, all we could see through stinging eyes was mist and ice. We could hardly tell whether we were climbing or losing height. My heart beat a little faster. Oh my God, have I made a mistake in my calculations? If so, then we are in deep trouble.

At 2030 hours we hit rock which appeared to be running in the right direction, so we left the compass-bearing and edged our way carefully down the rim of the rock. The clouds cleared and we glimpsed for a moment a breathtaking and intense blue sky. Then the mists closed in and it was gone as though but a mirage.

Without crampons, walking on the sloping, moving ice in rubber-soled boots was not easy. We did not dare to rope ourselves together for – if one of us fell – the other would not have held him and both of us would have slid over the edge together. We could not tell where the terminal rim of the ice lay, though it must have been close for the wet crunch of our boots was drowned by the background roar of water pouring off the glacier.

I felt we might be walking around the wrong outcrop – perhaps we had gone too far north and were in the middle of the main glacier; having seen the force of the water melting off the

> ice, I wondered whether the camp had not been completely washed away. Even if it hadn't, we might miss it in the mist, for the successive outcrops of rock were most confusing. Each new bay in the rock-piles looked like the one with the camp. By now finding the camp was the be-all and end-all of our lives. To sleep in a tent with a sleeping bag, no matter how wet, seemed the ultimate luxury. We wanted nothing more than that, and did not think further.
>
> Suddenly Peter pointed to the front and I quickened my pace. 'That's it, I'm sure that's it!' he shouted against the wind. I could not see anything in the swirling gloom. 'Are you sure?' I asked with my heart pounding. 'Yes, I can see the tents.' We ran the last few yards into the camp in our relief. We were numb with cold and awkwardly stripped off one another's clothes, climbed into the tent where Ran was, and crawled into one sleeping bag so that the meagre warmth from our huddled bodies could warm each other's frozen limbs. Both of us had uncontrollable shivers and Ran produced a flask of brandy. It tasted good as it burnt its way down my throat then swelled up with heat in my stomach.

Relieved as I was at the arrival of Peter and Roger, I noticed their poor state, which did not bode well for the other groups. They had crossed over no crevassed ground, however slippery and sheer their route, whereas Henrik's team must pass right across the rotten snow of the moving ice tongue, dangerous enough in daylight. Both Roger and Peter were having difficulty in speaking and, though obviously exhausted, they were shivering convulsively and unable to sleep. Their skin was a mottled green in the torchlight, their lips cracked, and icy particles of sleet clung to their hair. They lay together shuddering and sucking numb fingers. Bob's diary recorded the nightmare experience of his benighted group:

> Reflecting on our plight, I realised we had fallen into a common trap; the day had earlier seemed bright and clear so we had left without protection kit or adequate rations. Now, in a blizzard, we

> faced the prospect of huddling together under our three groundsheets or the equally unpleasant alternative of a blind traverse of the Fåbergstølsbre crevasse field.
>
> What followed was not exactly an argument; we were far too cold and worried to waste time arguing, but – whereas I favoured finding some form of shelter – Patrick was adamant that, with no tent in the freezing wind, we must attempt the crossing. Henrik was undecided but, swayed by our lack of food or dry clothes, agreed with Patrick and the decision was made.
>
> The next four hours were an unforgettable hell. The earlier sledge crossing of the area had been a picnic by comparison, since we had then been able to see the dangers: now they were obscured and increased, for the driving rain had melted all but a few of the remaining snow bridges and those that still existed were rotten and difficult to find in the gloom.
>
> I followed only the black line of the rope as Henrik, leading with his compass, was hidden in the misty gloom. God knows how he managed to sort out any useful bearing from his compass – we were spending more time detouring the black lips of crevasses than heading in any particular direction. I had long since lost any sense of orientation.

This group was also lucky, and finally found the campsite lit by our torch. Bob's diary ended: 'Peter, Ran and Roger were in one tent. We climbed exhausted into another. Everything was wet but at least the wind could no longer cut into us. We polished off a half-bottle of whisky between us, and Henrik climbed into a sleeping bag with me. I shivered uncontrollably for the five hours before dawn; decidedly the most miserable night of my life.'

Having established hundreds of sightings from their control points over the next week, our seven 'surveyors' moved down on to the ice tongue itself. Using crevasse ladders, survey poles and metal stakes, they threaded their way up and down the broken ice like so many flies on a fractured wedding cake.

I sat one night with two others in a tent. Munching an oatcake,

Roger reflected how very transitory and puny man was when seen against so massive, so eternal an element as the glacier. The blue-white mass below us had contemplated the heavens for aeons of time and doubtless would continue to do so for countless years to come. The spirit of the ice must laugh to itself to see our clumsy efforts at recording its movement, its shape and its nature. In a while it would change absolutely and our records would soon be outdated. The ice will continue to alter when we are long since dead, like the lemmings frozen for centuries in its icy veneer.

The Ice Age known as the Pleistocene began 2½ million years ago, and is still with us today. Within its overall existence there are fluctuations of the average temperature on Earth and, in response, glaciers advance or retreat. Advances are called glacial periods; retreats are interglacials.

The last glacial period lasted from the fourteenth century to about 1850. So, whether or not man-made global warming is currently having a big effect on ice the world over, we would anyway be experiencing an interglacial interlude during our lifetime and that of our children. Greenhouse gases do undeniably affect the behaviour of our ice-covered zones, but so too do natural phenomena like volcanoes that cool the Earth down.

In the three years between 1812 and 1815 three volcanoes blew their tops in a major way: Soufrière in the Caribbean, Mount Mayon in the Philippines and Tambora in Indonesia. Over three thousand feet of Tambora literally disappeared, sheared off by unimaginable forces. Twelve thousand of the local islands' inhabitants were killed, many thousands starved when their crops were buried under ash, and dense volcanic dust clouds blocked out the sun's warmth far more effectively than did the subsequent and more famous Krakatoa explosion. Tambora altered global weather patterns and lowered normal summer temperatures by as much as 8°C – enough to ruin crops and cause mass starvation.

Sitting outside the tent in warm sunshine with the others, I pictured the entire Jostedalsbreen as a giant bath and tried to imagine the amount of water, should the Earth warm up a bit, that would result from the melting of an equivalent-sized ice chunk of 600 square kilometres with a height of 300–600 metres.

I was distracted from my thoughts by the sudden appearance of a group of shirtless climbers wending their way up the ice. Three were tough-looking men with ropes and ice axes and the fourth was a young woman, blonde hair tucked up under a peaked cap. All conversation stopped outside our tents. Our group was mesmerized. The girl was very pretty, well tanned like the men she was following, except for her breasts, which swung free as she walked. They were as white as ice. The vision passed on up the glacier and we heaved a communal sigh.

Back at work on the ice tongue, we planted survey poles at 200-metre intervals all the way down the 2-kilometre-long frozen river. Half the team then worked from the top of the tongue downwards with a subtense bar, whilst the others started down at the glacial snout and moved upwards with a theodolite and 16-foot-long measured staves to complete a tachymetric traverse which would give us accurate readings of the complex contour lines of the whole glacier.

Darkness sent everyone back to their tents, and next morning Geoff, with his nose hugely swollen from his parachute jump, gave out bad news. The heavy rainstorm and the resulting ablation had messed up all the previous day's sightings due to tiny movements of the poles. Twenty-four hours later Geoff announced over the radio, 'The ice movement is negligible now, but would you believe this? During the night, all the survey poles have popped out of the holes we drilled.'

So we went back to work with hammers and stakes, replacing poles and substituting new ones where originals had fallen into deep crevasses. I glanced into one such hole. There was no visible bottom, just a faint gurgle from water flowing far below. 'In a hole on a nearby glacier,' Geoff told me, 'village children recently spotted a corpse, and police fetched up the perfectly preserved body of an old man dressed in the style of clothes worn by local shepherds four hundred years ago.'

The work finally complete, two of our group departed down the ice to our valley base with the precious notebooks containing our survey results. We would have followed them, but the tricky terrain would have meant hiring porters to get the heavy and more bulky gear down the precipitous route to the valley five thousand feet below. And we would have needed many hours of good weather as well. So I had hired glacier guides to take us down the Briksdalsbreen, which was the steepest of the glaciers and would, in theory, allow us to use gravity and our ropes to lower the gear on sledges to the base of the Briksdal, where we would have easy road access to our Land Rovers. No porters, no sweat and an added bonus that the 40-kilometre route from Fåbergstølsbre to Briksdalsbreen would follow an original, much-used drift trail.

Our two guides arrived on time but were apprehensive about our plans. Henrik spoke to them in Norwegian and told us that they were prepared to guide us for some thirty kilometres but then we would be on our own. Henrik's diary recorded the guides' worries: 'They advised us not to go down the Briksdal because of the weather conditions. They emphasized the danger from deep crevasses. I agree with them for three reasons. Firstly, it is the maximum melting period with danger of avalanches; secondly, we have no proper ice ladders, no ice nails – only ropes; and thirdly, we have no experience on ice!'

I tried to persuade the guides to make the journey. Henrik translated. One explained:

> Many times I have led people over the Jostedal. I have even skied by myself over its entire length in one journey. But not in such weather as this. You do not know the crevasse fields to be crossed, nor do you know the zigzag route we must follow if the dangerous areas are to be avoided. As to your hopes to descend the Briksdal, there are areas above it which will be perilous to transit, and the ice tongue itself I have never descended: indeed I know no one who has, for the old cattle route has long since fallen into disuse.

The other added: 'I know the weather in these parts – a mist like this may lie over the plateau for days on end and with it you will get the rain. Many of the snow bridges will fall away and, as for the Briksdal, all day and every day it will move with tons of falling ice. If you have any sense, you will abandon what equipment you cannot carry and descend to Fåberg.'

Further discussion ended in compromise, with the guides agreeing that after the thirty kilometres they would advise us on a specific compass bearing, mist or no mist, which would take us to the upper reaches of the Briksdal.

For five hours we sweated, strained and cursed up the endless slopes. Each time we came to the top of a gradient, another expanse of grey mush ice climbed to a misty horizon above us. Yet, when a gap in the mists allowed us good vision ahead, the shimmering white plateau rolled away to the west seemingly flat as a pancake. If there were gradients, they were undetectable. Of the guides, who had gone on ahead, there was no sign; to our front we could see their spoor running on for little more than fifty yards before it faded into the overall glare. I began to wish that I had snow goggles, but they had been lost earlier that week.

A wind howled about us, lashing the sleet viciously into our eyes and lips. We needed more grip with the skis to gain leverage for tugging our burdens but, as time passed and the crust grew wetter, our skis increasingly slid backwards. Just as we tried to pull hard to tug the pulk over a hummock, one of our langlauf skis would slip away backwards, lashing into the sledge and causing the others to curse.

Langlaufing is a type of cross-country skiing that is popular in Scandinavia but practised by very few Britons. Pioneers have tried to enthuse the British with its simplicity and economy, but the countryside and weather conditions in Britain do not favour langlaufing as they do in Scandinavia or Bavaria. Nor, it seems, do we take kindly to a sport demanding a fair amount of exertion and strength when the expanding potentials of downhill skiing are effortlessly available all over Europe and even in Scotland.

One can langlauf in any clothes, so long as there is freedom of limb movement. Specially made boots must be bought with thick rubber soles that protrude beyond the toecaps so that the overlaps can be fitted into metal brackets on each ski. A spring retaining clip holds the toe of each boot in position and the skier can virtually run on flat snow or, with the aid of his ski sticks, up 40° inclines.

The skis are prevented from slipping backwards when climbing by the application of specially prepared waxes and klisters. For every conceivable type of snow there is a different colour of wax, and for each degree of changing temperature a further change of wax is required. But Henrik was an expert at gauging the temperature and texture of the coarse snow by rubbing some in his palms. He selected green and blue waxes and applied them with aggression to the base of our skis, finishing by massaging the now shiny wood with a cork. If too smooth a wax is applied, the skier will slide fast on a downhill stretch but will find climbing difficult, for his skis will gain little or no grip and will slide away backwards, giving a treadmill effect to his efforts. On the other hand, an over-glutinous wax such as a klister resin, which is for wet or slushy snow, might be ideal for climbing but will cause clogging, allowing no free slide at all. When the correct wax is applied, fast movement up and downhill is possible, and once the rhythmic glide of the professional is learnt, distances of over fifty miles in a day can be attained without undue exertion.

Even Henrik did not always get it right. After some seven hours of skiing, he bade us stop: he would re-wax our skis with a klister wax. Thankful for any excuse to rest our aching shoulders and thighs, we crouched down in the poor shelter of the sledge. The others were not visible behind, but our own trail was plain to see, since the whole floor area of our sledge flattened the slush as we passed. Henrik shook his head, running a gloved hand up one of his skis. Then he swore in some other tongue.

'Look at this. The abrasive texture of the surface crust has ruined my skis. It will be no use at all trying to re-wax them, and yours will be the same. New wax must always be applied on to a base wax, not direct to the wood, or it will rub off in minutes. But look – all the base wax has gone and much of the wood has been filed off too.'

He was right. No wonder we were slipping about. The others caught up with us. They too were slipping on the spot, 'tread-milling', as Roger described it, and they had stopped to repair their manhaul harness, which had come apart.

A gradually descending slope helped us for two hours as we slid smoothly, silently, through the yellowish gloom, the driving sleet coming from behind us now, the cadence of its hiss on our anoraks rising and falling with the wind squalls. We changed over our harnessed positions every half-hour, the lead-hauler making sure to look only before him, some five yards in front of his skis, to pick out the blurred marks of the faint piste.

Henrik prodded me with his ski stick and pointed to the left. We stemmed our skis and came to a grinding halt, for there, like some long-sought signpost to Mecca, stood our ice axe where the guides had left it. Scrawled in thin snow beside it were words and an arrow. The letters were almost obliterated, but Henrik peering at them shouted, 'To Briksdalsbreen! To Briksdalsbreen!'

Henrik decided that he would leave us at that point and follow the ski tracks of the guides back down to the valleys. He was the only one of our group with previous glacier experience and his reaction to the guides' advice was that to attempt a descent of the Briksdalsbreen in the prevailing conditions was less than sensible. As a family man, he made his decision accordingly and we all respected it.

Bob moved out ahead of us with his compass. Following him, we moved carefully, finding that the gale was forcing the sledges to the left. Particles of icy sleet stung our cheeks and foreheads, and the murky ether hissed with white pellets seemingly bent on our discomfort. Without goggles, I kept my eyes half-open and my head down, letting Geoff do the steering. I looked behind briefly from time to time: Patrick was there, swathed in mist and often stumbling as he checked Bob's direction on his own compass and called out some new correction from time to time. Of the other sledge there was no sign, but they had our tracks to follow so long as they kept going. None of us wished to stop, even briefly, now: it was far too cold, with the icy blast blowing straight up at us from the crevasse fields down to our right, from where came alarming noises of falling ice, sometimes quite close. I expected at any moment to find the sloping shoulder which we were traversing falling away sheer beneath us.

Bob must have had similar thoughts, for he was moving more slowly now, peering myopically into the gloom and stemming his skis carefully. I did not envy him his guiding role, for a crevasse can remain invisible in the mist until a skier is on top of it. It is difficult to stop quickly on langlauf skis when the surface is hard and icy.

We had been moving for two hours after leaving Henrik when Bob came to a sudden halt. 'Crevasses,' he shouted. 'All over the place. We must have been moving with our eyes shut, for they're on every side.'

The snow bridges in this part of the glacier were firmer than those of the Fåbergstølsbre, but they spanned wicked-looking gaps which ran on for hundreds of yards before tapering to some six feet in width. Only then did snow bridges seal their lips and we could attempt to cross them, our hearts thumping as the whole length of our sledges weighed down on the teetering spans. We knew we should be roped but were too cold, too exhausted, to do aught but stumble on with heads down and shoulders bunched. Slithering skis catching in the crust, we shouted and swore at each succeeding chasm that forced us from our compass bearing.

I called to Bob to stop. We had no idea what lay ahead. We were dog-tired, so we needed to camp before dark and while there was still a flat spot. We were traversing between two great splits, moving on an apparently solid platform as wide as a Roman Catholic altar is long. It offered no protection from the gale, but on the Jostedal plateau it is useless to look for shelter. There was just enough room for our two small tents. Unleashing the taut straps of the sledges with numb fingers was a slow business. With four of us gripping the corners of a tent, the fifth secured it, not with ice pegs, which were immediately whipped out by the wind, but with ice axes pushed deep into the crust. Inside, each of those tents was a pocket paradise.

Towards five o'clock next morning the mists cleared suddenly from below, leaving us as though on the edge of a monsoon cloud. Immediately above us the mists still lay thick, but elsewhere the world was a sun-dappled place beneath a clear friendly sky. The events which followed were best witnessed by Bob Powell, as he was behind the rest of us. His diary records the start of the descent:

> 0545 hours. To our relief the clouds of mist rolled away and revealed a cold clear morning. We crawled from our tents and the whole of the top of the Briksdalsbreen was visible. By backbearings, we established that we were in the position we had hoped for, so we stowed the kit on the pulks, fitted skis and set off on our descent to the Briksdalsbreen's upper ice field. Almost immediately disaster struck, for one of the pulks ran headlong out of control. Roger and Patrick fell sideways, releasing their grasps on the handles as the sledge plummeted into a deep fissure, along with its valuable load. We counted the cost of this loss – one boat, tents and parachutes, six hundred feet of rope, and an assortment of personal and scientific gear, camp beds, lilos, etc.
>
> We continued on down since, despite the loss, we still had all the necessities for the ice descent. We did take the precaution of transferring loose items of personal kit, such as crampons, and all the ropes we had from the remaining sledge to our backpacks. Helmets were donned, and we found a relatively simple route down the next steep gradient. Already, though, the crevasses were more formidable than those at the centre of the Fåbergstølsbre – some indication of what was to come.
>
> No sooner had we congratulated ourselves on the speed with which we had navigated this first pitch – perhaps relaxing at the relative ease of the descent – when the second pulk went out of

control. So heavily laden were the two sledges that traversing crabwise across the slope and having to turn through 180° was sufficient to throw them off balance, and the second one rolled a bare three metres before plunging into a crevasse running parallel with our course. This time Patrick was on the downward side of the pulk and narrowly escaped being caught by the load as it rolled over. Roger was in the traces and was flicked bodily over. Ran and Geoff, navigating some two hundred metres ahead, turned but were in no position to help. We grouped around the crevasse, staring into the depths.

We had by now switched from skis to crampons, and one of the losses in this second incident was six pairs of skis and sticks strapped on the top of the pulk – indeed it was probably their bulk which had unbalanced the load and made it so ungainly. We examined our kit, laying it out on the snow to reassess whether we had the bare minimum for the ice descent. Although much rope had been lost, we decided that we should have sufficient lengths of 300 foot, 200 foot and 100 foot line, if single fixed ropes were used for abseils. Each team member had crampons and an ice axe, and there was adequate food for twenty-four hours.

I winced as I thought of the amount of equipment lost. Perhaps it would have been better to have abandoned it above the Fåbergstølsbre and saved much sweat. On the other hand there had been a sporting chance of successfully lowering the sledges and a chance is always one up on a negative certainty. However, there was little good to be had in worrying about that argument now. At least we still had sufficient gear, it appeared, to descend three thousand feet of ice, however sheer.

Beneath us lay a vast field of jagged ice blocks; a nightmare in blue and white. This was the first icefall. The glaciological definition of an icefall is a heavily crevassed area in a glacier at a zone of steep descent. There would be four more, but only this one could safely be skirted by descending the black cliffs enclosing either edge, for here the rock was broken in many places and the route beside the icefall would be an uncomplicated rock descent, saving valuable hours of light. Time was all-important for, with our remaining rations and all but a single two-man tent lost in the crevasse field, we could ill afford to spend another night on the ice.

A waterfall precluded further movement between ice and rock; a thunderous deluge issuing from the heavens, so it seemed, for the water's source was invisible to us huddled down below. Flashing cascades poured forth from the black granite many hundreds of feet above us, thundering past ice and rock into some bottomless canyon.

Looking carefully around, we saw that instead of the usual giddy divide between rock and glacier, we were faced, through some anomaly of nature's forces, with a temporary bridge of ice spanning the abyss. It looked as if a great chunk of ice had lodged itself in the bergschrund when the last avalanche had descended from the ice face above. Other smaller bits of ice had then become wedged upon the original chunk so that, although the giant block had melted down and might at any moment drop away into the gorge, a complex of crazily balanced smaller blocks led the way before our doubtful gaze out on to the main ice arm. Roger was with me and viewed the teetering bridge leading from rock to ice with equal distaste.

I contemplated the ice bridge as we clung to the rock. I was annoyed by the slow progress of the others. I knew why I felt irritated: I was frightened. I glanced at Roger, but he seemed unaffected by his surroundings. Did he feel that he should be leading us? After all, I had never climbed on ice before, any more than had the others. Our week's clambering about the Fåbergstølsbre was the only experience any of us could boast. A few days ago we had strapped on crampons – probably incorrectly, since no one knew how the experts wore them – and, grasping the alien weight of short ice axes, taken our first steps on the treacherous medium of glacial ice. The Fåbergstølsbre was a gentle slope compared with this monster, both in length and degree of incline.

This was no time for lack of self-confidence. Ice is not so very dissimilar to rock when it comes to methods of descent, and I had spent much of my life in various mountain ranges. The others had not; so I was, I tried to persuade myself, the best qualified to pioneer a route down the Briksdalsbreen.

As the others readjusted their packs and tightened their crampons, Roger tuned the radio and tried to contact the camp far below us. Johnnie, the boss of our vehicle group, answered him. He had bad news; news which he had learnt from some locals earlier that morning and which he had been trying to tell us about ever since. Now, hearing us at last, Johnnie was voluble. He couldn't understand why we had not been told before – since it was common knowledge amongst the local Norwegians – that the glacier we were descending was notoriously dangerous throughout the year owing to its unusually steep declivity, but during mid-August, the period of maximum annual melting activity, it was especially hazardous. Some forty local farmers and guides had walked up to the lake and sat with Johnnie discussing our plight – for such they unanimously considered it to be.

Fifty years ago, they said, a Briton called William Slingsby, a climber of much repute, had managed to scale the glacier; but his attempts at descending it had been frustrated by the falling ice and the impossibility of working out a plausible return route. He had planned his upward route carefully in advance but he could not retrace it once up, for such is the nature of the ice that crevasses may be jumped across in one direction, but often not the other. Going up he could see to avoid the more perilous pitches. Not so descending, for the ground below was dead ground visually.

For half a century the great face had remained inviolate, and then, only five days before our own arrival at its summit, a team of Norway's ace glacier climbers had set out at dawn and, after forty gruelling hours – and an accident when the leader had badly sprained his ankle – had been forced to give up only a thousand feet from the top. Later they were to describe the ascent as their most difficult climb ever. Their achievement was the culmination of months of training and numerous ascents of other tamer glaciers. They acknowledged the Briksdalsbreen to be the Everest of Norway's glaciers They had been equipped with the latest in ice-climbing gear: specially stressed screws and pitons, and periscopic ice ladders for traversing the many wide crevasses which more often than not split the entire width of the glacier.

Johnnie ended with the words, 'All the folk here say you should go back up while you can.' I replied, 'We cannot go back, Johnnie. Both sledges and most of the survival kit were lost this morning. We're virtually out of food, with no spare radio batteries, and only one two-man tent between the five of us. Getting this far has meant traversing a maze of crevasse fields and a long descent. It's unlikely that we would ever find a way back even if the weather remains fine.'

Johnnie, as tape-recorded for ITN film, then said:

> There are already two helicopters on standby within an hour's journey, but Jan Mickelbust here says that they could never do it. For one thing the thermal wind currents up the glacial valley would make it impossible to hover above you and between the narrowly separated cliffs. For another, the helicopter's engine noise and the downward blast from its blades would set off many avalanches and bury the lot of you.
>
> You don't seem to understand that you've chosen the very worst time of year for this. Everything's melting. From down here it's like listening to Tchaikovsky's *1812*. Each new explosion is followed by a minute spume of white spray. Looking at these through binoculars we can see whole areas of the face break off and fall away; chunks of ice bounding down the glacier below.
>
> If you really can't go back, for heaven's sake be careful and take your time. I'll keep the radio open, so let me know if you get into difficulties. We can't actually see you as yet, so I can't tell you much about the conditions immediately below you.

I trod warily on two of the balanced blocks that provided the only visible way down, but both pivoted wildly and I withdrew my questing boot rapidly as from a too-hot bath. There seemed no way over this crumbling ledge. Geoff whistled with low cadence and indicated the far side of the ice pillar. Slithering around it, I found a narrow, but firm block wedged at its base, and I eased round the pillar with caution, for the weight of my pack tended to pull my body outwards. I noticed the pillar was red where I had clutched it. My woollen army gloves must have succumbed to the abrasion of sharp rock and ice and now my skin was also being torn by the file-like surface of the eroded blocks. Ten minutes of intricate movement and I was across the bridge and, cutting holds up the face of the solid ice, climbed on to a narrow ridge where it was possible to belay to a home-made ice bollard.

Bob recorded our arrival below the first icefall in his diary:

> The icefall negotiated, we traversed across to what looks to be the quicker central route. Ran has, by the time I reach the centre, already fixed a double 200-foot abseil rope, and one by one we lower ourselves to the plateau above the final 2,000-foot pitch. The plateau itself is some 400 yards wide, and crossing this is no mean feat in itself. It is difficult to recapture the sheer hard work and time it takes to perform even a simple manoeuvre. The negotiation of the icefall, for example – all carried out with whispered commands, for even a whistle can bring a ton of ice crashing down – took about one and a half hours.

Rushing rivulets flowed down every cranny in the ice and, thirsty with apprehension and fatigue, we lay on the ice to lap up the nectar-like water and bathe bloody hands. It had not been apparent from above, but the plateau was split by a series of parallel fissures. It resembled a ploughed field, with each furrow being many feet deep and from three to six feet wide at the lips. We began to zigzag through this crevasse field wishing that we had but a single ice ladder – or even a sledge – to span these alarming gaps. To begin with the fissures would narrow towards either flank and, by side-tracking to left or right, we could find places where it was possible to jump across the gaps, cramponed feet scrabbling for a hold on landing. But, not halfway across the plateau, we came to a great crack that stretched across the whole breadth of the glacier. No one would volunteer to jump across with a rope: all were apparently still sane.

Looking back to the plateau, I saw one orange figure lying crumpled on the ice, well behind us. 'It's Patrick,' said Roger. 'He's whacked and resting.' Evening was nigh, with the five of us in the middle of an ice wall which at any moment might prove impossible to descend. Already a cold wind was blowing up the gully, and even a five-minute halt had us shivering uncontrollably. We needed sustenance and warm shelter, but had neither. This was no time to rest and my temper flared.

I swore at Patrick, yelling at him to join us at once. This had no immediate effect on him, but the echoes of my voice melded with the booms of responsive ice falls above and below, adding weight to my urgency. He got up, teetering as the pack settled on his shoulders, and plodded on in a daze to join us. Roger, Bob and Geoff descended into the gloom and I lowered their packs to a narrow rock ledge on a separate rope.

The ledge was scarily narrow and water from the cliffs above dripped down the backs of our necks, but at least it went in the right direction. We followed it for three hundred yards and assumed that we must have circumvented the great fissure which had blocked our way on the surface above. The rock ledge kept its level of incline, but the glacier ice began to descend rapidly and was soon well below our little ledge. Dusk arrived with scant warning, and a freezing wind blew steadily up the Briksdalsbreen. Even if we could get back down to the ice, it would be unwise to do so in the poor light. We agreed to spend the night on the ledge, there being no reasonable alternative.

We had a single tent designed to sleep two average-sized soldiers in comfort, so long as they had lilos or soft ground beneath them. We brushed the wet gravel from our minuscule camping ground, erected the tent and crawled inside through the small entrance flap.

What a squeeze. It was too cold outside to do aught but take spare clothes from our rucksacks and leave them wedged against the rock, together with vital ropes and axes, in the hope they would not be blown away.

The maddening business of removing boots from swollen feet with numb and bloody fingers was conducted inside the tent, one man at a time, whilst the others laughed at his ineptitude. Blood began to return to our toes and fingers with a painful throb. There was nothing to clean them with, for no one was willing to leave the shelter of the tent for water, but Patrick produced some evil-looking yellow cream from his anorak and this we applied to the raw areas of our fingers. The tin's instructions were in Norwegian, so it could have been ski wax. Whatever the cream's true purpose, its effects were agonising and my fingers kept me awake much of the night. Patrick, Bob and Geoff had tough civilian gloves, and their fingers were but slightly cut. Roger, like me, had army woollen mitts, so his hands were also raw and swollen.

'Good heavens!' said Patrick, with unusual animation. 'It's my birthday today!' He was allowed an extra dessertspoonful of the mashed curry gruel which Roger prepared in the centre of the tent: this meant two spoonfuls instead of one, and three sips of weak tea instead of two, for we were each rationed to a fifth of one man's 'dehydrated meal'. We knew that tomorrow we must find a way down the steepest section, the last two thousand feet of the icefall: the famous 'avalanche icefall', which tourists from all over the world come to see, recording the drama and beauty of the tumbling ice for their home movies.

We decided that we would sleep like sardines – one up, one down and head to toe. This made for more room, true enough, but our hips were jammed solid in the middle of the tent. Furthermore, with due respect to Patrick and Geoff between whom I was wedged, so overpowering was the aroma from their four feet that I was soon nodding off, despite the nearby crunch and rumble of the ice.

After two hours in this 'black hole of Calcutta' I awoke with someone's bony hip jabbing my ribcage, to find I could hardly breathe. I knew I might vomit. Even the freezing wind outside might be an improvement, but how to extricate myself from the tightly packed bodies without waking them? Being a captive in my sleeping bag, it was impossible, and foul mutterings from unidentifiable mouths followed me as I retreated through the tiny entrance hole.

Much was my embarrassment when I found that the ledge on the Briksdalsbreen was so cold that even the evil atmosphere back inside could only be an improvement. During my brief absence from the tent, the other four had fallen asleep again and seemed to have swollen. I tried to drive a foot between two of the bodies as a thin end of the wedge, but there was no room at the inn and I spent the night outside, regretting my lack of staying power.

Dawn came cold and clammy, creeping up the deep blue surface of the icefall. Breakfast was three-quarters of a biscuit: exactly three-quarters, for I checked carefully lest there had been a mistake and I was due the whole. A tin mug full of steaming water well boiled with used tea bags was passed around under Bob's stern eye. Should a drinker's Adam's apple jerk more than once, or the tilt of the mug be too acute, Bob's large hand would strike and the mug passed to the next man. I had visions of scrambled egg and fruit juice.

Hands ached and refused to operate efficiently with bootlaces, zips and rope coils. Blisters squelched and complained bitterly at the first pressure of boot leather. Geoff's ribs were as tender as ever, but he was up first and, lying along the ledge to peer downwards, he pondered our next step. He decided on a long abseil down the sheer wet rock to another ledge nearly three hundred feet below which protruded from the cliff so that it lay over and above the ice, bridging the bergschrund neatly though precariously.

There was a 300-foot length of rope coiled around Bob's rucksack which Geoff used, securing it by a sling and carabiner to a hefty boulder on our ledge. The descent was unnerving and served to jolt us wide awake, stretching stiff limbs and bringing unwelcome feeling to our hands. To prevent rope-burn, my tattered gloves being worse than useless, I wrapped socks around my hands. These were soaked in blood on my breathless arrival at the guttering below but, for the first time since the previous morning, my hands felt warm and the throbbing had ceased.

Patrick was unusually quiet, although his progress was as noisy as ever, loose rocks and gravel particles showering down on those of us below as he jerkily descended the rope. He must be a brave man, I thought, for he had a strong dislike of heights, and that first abseil was of a decidedly exposed nature. Our rope reached the ledge with some fifteen feet to spare. Geoff's estimation had been precise, but the view from above proved misleading, for although our narrow platform effectively bridged the bergschrund, it was higher above the ice than we had thought. To jump from rock to ice would be suicidal, even with crampons, since the surface was hopelessly fractured, being the jagged spoil of many previous ice falls lying poised in unstable confusion over a criss-cross network of fissures.

The sun was not yet over the mountains, and the narrow ledge where we clung to the wet granite was a dank, chilly place. The ice below looked, to my inexperienced eyes, totally impossible. It was a hostile area of innumerable death traps, where one step on an ill-balanced ice block would cause a whole delicately poised platform to collapse into the void below. A noise, too, might be enough to set in motion the tumbled fragments from above and bring them bounding through the air to sweep the face and fall to the unseen lake a thousand feet below. I shuddered involuntarily and looked upwards over my shoulder. The rope swayed gently, running out of sight up the slimy cliff. We could not get it down – a fact which delighted Bob whose load was that much lighter. We would not get back that way, I mused, so we had no choice but to descend, having thoroughly burnt our boats.

It was getting cold standing tight against the rock and staring at the frozen waterfall of ice so near to us, yet so unattainable. Again Geoff's keen and practical eyes found us a way out. There was, he said, a series of sharp runnels in the rock running diagonally across the cliff to our left as we faced the ice. If we could make our way down by way of them, we would reach a point where a large tumble of ice had jammed over the bergschrund. This, Geoff felt sure, was our only way out, up or down. Patrick, following behind in his usual unsteady fashion, lurched up to the obstacle and verbally indicated his reluctance to follow such a precarious route. 'You must be joking,' he muttered, inspecting the route indicated by Geoff. 'A monkey with sticky fingers would look twice at that.'

I must have somehow annoyed Patrick at that point, for I sparked off a violent soliloquy which indicated very clearly what he thought of the whole proceedings. I was accused of being totally unaware of the perils of the situation, of abusing his friendship by deceitfully luring him on to the expedition with false promises of trout fishing in Norwegian lakes and little physical discomfort, apart from the odd night in a tent. Once this indignant tirade had abated, Patrick obviously felt better and crabbed his way past us to inspect the rock face.

Only the sharply eroded runnels in the granite provided holds. Some were too smooth to grip, but with a fist clenched within them, good chock-holds served to keep us from falling away from the bluffs. We clung like limpets to each little hold, cursing the outward pull of the rucksacks and sweating at the thought of what lay below. But we made it and reached a hollow in the rock on a level with the giant blocks of the icefall. Here we strapped on crampons and loosed the ice axes from our packs. And so began the most hair-raising morning of my life.

The upper cliffs of the Briksdalsbreen are at no stage predictable, but at least their dangers can be minimized with care and common sense. That is no longer true when one comes to the bottleneck region which crests the final majestic sweep to the lake, a sheer thousand feet of brittle ice swept by avalanches throughout the summer months. From the first few testing steps over the icefall, it was obvious that only luck would see us safely down the next unstable gradient.

I halted abruptly as a grinding rush of smaller fragments slid away below me, to disappear as though through a trapdoor. Where they had been, a deep blue cavern lay revealed, and the rectangular block on which I crouched lurched sickeningly, slipping towards the newly opened hole with other bigger blocks moving beside it. I wanted to scream or shout or something, but stopped instinctively. Another block, sliding down before mine, moved across the gap and plugged it.

For minutes we surveyed the chaotic scene below. Layer upon layer of fallen blocks were scattered crazily between tall chiselled pillars. The blue sheen of newly fractured ice was covered by a coating of moist black gravel, for the alluvial muck of the bergschrund higher up had spewed some of this mud through diagonally inclined fissures and down to the ice cliffs below.

A thunderous roar sounded above us, coming immediately after a report much like a pistol crack. I ducked instinctively, wondering if the entire face would be covered by what was to come. The shoulder on which we kneeled seemed to shudder and vibrate as the whole ravine reverberated with sound. A squadron of Concordes passing directly above might have produced a similar volume of sound, but I doubt it. All around us the smaller ice fragments slid away as the first great chunk bounded past, well to our front. Then the main body of pounding, gyrating white boulders passed with alarming speed, sending slivers of glinting ice all about us. As the initial pulsating roar passed away, echoes and re-echoes pursued the mother sound down the enclosing cliffs of the gorge till silence came and we looked at one another, saying nothing.

It was already ten o'clock, and the sun would soon climb over the mountains. Then we would be in trouble, for the melting process would accelerate ice falls. Already the little mountain track far below was moving with pinpricks of colour: the first tourists from Loen trekking up from the roadhead to watch and photograph the fabulous icefalls of the Briksdalsbreen. The thought was ironic. Here we were, dreading the next fall, praying that the sun delay its climb, whilst down below, on the far side of the lake, the tourists gaped up, impatient for an avalanche, the bigger the better, and wishing the sun was up. They could not know that five fellow humans were moving snail-like down this wall of death.

Patrick, in the middle of the rope, had disappeared through a heap of loose ice shale. Now he dangled somewhere below the surface. As Geoff reached the area of the slide, he slipped and further fragments fell in on top of Patrick, one large block closing over the hole to form a tomb. Geoff began to haul on the rope with Bob's aid. Patrick surfaced a few minutes later, numb with cold but unhurt.

Using two short ropes joined together, we descended a cliff below the tumbled section and found, to our dismay, evidence of fresh falls across the entire width of the glacier. Only immediately beneath our cliff was there a narrow couloir of smooth unlittered ice, and here we rested briefly, flinching as each successive crack and rumble shook our perch. Now at last we could see the lake, or rather that half of it farthest away from the glacial snout, and watch the slowly gyrating ice floes sailing towards the outlet torrent where they jammed its mouth, fighting for release into the fast current.

Johnnie's diary describes his reflections whilst observing our descent:

> There were many local guides and farmers in groups round our Land Rovers, watching the little dark figures on the ice face. I also met the four Norwegian climbers who had tried to scale the glacier three days before. It had taken them twenty-four hours, they had had a slight accident and had been forced to abandon the attempt before reaching the final 1,000-foot pitch. They had then descended by a rock trail – possibly the route Henrik had taken.
>
> I read a translated local newspaper describing their feat: 'The four climbers had wanted to climb the Briksdalsbreen for a long time, but only this year, they say, have they pulled enough guts together to see it through. They have been climbing a lot around Norway, both mountains and glaciers. Among glacier experts the Briksdalsbreen is said to be the most dangerous one in Norway, and this is no doubt the reason that it has been left so much in

peace by climbers. The four soon discovered that the least dangerous area was the centre where there were less avalanches. The glacier was full of cracks, the biggest ninety feet deep and thirty feet wide. They had to descend deep inside some in order to pass. In places the ice was so solid that they could not use regular nails, but they were well equipped . . .'

On meeting these four climbers, I asked them what they thought of our team's chances. It was dangerous, they said, there were too many avalanches. Did our party have all the right equipment? I said that they had many feet of rope, but no ice screws. This was not wise, they said. If they were to make the descent, they would try to climb up first to mark the best route, and then come down. But to descend it unseen, that was most unwise. Overall, the locals gave our team little chance of getting down alive. Either the avalanches would get them, or lack of the right equipment would. This was not very cheering, but I was not unduly perturbed at this stage.

Watching the painful progress of the small figures down the glacier was an exciting experience. There was the feeling that at any moment an avalanche would obliterate them. They were at the glacier's mercy, no matter what route they selected, and by the lake the crowd of Norwegians and tourists watched in silence: the tension had communicated itself to them. Someone with binoculars had noticed a rope hanging near the top of the glacier, presumably abandoned the day before. I wondered how much rope they had left; perhaps they would not have enough to complete the descent: then what?

The sun was moving on to the very face of the ice as we watched. By using binoculars, I could almost identify the individuals. It was like a cine film. Suddenly there was a tremendous cracking noise, followed by a rumble: huge lumps of ice could be seen bouncing down the glacier, shattering as they went and triggering off further falls. At the sides, avalanches rolled down with regularity. It was the speed that was terrifying to watch: within seconds of the first crack and boom, tons of ice swept

> down the almost vertical slopes. Anyone in the path of these falls would have stood little chance. During the morning no one in our team was hit, though on occasions I saw ice blocks pass uncomfortably close to them, blotting them from view.

On our ledge the sun was making itself felt through the weight of our sweaters and anoraks. We rolled our sleeves up and drank our fill from the dripping ice. There was a feeling of unreality about that morning. Glancing at the others, I thought Bob showed signs of actually enjoying himself, unlike the rest of us. Reading through his notes on the expedition later, I noticed that he had given considerable thought as to the varied motives that drove each one of us. He felt that personal background had little effect on a man's reasons for proving himself: illegitimacy might help to trigger off the ambition of a Lawrence, but he did not think the vagaries of our respective parents had impelled any of us on to the ice; three of us came from military families, one had a mining father, and another a steelworker. This, Bob mused, had influenced us little. Rather it was our individual outlooks on life that had prompted our presence on the glacier. During a lifespan there are highlights in everyone's memories which they try to recapture: some get their kicks from drugs, perversions, or financial gain; others from conquering the elements for the thrill of it. And the more hostile those elements, the more treasured will be the memory of dangers narrowly avoided.

Falling away beneath us for some seven hundred feet, an ice wall of great frozen chunks reached down to the lake. Geoff felt that we would only manage this region in relative safety by firm speedy action. He had a 400-foot length of thin red Marlow Terylene and, while he checked and uncoiled it, we hacked away at the base of our ledge with axes, making narrow grooves to anchor the rope as firmly as possible. In the absence of ice screws, home-made bollards were a relatively safe alternative.

The rope made ready, we hurled it into the abyss. For fifty feet it was visible, snaking straight beneath us, then it disappeared over a bulging shoulder. Henrik's voice came over the radio then, advising us that the rope had snagged in a deep crevasse: anyone descending it would be trapped. Geoff tried again, this time throwing the coils well to the right of the ledge. Henrik confirmed that the rope now hung free, its end hidden from his view but in the area of a small ice platform only three hundred feet above the lake.

That abseil was possibly the most perilous passage of the descent, spanning as it did some four hundred feet of broken ice, which might or might not hold firm at each descending bound of our roped bodies. We went down wearing our rucksacks, for these could not be lowered separately in safety. Bob and I reached the platform without mishap and descended another 50 metres clear of the rope end for safety's sake. The others were invisible for a while, then Patrick appeared sliding down the rope at speed. Geoff came next, and Roger appeared over the lip as Geoff reached the central marked tag. They were sliding easily, smoothly down, when – without warning – a wide area of the ice face between them teetered briefly, as though in slow motion, and then, as a numbing roar marked its fracturing, came rushing down the gully towards us. I glimpsed Patrick flinging himself flat as the great mass of ice rolled over his ledge, cascading down the couloir to our immediate right.

Geoff's language was imaginative when he reached us. He was lucky to be alive, but we were all badly unnerved. The lake was close now and the very proximity of success seemed to amplify the dangers. Some way past the platform, I was belaying Bob down a gully chimney when I heard a scream of pain. Scrambling back up to the platform, I found the other three bunched together in a huddle. Patrick was pressing ice against Geoff's leg, and Roger was unravelling a dirty bandage. It transpired that Patrick had been swung off balance by his rucksack as he edged down the face of the bluff. He had fallen on to the ledge below where Geoff was waiting, and one wildly flailing crampon had dug a metal spike into Geoff's skin, scraping down along the bone.

Calling for advice from below, we were counselled by Henrik to move to the left flank of the snout and descend on to the steep slipway which runs between the bergschrund and the crevasse field.

Henrik warned us of its character: 'It is a steep shoot of loose ice and muddy slime lying over a smooth surface. All day we have watched successive avalanches channelled from above crash down it into the lake. But if you wait for a calm spell and go across fast, one by one, you will reach the ledge of rock which flanks it.'

'What happens when we get on the ledge?' asked the ever-practical Bob. 'It looks like a dead end to me.' But Henrik had also thought that out. 'Its far end is directly above the lake, perhaps two hundred feet above it. If you have rope left, abseil down and we will collect you by boat.'

Two ice falls sounded high above, and we watched anxiously as the avalanche spoil hurtled by, bounding down the dark chute as though it were a skittle alley. One by one we moved over that treacherous slope, as fast as we dared and the loose surface allowed. As Bob joined us at the far edge of the chute, God had the last word, a sort of Amen to a day of pent-up tension. The rumble of distant thunder grew ever louder from out of the gathering gloom of dusk. Then the whole grey slipway shuddered under a deluge of rushing ice spoil, as a railway vibrates beneath a passing express.

Our very last rope took us down to the waiting rubber boat with a grinning Johnnie at the helm. 'I never thought you'd make it,' he said.

Reaction began to set in as we landed on the far side of the lake amongst a small crowd of reporters, television men and locals, all interested to see the faces of the little orange figures they had been so keenly observing. Soon we would be back in England and would return to the daily grind of nine till five. None of us would forget the Jostedal, the special noise of falling ice, the roar of pounding water or the rush of freezing air on leaving the aircraft as you plummet from 10,000 feet.

Two weeks later I married Ginny. We had loved each other for ten years, and certainly since well before the age of consent. Neither of us had money in the bank nor a job, but she was lent a bothy in Wester Ross for a minimal rent and we lived there whilst I wrote a couple of books. We agreed to make our living through expeditions.

After Norway I found myself addicted to ice and was determined to learn all I could about extreme cold, about the great polar explorers, indeed about all aspects of the wonderful world below zero, for which the Jostedal experience had served as the first stage of a long apprenticeship.

Chapter Two

At first, the expeditions that Ginny and I planned and organized lacked the sort of major ambition which would switch us from the comparative ease of temperate climate challenges to our true goal of pioneering polar records. The reality of our financial constraints (in other words, being on the breadline) led to our first three projects having no polar involvement at all. Then, late in 1972, Ginny came up with her first polar-oriented idea.

At that time there were still a few places on Earth where no human had trodden (or even seen, since satellites were yet to orbit the polar regions). Ginny's tentative suggestion was that we navigate Earth's circumpolar surface without flying one metre of the way. Our route, where possible, was to follow the Greenwich Meridian, or the north–south line of longitude 0/180°, for some 37,000 miles, passing through both poles. Little did we know that this project would involve both of us full-time for the next ten years. We would need an ice-strengthened ship, a resupply aircraft with skis, and, as it turned out, £29 million in sponsorship plus a team of 52 volunteers, many with specialist skills, who would give up at least three years of their lives unpaid.

One of Britain's polar veterans, gurus and an ex-director of Britain's only active body in Antarctica, the Falkland Islands Dependencies Survey, Sir Miles Clifford, represented the negative reaction of the UK's polar establishment when he responded to our plan without enthusiasm: 'You are saying, Fiennes, that your group will, in the course of a single journey, complete the great journeys of Scott, Amundsen, Nansen, Peary, Franklin and many others. You must understand that this sounds a touch presumptuous, if not indeed far-fetched.'

We clearly needed some sort of official status and an office base from which to attack all the relevant official bodies and government departments, especially the Foreign Office who would, we knew, stand in the way of any proposal for a private expedition to Antarctica. Our only income was from my Territorial Army unit, the 21st SAS Regiment, based near Sloane Square in London. I approached my commanding officer. Would he approve our project? If so, would he loan us an office and storage facility in the barracks?

When a captain in the Regular SAS six years before, I had been arrested for blowing up civilian property with army explosives. So my Territorial SAS boss, who had not forgotten my indiscretion back then, agreed to lend us the requested support only on condition that the officer who had originally sacked me from the SAS, Mike Wingate Gray, became the official boss of the Transglobe Expedition (as Ginny had by then named our endeavour). This was agreed, and the two of us moved into a redundant indoor rifle range in the attic of the regiment's HQ.

On the six-inch school globe which Ginny had originally used to plot our route, the Arctic Ocean sector was clearly a greater obstacle than the Antarctic ice cap because sea ice, blown about by winds and currents, was bound to produce more problems than static land ice. Or so we assumed. We agreed that if, as we suspected, the Arctic obstacle was indeed the worst problem, we must leave it until last. This, of course, would entail heading south from Greenwich through Europe and Africa by Land Rover and thence by ship to Antarctica, which we would traverse with either dog teams or some form of snow machine. On reaching the far Pacific coastline, we would be collected by our ship and taken north to the Arctic. How we crossed that would be an issue to solve later.

I was assigned the task of studying every minute detail of all those expeditions that had previously attempted to cross one or other of the two great icy features. Locating data on previous crossings of the Arctic Ocean was not difficult, since only one team in history had successfully managed the journey of 3,800 miles (6,100 kilometres) over moving sea ice: the team led by Britain's Wally Herbert in 1968–9. Wally Herbert had completed his polar apprenticeship with the British Antarctic Survey (BAS) and had gained an impressive reputation as a field leader and surveyor with dog-team expeditions. Since leaving BAS, he had led major expeditions of his own in the Arctic and Antarctic, to the point where, when I approached him, he was undoubtedly one of the top polar explorers in the world.

In 1968, with three others and 34 huskies to pull their sledges, Wally set out from Point Barrow in Alaska to attempt the first ever journey across the semi-frozen Arctic Ocean via the North Pole. Before departure he told the press, 'Man has crossed all the deserts, climbed the highest mountains, probed the oceans and space, so only one pioneer journey is left on the surface of the Earth – a journey across the top of the World.' He added, 'I think the appeal of this trip is, in every sense of the word, the bigness of it – in time, in distance and as a challenge – a challenge of human endurance.'

Wally, knowing all about the behaviour of Arctic currents, estimated the total distance to be covered at 3,800 miles, including the effect of the strong currents drifting the ice floes over which his team would move their heavy sledges. In darkness for twelve hours a day and moving over fracturing sea ice, they eventually made it to a substantial-looking ice floe where they set up a winter drift camp, some three hundred miles short of the pole. In April 1969 they reached the North Pole with a desperate race on their hands in order to make faraway Spitsbergen before summer conditions rendered the ice floes too soggy and fractured to travel over. In the nick of time, Wally's men achieved the great traverse which was a major chunk of Ginny's plan.

Wally's answer to my request for his advice on the viability of our plan and on the best means of transport pulled no punches. 'The partnership of man and dogs', he wrote, 'is the safest form of surface travel in the Arctic Ocean when beyond the range of light aircraft ... If a dog dies, he and his food supply are eaten by his teammates, and the team carries on.' But he also stressed that we should not use dogs unless we were prepared to dedicate a year or two to learning how to handle them.

Another great dog-team leader, with both Arctic and Antarctic experience over four decades, was Dr Geoffrey Hattersley-Smith, who had also worked with light snow machines along the edges of the Arctic Ocean. He was adamant that his dog teams could move a great deal faster over rough sea ice than could any type of snow machine. 'Dogs do not refuse to start at low temperatures, nor do they have breakdowns and waste days, even weeks, of good travel time as a result.'

Ginny, a dog lover, agreed that we would not be able to afford the time or the money for two years learning doggy tricks. And, she pointed out, our expedition would, of necessity, be under some public scrutiny and the media can be quick to spotlight any real or imagined cruelty to animals. Our intentions might be humane, but the results could easily misfire. One of our most helpful polar advisers, Colonel Andrew Croft, a man of great polar experience from the 1930s and 1940s, had once completed the longest unsupported trip across Greenland. On returning to the UK, he readily admitted to the press that the only way he had made it was by feeding his weaker dogs to his stronger dogs, a truth which, he later admitted, he wished he'd never shared, given the public's outrage over such matters.

So we decided that the ice caps, both north and south, should be attempted with some form of machine. Not dogs, ponies or, especially, polar bears (as Amundsen had once envisaged).

I was now convinced that the Arctic Ocean crossing, which had taken Wally two summers and a winter to complete, would be our greatest hurdle, and since our journey was already looking like three years of travel, we really ought to find a way of crossing the Arctic in a single year. This meant finding a new route that would be quicker than Wally's.

I looked at Ginny's planning globe and found only one possible alternative to the Wally route. Instead of setting out over the sea ice from Point Barrow in Alaska, I drew a pencil line from Barrow east along the whole northern coastline of Alaska and Canada; it then zigzagged its way between various islands to Ellesmere Island in the far north. If we set out seawards from the most northerly point of this island, where I noticed a place with an airstrip called Alert, the distance was far shorter to the pole than from Point Barrow. This meant that we could probably reach the pole with time enough left in the summer of the same year to travel on down to Spitsbergen and meet up with our ship on the ice fringe somewhere east of Greenland and roughly where Wally's team had been collected by the Royal Navy. I put this to Ginny and to our SAS boss, Mike Wingate Gray. Both agreed that we should also try to work out how we could make it to our ship if we reached the pole too late to make Spitsbergen in the remains of summer.

I had learnt of a little-known voyage made in 1937–8 by a Soviet Union team. Even back then the USSR considered all territories to their north to be theirs, and in order to find out about the behaviour of the Arctic ice drift patterns, they had air-landed a team of four under the scientist Ivan Papanin on a North Pole ice floe. The main idea was to see where they would end up, and thereby to work out plausible navigation options for future commercial and naval operations.

After a dangerous flight and landing at the pole, Papanin and his team of three began a 274-day float in a prefab hut built on an old floe that gradually broke up as it headed south. En route they discovered an underwater mountain range and had encounters with bears. As the remnants of their floe eventually approached the northern shores of Greenland, they clearly needed rescue. The first ship sent to find them became trapped in the ice, an air balloon failed to locate them and two Soviet submarines could not surface anywhere near them. Eventually a small ski plane evacuated them and they returned to Moscow as heroes.

When the Second World War ended, the scientific results of their long, icy float were published, and in 1974 Ginny and I deduced from their data that, assuming the currents which took Papanin's men from the pole down to the Greenland Sea were unchanged, we would eventually be floated out of trouble if we did reach the pole later than planned.

A year after Ginny came up with her idea, we had worked out a travel schedule which should stand up to scrutiny by the Foreign Office experts. Its final link was the Arctic drift pattern, as proved by Papanin. We would go from London south through Europe and Africa, and our ship would drop us off where the Greenwich Meridian hit the coast of Antarctica. For eight months we would wait out the dark super-cold winter in some insulated prefab, then complete the first one-way-only crossing of the frozen continent, an area bigger than China plus India.

Our ship would then collect us from the Pacific coast and take us up the Greenwich Meridian past Australia and California. Before entering the lethal ice zone north of the Bering Strait, we would leave the ship in small inflatables, ascend the Yukon River and then follow the Mackenzie River to its mouth on Canada's northern coast, just east of Point Barrow. The next section, the Northwest Passage, might prove a stopper if the ice conditions that year were severe, but if our boats were small enough and had ice skids, we could haul them over ice floes. Thence to the North Pole and finally the Papanin float.

Mankind had reached the moon, yet nobody had ever been vertically around the surface of our own planet. In terms of the main historic overland polar journeys, Norwegians were the first to the South Pole, Americans to the North Pole, and the double prize of first to both poles was yet up for grabs. My Minnesota-based sister told me of four Americans who had, just before Wally Herbert's trip, reached the North Pole over the ice, possibly the first team ever to do so. One of them, Walt Pedersen, was now hell-bent on making it to the South Pole to become the first man to reach both poles by surface travel. He had a few years' start on us, planning-wise, but we might still beat him to it.

Our favoured route for the thousand-mile stretch across the Antarctic – along the Greenwich Meridian, from the point where we would spend the eight-month Antarctic winter to the South Pole itself – turned out to be literally unknown to man. I was keen to avoid such unexplored areas, since they could present show-stoppers, such as huge crevasse fields or monster regions of sastrugi, high walls of ice cut out by the prevailing winds like furrows in a ploughed field. So I investigated the possibility of switching to the only known traverse route, that of Vivian Fuchs and Edmund Hillary in 1957–8. Fuchs set out from Shackleton Base on the Weddell Sea some eight years after he and a colleague had decided to copy the traverse plan drawn up by Shackleton forty-three years before.

Shackleton's plan involved two separate expedition teams: his own from the Weddell Sea and, in another ship, a group who would drop food dumps off for him between the pole and the far Pacific coastline. The Fuchs plan also relied on a subsidiary expedition, based from New Zealand, who would lay depots along a marked route from the coast (near Scott's old hut) to the pole, by way of the Skelton Glacier. Sir Edmund Hillary, of Everest fame, was to lead the New Zealand team, using Ferguson tractors. Fuchs himself planned to set out from the Weddell coastline, having set up a scientific base there, then climb to the inland plateau, establish a second base and then go hell for leather for the pole and the Pacific coast in what he knew would be a tight race against the onset of winter.

In 1955 Fuchs' ship, a Canadian sealer, the *Theron*, entered the Weddell Sea and, after a difficult 33 days smashing through pack ice, unloaded a mass of equipment on to the sea ice, two miles from the ice edge. Two flights from open water leads were made by a little Auster floatplane, and two new mountain ranges were discovered. The ship then left in a hurry, for the danger of entrapment by ice, as had happened to Shackleton's *Endurance*, was extreme. Eight men stayed behind on the ice to establish Shackleton Base over the coming winter.

The eight men lived in a metal ship container whilst sorting out 300 tons of gear to move to safer ice. A blizzard trapped them for a week in the comfortless container, and when they were able to emerge they found many vital supplies had disappeared, open water channels were perilously close and the nearby stores still with them were buried under tons of drifted snow. By the time they had dug out, moved 'inland' and constructed their prefab wintering hut, it was almost 'summer'.

In November 1956 Fuchs and the main UK-based team sailed south in the Danish ice-strengthened ship, the *Magga Dan*, which reached Shackleton Base far more quickly than had the *Theron* the previous year. After completing a thorough and valuable science research programme, Fuchs and four others, in three Weasel vehicles and a Sno-Cat, headed south over the heavily crevassed Filchner Ice Shelf and then up to their South Ice Base, which had meanwhile been established some three hundred miles towards the pole by twenty cargo flights.

Two dog teams moved ahead of the snow vehicles to reconnoitre the best way through the crevasse zones and sastrugi fields. Overall speed was 3½ miles per hour, and the steel-link tracks of the heavy vehicles often broke through the snow bridges spanning deep crevasses. Light alloy ramps, hours of heavy shovel work and ingenious winching systems somehow saw all vehicles through to the high crevasse-free plateau, but way behind schedule.

A message came from the Hillary team, who had decided to ignore pre-agreed arrangements to remain at the upper limits of the Skelton Glacier and wait for the Fuchs team to join them there. Instead, they had raced on to the pole and become the first team since the days of Amundsen and Scott to get there overland. Hillary advised Fuchs that when he did reach the pole, it would be too late in the short polar summer to carry on to the coast, so he should wait at the pole until the following summer or risk serious trouble. Fuchs was naturally unhappy with Hillary, to put things mildly, but he kept his cool and eventually made the traverse just before winter closed in.

The South African Ministry of Transport sent a ship every year to Sanae, their country's scientific base, which was, by happy chance, almost astride the Greenwich Meridian where it crossed the

Atlantic coastline of Antarctica. I wrote to an old school friend in Cape Town who had spent a winter at their base, and he assured me that the inland plateau could be reached with far fewer problems from Sanae than from the base which the Fuchs expedition had used on the Weddell Sea side of the continent. Our planned approach to the great circumpolar challenge was almost complete.

Our most approachable and experienced Antarctic adviser, even in the early days when no other polar person would be seen dead involving themselves with our project, was Dr Charles Swithinbank, whose Antarctic credentials as a glaciologist were without equal. His many Antarctic activities had included membership of the 1949–52 Norwegian-British-Swedish Expedition which explored deep into the continent, a two-year attachment to the great US base of McMurdo, and a year at the Russian base of Mirny. By the time Ginny and I first met him in 1972, he was working at the Scott Polar Research Institute in Cambridge. The exact route we were to take in Antarctica was largely based on his advice.

So, using information garnered from the experiences of Fuchs, Herbert and Papanin, with additional advice from Andrew Croft and Charles Swithinbank, we had made up our minds on exactly how we would become the first people not only to reach both poles and cross both ice caps, but the first to circumnavigate the entire vertical surface of Earth.

How long would this 37,000-mile round-Earth journey last? There were certain immutable obstacles which no cunning detours could avoid. Neither ice cap could be crossed in winter, nor could the Northwest Passage. The Yukon River was only navigable when ice-free. So, even if all went exactly to plan, we would be away for three full years before completing the full circle back to Greenwich.

It was a nice idea but, as each day passed, year after year, and we received ten negative replies for every cautious yes, the idea remained just that: my wife's pipe dream. A married couple with no funds and no polar experience but with an ambitious idea which, given some £30-million-worth of support in kind, might become a reality, would need to convince many influential people of the viability of their scheme. We were soon to discover that we would get nowhere fast, especially in the two polar zones, without the approval of the Foreign and Commonwealth Office (FCO) and, in particular, their Polar Regions Unit (or polar desk), an offshoot of the Latin American Department.

We could never cross Antarctica without support from those countries that operated scientific bases at the beginning and end of our proposed route, namely the South Africans and the New Zealanders. Plus, at the South Pole itself, the Americans. None of these countries' polar authorities would move a muscle for us without the nod of our own FCO. For the next four years we battered our heads against an unyielding wall of officialdom, until at length Dr John Heap took over at the polar desk. He could not and would not break FCO rules, but he said he would advise us how to plan things in such a way that he would be able to give polar desk approval, once we had assured him of our full competence. He also advised us to put together a committee of Britain's polar godfathers and gurus who would act in a similar capacity to non-executive directors of a business corporation. We started to recruit such a committee, and Sir Vivian Fuchs became, soon after his retirement in 1973 following many years as director of the British Antarctic Survey, the most influential of our committee members.

Our preparations ignored the 'hot' parts of the world, for Ginny and I had already planned and completed journeys in Oman, the Sahara and on the Nile. Everything we now discussed centred on the polar regions, on cold-weather gear, on the effect of cold, of snow and of ice on people and equipment, even on the metal in teeth fillings.

In the Welsh mountains during winter weekends we selected our team from a great many applicants. Ginny's plan involved a ship's crew to deal with the Atlantic and the Pacific, an air crew for a ski plane for resupply only, herself as base boss and radio expert, and two men plus me actually to complete the entire 'vertical' journey without flying one metre of the route.

We advertised for volunteers in free-space magazines. First to apply was Oliver Shepard, who looked overweight. He was a Chelsea area salesman for Whitbread beers. Then came a rugged-looking ex-infantry soldier, Charlie Burton, and Geoff Newman, fresh from a job in a printing firm. Mary Gibbs was a part-time secretary who applied to join us as nurse and mechanic. Of the many applicants who we checked out over a three-year period, these four were the pick of the bunch, though not one of them had been anywhere cold.

We all joined the Territorial Army (TA) in line with their sponsorship of our barracks office. Charlie and Geoff were accepted as TA SAS troopers. Ollie and I were captains. Ginny and Mary, respectively, joined signals and nursing units. Because Ollie was the only one of us with 'A' levels, he was selected to be trained for any skill we might require that needed a reasonably high IQ. He took numerous courses. On 25 April 1976 his diary recorded, 'I am now a Doctor.' On 18 May, 'I am now a Dentist.' This after a one-day course with the Royal Army Dental Corps.

'What's the secret of good dentistry?' I asked him.

'You've got to be cruel to be kind,' he said.

I made a mental note to keep my teeth well away from him. Two weeks after his general hospital course, he was itching to get at our appendices, but two years later, out on the ice, it was all he could do to remember which side they were on.

During the seven years of planning we approached over 3,000 companies, asking them to cover everything we would need from a ski plane to drawing pins. By early 1976, 760 companies had come up with the goods. After more than four years of full-time work, we had millions of pounds-worth of hardware, including a 42-year-old ice-strengthened ship, the *Kista Dan*, one of the ships used on the expeditions of Vivian Fuchs and Charles Swithinbank, going back to the 1950s, and Land Rover had agreed to supply vehicles for the Sahara, Alaska and other non-sea, non-ice stretches. In the end it took me five years to find a sponsor for a resupply aircraft suitable for use on bumpy polar airstrips, but gradually the idea was creeping, snail-like, towards realization.

Sir Vivian, by now actively doing his very best to help us get going, advised me that we could not hope to achieve Transglobe without polar experience. On previous expeditions, whether hovercrafting up the Nile or plunging down roaring rapids in British Columbia, we had never wasted time and hard-to-get sponsorship by doing dry runs. But this time, neither the SAS nor our own committee would let us loose in the unforgiving polar zones without previous experience. We would need, they insisted, to learn to be cold.

Chapter Three

I began to plan two separate trial journeys. The first, in the summer of 1976, would be in Greenland, its terrain being similar to Antarctica. Then, as there was nowhere suitable to simulate the Arctic Ocean between the Alert Base and the North Pole, we would try a dry run on that same route, in 1977.

In the early summer of 1976 Ginny produced a meticulously detailed paper on our planned logistics for both training journeys, which we passed to the Ministry of Defence and, that July, the RAF flew us to Greenland with 30,000 pounds of sponsored equipment, including two tracked snow vehicles, which we called 'groundhogs'. Each of them pulled two sledges of our own design, made for us by British Steel apprentices. The groundhogs had little raised cabs that were big enough for two people at a squeeze and they looked like the cartoon vehicles on a Sugar Puffs cereal packet which are called groundhogs, and so that is what we christened them.

The Cold War had hauled Greenland from the status of a political backwater to centre stage in terms of the US preparations for nuclear war, for the northern coastline provided the speediest air route between the opposing superpowers. In the early 1950s, in the heyday of the strategic bomber and with recent memories of Hiroshima, a radar shield on friendly terrain but as close to the enemy as possible was a valuable asset and, in 1952, a giant US airbase was accordingly set up at Thule, in Greenland's far north-west. This was at the time the northernmost navigational limit for the bombers. With the subsequent advent of ballistic missile technology, the Ballistic Missile Early Warning System (BMEWS) was added, with its capability to detect Intercontinental Ballistic Missiles (ICBM) fired at North America over the Arctic Ocean.

We landed at BMEWS, which, for its far-from-home technicians, stood for Barmy Men Existing Without Sex. The site was manned by a mix of Americans and Danes. The Eskimos who had originally lived there had been moved by the Danish government to Qanaq, a site some sixty miles to the north where hunting and fishing prospects were known to be good. We were briefed on arrival as to the strict security rules. The site, along with two others in Alaska and England, ensured that any rocket, or even a snow goose, flying in a straight line towards the USA from the Soviet Union would be instantly spotted and destroyed. In theory at least.

From our quarters at the coastal base we could see the rim of the Greenland ice cap, and after a few days' preparation in an empty hangar, a flatbed took us and all our gear to an abandoned US Army site, Camp Tutto, at the base of an ice ramp with access to the glacier. The plan was to learn from scratch how to travel over glacier ice with our groundhogs and sledges, how to detect and avoid crevasses, and how to survive in cold temperatures. Each snow vehicle, towing its two sledges, would carry only one man (the driver) in the cramped cabin, and I would ski ahead to navigate and spot obstacles. Ginny and Mary manned our radio and sorted out a mountain of gear they would need to know how to use in the dark and cold in the months and years ahead.

Ginny had watched our three chosen team members closely over the past two years in the office. We had decided that only two out of the three would form the expedition's main travel group, on the basis that three is a far better unit than either four or two. Our advisers all agreed on this. To generalize, on long hard journeys in hostile places it is relatively suicidal to take only two men. Four men can create cliques of two. With three, two can gang up against the leader. There was no easy answer.

I liked all three of the men, but needed to watch them in action before finally deciding who we would need to discard. Since our tent only accommodated three, the Greenland trials would be split into two periods of a week each with Ollie, our only 'mechanic' on both. Geoff would drive the second groundhog for the first trip, an 80-mile loop around the Hayes Peninsula passing through two known crevasse fields. Then, back at Camp Tutto, Charlie would take over from Geoff for a second, more ambitious, journey heading east towards the interior of the ice cap for 150 miles along the fissured slopes which parallel the jagged coastline of Melville Bight.

If both trips went well, we would get back to Tutto by the end of September with a sound knowledge of the problems likely to be met in Antarctica.

On the first foray I skied ahead on a series of compass bearings, whilst Ollie and Geoff learnt to drive the tracked groundhogs up ever-steeper gradients. For the first time we erected our pyramid tent and camped in deep snow at temperatures below 5°C. Two days later, a strong wind from the inland plateau forced us to camp early in order to shovel blocks of snow onto the tents' valances and to sit out our first blizzard for the next three days and nights.

By chance we had struck a good year for blizzard and snowdrift learning. More snow fell on Greenland in 1976 than had ever been previously recorded. The climate experts at the University of East Anglia announced that the Greenland ice cap had been made unduly heavy, in terms of the world's balance, and that may well have caused the Earth to wobble in its orbit, leading to a change in fragile weather patterns.

An early lesson of tent life was to avoid contact with the inner lining of the tent and thus avoid having wet clothing. And we learned to keep brushing snow under the floor lining. Brushing became obsessive. If the cooker was on and the tent warm, moisture ran down the lining, the rubber tent floor got wet and so did parts of our sleeping bags. Additionally, the moisture in the air permeated the down in our sleeping bags, so we made a note to get outer vapour-barrier bags. After a few days we further noted that our body sweat wet the inside of our bags, so there was a need for inner vapour-barrier linings as well. The warmest, driest position in the tent was the central one but, since both outer sleepers were at all times pressing away from the tent lining and edging inwards when possible, there was little privacy. The act of peeing without causing mayhem in the tent was slowly learnt. More serious calls of nature meant going outside whatever the blizzard conditions. This was caused by sensibilities, certainly not by common sense.

We knew that Wally Herbert had experienced winds of 207 m.p.h. near Thule. Not bad considering the world record is only 225 m.p.h. During a lull in the blizzard, our first experience of a Greenland coastal wind, we donned our outer clothing and, after struggling with the entry flap tie knots which were frozen, we battled through a high drift half-covering the entire tent. Standing up with difficulty, we found that we could not look into the wind and visibility was, in any case, virtually nil in every direction.

The radio antenna wires that I had laid out between two ski sticks when we first arrived at the site had disappeared under drifts. They would need digging out with great care so as not to cut the cable. The PVC covers of the sledge loads had all blown away, for their rubber ties had cracked in the cold. The groundhogs were snow-covered up to the catwalks around the cabs, and our shovels, somewhere on the back decks, were not to be seen. Various things we should have done on camping, and others that we should not have done, crowded my mind. Still, we would know the next time. No more foolish virgins.

'Keep close to the tent!' I yelled. But nobody heard me. I could hardly hear myself. In five minutes we were all back inside the tent, bringing with us lots of snow which we needed to brush off quickly before it could melt. Another point: we would need three brushes, not just one.

We were lucky that none of us was too fussy about the exact amount of tent space we needed, perhaps because of the years we had already spent together in a chaotic and crowded office, sharing one phone and various communal desk spaces. The American explorer Will Steger wrote of a polar tent colleague, 'Being the perfectionist he is, he knows immediately if I try to grab a few inches more space than I've allowed myself in previous nights. He knows exactly where the strings (for drying kit) line above his head and, if I move over just an inch and a half when we set up camp, he knows immediately and takes back his space by not so casually pushing things aside ... To keep peace, I am not complaining.'

On the fourth day the winds abated and the sun shone. Once the shovels were thankfully located, the big dig began. The sledges, although 4 feet high when laden, were well buried. At −10°C we were soon sweating and life felt good. But not for long, since Ollie could not start his vehicle. An hour later, during which we found that all the vehicle repair manuals were in German, Ollie established that the starter motor was not to blame and that somebody (meaning himself) must have inadvertently knocked forward a small hidden knob which disengaged the battery from the power circuit. Ten and a half hours after emerging, we had everything packed (including quite a heavy load of excess blown snow), the sleds and groundhogs were dug out, and both engines were ticking away sweetly.

On my skis, I waved back with a suitable 'Wagons ho!' signal. Both drivers eased down their accelerators. Engines roared. But nothing happened. The tracks were frozen into the caked and frozen snow. After two more hours of digging, one groundhog came free, and we used this to tow out the other one.

Due to the newly drifted snow, the going was slow: one mile an hour at best. How long until the next big blow? We resolved to travel round the clock whilst the weather allowed. I kept some fifty yards ahead of the vehicles in order to avoid compass error. Magnetic variation was 76° to the west. After five hours, we reached the first signs of crevassing around the flanks of a great glacier. This was the Harald Moltke, our first main objective.

A ground mist descended. Not good for our first crevasse foray, so we camped above the glacial valley down which poured the inland ice on its way to the sea. The normal silence of the ice cap, riven only by the wind, was now replaced by booming sound waves from the Moltke, for the sea was not far away and the crash of huge icebergs calving from the ice front rose against the granite cliffs to echo back and forth with thunderous power.

Outside in the mist a lone bird called. How, I wondered, did it survive in such a barren land? Surely it should stay in the coastal ice-free stretches to find food? And how did it navigate? By following the shoreline or cliff faces? By listening to calving glaciers in the gloom? I had heard that they use the sun and even the stars. In Antarctica I, too, would mostly depend on the sun for our heading.

For thirty years I had depended on my hand compass. Basic skills with this little instrument had hugely helped me in the army when orienteering in Europe, in the Borneo jungle, in the SAS after being selected, and later as navigator on many expeditions. Sometimes the key variable, the magnetic deviation, was as much as 190°. I remembered my first army lessons at the Hermitage School of Survey. 'You need to comprehend the variation,' the Sergeant had intoned, 'not just accept that it's there.'

In the sixteenth century European mariners began to crave more reliable compasses. They knew that lethal errors which caused shipwrecks would be avoided if only they could discover why the compass needles dipped more and more as they headed north. In 1600 an English scientist, William Gilbert, realized that there must be some powerful pull from within the Earth itself. We now know that the swirling molten iron in the Earth's outer core, electrically charged, creates a constantly changing electromagnetic field. Depending upon where on the Earth you use your compass, the strength and direction of both the horizontal and the vertical parts of the magnetic field will vary. Approaching the polar regions, the amount of dip increases as the field sweeps around the Earth and returns to the magnetic poles.

Whereas I was confident to the point of being cocky as to my directional navigation abilities, I had no confidence at all in knowing where I was once in a land with no features and where the only markers that can provide backbearings are stars or the sun. So on the high rim of the Moltke when the next day proved sunny, I set up my sponsored theodolite at 4.30 p.m. Greenwich Mean Time, which was local noon, and I recorded the height of the sun. Back in the tent I used a complex set of tables to compute our position. Checking this against the map, I found that I was some sixty-two miles too far west.

Later, Ollie asked how accurate my first practice had proved.

'Only one degree out,' I told him in all honesty, since one degree of latitude is sixty miles.

'Well done,' he congratulated me. I resolved to put in a lot more practice. There was plenty of time for this between blizzards, since Thule experienced four months of continuous daylight from April till August. This is great for the polar Eskimos, but the downside is the four months of perpetual darkness from October till February. In Finland and Russia there is much gloom and suicide in the dark times but, according to Eskimo expert Wally Herbert, native Greenlanders see their long night as 'a magical period' with 'the light of the moon and the stars not only reflected but magnified by the snow and ice, contradicting the very concept of darkness and lightening the heart.' Nonetheless, they have a word for the depression that comes in winter. They call it *perlerorneq*, or 'the burden'.

Ollie, I was discovering, possessed a great but quiet sense of humour and a very placid nature. He did not get excitable, and I decided quite early on in Greenland that he must be, along with Ginny, the key member of our expedition.

He was also an extremely keen twitcher and avid note-taker of bird sightings. Knowing this, Geoff and I had prepared a tape recording of some exotic birdsong heard only in the tropics, and at night, above the intermittent roaring of the Moltke, Ollie woke to hear the raucous twittering of a lesser-known Nigerian parrot just outside the tent. He sat bolt upright in his bag, his eyes out on stalks. He beckoned to Geoff and me to keep quiet as he stealthily eased out of his bag and reached for his camera. Unfortunately, the battery of the tape recorder gave out and the parrot noise died to a low groan. 'You bastards!' screamed Ollie. But he soon joined in the general mirth at his expense.

Next day we entered a fringe crevasse zone where the upper rim of the Moltke began to spill its ever-creeping burden, like wet icing oozing off a sponge cake, down towards the sea. The ice sheet of Greenland's interior plateau is 10,000 feet deep and the ice we were crossing was somewhere between 3,000 and 6,000 years old.

Despite the ongoing din of its descent, the Moltke ice only moved fifty yards in an average year. The Director of the Met Office in the UK, who had arranged training for Geoff to conduct certain experiments whilst we were in Greenland, had shown us impressive figures for the glaciers in our area. The Daugaard-Jensen discharges enough ice into the sea each year, mostly in summer, to meet all the freshwater needs of the USA. The Humboldt Glacier, 60 miles wide where it flows into the sea, is the biggest glacier in the northern hemisphere. The Petermann and Jungersen glaciers specialize in calving off huge table-shaped icebergs known as ice islands, such as are normally to be found off Antarctica. Altogether, the north-west Greenland glaciers, including the Moltke, spew out over 40,000 major icebergs a year. In 1912 one Greenland-sourced iceberg drifted into a shipping lane off Newfoundland and sank the *Titanic*.

In the Moltke crevasse field I skied a zigzag route between crevasses, and Geoff in the lead groundhog followed my trail, which was easy when the visibility held. But the mists came back, and, dodging crevasses in the gloom, I lost our main bearing. While climbing a steep slope we came to a gradient our machines would not ascend. We had to take the sledges up one by one, and even then the tracks would often spin and dig in. The steering on Geoff's groundhog suddenly failed. We found a main drive sprocket had sheared off from one track. Oliver proudly announced that he had a spare. We dug a service tunnel under the stricken machine and, ten hours later, Ollie the beer salesman had gained his spurs as a field mechanic by replacing the sprocket.

The temperature dropped and Ollie, the toughest of us, wrote in his diary: 'Minus 14° centigrade. It is unbelievably cold. This morning my groundhog refused to start, so I poured my Thermos of hot coffee over the starter motor with immediate results.' Geoff, who had made the coffee, was annoyed.

More or less on schedule, we came to a rock feature near the coast which, for some reason, had a name on the map Puissitdlussarssuaq, renamed by Geoff as Loosepussy. Here another drive sprocket broke, and this time there was no spare part. Geoff, with lateral thought, sawed a chunk of aluminium off a crevasse ladder and, using my navigation dividers, designed a hexagonal sprocket adaptor, which proved to fit precisely. Ollie, meanwhile, attacked a jammed hub ring with a blowlamp and sledgehammer. He blackened two fingers with misjudged blows and singed off one eyebrow. He worked hour after hour in a snowhole under the broken track and finally, with a chisel and a paraffin jelly heater, managed to prise away the jammed ring. Geoff's adapted sprocket then fitted Ollie's hub, and I felt warmly proud of their achievement. It was as though two farm labourers had repaired a computer.

Some days later, after only minor breakdowns and good weather, we arrived back at Camp Tutto. I told Ginny that Geoff and Ollie were great material. But she and Mary had found Charlie 'dead lazy'. He had made friends with the local Danish fire chief and often disappeared on boozing sessions in one of Thule's many private bars. Ginny and Mary were left to maintain the base, fetch water, service the generator and man the radio watch. 'If he behaves with you on the ice like he has down here,' Ginny warned me, 'you're in for trouble.'

Ginny had made friends with local Eskimos whilst we were away and one of them was a lovely, rotund, ever-smiling lady seamstress called Emilie. She lived in the neighbouring village of Dundas, which had been a trading settlement until BMEWS was built and the Eskimos moved north to Qanaq. Only a dozen Danes and Eskimos with their families now lived there and they ran the place as a radio transmitting station, in a quiet and different world to the sprawling tin huts of the adjacent bustling airbase.

On Wally Herbert's advice, Ginny had decided that we should use Eskimo jackets for our polar travels, on the grounds that they had worked well for Wally on all his extreme cold expeditions.

Wally had recommended Emilie as being the best seamstress around and the Hudson's Bay Company in London had sponsored us with enough Russian timber-wolf skins to make six hooded parkas. Ginny gave these to Emilie, and marvelled at her expertise in the rare skill of tailoring fur.

We had listened to arguments by various scientists about the evolution of Eskimos on a Darwinian basis to the point where they are far more capable of surviving extreme cold conditions than us, so that even the best fur jackets might prove insufficient protection for our more cold-susceptible bodies. Some authorities point to the generally short and rotund Eskimo body shape, which reduces the ratio of their surface area to their body mass and heat generation. They lose less heat through their limbs, and they have more blood vessels in their feet and hands so that they can often use them ungloved in temperatures as low as −40°C. The sweat glands on their faces are more numerous than elsewhere on their bodies because their faces are more exposed to extreme cold temperatures, and their cheeks and eyelids are much fleshier for the same reason.

But although in theory humans, like other animals, may acclimatize to cold on an individual level, proof of such an adaption process is lacking, except in the case of Japanese *ama*, women pearl divers who have a unique tolerance of cold water. Their bodies show a marked ability to shut down their surface blood vessels so that the blood flow to the skin, and even to the underlying muscles, is limited. This reduces heat loss.

As with the *ama*, the act of growing up in a very cold climate will also have a direct influence on cold-protective mechanisms. Studies of laboratory piglets raised in cold rooms have shown that their legs will be shorter than the norm, due to less blood circulating in their limb growing points. A similar effect may underlie the general stature of the Eskimo.

Whatever the reality of the relative ability of Emilie's body compared with, say, Ginny's, to tolerate the cold, we could find no scientific evidence that newly developing artificial materials, like Gore-Tex, would improve our chances in extreme polar cold. So we looked forward to trying out the results of Emilie's workmanship in a Cold Chamber back in the UK.

In our absence Ginny had been busy in the station library, studying the various histories and myths of the great frozen continent, home to 55,000 people. Locals call their country Kalaallit Nunaat, meaning the Land of the People. Archaeological work indicates that, around 3000 BC, nomadic people, originally from Alaska, travelled slowly east across the barren lands of northern Canada and Ellesmere Island, eventually crossing Smith Sound which, at its narrowest point known as the Eskimo Bridge, is only sixty miles wide and when frozen is easy to cross. On arrival on Greenland's north-west coast, some of these original nomads headed south down the west coast, but most headed north and east to the now uninhabited region of Peary Land, which in warmer times was good hunting country. The descendants of these original nomads, the so-called Sarqaq tribes, thrived from 1400 to 700 BC, after which, in terms of archaeological evidence, they disappeared.

Meanwhile, a different Palaeo-Eskimo people, termed the Dorset or Thule culture, were settled in many northern regions of Alaska, Canada and, between about 700 BC and AD 1300, in Greenland. Unlike the Sarqaqs, they used skin boats and sledges. Described by the first Vikings to reach Greenland, in the tenth century, these natives were known as Skraelings and their settlements were spread around all of Greenland's ice-free coastal zones.

The first description of land to the north of Britain came as early as the fourth century BC from the Roman navigator Pytheas of Marseilles, but no other Roman ever sailed north of Scotland. Irish monks in about AD 400 followed the flight of migrating snow geese and were the first to settle in Iceland. In the sixth century Vikings joined these original Irish monk settlers in Iceland, and in AD 900 a Viking named Gunnbjorn, lost at sea in a gale, sighted East Greenland's coast. Although he told the people back home, it was not until AD 950 that a Norwegian, banished to Iceland for manslaughter and thence banished again for murder, sailed to find Gunnbjorn's reported land. Having found it, he settled there and over the next decade encouraged other Icelanders to do likewise and to trade with native Eskimos.

In 1100 a Norwegian bishop established Christianity as Greenland's official religion, and in 1261 Greenlanders voted to become a crown colony of Norway.

Over the next century the climate changed and in 1492 the Pope wrote that, due to frozen seas, no ship had called at Greenland 'for 80 years'. Archaeologists record that the last Norse colonists of Greenland must have died in the fifteenth century. Bodies show signs of starvation, but also of wound scars. Nobody can say for sure what wiped out the colonists. Suggestions that Thule Eskimos hunting to the south exterminated the settlers have never been proved. Starvation and in-fighting brought on by climate change is more likely.

In the sixteenth century, European explorers such as John Davis came looking for the Northwest Passage. Heading north, with Canada off the port bow and Greenland to starboard, they met up with the Thule Eskimos and reported their presence. One of Henry Hudson's early voyages at the beginning of the seventeenth century had explored the seas to the east of Greenland, and his reports of great numbers of walrus and whale led to many whalers, in between their massacres of both species, heading ever further north between Spitsbergen and Greenland. By the mid-seventeenth century, a surge in European whalers operating off Greenland and calling at settlements there resulted in the Eskimo race becoming adulterated with European blood, and this ethnic mix has continued ever since. Today, the natives of Greenland are not called Eskimos, Inuit or Danes; they are simply Greenlanders and they call their Eskimo language Greenlandic. Many also speak Danish, which is taught in all their schools.

When writing about Eskimos today, there is a minefield of political correctness to be observed. In the USA the term Eskimo is usually used to describe the groups of culturally similar indigenous peoples who live in the Arctic regions of Canada, Alaska and other US territories, Greenland and Russia. There is no collective term that covers all these different people other than Eskimo. Having said that, it should be recognized that many Canadian and Greenlandic natives nowadays view the term Eskimo, originally a French corruption of a Cree Indian word meaning 'eaters of raw meat', as rude, to the extent that in Canada the Constitution Act of 1982 named the Inuit as a distinctive group of aboriginal Canadians. The word Inuit can be translated as 'real men' or 'the people'.

Most of Greenland's 55,000 inhabitants live along the west coast, with only a few along the south-eastern tip. The east coast is blocked for most of the year by ice and remains a vast game reserve. The stretch of the ice cap between the two coasts is 800 miles at the widest point, and the whole island is ten times the size of Britain.

North Pole explorers from America, especially Admiral Peary and Dr Frederick Cook at the turn of the twentieth century, exploited the Thule Eskimos' travel and hunting skills on their pioneering journeys. Many of the Thule Eskimos still make a good living using the age-old hunting skills at sea and on land. They fashion their trousers from polar-bear pelts, and use the longest bear hairs to trim their wives' fox-fur leggings. But Emilie told us, with a big grin, 'The men like the bear hunt anyway.'

Elsewhere in the Arctic countries the polar bear is a protected species, and the Greenland Eskimos are among the few peoples who are still allowed to bear-hunt. Over nine months of frozen sea ice, the hunters of Thule, or rather Qanaq, with their backs to an ice sheet devoid of life, make their living hunting seal, walrus and polar bear. Some travel five thousand miles a year, often alone and by dog sledge, on hunting forays over shifting pack ice. Eschewing the cosy ways of most southerly Eskimo citizens, cosseted by the welfare state, the hunters of Qanaq have elected to maintain their traditional way of life. This naturally depends on the continuing presence of animals to hunt and, fostered by Danish conservationists, the hunters have become increasingly conscious of the need for wildlife conservation. Controls on the use of rifles, as opposed to harpoons, help to ensure that the narwhal and walrus are not overhunted. Polar bears that are in cub may no longer be shot. Fox trapping has a similar ban and caribou, hunted to extinction in the district during the nineteenth century, are being reintroduced from Southern Greenland.

Wally Herbert quoted a Thule hunter as stating, 'The great hunters are those who go out in all weathers to bring back meat while the dreamers are sleeping.' Wally explained the hunters' driving force as being 'a phenomenon as old and powerful as life itself, the need to take part in the ritual game of life and death through which man seeks and finds an affinity with his environment ... prove himself the master predator in a savage world ... for in this society the hunter is supreme and the greater his exploits in the dark, the greater the respect he commands.'

The most prized possession of the Eskimo hunter is his dog team, usually between 5 and 15 in number, depending on his wealth. The team's ability, learnt through complex training and harsh discipline, to cross snow and ice in all weathers, is unparalleled. Wally summarized the abilities of a great pack with an efficient master and top-notch king dog. Their performance, he wrote,

> has to be seen to be believed. With whip-cracks as loud as rifle shots, plus special calls and whistles, a skilled hunter can weave a team of dogs at full speed across the roughest stretch of ice, slow them down, stop them and get them to lie flat. He can make a 17-strong pack divide during a dangerous descent so that his sledge overruns the dogs' long traces and the team ends up behind the sledge to serve as 17 clawing anchors in the polished snow ... He can spread them out when they are on bending ice and thereby distribute their weight for safety; and at any time he can unhitch and make them follow him as meekly as a pack of well-trained pets.

The team dogs have individually tailored sledge-harnesses, which are only removed for adjustment or repairs. To discourage dogs with escapist tendencies from chewing through their straps, their teeth will be filed down. To protect the soles of their feet from sharp ice crust, they are fitted with rubber and canvas boots with claw holes. They sleep curled up outside in all weathers, covering their sensitive noses against frostbite with their bushy tails.

'Dogs', Emilie remarked, as she patted a pet husky pup, 'are needed to hunt all our meat except for the bird meat.' She explained that springtime in Thule produced an explosion of life, whether flowers or insects or teaming bird life. Beautiful, but tiny, blooms carpet the gravel coastal plains, and larvae or eggs hatch in their millions. Whether mosquitoes, bees, spiders, beetles or butterflies, they proliferate to enjoy the short Thule summer when, for three months, the average temperature is above freezing.

The birds that wheel screaming above the cliffs of the Thule coast include glaucous gulls, eider ducks, snow geese, kittiwakes, gyrfalcons, arctic terns, fulmars and, in their millions, the little auks or dovekies that are annually trapped by the Eskimos based, for four- or five-day outings, in cliffside camps. One hunter will, in that period, expect to net over a thousand dovekies, which he will use to feed his family, his dogs and his house guests. Hundreds of thousands are eaten annually as a welcome supplement to the diet.

Often the dovekie corpses are simply plucked, whilst still warm, and eaten raw, but they are more usually cooked unplucked in boiling water along with lumps of seal blubber. Then, once cool, the eager Eskimo gets to break off the wings and strip off all the skin and feathers in a single movement by pinching the skin at the back of the bird's neck and pulling gently, like removing a sock. Only the bones and beak get spat out.

The most exotic of dovekie dishes is the *kiviaq*, where literally hundreds of corpses are bound up in a sealskin with chunks of seal blubber for at least six months until the contents reach an advanced stage of decomposition. The lucky family then consume the *kiviaq* in its putrefied state, picking out the feathers, bones and beaks as they go.

Conservation of birds is also now commonly practised so that, for instance, the eider duck, which was once on the edge of extinction, has now re-established vast colonies and has added a rich new taste to the Thule menu. When a Danish friend muttered to Ollie, our resident twitcher, about 'all the poor birds the locals kill round here', he replied with the observation that, in the USA and Europe, statistics of annual bird-kill included 100 million killed by cats and the same number by window-crash plus 50 million by car-crash.

Between 1910 and 1929 the explorer Knud Rasmussen from Denmark devoted his life to studying the Thule Eskimos and to protecting their way of life. He encouraged their trade with the main centres of life further south. And, in Thule, he set up the first trading post, school and rudimentary hospital. In 1814 Denmark had ceded all of Norway to Sweden, but Greenland, which was until then a Norwegian possession, became a Danish colony, and after Rasmussen's death in 1933, the Danes took over his good work in Thule.

The music of the Thule Eskimos, uninfluenced by the music of any neighbouring land for many centuries, is rhythmic but not, to the Western ear, stimulating or exciting. Often performed by a single person, beating a sealskin tambour on a wooden frame, he or she will keen a long, repetitive refrain about everyday life or some long-ago hunting saga made up on the spur of the moment. Sun and sex sometimes get a mention, but no more than do the moon and geriatric existence.

The Eskimo (or Inuit) Sun is a woman who, after being raped by her brother the Moon, cuts off her own breasts from shame and flees heavenwards after blackening her face with soot. This saga also adds that, in his ongoing chase of his sister, the Moon often forgets to eat. All this explains why the Moon is dimmer than the Sun and appears to get quite thin from time to time, whilst the Sun-woman simmers with incandescent anger.

Sex is surprisingly poorly represented in the saga songs, bearing in mind that gonorrhoea is widespread and sexual free-for-all is traditionally accepted between husbands, wives and visitors, with a ritual ceremony organized by the shaman or *angakoq* in the local equivalent of the village hall where lights are put out and partners are briefly exchanged. Another custom is for lonely wives to offer one-night stands to visiting hunters when their own husbands are out hunting. This must have helped avoid inbreeding in isolated hamlets. But despite these loose sexual mores, Greenland Eskimos were and are basically monogamous.

In terms of geriatric tales from the grave, a friend told me how dead relatives were wrapped in blankets or furs and left to the elements and to wandering meat-eaters. 'Long ago', the story went, 'we put our houses below ground and our dead above ground. Then the *kabloona* [white man] came and told us to put our houses above ground and our dead down below.'

Knut Rasmussen recorded that the death of elderly Eskimos by suicide was common, usually by drowning or hanging themselves or by asking their relatives to put them to death by stabbing or strangulation. Old folk who had become a burden to their family and who recognized this would customarily ask for death assistance three times. Infanticide was also carried out when the threat of starvation faced isolated families. Orphans or disabled children would often be left outside to die.

In her book *The Snow People* (1973), about the time she spent living with Eskimos on an island near Thule, Wally Herbert's wife, Marie, recorded:

> In the old days there were a lot of murders and when one person was killed, his relatives would take revenge. Sometimes a whole village would be wiped out this way. In the old days a woman in labour was put outside in a snow house and she had to deliver the child herself. Occasionally an old woman who knew about such things might help her, but very often she was left to fend for herself ... Also, if a husband died, the wife and children were not allowed to eat meat for weeks. They sometimes nearly starved. There were lots of strange customs.

One admirable aspect of Eskimo philosophy is that the Thule Eskimos have no real word for war, and their children do not play games of war, unlike most children the world over. Their games with imaginary guns or harpoons will be directed at imaginary bears, not other people. Wrestling in their homes, they ape dog-fights, not human strife.

As with many aboriginal peoples, new visitors from other lands brought their diseases and their way of life with them. The European whalers brought death to the Greenland Eskimos over many years, and during the nineteenth century the Greenland coastal populations died in their hundreds from pneumonia, trichinosis, tuberculosis, measles, smallpox and various sexual diseases, and there was general social disruption, along with the birth of illegitimate children and drunkenness. Whereas in the old days of hunting for survival Eskimos' teeth were remarkably good and worn down only by old age, now Western foods cause dental decay.

The Danes have done their best to cut down the uncontrolled availability of alcohol. They have also made available creature comfort benefits and central heating to those Greenlanders who prefer that way of life, whilst still enabling those few hardy souls who wish to cling to the old ways to do so. Nonetheless, a deep-seated malaise has, of course, resulted, as with every other scene of social upheaval around the world. The older generations are upset at losing the status quo that they loved and still try to cling to. There are sad suicides motivated almost certainly, as their friend Wally Herbert has surmised, by a terrible form of identity crisis, a fatal loss of self-esteem ensuing from the clash of two very different cultures.

Emilie duly produced our Eskimo fur parkas in time for our second and last journey on the ice cap. Because they proved very warm indeed and the temperature in mid-summer Thule was often above freezing by day, we kept them for colder times. Ollie and I left, this time with Charlie, for Camp Tutto and thence, in the groundhogs, up the ramp to the ice field.

I began the second inland journey with critical glances at Charlie, but he showed no signs of evil humour. Instead he seemed happy to be away from Thule; he pulled his weight at whatever we did and was unusually quick at copying our actions for, with our earlier journey behind us, we thought we were experts. This might have annoyed Charlie, but he never showed it. When disaster threatened he turned up trumps.

We had been travelling for several days when we hit a field of crevasses. The first I knew about it was when one of my ski sticks broke straight through the surface snow and disappeared. My arm followed up to the shoulder. With slow movements, carefully keeping my body weight over both skis, I moved away from the small black hole in the snow, the only indication of hidden danger. I cursed myself for a fool. The trouble was that we had been taking too long over this second journey and we were trying to push on too fast. It was a misty day and getting dark now, but this was no place for travelling in poor visibility. I was descending a steep slope without any idea of what lay below. The angle was too great for a groundhog to get back up, if need be, and too steep to pitch our tent.

I waited for the groundhogs to catch up, and then explained our predicament. Both drivers gave the thumbs up and travelled on in first gear, using the steering brakes as sparingly as possible, and I skied carefully on in front. The farther we descended, the darker it became. It seemed an age before the slope levelled out, and only then, when I was well and truly committed to the valley, did it reveal its unstable nature. I kick-turned my light Norwegian skis and langlaufed back up my trail. Suddenly a groundhog appeared with Charlie half out of its cab. Oliver, he said, had gone down a crevasse.

At first I could see nothing. Charlie pointed to a vague blotch of darker gloom. I skied towards it. Oliver's groundhog had a flag on its cabin roof and it was this that Charlie had seen. The rest of the vehicle had disappeared from view. Then cresting the rise, I saw the trapped groundhog and, catching my breath, came to an abrupt halt. My ski tips hung over a narrow canyon in the snow which led zigzag fashion to the hole that engulfed the machine.

Gingerly I inspected the fissure, but could see no bottom to it.

Oliver had been driving almost parallel to its course when his groundhog's right-hand track had punctured the rotten bridge concealing its presence. The vehicle must have lurched sideways and downwards. Fortunately, for the moment at least, the left-hand track had caught upon the lip of the crevasse and balanced there. But the least movement could dislodge the machine and send it plunging downwards.

As I watched, Oliver began to wriggle out of his tiny cabin door, his parka catching on the controls as he did so. The groundhog rocked to and fro; snow fell away from the bank which held it, and Oliver, realising his danger, redoubled his efforts. Soon he was on the catwalk beside the cab. Keeping his weight central, he edged towards the safer side, and away from the void. Each time the machine lurched and slipped a bit, he froze. When it quieted he moved, eel-like, nearer terra firma. He did well, escaping without disturbing the machine. Now we had only to pull it out, an event we had long prepared for. Oliver, without the safety of skis, stayed where he was. I moved over to Charlie and beckoned him forward.

On paper we had agreed on the best method of recovery: a straightforward pull by the still-mobile groundhog using Kevlar, a tow rope endowed with a great deal of elastic strength. Once enough elasticity was induced by the towing machine, the other should, by rights, pop out of its predicament like a cork from a champagne bottle.

Charlie reversed, then slowly nosed through the mist into the best approach angle. He was perhaps eighty yards from Oliver and well away from the crevasse when it happened. The only noise was a sharp thud as Charlie's head hit the windscreen. I watched fascinated as the snow unzipped in front of me, revealing a long black cavern.

The groundhog was moving slowly at the time and Charlie was quick. He slammed on both steering brakes as he felt himself fall, coming to an abrupt halt as his vehicle jammed its upper catwalks between the lips of the new crevasse. Then, unseen, the moon edged behind the southern hills and the darkness was complete. By torchlight and wary as long-tailed cats in a room full of rocking chairs, we tested the snow yard by yard until we came to Charlie. He was out before we reached him and unlashing his tent from his leading sledge.

We made camp between the two crevasses, hoping that the spot we chose was solid. We were tired, many miles from anywhere, and caught between an escarpment that we could not climb and a deeply crevassed valley through which we must travel to escape.

Above the Camp Tutto ramp we had noticed various missile-detection installations, domes and outhouses, built on high ice-field features, and we knew that there were others way out in Greenland's vast interior heights. All were supplied by ski-equipped cargo aircraft and back in 1942, even before the Cold War, an American Flying Fortress aircraft had crashed high up on the ice cap. An attempt was made to rescue the crew, but the rescue aircraft crashed, killing its own crew. Then one of the two snow tractors sent to the rescue fell into a crevasse a few yards from the Fortress crash site, killing the vehicle's occupant. The remaining tractor took three survivors from the Fortress and its own four-man crew back towards the coast. In another crevasse another man died, and all the survivors had to spend a winter on the ice cap prior to their eventual rescue the next spring.

From the site of our predicament we found that we could see the ocean beyond the Thule coastline and just south of the narrows between Greenland and Canada's Ellesmere Island. The northern section of these narrows, Robeson Channel, is only 60 miles wide and is normally frozen solid through the long winter. Wally Herbert had once told me of an amazing journey by an Eskimo group led by a Canadian Eskimo named Qitdlassuaq from faraway Baffin Island. He was a shaman and, in a self-induced trance, felt urged to visit the descendants of his ancestors who had travelled east from Baffin three hundred years before and never returned. Qitdlassuaq persuaded his 38-strong extended family group to travel with him into the unknown.

In 1856 they set out on what turned out to be an epic seven-year journey over frozen seas via Ellesmere Island. Sixteen of them eventually made it to their 'long-lost relatives' in Thule, who, at the time, were very demoralized and hungry.

Qitdlassuaq perked them up and taught them forgotten survival skills. After six years he felt homesick and, with his original followers, set out back to Baffin Island. He died some time later and his leaderless group ran out of food. They resorted to murdering and eating their weaker brethren one by one, but five years after they had set out, two or three survivors came back to Thule.

For two days we shovelled, dug, chipped and cursed. At first the task seemed beyond us. To extricate the groundhogs from their dizzy perches meant moving them backwards or forwards. Yet the slightest movement in either direction would only serve to widen the gap in the delicate snow bridges and send the machines plunging downwards. Oliver's diary records: 'We spent the day roped together as crevasses are all around us. One, close to the tent, is about five feet wide and has infinite depth.'

After many hours we completed tunnels for our aluminium crevasse ladders well below the sunken groundhogs. The recovery operation was dicey, but it worked.

Our timetable was now well into the red. Winter and darkness were upon us. The journey back to Thule was splattered with crevasse alarms, boggings and many breakdowns. But Oliver always coped. With spindrift settling down his neck and some of his fingers split from the nails back to the first knuckle, he continued patiently and thoroughly 'botching up' where he had no spare part to do the job. As he worked Charlie watched, helping where he could. Oliver was often short and sharp with him, but he ignored this. He decided it was just 'Ol's way' when embroiled with details, and lived with it. Theirs was a close and easy friendship. Luckily, however, the two did not form an alliance against me. In the back of beyond where there are no links with normal life, friendship is important.

We returned to Thule not a day too soon. The weather clamped down on the ice cap and stayed there, a grim, grey blanket hiding the whole feature from the camp. But the wind spilled down the valley, battering at the man-made installations and tearing through Thule to lash the icebergs and the black islands beyond. Once again six in number, we stored all the kit, cleaned and greased for the winter, and told the authorities, Danish and American, that we hoped to be back in about three months' time to transport all of it by plane to the Canadian Arctic for another dose of polar training.

I returned from Greenland fit and weighing 185 pounds. Ollie, Charlie and Geoff had all done well in Greenland, which did not help my ongoing intention to keep only the best two. I did remember that a short while before Captain Scott set out on his second Antarctic expedition, he had to select a handful of men from 8,000 keen volunteers. So I had a far easier task.

Ginny and I continued to look at volunteers long after our three Greenland 'apprentices' became our first choices. Between 1972 and 1978 120 volunteers tried their luck. Some lasted no longer than the interview stage. I had a stock approach, which I called the 'black talk'.

'If you want to join, you must apply to the Territorial SAS Regiment in the corridor just below this attic. They have a weekend selection course in Wales.'

'What, just the weekend?'

'No, twelve weekends and a final two-week test in the hills. You will need to get rid of your beard and some of that hair, of course.'

If this last point did not put them off at once, the black talk continued. 'If the SAS accept you as a trooper, come back again and we'll have another talk. If you are still keen, you must leave your job and help us here full-time to get the expedition going.'

The bulk of them we never saw again. But some made it into the Territorial SAS and worked on and off to help us, and a few made the final decision to fling in their jobs altogether.

Whoever made the grade I took on weekends in Snowdonia each winter and spring from 1973 until 1978 to train for the annual army race, the Welsh 3000. Usually there was freezing rain, thick mist and strong winds, and sometimes snow and ice. Starting on the summit of Snowdon, the whole team practised covering 25 miles to the top of 13 Welsh peaks over 3,000 feet within 24 hours while carrying 25 pounds of safety gear on their backs. In 1974 we won in the record time of seven and a half hours and brought the Territorial cup back to the Duke of York Barracks in triumph.

It wasn't a perfect method of selecting people for polar travel, but it was the best I could manage at no expense. I wasn't after physical prowess, but reaction to stress and strain. I looked for good nature and patience. Ginny and I might not have either, but there wasn't much we could do about that: at least we could ensure that the rest of the team were suitable. Once I'd found my paragons, I hoped that the army would train them as astronavigators, mechanics, radio operators and medics at no extra cost.

Whilst we searched for ideal people, a thousand and one other problems needed solving, including the need for a ski plane to resupply us in the polar zones, an ice-strengthened ship to take us southwards down the Atlantic and, after we crossed Antarctica, to take us northwards up the Pacific to the Arctic. And snow vehicles suitable for both the land-based ice of Antarctica and for the moving sea ice of the Arctic Ocean.

We showed our committee some film footage that we had taken of our groundhogs in Greenland, and we were told in no uncertain terms by one of our Arctic advisers that however suitable they might be for Antarctica, they would very soon be 'lost at sea' in the Arctic. He explained why. So, with little time to go, I followed his advice and found sponsors to buy us six Bombardier 640cc skidoo snowmobiles, which weighed about 600 pounds and could be manhandled over high walls of pack ice and over fairly thin sea ice without sinking quite as easily as our heavy groundhogs.

Not long after our return from Greenland, a scruffy-looking man with a black beard answered Ginny's advert for a ship's deckhand. Anton Bowring was quiet and unflappable. He listened impassively when I explained that there was no ship as yet for him to be a deckhand on, but his first job could be to find one. A year later he located a thirty-year-old strengthened vessel once called the *Kista*

Dan, and persuaded the giant insurance brokers C.T. Bowring, once owned by his family, to buy her on our behalf. This they did, with an eye to the fact that they had sponsored Captain Scott seventy years previously with his ship, the *Terra Nova*.

Five years after I had first started trying to find a sponsor to loan us a second-hand Twin Otter ski plane (worth about £2 million), the Chubb Security group kindly did so for a three-year period. Through good luck we then obtained the services, on a volunteer basis, of Britain's most able Twin Otter polar pilot, Captain Giles Kershaw, and, through the army, a brilliant flight engineer, Gerry Nicholson.

One weekend in that summer of 1976, while visiting my sister Gill's farm in Yorkshire, Ginny's pet terrier drowned in a slurry pit. For weeks Ginny was inconsolable. I chanced to tell Peter Booth, who kindly gave Ginny a Jack Russell puppy with whom she fell instantly in love. We called him Bothie in honour of his donor, and Ginny informed me that she was not going on Transglobe without him.

After Greenland we were in a much stronger position to persuade the reluctant authorities to give us the polar go-aheads that we desperately needed. Although not exactly polar veterans, we had at least mastered the art of deep-snow ice-cap travel in temperatures of –15°C. We knew, on the advice of our venerable committee, that polar doors would still not be opened until we had also gained successful experience of the very different problems of Arctic sea-ice travel at –40°C. To save postponing the main expedition for yet another year, we must complete a genuine attempt at reaching the North Pole in the spring of 1977.

We had over 30,000 pounds of polar gear in store at the Thule missile-detection base. The only place we could use from which to set out for the North Pole was Alert, the Canadian Army base on the northern coast of Ellesmere Island, but how to fly our gear from Thule to Alert? If we could find the money for that operation, the next financial need would be to pay for Twin Otter resupply flights en route from Alert to the pole, since our own Twin Otter was not yet available. The necessary total of £60,000 came from a generous Omani businessman, Doctor Omar Al Zawawi, and after great troubles getting permits from the Canadian, British and American Ministries of Defence, the six of us flew to Alert via Thule in February 1977, keen to learn to be colder yet.

Chapter Four

Even a man with perfect circulation and the best clothing combinations designed by man will suffer terribly under the worst Arctic conditions

WALLY HERBERT (1974)

Alert Camp, the world's most northerly settlement, is supplied only by air, since there are no roads for hundreds of miles and all sea access is permanently frozen. Sixty Canadian soldiers and scientists, known as the Chosen Frozen, manned the base at that time, and none of them stayed for more than six months at a stretch lest they become 'bushed'. They spent most of their time in their heated offices or mess hall because the outside weather, except for a short two-month 'summer', is hostile in the extreme. Precisely what went on in the highly secretive confines of the base was, the commanding officer told us with a wink, 'To do with reporting the weather.' But it was an open secret that the actual task of the Chosen Frozen was to monitor each and every movement of any submarine that passed into or out of the narrow Robeson Channel, between Canada and Greenland. At the height of the Cold War more than eighty nuclear submarines patrolled around Arctic waters and under the sea ice, all carrying weapons of mass destruction, playing a potentially lethal game of cat and mouse.

On the day of our arrival at Alert the temperature was –48°C and the night was pitch-black. There would be no sign of the sun for a month. Our own camp, a deserted huddle of four wooden shacks, was perched along the very shore of the frozen sea some two miles north of the army camp. Between our huts and the North Pole lay nothing but miles of jumbled ice and smoking seams of open sea: 425 nautical miles in all. To stand a chance of reaching the North Pole, an expedition must set out on or close to 3 March, the day the sun reappears at the latitude of Alert.

Of our first night at Alert, Oliver wrote: 'The huts are deplorable. Two of them are just habitable, the remainder full of ice and snow. Our predecessors must have left in a hurry, many years ago. No heater and so, so cold. I slept wearing ten layers of clothing. It is impossible to get warm.' Quite how Ollie managed to put on ten layers, I have never managed to work out, but we had done our homework on the history and evolution of cold-weather clothing and had various alternative choices to cover all parts of our bodies.

As well as considering the merits of natural fur, we had also looked at 'clever' artificial materials, including nylon, polypropylene, Polarguard, Hollofil, Quallofil and Gore-Tex. Although the Arctic Ocean and its coastlines are, in winter, extremely cold, humidity is high so sweat going into clothing and sleeping bags is an important factor in the choice of materials. Certain breathable fabrics like these allow mist-like water vapour to escape through the pores but keep out actual rain.

At different times on our main expedition we would be driving open snowmobiles or small boats and using minimal energy, whilst at other times we would be manhauling heavy sledges using maximum energy. An unproofed parka will allow sweat to escape but won't be windproof or waterproof, whereas a proofed one will protect against both at the expense of not being breathable so that your own sweat will make you wet and, in due course, cold.

Our answer was our Inuit fur parkas for skidoo-wear and Ventile cotton parkas for sweaty manhaul work. Ventile is a closely woven pure cotton that, when dry, is fairly windproof, breathes efficiently and avoids sweat-caused condensation.

We used Canadian Army canvas boots with thick felt insoles worn over nylon mesh insoles. At the end of the day we battered away the ice formed from sweat which had collected in the mesh. We also wore latex rubber waterproof socks next to our skin and under our woollen socks to ensure that no sweat froze in our socks.

On our second morning at Alert we awoke to find the daylight hours as dark as night. Torches with new batteries went dead after six minutes' use outside the huts. Flesh glued itself to metal and, if you tore your hand away, the skin remained behind. Ginny went outside to our makeshift lavatory and, knocking the wooden seat aside by mistake, made contact with one side of the steel-rimmed bucket. She received a painful cold burn down one cheek of her bottom and rushed into our hut to warm up against the oil-fired stove. She stood too close and singed her other cheek with a hot burn. This must have been some sort of a record.

With only two weeks to our departure date, we worked around the clock, making frequent visits to the kitchen shack for flasks of hot tea. We could manage about an hour outside in a stiff breeze before retreating to thaw out. When a 30-knot wind was blowing, twenty minutes was the limit.

Oliver and Charlie prepared our new skidoo snow machines. Much lighter than the groundhogs, they were powered by 640cc two-stroke engines and were steered by way of handlebars controlling a single short front ski. Skidoos are the snow traveller's motorbike: they provide scant protection from the elements. In the meantime, I practised with my theodolite in a 28-knot wind at temperatures of −45°C, fairly average conditions for the time of year.

One night the shooting of a single star took an hour and fifty minutes. In England I would have shot a dozen in twenty-five minutes. My eyelashes stuck to the metal of the scope and my nose cracked with the first symptoms of frosting. If, by mistake, I directed my breath, even briefly, on to the scope, it froze; if I then wiped its lens with my bare finger, this brought on circulation problems. Each time I tried to turn my head, my beard hairs were tugged by the ice that meshed them, my eyes watered and more ice formed on my lashes. I persevered all week, for my ability to keep track of our position on the Arctic Ocean, whether by the sun or stars, would be key to our survival. An error of four seconds would put our position wrong by a mile.

Since we needed good photos and a reasonably produced movie film of all our training in Greenland and on the Arctic Ocean, and since I was the only one of the group to have done previous camera work, I had to cover any and all activities with both a still and a movie camera. So if, for instance, Charlie was to break through sea ice and shout for help, or if Ollie was attacked by a bear, I would need time (before helping them) to unpack both carefully stowed cameras in order to record the event. Good photos and film of their equipment in action is a key way of making existing sponsors happy and of gaining new ones.

I was sponsored with a robust Nikon F2 camera, a Bolex 16mm movie camera and a good supply of Kodak film. Changing film reels at –40°C, even though both cameras had been fully winterized by the sponsors, was a challenging task wearing mitts. I had discovered that Kodachrome II was by far the best film in the cold in terms of its patience in not cracking when its acetate chilled into rigidity. When both cameras came into the warm moisture of the tent at night, I always put them in sealed polythene bags to keep them dry.

Each morning, once outside, I would set the exposure at f5.6, the focus at infinity and the flash sequence at 'fill-in flash'. Because the sun always circled for 24 hours at more or less the same altitude, the light value hardly changed all day. I used only lithium batteries, the best in the cold. On the clockwork camera I set the speed at 24 frames per second, in order to allow for the cold slowing down the clockwork and thus prevent the appearance of us walking like Charlie Chaplin characters.

We set out on 1 March and travelled five miles along the shoreline west of our camp before driving on to the sea ice to cross Black Cliffs Bay. A mile later we camped at –51°C, two men to a tent. Geoff tried to send a message back to Ginny, but his Morse key froze up and his breath simply froze inside the fine wire mesh of his microphone. Then the main coaxial power line cable cracked when he tried to straighten it out from its coil. Next morning, after an unforgettably evil night, none of the skidoos would start.

Over the next four days of mechanical delays we all learned the nature of tent life at −50°C. A useful lesson for the future. Geoff found the extreme cold especially difficult and, in a demoralised state, allowed six of his fingers to go numb while driving his skidoo. At the time he was wearing silk gloves, woollen gloves, heavy quilt gauntlets and thick leather outer mitts, but the numbness nonetheless quickly turned to frostbite. We limped back to base and Mary sedated Geoff, who was obviously in pain. With cobbled-up heating systems for the skidoos, we set out again on 8 March, but this time without Geoff.

The torture of the cold at night was such that we could not sleep without taking Valium tablets. For two or three hours after nestling down into our bags life was bearable, but then our metabolisms would begin their involvement in the process of digesting our evening meal and blood would circulate less in our extremities. At this point each tent inmate was bound to curl up into the tightest possible foetal position. Our SAS doctor's notes advised us that our inevitable shivering overnight would lose us an average of 2,000 calories each. I spent many minutes each time I woke banging one foot against the other for fear of frostnip, an early stage of frostbite, in my toes; and I hated the inevitable need, usually about two-thirds of the way through the sleeping hours, to have a pee. The doctor's comments suggested that a pee bottle should be stored inside each person's sleeping bag, and that it was possible, with practice, to use it without wetting the bed, unless you were female. No advice was given for females. Apparently getting cold at night causes the brain to order the body to withdraw any excess fluids from cells and place them in the bladder for excretion.

Despite the fact that I never felt even vaguely warm at night, I was, according to the notes, losing an average of one whole pint of moisture through sweat into my sleeping bag every night. In Greenland, where it was much warmer, we had first noticed this sweat problem but, in the subsequent rush, had forgotten to order inner vapour-barrier liners. I vowed to correct this omission once back home.

The sea ice was at first only slightly fragmented and for four days we followed the coast to the west, gaining slowly in northerly latitude. At a mountain called Cape Albert Edwards, I set a course due north. Where the land ice meets the ever-shifting sea ice there are often long stretches of open seawater, even in winter, and we were lucky to coincide with an unusually cold year which kept these leads frozen, even when the rising tides of the full moon were fracturing many ice floes.

Choosing the right place to camp was not a casual task. Multi-year ice floes were best. Sea ice grows at a rate of two or three feet a year, and three-year-old floes have had time to mature. They begin to look weather-beaten to the practised eye. Winds have rounded off protruding ice blocks and the floe surface usually provides good flat camping areas with a surface from which much of the sea salt has been leached by past summer sunshine. Salty coffee or tea in the tent will quickly earn rebukes over poor camp spot selection.

For a week we struggled through our first pressure ridges – walls of broken ice blocks, many over twenty feet high. The heavy sledges overturned, as did the skidoos. We sank up to our hips in deep snow, cut passageways for the machines using heavy axes, shovelled for hours to form snow ramps, sweated in our fur parkas when it was −52°C and, on relaxing, felt the raw coldness rush through our clothes and our bones to the very core of our bodies'. All day we ached for the protection of our tents, but by night, shivering out of control in our bags, we only wished to be moving again.

Oliver wrote: 'What a night! I had to thaw out my bag which was solid with ice and the zip was frozen. The cooker would not start so the tent was unbearable. When I did start it, the fumes stung our eyes. I shivered all night and woke with a frozen nose. I hate this f. . .ing place. The cold is so intense and my hands are letting me down badly. The pain is indescribable and non-stop. I cannot sleep because of it.' Oliver was suffering. We all were, but not as severely as did those European explorers who, over a period of four and a half centuries, inched their way northwards on their sometimes hell-like voyages, eventually to the latitude of Alert and beyond.

A pocket history of all the mariners, whether from their countries' navies or on whaler ships, who opened up the Arctic by sea would be a book in itself. As would a description of the land- and river-based Arctic journeys. Those that have most impressed me go back to the seventeenth century and the first landfall on the Greenland coast since the Norse colonies there disappeared for no known reason. And many later voyages pressed on and on, forever seeking to fill in the blanks in the known charts, despite every conceivable hardship and the knowledge that so many of their predecessors had disappeared without trace in the cold, cold Arctic seas.

The most famous Norse explorer of all, Fridtjof Nansen, summarized the early days of northern exploration:

> Long before other seafaring nations had ever ventured to do more than hug the coastlines, our ancestors had traversed the open seas in all directions, had discovered Iceland and Greenland, and had colonized them.
>
> The strength of our people now dwindled away, and centuries elapsed before explorers once more sought the northern seas. Then it was other nations, especially the Dutch and the English, that led the van.
>
> Though everywhere ice was met with, people maintained that this open sea must lie behind the ice. Thus the belief in an ice-free northeast and northwest passage to the wealth of Cathay or of India, first propounded towards the close of the fifteenth century, cropped up again and again.
>
> England has to thank these chimeras in no small degree for the fact that she has become the mightiest seafaring nation of the world.

For several centuries the British sent expeditions north to find a quick route to trade with the fabulous riches of China. They believed that, should they find such a route, their voyages would be far more economical than sailing all the way round the tip of South Africa. At first they concentrated on heading north-east and over the top of Norway and Russia, in search of the Northeast Passage.

Some two hundred and fifteen London merchants, headed by the famous Sebastian Cabot, financed two expeditions. Three ships sailed north in 1553. Two, under Sir Hugh Willoughby, wintered on the Kola Peninsula near what is now Murmansk, and fishermen eventually found the crews of both ships. All 63 men were dead. Their report noted 'strange things about the mode in which they were frozen, having found some of them seated in the act of writing, pen still in hand, and the paper before them; others at table, platters in hand and spoon in mouth; others opening a locker, and others in various postures, like statues, as if they had been adjusted and placed in these attitudes.'

The third ship, under the command of the pilot Richard Chancellor, reached a point on the coast of the White Sea from which he travelled overland to meet the Czar, and in 1555 a joint trading venture called the Muscovy Company was set up which organized various voyages over the next twenty-five years, none of which found a Northeast Passage.

In the same period, the Dutch sent off three voyages under pilot Willem Barents with similar aims as the Muscovy Company. The third of these penetrated further north, at 80°N, than all the others and discovered Spitsbergen, but the ship sank and Barents died. After this the Dutch switched their commercial focus on to southern voyages round the Cape of Good Hope, which left the search for the Northeast Passage to the English, but after the Willoughby tragedy, English eyes swivelled to the apparently less threatening route to Cathay between Canada and Greenland. By the end of the sixteenth century they were focussed on sailing west from Britain to the north-eastern flank of North America and then heading north and west to find a way over the top of Canada, the so-called Northwest Passage.

When Queen Elizabeth selected her sea captains to search for this fabled route to the riches of the East, she chose Martin Frobisher. In his youth he had been licensed (which 'proper lawless pirates' weren't) to seize ships operated by the French in the Channel and elsewhere. It was said that he would plunder anything worthwhile from ships of any nation, including his own. The Queen paid for his two 35-ton ships and their crews, and he was also granted a licence for his voyage by the Muscovy Company, who approved of the ambitious plans of the Queen's oft-times adviser, Sir Humphrey Gilbert, half-brother of Sir Walter Raleigh. He had published his *Discourse of a Discoverie for a new Passage to Cataia* in 1576, as an optimistic prospectus for the search. It was accompanied by a map showing open water around the top of North America.

Frobisher was briefed at the Queen's personal dictate by a famous courtier, John Dee, and told that his voyages were valued mainly for the claims they established on newly discovered lands that would consolidate her historic rights to possession of the northern portions of North America. John Dee, who phrased the relevant documents, is credited to this day with inventing the concept of the British Empire and for setting out the legal basis for such an institution.

Frobisher set sail in 1576, but, unfortunately, one of the charts he was given by Gilbert and Dee was full of geographical errors, which led his voyages into various mistaken claims. So when he sighted Greenland, he thought that he'd merely spotted an island which had been christened Friesland by the fraudulent captains of a fourteenth-century voyage, the notorious Zeno brothers. Friesland, in fact, did not exist. What Frobisher actually saw was Resolution Island, off the southern tip of Baffin Island. He sailed on in a northerly direction for 150 miles into what he thought was an opening to his goal, the Northwest Passage. But this passage was, in fact, merely a long inlet and cul-de-sac now named Frobisher Bay. Since he had turned back before reaching its end and verifying its true nature, he believed and claimed that he had found an entrance to the desired passage to Cathay.

Meeting a group of Eskimos there, Frobisher gave them various trinkets, mirrors and handbells, and they offered to guide the ship to a good harbour. The only ship's boat, with five crew members, followed the Eskimo kayaks out of sight and were never seen again. Frobisher managed to entice a single Eskimo back on board as a hostage, but when no others, nor his missing men, had reappeared after fifteen days, Frobisher sailed back to England.

A merchant, named Lok, who had part-subsidized the voyage was given the only item that the boatless Frobisher had been able to obtain as a souvenir of the unknown land: some black rock obtained from one of the Eskimos. Lok was told by a London alchemist that the rock was gold ore, so he eagerly commissioned Frobisher to return with a new crew, including 120 miners, to the place where he had met the Eskimos. He was ordered to obtain as much of the black rock as he could, and not to spend any time 'exploring up the passage'.

This time, in 1577, Frobisher actually landed on the Greenland coast, a great feather in his and Britain's cap, had he but known it! He then went back to his inlet and managed to load 200 tons of black 'gold' on board. Back in London, then alive with gold fever, the Queen was over the moon, Frobisher was knighted and immediately commissioned for a third voyage, this time with fifteen of the best ships in the Queen's navy and with a secondary aim: besides getting more ore, he was to leave behind a hundred colonists, together with prefab huts and three of his ships.

On his way this time, in 1578, Frobisher sailed up a different passage, now named Hudson Strait, but on spotting his error he turned back just before entering it and therefore missed out on the discovery of Hudson Bay. Storms then lashed his fleet, sunk one ship and forced a speedy retreat back home with 1,000 more tons of ore. Due to the loss of huts and food in the storms, no colonists were left behind.

By the time Frobisher was back in London, alchemists had come to the conclusion that his first consignment of ore had contained no gold at all. Lok was imprisoned, the general opinion being that he had been duped by the initial alchemist, who was a Spaniard and thus suspected of being a Catholic agent out to ensure that the Protestant Queen of England suffered heavy financial losses. A fine example of an early conspiracy theory. Frobisher himself somehow avoided a tarnished reputation and went on to command the biggest English ship at the defeat of the Spanish Armada.

Britain, the great claimant of new territories, never did press a claim for Greenland. The Danish-Norwegian government of the time reacted speedily to the Frobisher voyages and engaged an English navigator to lead an expedition in 1579 to claim the territory for their government. This mission failed due to storms and ice.

In 1586 the whaling captain John Davis located a hopeful west-leading inlet to the north of Frobisher Bay and managed to sail well north of any previous voyage up the west coast of Greenland. His inlet proved to be a cul-de-sac, like Frobisher's before him, but he made his mark in history by meeting and later describing the Greenland Eskimos, and by promoting the Labrador Sea and its coastlines as a rich fishing area. The area of sea he explored, between the west coast of Greenland and Baffin Island, was later named the Davis Strait.

Among the many memorably hell-like voyages of the time were several funded by King Christian of Denmark-Norway, who sent navigators to explore Greenland's west coast and search for silver. One of these navigators, James Hall, pursued a sideline of abducting Eskimos to serve as exhibits at popular sideshows. Various Danes and some Eskimos died on Hall's voyages, and instead of walking the plank, mutinous crew members were singly put ashore and abandoned. An Eskimo eventually knifed and killed Hall in 1612.

The Norwegian, Jens Munk, was also sent by King Christian to locate the passage and claim land. Munk reached Hudson Strait in 1619. Overwintering on the west coast of Hudson Bay, the crew began to get scurvy. Munk wrote: 'All the limbs and joints were so miserably drawn together, with great pain in the loins, as if a thousand knives were thrust through them. The body at the same time was blue and brown, as when one gets a black eye, and the whole body was quite powerless. The mouth, also, was in a very bad and miserable condition, as all the teeth were loose, so that we could not eat any victuals.'

Day by day men expired, and their burial was difficult in the frozen earth. The surgeon then died, which did not help. When everyone was too weak to dig, bodies were left on board. Eventually only Munk and two others were left. They began to eat berries and miraculously started to get their strength back. Somehow they refloated their ship, threw the corpses overboard and sailed back to Denmark minus 61 members of the original crew.

By now the British were recovering from decades of Spanish maritime warfare and were turning their attention to more peaceful and commercially gainful goals. The East India Company had been formed in 1600, to trade with the East Indies. In order to avoid the long voyage around Africa, a shorter northern passage was urgently needed, as well as a quick route to China, which would avoid Dutch warships.

In 1610 Henry Hudson, who started out as a cabin boy and gradually worked his way up to being a ship's captain, was sent by London merchants to concentrate on possible entrances in the Hudson Bay, which was thought (correctly) to be a gateway to the passage. He sailed into the bay and right down its east coast, and discovered that its southern boundary had no likely outlets. Another cul-de-sac. His crew grew mutinous and eventually cast him afloat in a small boat, to certain death, together with his 7-year-old son and several sick crewmen. On their way out of Hudson Bay the crew were attacked by Eskimos and a number were killed. Robert Bylot (who had not been a mutineer) eventually piloted the ship back to London.

There was yet hope that somewhere up the Bay's west or northern side there might be a westerly channel which would lead to the passage. A career sailor, Thomas Button, was sent north in 1612, with Robert Bylot as an adviser. They sailed up the west coast of Hudson Bay after a winter of many deaths and reached the northern end of the bay at Southampton Island.

In 1615 Bylot was sent back to the bay, with William Baffin as his pilot, a navigator more skilled than any other of the time. Their voyage, crucially, sailed north of Southampton Island for the first time, not south into Hudson Bay. When blocked by sea ice, they turned back and Baffin concluded that the Hudson Strait way to the passage was a no-hoper and the best route must be to follow the Davis Strait up the west coast of Greenland for a greater distance before turning west. This he and Bylot did, when they returned in 1616. They soon passed the furthest north reached by Davis before entering what would be named Baffin Bay. Three promising channels were observed, each heading west or north-west. They named them Lancaster Sound, Smith Sound and Jones Sound.

Two hundred years later, Lancaster Sound would prove to be the start of the best, although a labyrinthine, way to the passage. But Baffin and Bylot found ice blocking the way into all three straits. On their return to Dover, their failure to find the passage and the great Baffin's pessimistic opinion that a passage would never be found, led to the end of marine exploration to find the passage for the next two hundred years. Man's knowledge of the cold places was gradually – very gradually – expanding, but at great cost in terms of the sufferings of the crews involved.

Most of these crews were used to sailing off and around the English coastline, or, at most, in the southern hemisphere. They had no inkling of the conditions that they were to experience in Arctic waters. There was little comprehension of the way sea ice behaves. Icebergs bigger than ships could advance with speed and crush their wooden hulls. Vice-like pack ice could, and often did, ensnare and sink the toughest of their vessels. Standard sailing responses to imminent danger were impossible when the cold froze rigging lines and the very cloth of sails became unmanageable in the raw blistered hands of desperate sailors. Navigation, as I was soon to discover in 1981, was next to impossible with any degree of acceptable accuracy due to the nearby location of the North Magnetic Pole and the freezing fog which obscured the sun more often than not.

Scurvy was a great killer on many of the voyages, and many, if not most, of the early expeditions were sooner or later forced to face the decision of whether to flee from advancing ice or risk entrapment for one or maybe more winters. These problems would continue to dog later expeditions.

However, the mainland region, now called Manitoba, was gradually settled, and Churchill, halfway up the west coast of Hudson Bay, became an important headquarters of the fur-trading, mineral-prospecting Hudson's Bay Company (HBC), founded in 1670. Just as keen as the Admiralty on finding the passage, the HBC sent many exploratory sloops around Hudson Bay and many land and river-based expeditions north to locate the passage, in the hope that it might lie just off the northern coast of the Canadian mainland.

In 1770 the HBC sent their employee Samuel Hearne north, both to search for copper and furs and to look for the passage. He was accompanied by a large band of Indians and eventually reached the Coppermine River, up which they travelled in canoes. Eight miles from the sea, they came upon an Eskimo settlement, whereupon the Indians massacred all the Eskimos.

Hearne could do nothing to save the unfortunate victims. He later wrote of the horrors of that day: 'I solicited very hard for her life; but the murderers made no reply till they had stuck both their spears through her body, and transfixed her to the ground. They then looked me sternly in the face, and began to ridicule me by asking if I wanted an Esquimaux wife; and paid not the smallest regard to the shrieks and agony of the poor girl, who was twisting round their spears like an eel.'

The Indians had Hearne's own future in their unpredictable hands, and he could not persuade them to accompany him to the actual mouth of the river. His estimate of its position later proved inaccurate by some two hundred miles, which was to confuse future explorers in the area. Hearne called the place of the massacre Bloody Falls. I was to come across many such reminders of the past on my own journey.

*

Fast forward to our ongoing 1977 North Pole attempt. We suffered from the seriously cold conditions in a way that we had never encountered on our previous Greenland journey. One morning the wind blew at a steady 45 knots, with gusts above 50 knots. The wind-chill factor was –120°C and the natural liquid in our eyes kept congealing, making it difficult to navigate through the broken ice blocks.

Vision was all-important. To progress at all meant choosing the least nightmarish route through the rubble fields and ice walls. We never tried to drive skidoos and sledges north until we had first prepared a lane with our axes. After each section was cut, we would clamber up a nearby ice slab and peer north. I always hoped to see a sudden end to the rubble beds, but my hopes were always dashed. A chaotic jumble of blocks, large and small, invariably constituted the entire 180° view; that and the sky.

We dreaded axe work because of the body sweat it caused and, later, the shivering when sweat particles inside our clothes turned to ice, which cascaded down our underwear when we moved. A typical stint of axe work would last 9–11 hours in order to clear a skidoo lane of between 500 and 3,000 yards.

During the two months of our North Pole attempt, the chartered plane, an Otter with skis, visited us eight times. But there were other days when we were far out to sea and the pilot returned to Ginny with a glum face and a negative report: we were nowhere to be seen. Ginny sat at her radios for ten hours a day, often longer, knowing that we were passing through areas of unstable, breaking ice. She never missed a schedule, and at times of major ionospheric disturbance, when even the Canadian radio experts at the camp were blacked out, Ginny would tirelessly change antennae on her high masts, hop from frequency to frequency and yell out her identification sign hour after hour, in the hope that we might pick up her call. Out on the ice we were entirely dependent on her. Hearing her faint Morse signal or, in good conditions, her voice in the tent was the happiest moment of any day.

At first, aware of the danger from polar bears, we each carried a rifle, but soon dropped the practice through sheer exhaustion. Slipping, sliding and falling into drifts made it difficult enough to manage a shovel and axe. The work was thirsty and, with nothing to drink all day, we ate balls of snow. I once axed off a tantalizing lollipop-like chunk of ice from a block and crammed it into my balaclava's mouth-hole. There was a fizzing sound and a stinging sensation. I felt around with my mitt and removed the ice, which was stained red where it had taken the skin off my tongue. I tasted the blood for an hour, and my tongue was raw for days. 'You should eat more ice,' Charlie commented. 'It keeps you quiet.' Our daily ration of two frozen chocolate bars each wreaked havoc with our teeth. By the time we returned to London, we had, between the three of us, lost nineteen fillings.

Without Geoff in my tent, I noticed the lack of his body heat, but the absence of his companionship was the greater blow. Little things took on great importance. Some nights everything went wrong and I felt at the end of my tether. For long minutes in the dark I thought of nothing but my eyes. The pain was a live thing. I pressed against my eyeballs with my wet mitts, but the feeling of sharp grit moving about under the lids persisted. I can remember no dentist visit, no limb breakage, nothing in my life so painful as 'Arctic eye'.

A week later I moved in with Charlie and Oliver. It was a tight squeeze, but less intensely cold with the warmth of three bodies. The ends of Oliver's fingers had gone black, with layers of skin peeled off all but the little fingers. Deep cracks edged back from his cuticles and criss-crossed the tender subskin revealed by the frost removal of his epidermal layers. Most of his mechanical duties involved work with petrol and cold metal. My nose and one ear were frostbitten, and I could sleep only on my back or on one side as a result.

It is difficult to avoid outbursts of temper and hours of silent hostility in such conditions. For three years in London and four months in comparatively temperate Greenland, relations between the three of us had been idyllic, but the Arctic put an end to that harmony. The new level of strain was beginning to get to us. Apsley Cherry-Garrard, describing Scott's 'winter party', wrote: 'The loss of a biscuit crumb left a sense of injury which lasted for a week. The greatest friends were so much on one another's nerves that they did not speak for days for fear of quarrelling.'

Over the weeks we inched north until the pressure ridges were no longer an unbroken mass. We began to find flat 'pancakes' of ice where travel was easy, and quick flashes of hope, even elation, would then upset my determined cocoon of caution. I remember the thrill of exhilaration as ice flashed by, my skidoo making a jarring thud as it bounced off ice walls, or quick relief as my sledge, leaping behind like a live thing, settled back on its runners instead of overturning.

The fear came when my skidoo rolled over, down thirty-foot ramps of hard, sharp-edged ice slabs, and I flew off to land yards away, the wind knocked from my lungs, my head buried and my goggles stuffed with snow. Was I hurt? Would I be able to carry on? The ridge and rubble zones were most exhausting. The three of us together would slowly drag, shovel and haul an overturned sledge or a bogged skidoo from a drift to the tired, endlessly repeated chant: 'One, two, three – pull.' With only coffee for breakfast and two Mars bars for daytime snacks, we felt hungry and thirsty all the time. I would wake in the night to find my body liquid sucked away due to stomach rehydration of our dehydrated supper, leaving a raging thirst and no water at hand to assuage it.

During the second week of April, the pack ice showed the first symptoms of break-up. We found that at –30°C, or thereabouts, and with no wind to ripple the water, the surface would freeze overnight to the point where it was often, but not always, crossable. Nights of creaking, rumbling thunder gave way to mornings of brown steam-mist, a sure sign of newly open water leads. For days we crossed open ditches and lakes of nilas, which is newly formed dark grey sludge ice. As long as the temperature remained below –20°C, the delays caused by the fractures were a matter of hours not days, for the open water refroze steadily, providing no wind blew to provoke further movement of the pack.

Geoff, his fingers still bandaged, joined one of our Otter resupply drops in mid-April. He told us over the radio: 'There is a great deal of open water ahead of and behind you. The minor floe you are now on is floating free.' A shift in the wind pattern closed the pack overnight, forming new high walls of rubble where the floes, some, as we were later told, weighing over a million tons, crunched against each other.

Winds picked up surface snow and filled the air with the glint of freezing ice particles. White-out conditions resulted when clouds blocked the sun, and then we travelled slowly, for navigation was awkward without shadow or perspective. No hole in the ice was visible until you fell into it; no hummock or thirty-foot wall evident until you collided with it. One of us would walk ahead with a prod, feeling the way forward for twenty yards before the skidoos slowly followed. Axe work was hazardous in white-outs, since we could not see where our blades struck until they landed. We cut our way through high rubble, knowing that somewhere to the left or to the right a clear passage might well detour north, involving far less work.

Our words were swept away by the wind, so more often than not we communicated by hand signals. Around us the ridge walls, like giant sails, caught the wind and strained to respond. Floes split under the resultant stress, and the eerie boom and crack of unseen fractures flayed our nerves. Open water, being black, was clearly visible, but new ice, mere centimetres thick, was quickly covered by spindrift and formed traps for the unsuspecting. We prodded ahead to avoid falling in.

Conventional wisdom has it that 'white ice is thick and grey thin'. On one occasion I discovered that this saying is not always true. I was gingerly advancing over a recently fractured white ice pan. The ice felt spongy underfoot at first, then more like rubber. Suddenly the surface began to move beneath my boots, a crack opened up and black water gushed rapidly over the floe, cascading over my boots and weighing down on the fragile new ice. As the water rose to my knees, the crust under my feet cracked apart.

At such times, past information imbibed, and at the time seemingly unimportant, tends to come to mind: I had read that about

140,000 people in the world drown every year. Sailors in the World Wars, I recalled, survived one minute on average in the North Sea. Fat people survive for longer (I was pretty thin), and you should try to move as little as possible (I was thrashing about to stay afloat).

I knew that in laboratory experiments, at temperatures of –25°C, navy personnel simulating escape from sea-crashed aircraft could hold their breath at most for 37 seconds and, in shock circumstances, for considerably less. The body's cold-shock response, at any temperature below –12°C, is triggered by the activation of cold receptors in the skin sparking off a completely uncontrollable gasp, which fills the lungs with air or, if submerged, with water.

For victims of extreme cold induced by immersion who escape from the water but have no means of obtaining warm shelter, the process of dying is elemental. Blood vessels begin to constrict, and these are the conduits that usually carry your hot blood to your cold extremities. Your body hair, goose pimples, stands up in a vain attempt to trap more air close to the skin. In my circumstances these body activities would hardly help.

Shivering violently would, in theory, generate heat to delay the drop in my core temperature, but this would use up to 40 per cent of my body's maximum exercise capacity, along with a supply of my key fat and carbohydrate store. This shivering process, which initiates hypothermia, would continue until I ran out of the necessary energy fuels, at which point the shivers would die away, I would cool faster, and the electrical activity in my brain would begin to fail, leading to coma status and fading heartbeat. No heartbeat means no oxygen supply and death. In very cold conditions the actual point of irretrievable death will be delayed possibly to many minutes.

Another anomaly of cold-water immersion is often described by marine-rescue experts as 'rewarming shock'. When a number of individuals jump off a sinking ship into a cold sea, some with their clothes on will survive, whereas others, swimming with just underwear, may well survive for several minutes in the rescue boat, but later, as the cold blood from all their extremities returns to their hearts, they are likely to die one by one.

Children are at greater risk because their smaller body-to-surface area ratio means that they lose heat faster. And the elderly also have a higher death rate from cold immersion, due to their lower metabolic rate.

Humans thrive at a core temperature of just under 99°C. At about 95°C they begin to shiver uncontrollably and become 'sleepy'. At 93°C amnesia sets in, and at 91°C apathy. At 90°C the heart begins to slow down, and at 87°C hypothermia sets in: without help to rewarm, death will follow quickly. In all cases, profound hypothermia can simulate death, but the final diagnosis that a corpse is indeed truly 'gone' cannot be made until there is failure to revive after the core body temperature has been warmed back to normal. As the old saying goes, 'Nobody is dead until they are warm and dead.'

There is no better example of this than the Swedish skier Anna Bågenholm who, in 1999, was trapped in water, and under the ice, for eighty minutes. Her body temperature dropped to 13.7°C (56.7°F), the lowest survival body temperature ever recorded in a human with hypothermia. Although able to breathe in a tiny air pocket, her rescuers recorded that she suffered circulatory arrest forty minutes after her initial immersion. They would have been forgiven for giving her up as dead.

Back to me, also immersed and getting cold. I sank quickly, but my head could not have been submerged for more than a second because the air trapped under my wolfskin acted as a life jacket. The nearest solid floe was thirty yards away. I shouted for the others, but there was no one nearby, and there would be no passers-by. Each time I tried to heave myself up on to a section of the submerged crust, I broke it again. I crawled and clawed and shouted. Under my threshing feet was a drop of 17,000 watery feet, down to the canyons of the Lomonosov Ridge.

I began to tire. My toes felt numb and there was no sensation inside my mitts. My chin, inside the parka, sank lower as my clothes became heavier. I began to panic. After four, perhaps five, minutes, my escape efforts had weakened to a feeble pawing movement when, in an ecstatic moment, one arm slapped down on to a solid ice chunk and I levered my chest on to a skein of old ice. Then my thighs and knees. I lay gasping for a few seconds, thanking God, but – once out of the water – the cold and the wind bit into me. The air temperature was −38°C with a 7-knot breeze. At −29°C and 19 knots, dry exposed flesh freezes in sixty seconds.

My trousers crackled as they froze. I tried to exercise my limbs, but they were concrete-heavy in the sodden, freezing parka. For fifteen minutes I plodded round and round my skidoo, which I could not start. My mitts were frozen and the individual fingers would not move.

Oliver came along my tracks. He reacted quickly, erecting a tent, starting a cooker, and cutting off my parka, mitts and boots with his knife. Twenty-four hours later, with me in spare clothes and a man-made duvet, we were on our way again. I was lucky to be alive. Few go for a long swim in the Arctic Ocean and survive without frost damage. The fact that I wore animal leather all over my torso and hands, with heavy felt boots, was my saving grace.

During the latter half of April we pushed hard to squeeze northerly mileage out of each hour's travel, speaking to each other hardly at all, except inside the tent. Lack of sleep made us light-headed. We had lost weight and strength and we lived in a dreamworld of whiteness and weird shapes, intense glare and hard ice. The only certainty was north. We must go north. Every minute spent making northerly progress produced satisfaction, every delay frustration.

Only three teams in history had undisputedly succeeded in reaching the Pole. By 20 April we had exceeded the records of the Swede Björn Staib, the Italian Cagni, and the Norwegian Nansen. By the end of the month, we had surpassed all but the journeys of Peary and the three pole conquerors: Plaisted, Herbert and Monzino.

On 29 April we were brought up short by what Oliver called the escalator. This was an 800-yard-wide river of moving mush ice fringed for a mile on either bank by an unstable concoction of part-open pools and compressed pancake ice formed from broken floes of nilas and ice rind. A local storm must have devastated the pack all around this mushy river, for the floes were nowhere bigger than a dining-room table. Slabs leaned crazily in all directions and the thunderous crunch of fragmenting floes added to our feeling of unease. A river of porridge-like shuga sludge moved across in front of us at about two miles an hour, and everything on the far bank was, on closer inspection, also floating past from west to east.

We first attempted to cross the escalator in the inflatable rubber dinghy which Charlie always carried, but a wave of ice sludge climbed over the upstream tube of the inflatable, threatening to pour into the boat like lava and submerge us. We camped for two days and nights, awaiting a freeze-up. In the end we crossed the moving surface of the jellied river well before it reached a thickness that we would normally have considered 'safe'.

Every day we confronted more zones of swamp-mush and webbed fissures of open water, for the sun's ultraviolet rays bored down into the surface pack, rendering it rotten and susceptible to the slightest stress from wind and current. On 5 May we passed by 87°N, a mere 180 miles from the pole.

The transpolar drift stopped us. The two major currents of the Arctic – the Beaufort Gyral Stream and the Transpolar Drift Stream – meet and diverge somewhere between 87° and 88° of latitude north, causing surface chaos, tearing floes apart in places and jumbling others up to heights of thirty feet. On 7 May there were wide canals and slush-pools every few hundred yards. The entire region was in motion, slowly swirling and eddying. At this point the engine of my skidoo blew a head gasket and we could not progress without a resupply drop.

Finding a safe floe, we waited with mounting frustration while Ginny tried to cajole a ski plane from the nearest charter company, six hundred miles to her south. When she succeeded three days later, temperatures rose to −15°C and mist banks caused the plane to miss us altogether. On a second attempt they found us. By the time we had fitted the new skidoo engine, we had drifted sixty miles to the south and east, and a six-mile belt of sludge surrounded us. We waited for a further week, hoping for a freak temperature drop, but on 15 May, with the temperature at 0°C, I decided to call it a day.

Our funds ran out with the flight that extricated us from the floe and took us back to Alert. There Ginny gave me a radio message from London. Prince Charles had agreed to become patron of the Transglobe Expedition.

Back in the London office we carried on much as before, but the Arctic journey had humbled me. It was my first expedition failure. The cold had taught me a good deal about myself, as well as the others. Soon afterwards, Mary and Geoff were married and left the expedition. Mary's place as Ginny's base-camp companion was then taken by a young Cumbrian named Simon Grimes. By the end of 1978 we had over 1,500 sponsors, and 60 tons of equipment were stored in various parts of the Duke of York's barracks.

In the spring of 1979 Prince Charles opened the Transglobe's press launch in the presence of 900 supporters. He arrived at the controls of our Twin Otter on an appropriately snowbound runway at Farnborough and announced that he was supporting the expedition 'because it is a mad and suitably British enterprise'. Aiming to set out in September 1979, we worked hard through the summer with the help of many volunteers. Anton recruited 16 crewmen for his ship, which he christened the *Benjamin Bowring* after an adventurous ancestor.

In July and August we packed and labelled over 3,000 heavy-duty boxes bound for 18 different remote bases around the world. A year earlier I had, for the first time, opened an expedition bank account, and the day we left England with a mind-boggling array of equipment for the 110,000-mile journey, a team of 30, a ship and an aircraft, we were in credit to the tune of £81.76.

Late in the afternoon of 2 September 1979 the *Benjamin Bowring* left Greenwich with Prince Charles at the helm. He wore a black tie because his uncle, Lord Mountbatten, had been killed three days before. Of the expedition, Prince Charles said:

> Transglobe is certainly one of the most ambitious undertakings of its kind ever attempted, and the scope of its requirements is monumental ... Although so much has changed in the world since explorers first attempted to reach the Poles at the beginning of the century, the challenges of nature and the environment are still very much the same ... Above all, the human risks are still the same. They're all there today, the frostbite, the loss of body fat because of the cold and the protracted bouts of shivering, especially at night, the unsuspected crevasses and traps for the unwary, the thin ice ... Even though a decade has passed since man first set foot on the moon, polar exploration and research remain as important as ever.

There were many people lining the pier. I spotted Geoff, who was shouting rude messages at Oliver, and Mary, smiling through her tears. The *New York Times* editorial column, under the heading 'Glory', stated, 'The British aren't so weary as they're sometimes said to be. The Transglobe Expedition, seven years in the planning, leaves England on a journey of such daring that it makes one wonder how the sun ever set on the Empire.'

Chapter Five

Then the bright star appears – the man whose name will ever be remembered as ... one of the most capable seamen the world has ever produced – Admiral Sir James Clark Ross

ROALD AMUNDSEN, *THE SOUTH POLE*: 1910–12 (1912)

Our 30-year-old ship, the *Benjamin Bowring*, was crewed by a wonderful bunch of volunteers, all skilled in their jobs, whether chief engineer or first officer. They included Quaker, Buddhist, Jew, Christian and atheist, black, white and Asian. They came from Austria, America, both ends of Ireland, South Africa, India, Denmark, Britain, Canada, Fiji and New Zealand. None would be paid a penny for the three years of the expedition.

A senior Brother of Trinity House in London, the authority who selected many of the officers and crew of the early Arctic expeditions under the likes of pioneers Hudson and Baffin, had helped Anton select the crew. Our volunteer skipper was a retired bee-keeping admiral who grew roses and had never commanded a ship in ice. He was called Otto Steiner but, despite his name, he had helped to sink German ships in the last war. Ginny was not the only female aboard as there was a cook, Jill McNicol, selected by Anton Bowring, who later married her.

We reached Algiers and the land group of Ollie, Charlie, Ginny, me and Geoff's replacement, Simon, were dropped off with three

Land Rovers. As we waved the ship goodbye, we noticed that they left the harbour and continued in reverse until out of sight. This we later learnt was because the gear system had got stuck in reverse.

On reaching the Ivory Coast, more or less on the Greenwich Meridian, we met up with the ship again which took us down towards Cape Town. The electrics of the refrigerator room broke down in the tropics and a ton of sponsored mackerel turned putrescent. Much of the mushy, stinking results escaped into the bilges and the smell was all-pervasive for weeks. Three days before Christmas 1979 we left Cape Town, the last land for 2,400 miles, and set our course for Antarctica.

Ginny's dog Bothie made himself at home all over the ship and was about the only passenger who seemed completely unconcerned by the extreme rolling motion that the ship seemed to favour from just south of Cape Town and thereafter. Only one of our crew, a Pink Floyd fan from Leighton Buzzard, had sailed in Antarctic waters before, and even he seemed to think our ship had a 'difficult movement'. At all times, a couple of people were on bridge-watch for growlers – semi-submerged chunks of ice. I sought reassurance with a visit to Anton's cabin.

'Everything OK?' I asked.

'How d'you mean?'

'The ship,' I gestured downwards. 'The hull . . . you know?'

'Ah.' He understood. 'This is not rough, you know. It will get much worse.' Then he told me about a British expedition the previous year, same time, same latitude as us. Called the *En Avant* and ice-strengthened as we were, she was commanded by the famous polar sailor, Major Bill Tilman, with a crew of eight. Somewhere prior to reaching the ice she disappeared and was never seen again.

'It's my bet,' Anton concluded, 'that they were hit by a big wave. You get the biggest anywhere down here.'

All of the world's oceans mix together in the Southern Ocean, the circumpolar sea which cuts Antarctica off. This globe-girdling storm track breeds westerly storms which, unimpeded by land masses, become ever more impressive as you head south into the Furious Fifties and Screaming Sixties.

We were headed on a magnetic bearing of 220°. At the 50th parallel in late December the first iceberg passed abeam. Ollie, usually to be seen on the bridge wing with binoculars and notebook, noted black-browed and grey-headed albatross, skua, giant petrel, prion, and many more.

Then a Force Eight storm hit us. Our ship was of steel, but had worked for the Australians when Mawson, their most famous explorer of Shackleton's era, was still active in their polar ranks. Shackleton had been in these waters in wooden vessels only sixty years before us. I had met one of Scott's stokers, Bill Burton, whose memories of the fateful 1910 expedition were still vivid.

We were battered by giant Southern Ocean rollers. I found the most fearful moments were at maximum roll, when the ship stayed down for a while before the next re-righting move began. Charlie appeared for breakfast one stormy morning with a bruised cheek where his heavy glass bedside ashtray, complete with its load of stubbed dog-ends, had struck him after an especially violent roll.

Amidships, and close by the skipper's cabin, Anton had hung a brass inclinometer, the very same simple instrument that Captain Scott carried on *Discovery* and our only relic from that earlier southern voyage. One of our deck watch, an Indian officer called Cyrus, was at the helm one day soon after Christmas as a giant roller forced the *Benjy B* to keel to 47° both ways. Christmas goodies bit the dust, Bothie slid on his side a good six yards, and the Admiral nearly swallowed his pipe. Everyone together shouted, 'Cyrus!' For the next three years, whenever the *Benjy B* took a wave more violent than most, whenever somebody spilled their coffee at an imagined pitch or toss, poor Cyrus's name was mouthed like a swear word, whether he was in fact at the wheel or snoring in his pit.

I thumbed through one of the ship's small collection of sea books and learnt a few basic facts about waves. The size of a wave depends on the strength of the wind and how far it blows over the water. This is known as the fetch. With a short fetch you get a choppy sea and with a long one you get a swell of rolling waves. One in every 300,000 waves will be a monster some four times bigger than all the rest, and the biggest of all occur in the Atlantic to the south of South Africa – exactly where we were. Warships have recorded waves of over 120 feet in height. Sailors are familiar with waves known as Cape Horn greybeards which may exceed 2,000 feet in length and 100 feet in height. Their speed can be more than 30 m.p.h., which is considerably in excess of that of a sailing ship. There was certainly a problem with ships capsizing as a result of meeting them, should the helmsman be caught unaware.

The most notable feature that snakes around Antarctica, about eight hundred miles off its coastline and roughly between 50° and 60°S, is the place where two different bodies of seawater meet up in a zone about thirty miles wide. This so-called Antarctic Convergence is of special interest to oceanographers, and our two resident scientists were no exception, drooling over the contents of their trawl nets whilst we passed through this anomalous zone.

The waters of the Pacific, Atlantic and Indian oceans are at this latitude cooled from about 7°C to a mere 2°C. Cold dense water heads downwards, and warmer, northern-derived waters thrust upwards, bringing all manner of life forms to the surface, including algae, plankton and various micro-organisms. The resulting rich supply of nutrients feeds billions of krill, which in turn support some 35 million seals, 70 million penguins, plus countless whales, fish and seabirds. The seabirds alone consume nearly 8 million tons of krill each year. Each day, with one of the crew operating the winch gear, our scientists trawled for plankton. With bathythermographs they obtained depth to temperature profiles. Using these side by side with salinity measurements, they identified large-scale water movements. Their aim was to study current patterns and the interaction of the water bodies at subtropical and Antarctic convergences. The behaviour and condition of these currents influence the existence of tiny phytoplankton and thus of their predators, the zooplankton, including krill.

Chris McQuaid, one of our two oceanographers, showed me a jar of seawater solid with tiny crustaceans after only a ten-minute trawl. 'This,' he said, waving his hand at the great grey expanse, 'is the most productive ocean in the world. For a scientist, its richness and diversity are irresistible. Krill may well prove to be an important source of food for humans and it is so abundant that it can be harvested in thousands of tons. Already, commercial krill fisheries have been established by several countries.'

He dabbed a finger in the jar of slimy sea-life. 'Unfortunately, there are plenty of examples in recent history of what happens when commercial interests go on a spree and ignore the simple laws of nature. Here we have a source of protein which is valuable and, by modern methods, quite easy to harvest. It may take only a few years to be culled to the point of scarcity, even extinction.'

He was warming to his subject. 'Krill is the central link in the vast and complex food webs that form the ecology of the Southern Ocean. Remove too many krill and you endanger whales, seals, seabirds and fish. In the rush to cull a new source of food for man and exploit it profitably, commercial interests may cause havoc.'

Chris's Irish brogue grew stronger with emphasis. 'Unless we, the researchers, know all the facts, we cannot present a convincing argument for control. But our resources are limited in manpower, money and opportunity, unlike those of the krill fishermen whose backers feed on their own profit and mankind's necessity. That's why the voyage of the *Benjy B* is such a godsend.'

Of the many species of krill, just one, the *Euphausia superba*, our scientists told me, has a greater biomass – about 500 million tonnes – than that of any other species of animal on earth, including humans.

The *Benjamin Bowring* began to feel like home to us all, a feeling that would increase as the months and years of the expedition went by. As the *Kista Dan*, she had plied Antarctic waters for Australian expeditions between 1953 and 1957. She had a range of 14,000 miles and a thrust of 1500 horsepower, with a variable pitch propeller, the pitch and direction of which could be controlled from the bridge or from the crow's nest high up the main mast with excellent visibility of the pack ice ahead.

I joined Oliver on the bridge wing and borrowed his binoculars to watch the numerous albatrosses that seemed to follow the ship. Ollie was in awe of them. They have wingspans of 3.5 metres and are the biggest of all seabirds. They are, nonetheless, designed to use the wind and to float on it using minimal energy. They need at least 12 m.p.h. wind speeds because, at a lesser speed, they are forced to beat their wings; this becomes dangerously uneconomical and can strand them on the sea, unable to lift off until the next strong enough blow. When the winds favour them, they have been known (through radio tags) to fly more than 9,000 miles in 33 days. Their wings and their innate knowledge of wind usage are their vital assets. Each of their wings is muscled and programmed to adjust to tiny wind fluctuations.

The winds were mainly from the west for a week, but as we approached the pack-ice zone and the coastline, easterlies prevailed. Where the two wind systems meet is known as the Antarctic Divergence.

Once into the pack ice proper, we sometimes came to a complete halt, which was worrying since nobody on board had had any experience at crashing through polar pack. The next British expedition after ours, known as In the Footsteps of Scott, reached the same latitude as we had and in a very similar vessel when the pack ice closed in, crushed her hull and she sank within hours.

I had a copy of a book written by the boss of the Australian equivalent of the British Antarctic Survey, Phillip Law, who had spent anxious times in the 1950s on our ship, in her *Kista Dan* days. He had laid down a few tips on how best to progress through pack ice. Two factors are vital: the type of ice and the amount of open water. Large, heavy floes can be pushed aside if there is enough open water in the vicinity for them to move into. Thick ice can be broken for a short distance until it brings the ship to rest, after which the ship may reverse, then charge again, gaining a further short distance. This backing and charging manoeuvre, if skilfully done, can be most effective, but it uses up a lot of fuel. Narrow leads can be followed by cutting across the ice at the sharper turns; the momentum of the ship carries her through or pushes the ice into the water at the bend.

With an ice cover of 10-tenths in the area to be crashed through, even very thin floes will hold up progress, for the ship is pushing, in effect, against miles and miles of ice. Broken-up, pulverized ice, if more than a metre in depth, may stop a ship through sheer friction, even though the ice would appear, in its slushy consistency, to be quite negotiable. Such ice is particularly dangerous because the ship's wake closes up as soon as the ship has passed and, when forward progress is halted, backward motion is likewise impossible.

A ship with parallel, instead of curved, sides may be gripped tightly by ice through which it has forced its way. In the old days, running the crew across the deck from rail to rail helped to roll the ship and free her. A modern icebreaker has curved sides and uses 'heeling' tanks and pumps which achieve the same purpose as the running crew by transferring water rapidly from one side to the other.

Calm, still weather of any duration is a great disadvantage in heavy pack ice. Leads do not open up and freezing proceeds rapidly if the temperature falls. It the ship is to be left stationary, it should be left with the bows facing in the direction of ice drift. Areas of hummocked ice should be avoided as far as possible, for these denote pressure. Moreover, hummocked floes are generally thicker and harder than others. It is not safe to stop in thick pack near icebergs.

Phillip Law had one experience on a ship fairly firmly held in pack ice which was drifting before a 60-knot gale. Some miles away were a number of icebergs which, deep in the water, were more affected by ocean currents than surface winds, and they were moving in the opposite direction. As a result, one iceberg was seen to be approaching directly towards the ship at about 5 knots. Fortunately, by backing and charging for half an hour, the ship was able to extricate itself from a position similar to that of a child's toy car in front of an advancing steamroller.

Ginny and I had the cabin which was set up as a quarantine room in case somebody needed isolation, and a heavy steel safe with drugs was part of the furniture. One morning we woke to find that it had been flung from its corner to a position right up against our bunks. We must have been sleeping very soundly. But once we were within the pack ice the sea quietened down and, apart from the frequent shuddering jolts on hitting ice, the voyage became pretty peaceful.

On 4 January 1980 the watch spotted the white cliffs of Antarctica to our immediate front. I thought of our predecessors who came south not for commercial gain but for adventure. The history of great sea captains claiming the honour of finding Antarctica, on the assumption that such a place existed, was in some way a southern parallel to the northern quest to find the Northwest Passage.

As far back as the fifth century BC, Greek geographers theorized that a vast region of ice existed at the bottom of the world, and by the Middle Ages map-makers often decorated their charts with a southern land mass which they dubbed *Terra australis*.

Under the initial promptings of Portuguese Henry the Navigator, the likes of Columbus, Magellan and Dias gradually opened up new horizons in the fifteenth and sixteenth century. In 1520 Ferdinand Magellan sailed round the tip of the American continent at 53°S, and fifty-eight years later Francis Drake recorded 56°S by rounding Cape Horn.

In the mid-eighteenth century three French expeditions skirted the Antarctic pack-ice belt and discovered various subantarctic islets, whilst in 1772–5 the English sea captain James Cook circumnavigated the world just north of Antarctica's icy fringe. Cook's southern voyages were to inspire the poet Coleridge to write in *The Rime of the Ancient Mariner* (1798):

And now there came both mist and snow,
And it grew wondrous cold:
And ice, mast-high, came floating by,
As green as emerald.

Cook was a good example of a self-made man. Born to a farmworker's wife in a two-room cottage in North Yorkshire, he was the second of eight children. He became a grocery boy until, aged eighteen, he joined the coal-shipping business that operated from Whitby to London.

The trip down the east coast of England involved cautious navigation by lookout and local knowledge of tide rips, sandbanks and speedy reaction to storms. In the 1690s about two hundred ships and a thousand men were lost on the coal run. Every year hundreds of bodies were washed up on beaches, having come from sunken vessels taking 2 million tons of coal to London. In a period of just five hours on one day in 1738, records show that 3,000 coal ships passed through the Yarmouth Roads Straits.

By the time he was twenty-four years old, Cook had ended his apprenticeship and was promoted to mate. By the age of thirty-three he was in command of his own collier ship, but then he took the unusual step of joining the Royal Navy. Two years on he was a senior warrant officer on a warship and his subsequent meteoric rise to selection as leader of a great national voyage of exploration was nothing short of miraculous for the son of a farm labourer.

The British government sent Cook south because they were determined to claim whatever lands might lie to the south of Cape Horn and South Africa before the French. His first expedition in the *Endeavour* (1768–71) was highly successful and included many new discoveries. He introduced firm rules that fresh meat must be eaten on all his long voyages, which, in an unprecedented fashion, meant that they were all free of scurvy. He was not averse to having wayward crew members flogged, but preferred less brutal ways of keeping order. On his three-year-long round-the-world *Endeavour* voyage, Cook became a truly expert navigator, using astronomical tables. By the late 1700s, new time devices were enabling navigators to determine their longitude accurately, and James Cook's great southerly voyages took full advantage of this. In 1772, when he was selected for his second great voyage in the *Resolution*, he used the most advanced and new-fangled mechanical watches to obtain his longitude.

For three long years, between 1772 and 1775, the remarkable Cook circled Antarctica and, from three different sides of the world, headed into the pack ice in his attempt to find land there. Each time he was defeated by highly lethal conditions and each time he persevered. After achieving the first crossing of the Antarctic Circle in 1773, he went on to reach 71°10′S, his most southerly polar record.

By the time that Cook eventually returned home, he had demolished any British hopes of claiming some valuable polar land mass. However, the mechanical watches that he used to determine longitude had proved to be accurate and efficient, and the introduction of fresh meat as a means of avoiding the hitherto dread certainty of scurvy on such long voyages was highly effective. New lands had been discovered and the previously reported erroneous positions of many islands had been corrected.

One of Cook's reports mentioned the plentiful supply of seals and other blubber-bearing animals to be found down south, and this sent pioneering sealer ships, and subsequently whalers, to the subantarctic islands. They arrived over the next half-century, slowly at first as the best sealing grounds were located, but then in a rush when Antarctic sealing became carnage. Animals of either sex were clubbed to death or shot where they lay on the beaches.

Very often the bull seals of a particular beach would aggressively prevent any of 'their' females from escaping to the sea. Seeing this, the sealers would leave the bulls till last. Dead animals were skinned where killed, and pups stayed beside their mothers' corpses until they died of starvation.

When a bull charged at a sealer, one of his eyes would be blinded with a club. One sealer's diary recorded, 'We took the remedy of blinding them all in one eye. It was then laughable to see these old goats planted along the beach and keeping their remaining peeper continually fixed on their seraglio while our sailors passed unheeded between their blindside and the water's edge.'

By 1822 James Weddell estimated that the post-Cook fur-seal cull in South Georgia alone had taken 'not less than 1 million 200,000 seals. These animals,' he noted, 'are now almost extinct.' Other less frequently hunted seals included the killer or leopard seal, which eats penguins and other seals and takes the place of the shark, which is not to be found in Antarctic waters. The krill-eating crabeater seal was badly named by the early whalers, since there are no crabs in Antarctic seas. These seals were never hunted in great numbers and, today, are the most abundant of all marine mammals on Earth. The fish and squid-eating Weddell seal, a favourite of the sealers, feeds on the sea floor, which often involves dives of 400 metres and staying underwater for an hour or more.

The best known of the American sealer captains, Nathaniel Palmer, commented in 1820 that the fairly small sealer *Hero* recorded its cull of fur-seal skins taken in one short month as 50,000 pelts. That same year witnessed vicious fighting between men from different sealers, all claiming kill-rights on the same beach. Thomas Smith of the US sealer *Kitty* recorded: 'They walked overland to our beach and slaughtered 8,000 seals. The leading men of our party, seeing their audacity, instantly collared their leaders to prevent them from farther prosecuting their obstinate design. This act immediately threw the parties into confusion, which resulted in a general and bloody engagement, in which many were severely injured.' Most of the sealers that reacted to Cook's information were American, largely because the European countries were, as usual, at war with each other at the time. An exception was the Australian sealing captain who claimed Macquarie Island in 1810.

In terms of who was first to sight Antarctica, there were several potential claimants, including the Briton, William Smith, who claimed the South Shetland Islands in 1819. Separately, the Irishman Edward Bransfield made a similar claim. Slightly later, the

American Nathaniel Palmer made his claim, and on 28 January 1820 a Russian, Captain von Bellingshausen, diarized his own sighting of Antarctica. Nowadays it is the Russian claim that is generally accepted in polar archives as having achieved the prize at 69°21′S, only two days prior to the Bransfield and Smith sightings.

There were many other sealers ranging the southern ocean at that time and previously who may well have sighted Antarctica or subantarctic land but made no claims. As soon as a rich new virgin seal beach was discovered, crews were sworn to secrecy, logbooks and journals were burnt by order, and all locations were kept as closely guarded secrets by the ships' captains.

Captain von Bellingshausen's expedition reached Macquarie Island to the south of Australia, and he found that the seal colonies reported some forty years before by Cook were virtually wiped out, so that sealing crews had switched their murderous culls to sea elephants instead. He described what he saw on the island:

> One of the sealers accompanied us. He had with him an implement with which to kill sea elephants, which consisted of a club four and a half feet long and two inches thick. The end was bell-shaped, four or five inches in diameter, bound with iron and studded with sharp nails. When we approached a sleeping sea elephant, the sealer hit him with this implement over the bridge of the nose; the sea elephant opened its mouth and gave a loud and pitiful roar. It had already lost all power of motion. The man took out his knife, saying, 'It is a pity to see the poor animal suffer', and stuck it into its neck from four sides. The blood poured out in torrents forming a red circle. The animal then gave a few heavy breaths and died at once. Large sea elephants, after this blow which stuns them, are pierced through the heart with a lance so as to kill them on the spot.

A year after von Bellingshausen's first sighting of Antarctica, American sealer, John Davis, actually landed on the Antarctic peninsula and eleven men from the Liverpool sealer *Lord Melville* spent the first winter on the subantarctic King George Island in the South Shetland group.

Three famous expeditions achieved various new southern records over the next quarter of a century: the voyages of James Weddell, who penetrated the Weddell Sea, John Biscoe who completed the first circumnavigation of Antarctica, and James Clark Ross who, amongst many other achievements, discovered the Ross Sea, the Ross Ice Shelf and established a new 'furthest south'.

In 1823, the British sealer *Jane* under James Weddell was the first to enter a bay that he named after George IV, but which is now the Weddell Sea. Although he never saw or claimed that he saw land, he had easily achieved a new furthest south record (of 74°15′S). In most other years he could have found his route blocked by pack ice, but occasionally a large exodus of this pack ice occurs and a wide area of open water, or polynya, can remain right through the winter months.

An enterprising British sealer-explorer, Captain John Biscoe, in 1832 completed a circumnavigation even further south than von Bellingshausen, discovering new islands and a new stretch of the Antarctic peninsula which he called Graham Land. He managed to circumnavigate Antarctica in his little whaler, only the third expedition to do so.

In 1839 John Balleny, a contemporary of John Biscoe, discovered the remote Balleny Islands to the south of New Zealand and passed details of his excellent route south, between 180° and 170°E, to James Clark Ross, the captain of a Royal Navy ship HMS *Endurance* that he passed in the Thames on his eventual return to England. Ross had been selected by the Admiralty to lead two ships, the *Erebus* and *Terror*, to sail south of Australia and locate the South Magnetic Pole. He had already made his name leading the expedition that first reached the North Magnetic Pole.

In the 1970s and 1980s, I navigated to both North and South poles and through the Northwest Passage using my theodolite for location and my magnetic compass for direction. Nowadays I simply press buttons on my satnav. It is easy to forget the great problems and dangers of all early ocean navigation.

At the time when James Ross set sail for Antarctica in 1839, the Admiralty were determined to find solutions to the two main navigation problems: the inaccuracy of the magnetic compass and the difficulty in determining longitude. The latter problem was in the process of being solved by the work of watchmaker John Harrison and the magnetic formulae of the German Johann Gauss, which had been checked out by many voyages in the northern hemisphere but rarely in the very southern ocean passages, where world trade was increasingly requiring safe routes and accurate navigation systems.

Gauss's formulae theorized that a South Magnetic Pole should exist in about 66°S of latitude and 146°E of longitude. Ross and his two ships were, if possible, to locate the pole wherever it was. He arrived in Australia only to find that rival pole-seeking expeditions from America and France, under Charles Wilkes and Dumont d'Urville, had headed south the previous year down the very route that he had declared in public as his intended route. It was not playing cricket.

Ross's reaction was mild: 'I should have expected them to have chosen any other part in the wide field before them, than one thus pointed out [i.e. Ross's intended one] ... considering the embarrassing situation in which their conduct may have placed me ... I resolved at once to avoid all interference with their discoveries and selected a much more easterly meridian on which to endeavour to penetrate to the southward.'

Ross chose the 170°E meridian because of the report he had been given by John Balleny, who had used that longitudinal line with considerable success and had been greatly helped by areas of open water. In due course it became clear that the voyages of Wilkes and d'Urville had not settled the location of the South Pole, which fact greatly pleased the Admiralty in London.

Early in January 1840, after days of storm and fog in the pack ice, Ross's ships found open sea to the south. 'This large space of open water occurring in so high a latitude looks very promising to us,' wrote ship's surgeon, McCormick. At the end of the month they took on board three penguins of unusual size, later to be classified as Emperors.

In early February they made one of the most dramatic of geographical discoveries. Now known as the Ross Ice Shelf, it was a sight previously unimaginable. Ross wrote:

> This extraordinary barrier of ice, of probably more than a thousand feet thickness, is a mighty and wonderful object, far beyond anything we could have thought of or conceived . . . a perpendicular cliff of ice, between 150 and 200 feet above the level of the sea, perfectly flat and level at the top . . . What was beyond it we could not imagine, for being much higher than our mast-head we could not see anything but the summit of a lofty range of mountains extending to the southward as far as the seventy-ninth degree of latitude . . . Meeting with such an obstruction was a great disappointment to us all, for we had already, in expectation, passed far beyond the eightieth degree, and had even appointed a rendezvous there, in case of the ships accidentally separating. It was, however, an obstruction of such a character as to leave no doubt upon my mind as to our future proceedings, for we might with equal chance of success try to sail through the Cliffs of Dover, as penetrate such a mass.

Ross was naturally disappointed that the main aim of the voyage was thwarted and no overland sledging journey towards the magnetic pole could be made in the manner by which, years before, he had reached the North Magnetic Pole. However, he later discovered an active volcano which he named Mount Erebus and measured it at 10,900 feet high, situated next to an extinct volcano which he named Mount Terror, and he reconnoitred a deep bay beneath the two volcanoes. He then explored the adjacent coastlines in both directions for as far and as long as the ice and the season allowed, and in two subsequent seasons he continued further explorations along the coastline of what he increasingly believed was a gigantic frozen continent.

Erebus and *Terror*, in their first bold foray into what was later called the Ross Sea, may not have reached the South Magnetic Pole, but their voyage broke all previous southerly records by over a hundred miles and they completed many thousands of meticulous magnetic observations which later helped in a major way to establish the true and erratic behaviour of the magnetic poles. Vast new areas of the coastline and islands were also surveyed.

The famous Norwegian polar explorer, Roald Amundsen, so critical of many polar pioneers, wrote of Ross's voyages:

> Few people of the present day are capable of rightly appreciating this heroic deed, this brilliant proof of human courage and energy. With two ponderous craft – regular 'tubs' according to our ideas – these men sailed right into the heart of the pack, which all previous explorers had regarded as certain death. It is not merely difficult to grasp this; it is simply impossible – to us, who with a motion of the hand can set the screw going, and wriggle out of the first difficulty we encounter. These men were heroes – heroes in the highest sense of the word.

Of Ross himself, Amundsen wrote that he was: '. . . the man whose name will ever be remembered as one of the most intrepid polar explorers and one of the most capable seamen the world has ever produced – Admiral Sir James Clark Ross.'

Long before Ross returned to Britain, acrimonious arguments had taken place as to the claimed successes of Wilkes and d'Urville, both of whom stated that they were first to sight 'mainland' Antarctica and both on the same day! Even today there are polar pundits who debate which of them was first to sight the mainland. What is not argued is that the person who first reached the South Magnetic Pole was a Yorkshire-born Australian geologist, Douglas Mawson, who sledged there in 1909.

The Ross voyages were followed in 1872–6 by the purely scientific voyage of George Nares, in 1892 by a whaling-inspired Scottish expedition, and in 1892–4 by the famous Norwegian explorer Carl

Geoff Newman in one of our fur parkas, custom-made in Greenland by the Inuit, before in the late 1970s we gradually switched to Gore-Tex jackets

James Clark Ross, described by the great Norwegian Roald Amundsen as, 'the man whose name will ever be remembered as one of the most capable seamen the world has produced'

Captain James Cook. From Yorkshire farm labourer's son to Britain's greatest seafarer and a superb navigator

William Edward Parry, the ultimate searcher for the Northwest Passage

Ernest Shackleton and members of the British Antarctic Exploration on board the *Nimrod* (1907-1909)

Roald Amundsen and crew (1906)

Captain Robert Falcon Scott on early skis and using two sticks

Charles Hall with his two favourite Inuit

One of Scott's men with a white Mongolian pony and light laden sledge

At RAE Farnborough as part of one of Dr Mike Stroud's research programmes

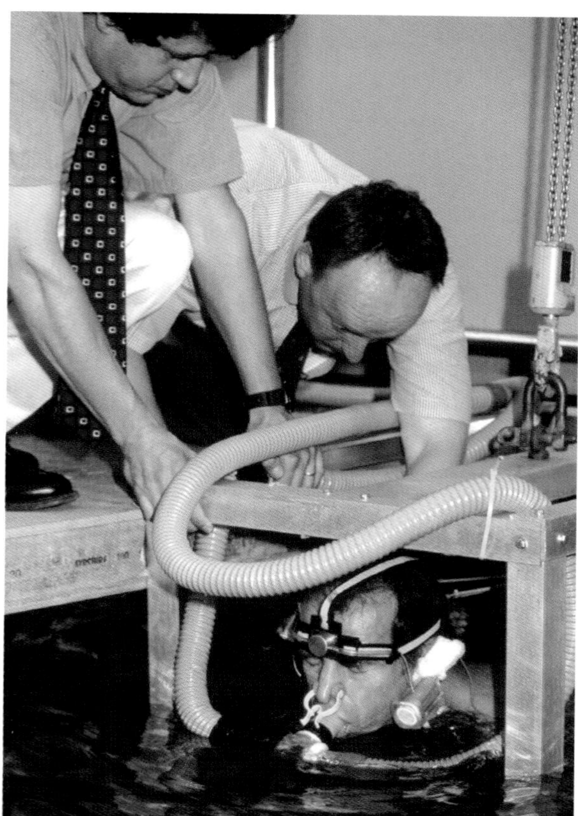

The team on the Fåbergstølsbre Glacier in Norway using Dexion shop shelving to cross a minor crevasse

The Transglobe ship, the *Benjamin Bowring*, on arrival in Antarctica in 1979

Ran Fiennes and Charlie Burton about to set out North from Alert in Northern Ellesmere Island

A major fissure is bypassed near the base of the Mount Erebus volcano

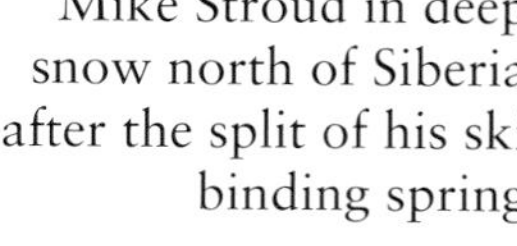

Mike Stroud in deep snow north of Siberia after the split of his ski binding spring

Our boat had to be abandoned when the sea froze (and stayed frozen for the next eight years) and we took to skis

Charlie Burton in the maze of deep canyons in Northern Ellesmere Island in 1981

Anton Larsen, but no further official exploration of the continent took place for some fifty years after Ross left Antarctica. The country most likely to have done so, Great Britain, was otherwise engaged, for the Victorians were hell-bent on expanding their empire, especially its commercial yield, and this imposed great demands on the Admiralty. Additionally, this was the period when Britain's polar fraternity was to spend fifteen years and more searching the Canadian Arctic for the very ships that Ross had used so successfully in Antarctica but which then disappeared in 1846 while searching for the Northwest Passage.

The only scope for commercial enterprise in the Antarctic in Ross's time appeared to lie in whaling. Ross had recorded on 29 December 1840, a few days before entering the pack ice at the entrance to the Ross Sea in about 64°S, that 'a great many whales were seen, chiefly of the common black kind, greatly resembling but said to be distinct from, the Greenland whale; sperm, as well as hunchback whales, were also observed; of the common black species we might have killed any number we pleased; they appeared chiefly to be of unusually large size, and would doubtless yield a great quantity of oil, and were so tame that our ships sailing close past did not disturb them.'

On the other side of Antarctica, south of the Falkland Islands, Ross later recorded, 'a great number of the largest-sized black whales, so tame that they allowed the ships almost to touch them before they would get out of the way; so that any number of ships might procure a cargo of oil in a short time.' These easy-to-catch whales became known as right whales.

Fifty years after Ross made his whale observations, a Scottish whaler, one Captain Peterhead, after checking many other whale reports and speaking to survivors of the Ross voyages, sent four vessels south to find right whales. They found none because, by then, mass exploitation of all whale populations further north than the pack-ice zones had virtually eliminated the right whales.

The blue whale, the largest of all mammals, roams Antarctic waters and was prized by the whalers. Killer whales or orcas, prowling off ice floes in packs to feast on seals and penguins, also target blue whales. Orcas, about 30 feet long and with distinct black and white markings, weigh in at about 7,000 kilograms each and they will attack a 100,000-kilogram blue whale just to eat the giant's tasty tongue. A sealer in 1923 described one such attack:

> Two of the pugnacious killers attached themselves, one on either side, to the great mammal's lower jaw ... two others kept making short furious rushes at the great whale. The fifth flitted between the point of the lower jaw, where he hung on with all his strength, and the broad back, where he joined the others in beating the life out of the poor whale. The harassed monster thrashed with his tail, beat his fins on the water with a terrible noise, and tossed his head from side to side, but all in vain ... He was visibly tiring, and before long lay quietly on the surface, while the five killers turned their combined attentions to his lower jaw and dragged it open. Then as it hung down in the sea, they flitted in and out of the great mouth, gorging themselves on the tongue. They touched nothing else.

In 1903 the Norwegian Svend Foyn invented the harpoon gun, and in 1923 his compatriot, Carl Larsen, sealed the fate of Antarctic whales by developing whale-hunt convoys consisting of a large 'factory ship' and several whale-catcher vessels. In their first two months in the Ross Sea, Larsen's little fleet harpooned 200 blue and fin whales. Over the next six years his company derived an income of some £2 million from 5,000 whales.

'Life aboard the factory ships was a toilsome monotony of cold, stench, and gore,' wrote Alan Villiers, a whaler crewman, in *Whaling in the Frozen South* (1925), and Thomas Bagshawe, an adventurer and onlooker of the time, reported, in *Two Men in the Antarctic, 1920–22* (1939): 'The whales that had been dead the longest were the first to be processed ... Any that have been lying for some time have swollen to a terrific size and look as if a mere pinprick would cause an explosion. In the early days, before stern-loading factory ships arrived in the Antarctic, flensing – the stripping of blubber from the corpse – was started as the whale floated in the sea next to the ship.'

'The flensers' hands were bare,' wrote Villiers. 'They can not wear even fingerless mitts, for they must have sure and steady hold of the greasy knives – one false sweep, one wild cut, might spell destruction for themselves or their mates. Frequently they must cease work for a moment, plunge the knife into the hot flesh, bathe their hands in the warm blood to bring life back to them.' 'Great joints are cut from the carcass,' wrote Bagshawe. 'The flensers wallow up to their waists in the body whilst they hack away with their sharp knives.'

On deck the crew continued cutting up the carcass. The blubber was further cut into chunks, passed through a chopping machine, and cooked in huge steam-driven meat and blubber boilers. The whale's tongue, the item so prized by marauding orcas, was also specially sought by the whalers. Intricately banded and cross-banded with muscles, and therefore 'wonderfully difficult to walk on,' in the words of one flenser, one blue whale tongue could yield up to 2,000 kilograms of oil.

Bagshawe wrote: 'As work on board got into full swing, the ship looked a disgusting site and had a still more disgusting smell. The decks were soon covered with a mixture of whale oil, blood and coal dust . . . The residue from the boilers was shovelled into the sea, to add to the heap of slowly rotting, frozen sludge that accumulated around the ship.'

While the packs of factory ships and their catchers scourged the South Shetland Islands, the South Orkneys and the Ross Sea, shore-based whaling stations were constructed on Deception Island and in the sheltered fjords on the eastern, leeward, side of South Georgia, on the same beaches that had been stripped of fur seals a century and a half before. The stations were mostly managed and manned by Norwegians.

Over the years a graveyard sprouted around the church, and wooden monuments could be found to men lost at sea or mashed by machinery. Despair and loneliness in the lady-less company of whalers frequently resulted in men being sent home as mentally deranged. A station manager on South Georgia reported that one whaler asked whether he could spare a new piece of rope; he wanted to hang himself, but the only rope he could find was rotten.

During the First World War, when humans turned on themselves the same destructive energies that they had once directed at the whales, the demand for Antarctic whales increased. It was the first 'modern' war, and the large-scale use of artillery bombs stoked the world demand for glycerine, then derived primarily from whale oil, to make explosives.

The whaling stations on South Georgia are now all derelict, the last having been abandoned in 1964. The buildings are ramshackle and cluttered with debris and spattered by squalls of snow and rain. Things move strangely in the wind, as if haunted; broken walls batter their frames, rusty cables sway, doors lurch on their hinges. Hymnals, blotched and mouldy, are still to be found in the pews of South Georgia's church, but the altar is caked with rat faeces. And today the blue whale, the world's largest mammal, is virtually extinct.

On 4 January 1980, after only nine days in the pack ice, we arrived at the coast close to where the Greenwich Meridian strikes Antarctica and, at 9 knots, moved west with the high ice cliffs of Antarctica to our south and the rim of the pack to starboard.

Ginny made radio contact with the South Africans at Sanae base, and their leader promised to send up flares from the ice bay at which it would be safest for us to unload: he called it by the Norwegian name. His base was only ten miles inland from this bight and the weather, he said, was good. His tone suggested that fine weather was not something to be taken for granted.

As many of us as possible now lined the deck, scanning the many indents in the ice cliffs, but we saw none where the ship might berth, let alone unload, since the cliffs were at least forty feet high. Then around midday we spotted the South African flares in a bay which was about half a mile wide at its mouth. Hemmed in by high cliffs, this bay tapered V-like for a mile and a half to its apex, where the cliffs fell away to a snow ramp which gave access to the interior. We would have to manoeuvre the ship as near as possible, unload fast on to the ice and then move everything inland some two miles across the ice to access the ramp.

Although the Antarctic summer was well advanced, the sun high in the sky and the temperature only around freezing point, the winter sea ice had not yet left the bay, and to my ignorant eye its surface looked solid enough. But Sir Vivian Fuchs had warned me not to trust such bay ice, as it only needed a strong northerly wind to start new fracturing, which would begin along the seaward edge where we were unloading. Sir Vivian's team had lost a great quantity of stores in this way, including 300 drums of fuel, a Ferguson tractor, coal, timber and engineering stores.

Our ship must leave Antarctica as soon as possible in order not to get iced in, so we would have to work fast to unload hundreds of drums of fuel, each weighing 450 pounds, and over a hundred tons of mixed cargo. I had long been planning the details of this and, if my paperwork was right, we should be able to finish in eleven days, using every single crew member, despite their ignorance of snow vehicles and cold-weather hazards. To accomplish this we had only one little groundhog from our Greenland trials and five skidoos.

As soon as Giles and Gerry appeared with the Otter, they would have to ferry close on 100,000 pounds of cargo inland some three hundred miles to the edge of the Antarctic plateau, where we hoped to set up a forward camp at 6,000 feet above sea level, near the abandoned South African base called Borga on the edge of the then known world. This base hugged the ice ridge of the Kirwan Escarpment, south from which man had never ventured. The mountain beneath which we planned to spend the long dark winter was named Ryvingen. For nine hundred miles towards the South Pole, a vast tract of unknown ice, probably over 10,000 feet above sea level, awaited us. As far south as Ryvingen we were simply travellers: thereafter, we would be explorers, in the true sense of the word, of one of Earth's last untrodden and unmapped regions.

It took Sir Vivian Fuchs a hundred days to cross the continent by a shorter route and using closed-cab vehicles which cut down the risk of exposure for his men. His team had great difficulties with crevasses. We must obviously count on at least as many days to complete our journey.

The Antarctic summer, the period when it is possible to travel, lasts but 120 days in all. Amundsen tried to challenge nature by starting his South Pole attempt a month early. He regretted his rashness when extreme cold forced his team back to their base for a further month's wait. Captain Scott failed to return from his own South Pole journey by early February, delayed by an unseasonable rogue blizzard that sealed his fate. To be isolated from a base on the polar plateau outside the narrow confines of summer is to invite a speedy demise. We hoped to start for the pole in October, the moment that the temperature rose to a bearable level.

The Admiral rammed the edge of the bay ice, known to glaciologists as fast ice, to make a nest for the ship from which a ladder could be lowered straight on to the ice. The *Benjy B* crew lost no time in disembarking in order to feel Antarctica under their mukluks and to talk to the South African men who had come to greet us. Tall, rangy men with unkempt beards, shoulder-length hippy hair and headbands, they had seen nobody for a year. Looking down from the fo'c's'le with Simon, I noticed two groups had formed: one of hairy South Africans bunched around our very feminine and petite cook, Jill; the other, a group of Transglobers, all armed with cameras, ringed around a single Adélie penguin which stared back at them with an arrogant expression. Simon and I couldn't decide which group was the more mesmerized.

The South Africans were one of several scientific groups from various countries stationed in Antarctica, including a group at the pole itself. Their leader took me up the snow ramp. A mile beyond it he paced out a relatively flat 600 metres.

'The prevailing wind goes this way. You can tell by the direction of the nearby sastrugi, the parallel ridges of snow. Your Twin Otter could use this as an airstrip and you can lay out your cargo alongside it.'

I thanked him and the South Africans left us after a feast on board of all those things they had long since run out of at their base – fresh fruit, vegetables, milk and whisky.

Whilst our crew drilled telegraph poles into the bay ice to act as anchors, I took Charlie and two hundred flagged bamboos to mark out a route from the ship to our inland cargo site, and on to the site of the hut where Simon and one other must spend the winter beside the cargo lines. Finally, poles with numbered flags were planted alongside the airstrip to mark off where different priorities of equipment and fuel must be placed. Every single crate – and there were close on two thousand, not including drums – was numbered and allocated a priority for its flight to the Ryvingen inland base. At any time a blizzard could drift snow over the cargo and cover it, so the numbered flags would tell us where to dig without delay for any given item.

That evening the South Africans brought a mobile braai, or barbecue, down to the site of our airstrip, and Transglobers trudged up the bay and the ramp in their party clothes to join in. An unlimited supply of South African wines filled the rear of one snowcat.

Two of the South Africans were penguin devotees and regaled us with facts about these Disneyesque birds as cuddly-looking as puffins, but smelly. Their nesting colonies can be smelt from over fifty miles away. The word penguin first appears in 1588 when explorer Thomas Cavendish, following in Drake's circumnavigatory footsteps, came to the Straits of Magellan and 'killed and salted a great store of penguins for victuals'. The word may have come from the Welsh *pen gwyn* meaning white-headed, or from the Latin *pinguis* meaning fat, or from the English *pin-wing*.

Fossils show that they evolved in Gondwanaland from flighted birds like petrels, and seventeen different species live in great colonies in Antarctica, the smallest being the Fairy penguin, which is only 40 centimetres tall. The largest, the Emperor, can dive deeper and longer than any other bird. One was tracked down to a submarine depth of half a kilometre, where it stayed fishing for 20 minutes.

Emperors nest in groups of up to 6,000 birds, all huddled together like rugby teams at half-time. In endless rotation, the outer birds slowly shuffle into the centre of the huddle to rewarm. Each bird keeps its precious egg on its feet while standing only on its heels, and the muscles that operate its feet lie deep within its body attached to long tendons. Wintering in this manner, often without food for four months at a time, they have evolved special anti-cold features, including a heat-exchange system in their nostrils which captures 80 per cent of the heat that they would otherwise lose through exhalation. Like all penguins, their wing bones are really just flippers designed, unlike any other bird, to push down, rather than up.

Penguin colonies are under constant attack, not by humans (although Francis Drake recorded revictualling his crew on a single day by killing 3,000 birds in the Straits of Magellan), but by skuas. These clever predators are up to every trick in the book. They may bomb nesting females to knock them off their eggs or, working as a pair, one of them pulls the penguin's tail feathers whilst the other jumps in to smash the eggs and slurp down the yolks. When penguins aren't nesting, skuas will live off black rats, human garbage at bases, and even rabbits. Some have been known to take milk from the breasts of lactating elephant seals. Humans who trespass in a penguin colony 'owned' by a particular couple of skuas will be aggressively dive-bombed. When at sea, away from their skua enemies, poor penguins are constantly at risk of being skinned alive and swallowed by leopard seals. What a life!

In the morning the unloading began. A light wind sprang up and the temperature dropped to –20°C, which was several degrees below what most of those involved had ever experienced, even briefly, so they wore polar mitts, parkas and mukluks. At the end of day two about a quarter of the cargo was logged in at the airstrip. But the third day saw a turn in the weather. The temperature shot up by

15°C, the northern horizon grew dark, the ship moved slowly against the ice as an increasing swell shifted her, and her anchor stakes started to work loose. The winch engine overheated and needed repairs. Unloading had to cease.

The Admiral had no wish to abandon the anchorage, but by midnight the wind had risen to over 50 knots and spray surged high as mounting waves crashed against the rim of the bay ice. Great icebergs began to shift ominously to our north, and soon two of our mooring stakes snapped. The other two followed shortly after and we were adrift. We had no choice but to head north to ride out the storm a safe distance from the coast. Ten drums remained on the ice near the ice front, and also Chief Engineer Ken Cameron's motorbike, which he had unloaded for personal reasons.

Soon after the *Benjy B* stopped to hover offshore, bows to the storm, Ginny woke me. Up on the bridge we watched whole segments of the bay ice ride out to sea. On one segment I counted eight drums of Twin Otter fuel, 320 precious gallons. They floated past and on into the wind-whipped white-out. We never saw Ken's motorbike again. I reflected that if some southern sailing skipper, after dinner and a dram, were to spot an ice floe bearing a gleaming Honda passing his ship, he would probably go teetotal for life.

Otherwise the unloading went well and Ollie, Charlie and I waved goodbye to the ship and our friends on 15 January. All being well, they would pick us up again in a year or so, two thousand miles away on the far side of the frozen continent. Ten days of careful preparation later, in conditions of nil visibility, we took our skidoos and laden sledges on a 370-kilometre journey inland to set up a base in which to spend the next eight months of polar winter and the long disappearance of the sun.

Navigation was tricky, for although there were numerous mountain features spearing the overall ice mantle, our route through them was confined to those slopes not riven by heavy crevassing. I came close to plummeting two hundred feet down a crack at a time when I was not roped up to my skidoo. We passed through a band of especially difficult crevasse fields known as the hinge zone. From there I followed a series of carefully selected compass bearings which wiggled us between the peaks of Draaipunt, Valken and Dassiekop to the 6,000-foot-high Borga Massif.

Two years after we passed through it, I read the technical description of the hinge zone in the *South African Journal of Antarctic Research*: 'The ice shelf rises gradually in elevation and increases in thickness until, about 110 kilometres from the coast at the so-called Hinge Area where it ceases to float, it has a surface elevation of about 100 metres and is some 600 metres thick.'

As we inched south, the Twin Otter crew flew over seventy round-flights to take Ginny, Simon and 100,000 pounds of gear to an ice field below Ryvingen mountain. There they erected four huts made of cardboard, which Ginny had designed. Once snowdrifts covered the huts' outer shells and insulated them, they would be proof against the worst Antarctic winter. Antarctica's 5½ million frozen square miles dwarf the United States, yet no more than 800 humans would spend the coming winter there, and none within three hundred miles of our four huts.

The site of our winter base was chosen because of its height above sea level and its distance inland, the furthest that the Twin Otter could be expected to reach carrying a 2,000-pound cargo load. We hoped, by wintering at 6,000 feet, to become acclimatized to the bitter conditions before the main crossing journey the following summer, when the average height would probably be 10,000 feet above sea level.

We reached Ryvingen without mishap and began a race to prepare our camp for the long winter. Simon returned to Sanae and the Twin Otter crew completed their 78th ferry flight from Sanae to Ryvingen. We wished them a safe flight back to Britain via the Falkland Islands and Argentina.

The weather clamped down on the ice fields, travel for any distance became impossible and we were soon cut off from the outside world. For eight months we must survive through our own common sense. Should anyone be hurt or sick, there could be no evacuation and no medical assistance. We must daily handle heavy batteries, generator power lines and heavy steel drums, but avoid the hazards of acid in the eye, serious tooth trouble, appendicitis, cold burns, fuel burns or deep electrical burns. Temperatures would plunge to –50°C and below. Winds would exceed 90 knots and the chill factor would reach –84°C. For 240 days and nights we must live cautiously and mostly without sunlight.

Chapter Six

They miss my little camp-fires, ever brightly, bravely gleaming
In the womb of desolation, where was never man before;
As comradeless I sought them, lion-hearted, loving, dreaming,
And they hailed me as a comrade, and they loved me evermore.

ROBERT SERVICE, FROM 'THE LURE OF LITTLE VOICES' (1907)

Cut off from any form of assistance for the next eight months, the four of us concentrated on trying to master the art of self-sufficiency before the sunless period of extreme cold set in.

Our cardboard huts soon disappeared under snowdrifts, and all exits from the huts were blocked. So I dug tunnels under the snow and stored all our equipment inside them. In two months I completed a 200-yard network of spacious tunnels with side corridors, a loo alcove, a 30-foot-deep slop-pit and a garage with pillars and archways of ice.

Since our huts were made of cardboard with wooden struts and bunks and our heaters burned kerosene, we were apprehensive of fire. A neighbouring Russian base, five hundred miles away, had been burnt out the previous winter and all eight occupants were found asphyxiated in an escape tunnel with blocked hatches.

Katabatic, gravity-fed, winds blasted our camp and snuffed out our fires through chimney blowback. We experimented with valves, flaps and crooked chimneys, but the stronger gusts confounded all our efforts. The drip-feed pipe of a heater would continue to deliver fuel after the fire was blown out, and this could cause a flash fire unless great care was taken when relighting the heater.

There was also the constant danger in each of our huts of carbon monoxide poisoning. According to Ollie's First Aid booklet, 'CO is colourless, odourless and poisonous. It locks up the blood's haemoglobin, preventing it from carrying oxygen.' Even low levels can be dangerous, and on a cold day in an airtight cabin warmed by a leaky woodstove, carbon monoxide levels can quickly reach hundreds of parts per million. Expose yourself to 200 parts per million for a few hours, and you will experience a headache, nausea and extreme fatigue. Expose yourself to 800 parts per million, and watch for convulsions and unconsciousness. Death will come within three hours.

Generator exhaust pipes tended to melt out sub-snow caverns which spread sideways and downwards. One day Oliver discovered a 15-foot-deep cave underneath the floor of his generator hut. He moved his exhaust system time and again, but nearly died of carbon monoxide poisoning three times, despite being alert for the symptoms.

Without power from the generators, Ginny's radios would not work, so our weather reports, which Oliver must send out every six hours, could not be fed into the World Meteorological Organization system, nor could the complex, very low frequency (VLF) recording experiments be undertaken for Sheffield University and the British Antarctic Survey. So we fought hard with shovels to avoid snow accumulation in certain key areas of the camp.

Some nights Ginny found communications were messed up by ionospheric disturbance caused by charged cosmic rays from solar activity funnelled into the magnetic field above the geomagnetic poles. At worst we had total radio blackout.

When this happened we would go out to the end of the hut's exit tunnel to watch in wonder the magical lights of the aurora set against the brilliance of a million stars and the silent gaze of the moon. On the backdrop of the greenish glow from the horizon, made jagged by mountains, fantastical shapes and images of many subtle colours billowed and waved like the folds in the skirts of an Eastern dancer. In less poetic terms, the spectacular light shows were the result of the corona, the sun's outer layer, squirting out great bubbles of plasma which entangle themselves with various magnetic fields. These giant bubbles then fly through space at 800 kilometres per second and strike our upper atmosphere, looking very pretty when seen from the right viewpoint.

Other unusual tricks of the light we observed that winter included rainbow-coloured haloes around the moon and vertical shafts above and below it. Sometimes mock moons can be seen to either side of the real one; scientists call these parasalenae, or moon dogs.

At night in the main living hut we turned the heater low to save fuel. We slept on wooden slats in the apex of the hut roof, and in the mornings there was a difference of 14° between bed level and floor temperature, the latter averaging –15°C. Ginny and I slept together on a single slat at one end of the hut, Oliver and Charlie occupied bachelor slats down the other end, and Bothie slept in a cavity behind the heater. The long black nights with the roar of the wind so close and the linger of tallow in the dark are still with me after thirty years.

There are few groups of individuals who will live together for long periods in the cold and the dark without dissension and tension rearing their ugly heads.

Careful team selection processes can minimize trouble from individuals, and many polar authorities use tests already devised by selection boards for police, top executives, army officers and air crew. The most apt for would-be polar winter base applicants is that used to select submarine crews.

In the 1890s, when expeditions first wintered on the polar coast or on their ships beset in the ice, there were violent arguments and mutiny and, later, long years of public recriminations. The journeys of the Belgian de Gerlache and the British expedition under Borchgrevink were riven with tensions. More recently, at a Soviet winter base, one inmate killed another with an axe following an argument over a chess game, and at the Argentine base of Almirante Brown, the base doctor forced his own evacuation by burning the base down.

Writer Sara Maitland, commenting in *A Book of Silence* (2008) on the effects of being away from accustomed norms of social contact, deduces that the most serious psychological risks are run by people who have not freely chosen their isolation or whose way out is barred. Back in 1928 when the American flyer Richard Byrd set up his first Antarctic winter base, he prepared for the effects that a polar winter might have on his men by taking ashore two coffins and a dozen straitjackets. A French polar writer, after a polar winter experience, summarized the negative moods of many polar winterers as progressing from resistance, depression and aggression to tolerance and indifference. In 1913 the Australian explorer Douglas Mawson had increasing troubles with his initially excellent radio operator who went slowly mad and, once back in Australia, was locked up in a mental asylum until he died.

Comments from British winter bases include, from a base leader in the 1980s: 'I kept the surgery door under lock and key. Already there were large amounts of Pethidine and Diconal missing. And, according to the little information I had, these were desirable drugs for undesirables – junkie material.' And, on first accepting the nominal role of Base Medic: 'Oh shit, I thought. This is a fucking madhouse. I'm locked in here for the winter with fourteen fucking weirdos! "I'll do it for fuck sake," I announced less than enthusiastically. I wondered what bits of bloody flesh and weeping penises would be brought my way during the winter. But I was the oldest and perhaps the best of a bad bunch. The sea was about to freeze over, barring any way in or out.'

In order to palliate the lack of available heterosexual intercourse, all British bases have ever-accumulating supplies of pornographic magazines and videos, libraries of which are kept by volunteers who are then known as Z-porn (in the same way that the chief base mechanic is always Z-mech). Another difficulty is that, of late, smoking is not allowed inside British bases, so smokers end up outside several times a day and very often in temperatures of 50° below zero.

As an Australian polar boss of many years' experience commented:

> Amongst men thus thrown together, trifling personal peculiarities can cause mounting exasperation and harmless peccadilloes produce serious resentments. The psychological strains are aggravated by physiological factors resulting from the disturbance of well-established diurnal rhythms of the human body during the long midwinter night or in the period of continuous summer daylight.
>
> Insomnia, or the 'big-eye', as the Americans call it, is an occupational disease in the Antarctic winter. In addition, there are the depressing effects of frequent high winds and dull, cloudy weather, and the constant battle against cold.

He also cautioned against the danger of cliques forming within a given base:

> The greatest obstacle to the building of a happy, contented and well-adjusted party is the difference in cultural levels of various men. What topics of conversation can be common to all? How does a leader prevent the development of an intellectual clique at meals, when the more erudite men gather at one end to discuss philosophical profundities, and the less informed members, tiring of the cultural high-brow conversation, sit and jeer and try to break it up? . . .
>
> A less healthy type of clique is that formed by malcontents, or men who, because of their unpopularity with the rest of the party, are forced to seek each other's companionship. Companions in adversity, men who lack friends gravitate together. I have seen some strange associations formed in this way.'

Over many years of polar expeditions and long periods spent crammed into a tiny freezing tent with one or two other men, I have sometimes silently hated them whilst there but, for decades, have kept going back on further testing journeys with them. A Norwegian friend, Ragnar Thorseth, a very accomplished polar traveller, wrote after a long and challenging journey with one other man:

> We discovered a lot of new things about ourselves and each other, some of them not at all to our liking. The antidote, we had found, was to have a good old booze-up every so often when we were ashore. Under the soothing influence of alcohol the most intransigent knots loosened and fell apart, and we found ourselves once more able to laugh at things which had once been seemingly insuperable obstacles; now they fell into their proper perspective as the over-inflated trifles they actually were.

Certain types of people, who may well be found acceptable in 'normal' society but who will definitely cause major troubles in a polar winter base include those with overweening egotism, the thoughtless, the selfish, the lazy and those with a strong sense of inferiority which will often lead to the development of a persecution complex and an ever-descending deterioration in morale. Conversely, the type of person most likely to improve, rather than darken, the atmosphere of a polar base in winter is one who is tolerant, patient, unexcitable, loyal, kindly and hard-working.

There was, of course, friction between us. Forced togetherness breeds dissension and even hatred between individuals and groups. After four years at work together, our person-to-person chemistry was still undergoing constant change, some days without a word being spoken. At times I knew that I disliked one or both of the other men, and that the feeling was mutual. At other times, without actually going so far as to admit affection, I felt distinctly warm towards them. When I felt positive antagonism towards the others, I could let off steam with Ginny, who would listen patiently. Or else I could spit out vituperative prose in my diary. Diaries on expeditions are often minefields of overreaction. Each of us nursed apprehensions about the future. The thought of leaving the security of our cardboard huts for the huge unknown that stretched away behind Ryvingen mountain was not something on which I allowed my thoughts to dwell.

On 2 May, the wind-chill factor dropped to –79°C. Windstorms from the polar plateau blasted through the camp with no warning. Visiting Ginny's VLF recording hut one morning, I was knocked flat by a gust, although a second earlier there had not been a zephyr of wind. A minute later, picking myself up, I was struck on the back by the plastic windshield ripped off my parked skidoo.

Many of these winds are katabatic, from the Greek *katabatos*, meaning descending. Air high on the polar plateau is dense and very cold. Because the continent itself is a high dome of ice, this heavy air 'falls' off the continent, rushing towards the coast until it gathers the momentum of a hurricane. As the hurtling wall of air encounters an object – be it a building or skidoo – the turbulence makes it drop its load of snow, leaving vast drifts to gather behind anything left out on the ice. These wind tails can grow as high as the buildings that generate them.

Even in 30-knot wind conditions we found it dangerous to move outside our huts and tunnels except by way of the staked safety lines which we had positioned all around the camp and from hut to hut. Charlie and I both lost the safety lines one day when an 80-knot wind hurled ice needles horizontally through the white-out. We groped separately and blindly in circles until we blundered into a safety line and so found our way to the nearest hut's hatchway. That same day the parachute canopy covering the sunken area of Ginny's antennae tuning units was ripped off, and by nightfall two tons of snow had filled in her entire work area.

A couple of years later a scientist at Casey, the Australian base, went outside in a storm to make a routine weather observation, and quickly found himself lost between two buildings, no more than a hundred feet apart. He was found frozen to death the next morning, sixty feet from the building that he'd left.

Before the sun disappeared for 24 hours a day, we trained daily at skiing. I taught Oliver and Charlie the rudiments of langlauf skiing, for I knew that if we succeeded in crossing Antarctica, we would meet many regions in the Arctic where only ski travel would be practical.

On a fine autumn day we left camp with laden sledges for a quick 16-kilometre trip to a nearby nunatak, or lonely rock outcrop. A storm caught us on the return journey and, within minutes, the wind had burned every patch of exposed skin and frostnipped our fingers inside their light ski mitts. At the time we were each moving at our separate speeds with a mile or so between us. This was not acceptable by current mountain-safety practices, but it was a system encouraged on all SAS training courses: the fewer individuals in a group, the faster the majority will reach their goal. This presupposes that the weakest link can look after himself. Oliver was last to arrive back at camp, his face and neck bloated with frostnip. For a week he took antibiotics until his sores stopped weeping.

Ginny's problems were mostly connected with her radio work. Conducting high-frequency experiments with faraway Cove Radio Station, she was wont to work a 1.5 kVA generator in the foyer of her hut. A freak wind once blew carbon monoxide fumes under her door. By chance I called her on a walkie-talkie and, receiving no reply, rushed along the tunnels and down to her shack. I found her puce-faced and staggering about in a dazed state. I dragged her out into the fresh –49°C air and told the Cove Radio operator what had happened. Next day we received a worried message from their controller, Squadron Leader Jack Willis:

> Even in a comfortable environment the operation of electrical radio components is a hazardous operation. In your location the dangers are considerably increased . . . Remember that as little as thirty mA can kill. Never wear rings or watches when apparatus is live. Beware of snow from boots melting on the floor . . . Your one kilowatt transmitter can produce very serious radio

> frequency burns . . . Static charges will build up to several thousand volts in an aerial. Toxic beryllium is employed in some of the components.

Only four days later, with all her sets switched off and no mains power, Ginny touched the coaxial cable leading to her 40-watt set. She was stunned by a violent shock that travelled up her right arm and felt, as she put it later that morning, 'like an explosion in my lungs'. The cause was static, built up by wind-blown snow.

Not being a technical expert, Ginny used common sense to repair her sets, replace tiny diodes and solder cold-damaged flex. When a 1-kilowatt resistor blew and she had no spares, she thought of cutting a boiling ring out of our Baby Belling cooker. She then wired the cannibalized coil to the innards of her stricken radio and soon had everything working again, the home-made resistor glowing red-hot on an asbestos mat on the floor. The chief back at Cove Radio described her as 'an amazing communicator'.

To keep our little community happy, Ginny listened to the BBC World Service and produced *The Ryvingen Observer*. On 6 May we learned that the bodies of US airmen were being flown out of Iran following an abortive attempt to rescue American hostages, that Tito's funeral was imminent, that SAS soldiers had killed some terrorists at the Iranian Embassy in London, that food in British motorway cafés had been summed up in a government report as greasy and tasteless.

We wore warm socks, boots and underwear all day inside the living hut because the wooden floors were constantly at a temperature not far above freezing, but we were, for the most part, comfortable, despite the extreme cold immediately outside our cardboard walls. As Ollie reminded me one day, when I commented on how clever we had been to design such a light but effective carapace against the elements, we were not the only creatures on the frozen continent to survive the long deep-freeze months of the Antarctic winter.

The largest terrestrial animal on the Antarctic continent is the

Belgica antarctica wingless midge, 2 millimetres long and the most southerly free-living insect on Earth. They mate in summer and lay eggs that survive winter in the muck of penguin colonies which, being close to the sea, seldom reach a temperature below −15°C.

Three other insect types also manage to survive winter on the principle that they keep water out of their systems: when water in a small delicate cell freezes, it expands and tends to burst the host cell. So Antarctic terrestrial invertebrates called tardigrades (eight-legged anthropods that live in moist environments) simply auto-dehydrate, repelling all moisture. Larval midges, on the other hand, are designed so that ice crystals form in between their body cells, rather than inside them. Thus their delicate body machinery is undamaged. Springtails produce a form of antifreeze which allows their body fluids to remain liquid at extreme low temperatures.

There are other terrestrial bugs that survive as parasites on warm-blooded birds. Each Antarctic bird has its own species of skin-sucking louse or blood-sucking flea, and these parasites have, over the aeons, followed the retreating southern continent down to its current polar setting, where they hide in the warm anal and genital folds of seals or cling to the feathers of deep-diving seagulls.

And in the sea there are ghostly icefish. Most Antarctic fish have only half the haemoglobin count of normal temperature zone fish, but icefish have no haemoglobin at all, the only such vertebrates in the world. Some fifteen species of icefish exist, and none have scales. Their transparent blood and resulting ghost-like colour, along with their spade-shaped head and banks of sharp teeth, make them ideal horror movie material.

Bothie, who never itched so I assumed had no parasites, spent his days following Ginny from hut to hut. She kept old bones for him in each shack and dressed him in a modified pullover when the winds were high. In charge of hut hygiene, I fought a non-stop battle with the terrier for eight months, trying to teach him that 'outside' meant right outside the tunnels as well as the hut. I lost the struggle. Sometimes, when outside the huts on rare windless days, Bothie would bark at the moon, and hearing the echo of his bark, would prick up his ears and bark again, hoping that he had heard another dog.

Charlie, in charge of our food, rationed all goodies with iron discipline. Nobody could steal from the food tunnels without his say-so, a law that was obeyed by all but Bothie. Our eggs, originally sponsored in London, were some eight or nine months old by midwinter and, although frozen much of that time, they had also passed through the tropics en route. To an outsider they tasted bad – indeed evil – but we had grown used to them over the months and Bothie was addicted. However hard Charlie tried to conceal his egg store, Bothie invariably outwitted him and stole an egg a day, and sometimes more.

The months of June, July and August saw an increasing workload in the camp, due to the scientific programme and our preparations for departure in October. The sun first came back to Ryvingen, for four minutes only, on 5 August, a miserably cold day. Down at our Sanae base hut, Simon, overwintering with one other Transglober, recorded a wind speed in excess of 100 m.p.h. Our coldest day was 30 July. With the wind steady at 42 knots and a temperature of –42°C, our prevailing chill factor was –131°C, at which temperature any exposed flesh freezes in under fifteen seconds.

One night there was little wind from the high ground above the camp, so I skied out for exercise and saw, high above the horizon, the most beautiful, pearly-white, noctilucent cloud formations that I had ever seen. They were luminous, almost ethereal, and they summed up the purity of Antarctica.

In August Ginny discovered the oscillation unit in her VLF timecode generator had failed due to the cold. To complete the VLF experiment without the instrument meant manually pressing a recording button every four minutes for unbroken 24-hour periods. Wrapped in blankets in the isolated VLF hut, she kept awake night after night with flasks of black coffee. By October she was dog-tired and hallucinating, but still determined to complete the three-month experiment.

As the sunlit hours grew longer, the ice fields reacted. Explosions sounded in the valleys, rebounding as echoes from the peaks all about us. Avalanches or imploding snow bridges? There was no way of knowing. With departure imminent, I realized how much I had grown to love the simplicity of our life at Ryvingen, a crude but peaceful existence during which, imperceptibly, Ginny and I had grown closer together than during the bustle of our normal London life. Now I felt pangs of regret that it was ending. Also tremors of apprehension. As the days slipped by my stomach tightened with that long-dormant feeling of dread, once so familiar during school holidays as the next term approached. 'I wish you weren't leaving,' Ginny said.

In the last week of October it should be warm and light enough to travel at 10,000 feet above sea level. Then we would attempt the longest-ever crossing of the Antarctic continent, and the first crossing attempt to use vehicles with no protective cabs for the drivers. The frozen land mass we must cross was bigger than Europe, the USA and Mexico combined, than India and China together, and far larger than Australia. The ice sheet was 4 kilometres thick in places and covered 99 per cent of the entire continent. Four days before we set out, a news release through Reuters quoted the New Zealand Antarctic Research Programme boss as criticizing our intended journey for being under-equipped and our skidoos underpowered. The official view was that we would fail: it was 'too far, too high and too cold'.

On 29 October we left Ginny and Bothie in a drifted-over camp and headed south. The wind blew into our masked faces at 20 knots and the thermometer held steady at −50°C. Clinging to a straight bearing of 187°, we crossed the 64 kilometres to the Penck Escarpment, a steep rise of several hundred feet of sheet ice. Spotting the curve of a slight re-entrant, I tugged my throttle to full bore and began the climb, trying to will the skidoo on with its 1,200-pound load – a heavy burden for a 640cc two-stroke engine operating at 7,000 feet above sea level. The rubber tracks often failed to grip on smooth ice, but always reached rough patches again before too much momentum was lost. Renewed grip and more power carried me on – just – to the next too-smooth section.

The ascent seemed interminable. Then came an easing of the gradient, two final rises, and at last the ridgeline.

Fifteen hundred feet above our winter camp and forty miles from it, I stopped and looked back. The peaks of the Borga Massif seemed like mere pimples in the snow, and Ryvingen itself just a shadow. At this point we left behind us the overall feature of the Kirwan Escarpment, the last known feature on earth along our line of advance until the pole.

This escarpment was first seen by members of the Norwegian-British-Swedish expedition of 1949–52, which was led by a veteran polar traveller, John Giaever from Sweden. At the end of the Second World War, Norway was keen to re-establish this sector of Antarctica as Norwegian territory because the very first exploration of its coastal area had previously been made by Norwegian Hjalmar Riiser-Larsen in 1929. The Ritscher German expedition had been sent south before the war by Adolf Hitler to dispute the Larsen claim. Hitler also sent bombers over the Weddell Sea coastline to drop thousands of small swastika emblems by way of a (clearly futile) territorial claim. Norway, eager to reassert its territory, paid most of the costs of the Norwegian-British-Swedish mission, including two ski planes from the RAF to assist with navigation.

The main scientific aim of the Norwegian-British-Swedish expedition included geological, surveying and glaciological exploration trips south towards the pole, and these were highly successful. One of the planes crashed, but nobody was injured. Later a tracked Weasel vehicle, taking a crew of four to the ice harbour close to their base, drove over an ice cliff in poor visibility, and all but one of the crew drowned.

In the summer of 1951, three of the team, including Gordon Robin and Charles Swithinbank, pioneered a route through the mountains and on as far as the Kirwan Escarpment. They obtained en route the first reliable and systematic (seismic) ice thickness measurements of Antarctica. These indicated that beneath the ice lay a region of mountains and fjords. In places the ice was 2,400 metres deep.

Late in May 1951, after a successful journey to the south, one of the team, the geologist Alan Reece, had lost the sight in one eye due to a rock splinter. After a while he had trouble with this blind eye, which became infected and had to be removed. The delicate operation was achieved by the others with advice over their radio from a specialist in Sweden. Having heard the gory details later from our friend and adviser Charles Swithinbank, and knowing 'Doctor' Ollie's medical limitations, we made sure to keep our eyes well covered when lowering 12-volt batteries down hatches after being charged and topped up with acid in the generator shed.

The first man to reach our part of the Antarctic coastline, some 120 years before Charles Swithinbank and his team, was James Weddell in 1823. Before that, navigational inadequacies and the fragility of ships precluded long sea voyages south from the civilized known world. With notable exceptions such as Biscoe and Ross, few explorers followed in Weddell's wake. Antarctica remained almost entirely unexplored.

In 1895 the International Geographical Congress was held in London, which debated the last great question of terrestrial exploration: was there a seventh continent down south? A Belgian naval lieutenant, Adrien de Gerlache, excited by the congress, put together an international crew which included the young Roald Amundsen, Lieutenant Emile Danco as magnetician, and as second in command, another lieutenant, Georges Lecointe. An Australian doctor, two Poles, a Rumanian and five Norwegians then joined up, as did Doctor Frederick Cook (later to claim priority in reaching the North Pole).

They set out in 1897, and dissension ruled throughout the voyage to Antarctica. In Punta Arenas, Chile, Gerlache had to call the police to restore order on board. Later a crewman was drowned and Danco nearly died in a crevasse. Overwintering in pack ice, the crew succumbed to scurvy and acute anaemia. Danco died, but recovering their health briefly in July 1898, Lecointe, Cook and Amundsen carried out the first-ever sledge journey on Antarctic sea ice. After three days and a few miles, they returned to the ship. Not long afterwards the bosun went mad. Overall, this internationally crewed venture discovered very little.

Also in response to the London Congress, in 1898 a Norwegian, Carsten Borchgrevink, led a British-funded expedition, which achieved the first planned overwintering on the Antarctic continent, the record furthest south by ship and by land, the first use of dog travel in Antarctica, and the first landing on the Ross Ice Shelf.

These successes were a touch clouded by bad publicity resulting from reports made by members of the crew. Relations between Borchgrevink and certain others became so bad over the winter that he pinned up a notice announcing: 'The following things will be considered mutiny: to oppose C.E.B [Borchgrevink] or induce others to do so, to speak ill of C.E.B., to ridicule C.E.B. or his work, to try and force C.E.B. to alter contracts.' Soon after producing this notice, Borchgrevink withdrew from the wintering hut to a stone shack, together with one Saami Laplander as his only companion. Although the winter conditions were bad, the team suffered less illness than did the Belgian expedition, and only one of them, the zoologist, died during the winter.

Two other responses to the London International Geographical Congress took place, one in 1901 by Swedes under Otto Nordenskjöld, and the other in 1903–7 by the French under Doctor Jean-Baptiste Charcot. The Swedes' ship was wrecked and the French narrowly avoided the same fate. The aim of both expeditions was to answer the main question posed by the Congress: what lay at the bottom of the world – a continent or a scattering of ice-clad islands? But this was not resolved. As the twentieth century dawned, mankind still had no answer to this fundamental conundrum.

From the Kirwan Escarpment we pressed south, and by dusk there was no single visible feature in any direction. Nothing to navigate by but clouds, and soon, once we left the weather-making elements of sea and mountains behind us, there would not even be clouds.

To begin with, despite our journey from the coast to Ryvingen eight months before and our Greenland jaunt, we were disorganized. We had never previously carried such heavy loads on our skidoos and our sledges, nor had we travelled on open vehicles in such extreme cold conditions. Maybe we had set out too early? If so, we would not be the first. In terms of disorganization, Scott in March 1902 wrote:

> I am bound to confess that the sledges when packed presented an appearance of which we should afterwards have been wholly ashamed, and much the same might be said of the clothing worn by the sledgers. But at this time our ignorance was deplorable; we did not know how much or in what proportions would be required as regards the food, how to use our cookers, how to put up our tents, or even how to put on our clothes. Not a single article of the outfit had been tested, and amid the general ignorance that prevailed, the lack of system was painfully apparent in everything.

Both Scott and Amundsen made depot-laying journeys from their bases out on to the Ross Ice Shelf to their south at the beginning of the polar winter, and both groups suffered frostbite as a result. Eight huskies died on Amundsen's foray, and his men recorded temperatures down to −45°C.

Our skidoos were identical to those we used in the Arctic in 1977, except that the carburettors were improved. Although our magnetic compass was usable, for the local error was a mere 18°, it had to be used with care, for the alcohol was cold and thick and this made the needle sluggish. I soon developed the habit of double-checking its final lie and tapping it gently in case it had yet to settle true.

Each skidoo towed a laden sledge which carried 1,800 pounds in all. Thirty-foot double ropes linked each skidoo to its sledge. In principle any one unit could plunge into a crevasse but it would soon be arrested by the halted weight attached to it. Of course, going downhill or on slippery ice the principle might not work too well if the skidoo were to fall through first. There would be no benefit to a driver whose skidoo dangled in an abyss anchored by its sledge if he himself carried on downwards. So we each wore a mountaineer's harness with a line attached either to the skidoo or to the sledge, depending on personal preference. Ollie and I believed the latter to be safer, Charlie the former.

Back in Britain when first trying to decide what size and design of sledge would be as unbreakable as possible and usable in both the Arctic and Antarctic, I had a hang-up over not using traditional wooden sledges as I thought it was likely that they would not be able to support the very heavy loads of fuel and spares we would need for our skidoos, in addition to normal camping gear and food. Steel seemed a better option, but Wally Herbert, my most experienced sledge adviser, was highly critical to the point of aggression, and felt that I was making a stupid decision. 'Personally,' he said, 'I would never take a metal sledge. A sledge must be flexible and easy to repair as well as strong.' Other Antarctic travellers I spoke to said the same thing.

Nonetheless, keen to take advantage of anything the twentieth century might offer, I approached the British Steel Corporation. They were interested. How would austenitic 316 stainless steel stand up to extreme temperatures? Using thin tubes welded by hand to the design of Professor Noel Dilley, four 8-foot 6-inch sledges for the Arctic and four 12-foot 9-inch sledges for the Antarctic were fashioned by young BSC apprentices as part of their training, all under the watchful eye of an expert steel welder. 'We'll show those wood merchants a thing or two,' he muttered as the sledges were handed over. Later they were coated at great heat and Tufnol runners affixed with epoxy and self-locking bolts.

On our second day of travel beyond the last rocky outcrop and at −53°C, we climbed slowly into the teeth of high winds and a white-out, the true plateau still 4,000 feet above us. After four hours Oliver staggered off his skidoo and lurched over to me, his speech slurred. 'Must stop. I'm getting exposure.' We boiled water and gave him tea. He was physically the toughest of us and wore five layers of polar clothing, but the cold was cruel and wore us down hour after hour. We travelled between ten and twelve hours a day. That night Oliver wrote: 'Very bad weather. I think we should have stayed in the tent.' I saw his point, but Greenland five years earlier had taught me that we could travel in high winds and white-out and every hour of progress, however slow, helped our slim chances of success. We had 2,200 miles to go, 900 of them unexplored.

I took a bearing check every ten minutes against the clouds: as these moved slowly and maintained their silhouettes for quite a while, they served me well. At times when partial white-outs hid sun and clouds, all I could do was aim my compass at imperfections in the snow ahead. When the sun shone I navigated by means of the shadows of a series of penknife-scratched lines on the plastic windshield of my skidoo. To check on the accuracy of this crude system and to put some life back into our frozen limbs, I stopped for five minutes in every hour. We normally maintained a space of a mile between each of us so, as soon as I stopped, a backbearing on the two specks back along my trail provided a good check on the angle of travel.

For four days and nights the temperature hovered around –50°C, with a sky aglint with ice crystals creating weird effects such as haloes, sun pillars and parhelia (mock suns or sun dogs). In the mornings the skidoos were difficult to start. Any wrong move or out-of-sequence action caused long delays. Try to engage gear too soon and the drive belt shattered into rubber fragments. Turn the ignition key a touch too hard and it snapped off in the lock. Set the choke wrong and the plugs fouled up. Changing the plugs at –50°C in a strong wind was a bitter chore which no one fancied.

Often the whole day would pass without a word spoken between us. Our routine became slick and included, after camping, the drilling of ice-core samples at every degree of latitude, a full coded weather report by radio to the World Meteorological Organization, and the taking of urine samples as part of our calorific intake programme.

Back at base, Giles and Gerry had returned from England with the Twin Otter, and they took Simon up to help Ginny. Every three or four hundred miles we would run short of fuel and Giles would have to locate us from my theodolite position. In ten days' travel we were 404 nautical miles from Ryvingen with a suspected major crevasse field just to our south. Since no man had been there before us, we had only the chance comments of aircrew from rare and high-altitude USAF flights from which to try to detect such obstacles.

On 9 November we ran into our first bad field of sastrugi: teeth of ice cut by the wind and resembling parallel lines of concrete tank traps. Due to the prevalence of east–west winds, these furrows were diagonal to our southerly direction of travel. The sastrugi were from 18 inches to 4 feet high and, being perpendicular, they often impeded any advance until we axed out a through-lane. The sastrugi buckled our springs, bogey wheels and skis. Oliver struggled to improvise repairs.

For weeks our progress was painfully slow. At 80°S we camped in one spot for seventeen days to allow Giles to set up a fuel dump halfway between the coast and the Pole. Once on the move again, frequent overturns caused minor injuries, axe work through sastrugi fields progressed sometimes at a mere 800 yards in five hours, and the ever-present fear of crevasses gnawed at our morale. One morning, stopping on an apparently harmless slope, Charlie stepped off his skidoo to stretch his legs and promptly disappeared up to his thighs. He was parked right over an unseen cavern, with less than 2 inches of snow cover between him and oblivion. We had been warned by Charles Swithinbank that crevassing might occur at any point over the unmapped area we must cross. He knew of crevasses 180 feet deep, but reckoned that 125 feet was a likely average depth.

Close to 85°S, in a high sastrugi field, we had stopped for repairs when we heard from Ginny that a team of South African scientists, operating at the rim of the coastal mountains near Sanae, were in trouble. One of their heavy snow tractors had plunged 60 feet down a crevasse together with its 1-ton fuel sledge. One man then fell 90 feet down another crevasse and broke his neck, and their rescue party, returning to their coastal base, became lost in the ice fields. They had, by the time Ginny contacted us, already been missing with minimal gear for five days.

At this point we learned that there were no rescue facilities available in the entire continent and, since the missing men were more than fifty miles from their base, they would almost certainly die. Already short of fuel and with a recurring engine start-up problem, highly hazardous in Antarctica, Giles nonetheless flew over a thousand miles to search for, and eventually save, the missing South African scientists.

From 85°S we struggled on, detouring east to avoid a mammoth crevasse field and running into total white-out conditions. Navigation became critical, and on 14 December, after nine hours of travel in thick mist, I stopped where I estimated the South Pole should be. There was no sign of life, although a 16-man crew of US scientists work in a domed base beside the pole. We camped and I radioed the Pole's duty signaller.

'You are three miles away,' replied a man with a Texan twang. 'We have you on radar. Come on in.' He gave us a bearing and, an hour later, the dome loomed up a few yards to my front. At 4.35 a.m. on 15 December, a thousand miles south of Ryvingen and seven weeks ahead of our schedule, we had reached the bottom of the world.

The American base at the South Pole, unlike any other in Antarctica, was protected from the elements by a metal dome. This was just big enough to house eight prefabricated and centrally heated huts and, in winter, when the temperature plunges to −79°C, its outer doors were closed. The dome was designed for the wintering of a dozen scientists and six or seven administrative workers.

In summer the South Pole is the sunniest spot on earth and often has 24-hour days of uninterrupted sunshine. Day and night are indistinguishable. The sun circles the sky at the same height above the horizon. Decisions about when to work and when to sleep are arbitrary. For convenience, the station keeps McMurdo time, which is also New Zealand time. The annual mean temperature, I learned, was –49°C; the lowest ever recorded at the Pole was –83°C, the highest –14°C.

The station was carefully sited upstream from the geographic South Pole, towards which the ice (and with it the station) moves at a rate of about ten metres a year. Once beyond the Pole, the ice will be moving along the meridian of 40°W of Greenwich towards the Filchner Ice Shelf and the Weddell Sea.

American scientists have been at the South Pole since 1957; the dome was built in 1975. It was an ingenious design and ultimately practical. The problem with any land base in Antarctica, whether on the plateau or the peninsula, is that snow very quickly covers any building, requiring base personnel to spend an inordinate amount of time keeping walkways and roofs clear. That would have been very difficult at the South Pole, due to its six months of darkness and low temperatures. By putting a dome over their buildings, the Americans eliminated the never-ending hassle of snowploughing and constantly monitoring snow-covered buildings, as well as the danger of getting lost when going from building to building in a storm. The downside of life spent month after month in the artificial light and dry air of the dome was the stale boredom it could induce in inmates, who described each other as 'dome slugs'.

Not willing to set out for the second half of the journey, which included a potentially unpleasant descent of the Scott Glacier, until Ginny had set up a radio base at the Pole, I asked Tom, the base commander, if we could stay at his place for a week or so. Washington had by now notified him of our impending arrival and had agreed that we could have 23 drums of aviation fuel. Anything else was at Tom's discretion.

We erected two pyramid tents about a hundred yards away from the dome and accepted his kind offer to eat with the Americans in their canteen in exchange for dishwashing and general clean-up duties. This released some of the base staff for much needed work elsewhere. Tom also let me visit the base 'doctor' who had dental equipment and, although he had never before worked on a real live mouth, he did a wonderful job on my cold-induced cavities and put an end to my incessant toothache.

Two weeks earlier the Americans had experienced a couple of worrying incidents. Down at the McMurdo base, the nerve centre for all US Antarctic outstations, helicopter and Hercules crews had helped recover 224 bodies from the remains of an Air New Zealand DC-10 which had crashed into Mount Erebus, the volcano overlooking McMurdo, whilst on a tourist sightseeing overflight.

At the pole station itself, their engineer had recently discovered that the dome's sewer outlet was causing big problems. Over a number of years the effluent, sinking into the ice, had opened up a cavern beneath the dome which was more than a hundred feet deep, with the bottom thirty feet consisting of chemicals and sewage. As a result the dome was slowly tilting one way and the stress on its nuts and bolts had already caused some of them to shear off. Given further strain and extreme temperatures, the situation could easily become serious. The overwintering scientists would not enjoy the twin threats of being crushed by falling girders or suddenly descending into a lake of sewage.

Underneath the dome's ice floor snaked a long tunnel carrying pipes and electric conduits. A good deal of ice had formed from past leaks and this had clogged up the footways. I accompanied Tom and two 'field hands', one an ex-B-52 bomber pilot, on an ice-chipping detail, armed with axes and empty sacks to fill with ice debris. On the way down Tom showed me a vertical vent shaft: 'One of our cooks tried to clear snow from that vent. A column of it broke off and crushed him dead.'

Luckily all our ice chipping took place in a horizontal shaft but I was beginning to think that life in the polar dome was more hazardous than out on the ice sheet. At least you could fall down crevasses out there and not drown in your own sewage.

'We have to watch germs here,' Tom warned me.

'But surely the cold kills all germs?'

'It does outside, but some of our scientists spend their entire Antarctic year in centrally heated huts either up here or down at

McMurdo. You say your wife will be bringing a dog here? It will have to stay outside in your tents, for there is a firm rule: No pets at the Pole. It would not be worth my while to even consider making an exception.'

'He'll be fine in our tents. He's very long-haired.'

'Good,' said Tom. 'And another thing. Be careful of cold germs. They are really virulent up here and we can't afford, especially during the summer season, to lose a scientist's working hours. It is said in Washington to cost a million dollars to keep just one scientist here for a year.'

He explained one of the methods for preventing the common cold. When a new arrival enters McMurdo, he is given special iodine-impregnated handkerchiefs in sets of three: one to blow the nose, one to wipe the nose and one to wipe the hands. At $1 per handkerchief, it costs $3 to blow your nose.

The dome at the pole has no overt political or economic purpose. Scientific research is the be-all and end-all of the polar base, as of all other national bases in Antarctica. By drilling deep into the ice and the ocean floor around Antarctica, the scientists learn about past events, both creeping and catastrophic. Past ice cores have recovered and analysed ice that has been around for 400,000 years. The inmates of the bases, from the world's universities, include geologists, meteorologists and glaciologists who study this least-polluted continent, the fifth largest of the seven and the least inhabited, to try to predict our future and find out how we are damaging our fragile environment.

The expeditions of Captain Scott began meticulous observations of weather patterns. His successors, the scientists of (initially) twelve nations with Antarctic bases, set up in response to the International Geophysical Year initiative fifty years later in 1957, have mounted the major research project which carries on today all over the frozen continent.

Earth is some 4½ billion years old, but primitive, slime-like life forms took a billion years to arrive and another 3 billion years to evolve into entities that left traces of their existence, such as fossils.

While all this was going on, the Earth's surface was cracking and moving around. Ice Ages have gripped the Earth on and off, going back at least to 700 million years ago when it was coated in ice like a golf ball.

At the time when today's Antarctica was ice-free and part of a massive continent a long way north of the south polar region, it was a green and pleasant land of forests, rivers and dinosaurs, which left a wealth of fossils behind. This great and temperate land is known to scientists as Gondwanaland. The land mass that now forms Antarctica broke away from Gondwana many millions of years ago and eventually floated south to settle around the South Pole and to ice over. All around it the oceans swirled with strong deep currents.

The break-up of Gondwana was slow, a few centimetres a year. Some 150 million years ago, today's Africa broke away. Later India floated off and collided with central Asia, which resulted in the formation of the Himalayas. In the Amazon basin, which was once part of Gondwana, there are now over 50,000 species of plant life, whereas in all Antarctica there are but two flowering plants.

Aquatic dinosaurs have been identified up to an amazing 15 metres in length, and the origins of the bird we call the penguin have been traced from the first flying form to today's flightless version that has learnt to dive and to swim. On subantarctic Seymour Island, etched into an area of mudstone, you can see the 18-centimetre-long footprints made 40 million years ago by the flightless phororhacos bird, which stood 3.5 metres tall, ran fast and sported claws capable of disembowelling even the armour-plated armadillo. Not far away, the mandible of a small crocodile-like creature and the remains of a long-extinct species of whale have been found.

Antarctica is geographically divided by a great mountain range which is largely hidden by ice, sometimes 4.5 kilometres thick, and known as the Transantarctic Mountains. East Antarctica lies mostly east of the Greenwich Meridian and is by far the largest sector of the continent, with an area of some 4 million square miles. The ice sheet that covers it, the East Antarctic ice sheet, holds most of Antarctica's ice.

Once consolidated at the South Pole with Ginny back in radio contact, we began the last leg of the crossing, from the Pole to the Pacific coast. En route our main obstacle would clearly be the 10,000-foot descent of the heavily crevassed Scott Glacier.

We set out on Christmas Eve. I thought with a twinge of sympathy of Captain Scott. He had left the South Pole 69 years before on 19 January, too late in the summer to be sure of a safe journey back. After his first expedition, Scott's meteorologists had sent their data to the famous Austrian scientist Julius von Hann who, in 1909, described the Antarctic winter as *kernlos* (coreless) or, as Scott's chief met-man George Simpson, wrote, 'The Antarctic begins and ends its summer at temperatures well below freezing, maintaining a continual reflective mirror of snow and setting the stage for a very cold winter.' During this coreless winter Antarctica is no place to be without good food and solid shelter. It is quite unlike the Arctic, where the coldest temperatures are restricted to the few months around the shortest day of the year.

From the South Pole every direction was due north. About 360 miles away in one direction lay the epicentre of the continent, the point furthest from the sea which is known as the Pole of Inaccessibility. And halfway between that pole and the Russian base of Vostok is the Pole of Cold, supposedly the coldest place on Earth.

Vostok was named after the ship in which the Russian explorer Thaddeus von Bellingshausen sailed in 1821, when he became the first person to sight the peaks of the Antarctic peninsula. The Russians established their research base at Vostok in 1957, the year they launched Sputnik. In 2012 at Vostok they succeeded in drilling down 2¼ miles (3.6 kilometres) to a remarkable lake which may hold many secrets. Until the 1970s nobody believed such a subglacial lake could be unfrozen, but then a British team used airborne ice-penetrating radar and located the lake, which was found to be as big as Lake Ontario.

Pitch-dark, isolated and unpolluted for 15 million years, the lake is surely a unique laboratory of evolution. Bacteria may have evolved even in such extreme conditions, and a method of research had to be worked out to eliminate the risk of polluting the lake, even at the moment of breaking through to its surface. Lake Vostok is the largest of some two hundred such subglacial lakes, and Russian, American and British scientists are hoping to unlock the secrets there of how life evolved on Earth and what it might be like on other planets. Microbial populations have already been found thriving in some of the smaller lakes.

At Vostok Station, 11,200 feet above sea level, a winter temperature of –89.2°C has been recorded. The average temperature there in June (midsummer) is –65°C. This is about the temperature that controversial scientists theorizing about conditions on Earth a billion or two years ago believe our planet was subject to when it was a ball of ice from pole to pole, known to theorists as Snowball Earth. Maybe deep polar lake research will prove them right.

From the Pole I aimed for Mount Howe, a single jagged peak 180 miles away which marked the upper rim of the Scott Glacier. I had chosen this route because it seemed to be the quickest line from the Pole down to the Ross Ice Shelf. Mount Howe was, for us, the first natural feature we had seen in a thousand white miles. Only one expedition had explored the Scott Glacier before us, one of Admiral Byrd's expeditions in 1933. I had read their description of conditions there: 'We picked a way through the maze around big gashes, seracs, rolls, ice holes and ridges … until the way ahead was barred by huge pits, holes, ridges and rolls. … A grander evidence of the overwhelming natural forces at work in this region is nowhere to be seen.'

In situations where the ice surface is under tension, it commonly responds by splitting up into a number of distinct slices. The crevasses which separate these slices of ice may be 40 metres or more deep, with sheer icy sides. Other crevasses, called splaying crevasses, may run almost parallel with the direction of ice movement; they commonly occur near glacier snouts where the ice spreads out or splits laterally. Where ice is stretched in more than one direction there may be intersecting sets of crevasses, giving the glacier surface a violently chopped-up or chaotic appearance. The greatest chaos of all occurs where a glacier is flowing over a rock step, giving rise to an icefall. Here the ice tumbles down in a series of separate blocks called seracs, which may be 20 metres or more in height and may lean well out of the vertical for several weeks before they collapse. The tortured surfaces of such icefalls are constantly on the move.

Our nightmare trail down the glacier led us into a cul-de-sac, surrounded by open crevasses. We retraced our tracks and tried again via another narrow corridor between blue ice walls. A maze of sunken lanes beset with hidden falls finally released us, shaken but unhurt, close by the Gardner Ridge and 6,000 feet above our ice-shelf goal. In 40-knot winds and thick mist, we followed the Klein Glacier for twelve miles until we were forced along a narrow ice-spit between two giant pressure fields, a chaos of gleaming ice blocks.

I knelt to study the map in order to find a way through, but the wind tore it away. I carried one spare chart with my navigation gear and, using it, plotted a course to the eastern side of the valley. Halfway through the smaller pressure field, a sudden drop revealed the lower reaches of Scott Glacier, a breathtaking show of mountain and ice-flow, rock and sky, dropping 600 metres to the far horizon and the pinnacles of the Organ Pipe Peaks. A crevasse field five miles deep crossed the entire valley from cliff to cliff and halted us short of Mount Russell, so we detoured east over a 1,000-foot-high pass and, three hours later, re-entered Scott Glacier – beyond the crevasse field – by way of a wicked ravine. We had travelled for fourteen hours and covered five days' worth of scheduled progress. The next day our mad journey continued. More ice walls, and skidding, out-of-control sledges. At the foot of Mount Ruth we cat-footed along the ceiling of an active pressure zone as rotten as worm-eaten wood. Charlie, careful never to sound excited about anything, described the subsequent downhill journey:

The descent was hair-raising, too steep for sledges which ran down ahead of the skidoos sometimes wrenching them sideways and even backwards over wide droopy snow-bridges. Some of the bridges had fracture lines on both sides and were obviously ready to drop at the first excuse, like overripe apples. How we made the bottom, God only knows. We camped on blue ice.

Some people will think it must have been easy, simply because we descended so quickly. All I can say is let them try. Ran and Ol were as frightened as I was, even if they don't admit it. That's why Ran kept going hour after hour without stopping. He zigzagged in every direction trying to avoid the worst areas. He didn't have much success and on one of the upper ledges we found ourselves right in the middle of a major pressure zone. Great ice bubbles and blue domes reared above us as we slithered along a maze of cracked corridors, totally trapped.

My sledge took an eight foot wide fissure diagonally and broke through the bridge. My skidoo's rubber tracks clawed at the blue ice, slipped sideways and the sledge began to disappear. I was lucky. A patch of grainy white ice gave the tracks just enough purchase to heave forward again. The sledge wallowed up and over the forward lip of the crevasse.

We had crossed Antarctica as a single team from the Atlantic to the Pacific. Only Sir Vivian Fuchs and Sir Edmund Hillary had completed such a traverse before, with two expedition teams pioneering two trails that met at the South Pole and by a far shorter route.

Sir Vivian himself was due to meet us in New Zealand to discuss the problems ahead. The expedition was still well short of our halfway point around the polar axis, but we were becoming better at dealing with the cold.

Chapter Seven

Eating people is wrong

MICHAEL FLANDERS AND DONALD SWANN
FROM 'THE RELUCTANT CANNIBAL' (1957)

On 19 January 1981 the *Benjamin Bowring* came through on Ginny's radio at Scott Base. She was seven miles out in heavy pack. On the same day, the four of us walked out past Captain Scott's wooden shack to Hut Point. It was not difficult to imagine the feelings of the pioneers in the early days when their masted ships had appeared on that same horizon. For weeks on end they had posted lookouts on Observation Hill to scan the northern limits of McMurdo Sound.

As our own little ship entered the bay between the ice floes below Scott's hut, strains of 'Land of Hope and Glory' came over the ship's loudspeakers. The two sections of the expedition were meeting up after a year and many miles. Not all eyes were dry, nor, in a short while, were many throats, for someone had saved some sponsored champagne.

We made a few sorties into the foothills of Mount Erebus with the crew and visited the site of Captain Scott's main hut, from which he and his four chosen companions had made their last journey. The site had been carefully preserved by New Zealanders on visits from Scott Base. It was just as it must have been seventy years back: pony harnesses hung on hooks, Victorian chemical bottles in the 'laboratory' and seal's blubber spread over the lobby floor. We felt a silent affinity with our dead countrymen, their journeys long done, ours but half complete.

Back on the *Benjamin Bowring* we learned that six weeks before, in these very waters, the 2,500-ton German research vessel *Gotland II*, ice-strengthened like ours, was crushed by encroaching pack ice. By luck her deck cargo was five helicopters and the pilots were on board. Everyone was flown to a nearby island and later to a coastal summer base. Our skipper, Les Davis, who had now taken over from Admiral Otto Steiner, took note of the Lloyd's report: 'The ship was of maximum ice security standard and her officers were experienced in Antarctic conditions.' Les knew that the Arctic Ocean pack ice would be twice as hazardous to any ship as this Antarctic ice, for it is harder and thicker in the north and individual floes are more massive. So his most testing time was yet to come.

We were rolling violently on 23 February when the cloud-hung mass of Campbell Island, on our route to New Zealand, was sighted. We entered the protection of its long natural harbour between green hills. After fourteen months without a blade of grass, this remote but fertile land was a wonderful sight, not unlike a Hebridean isle.

A dozen New Zealand scientists worked at a base beside the entry fjord, and they made us very welcome. According to the base leader, we were the first British registered ship to call since records began in 1945, and he had his men show us the island.

We came first to a colony of sea lions, famous for their lion-like roar, their harems of a dozen females and their artful slaughter of penguins. In 1622 on first observing them, the sea captain Sir Richard Hawkins described them as 'in their former parts like unto lyons with shagge hayre and mostaches'. Also present in the sea-washed kelp beds were lone leopard seals some three metres long, dark grey with blotches and, when they yawned, impressively sharp-looking teeth. They fed on penguins, krill and any nesting or swimming birds they could catch. Their only enemies, other than sealers, are killer whales and an impressive array of internal parasites.

Further round the bay past bogs of oozing peat, we came to the noisome nests of a dozen huge elephant seals whose noses resembled short trunks. We kept our distance from these monsters too because, although their body language was not aggressive, their breath smelt horrible.

We climbed up a muddy track and, as we constantly slipped backwards, our guide smiled and observed that it rained an average of 325 days a year. At the top of a long slope leading to a field of tussocky grass and many pretty flowers, we came to a couple of nesting albatross. We knelt down beside the nearest bird, which, like the seals, ignored us. It was white all over save for partly black wings, which have an incredible span of up to 11½ feet (3.5 metres).

Our guide was clearly in awe of the albatross. They can live, he told us, for sixty years, and electronically tagged individuals have been recorded as flying twice around the world in one go, pausing en route only to fish in the sea. They mate for life and, as more and more of these wonderful birds are killed by longline fishing hooks and nets, so increasing numbers of lone birds wait for mates who will never return.

A multitude of other birds thrive along the cliffs and crags of Campbell Island, but thousands are killed and their eggs smashed by the highly aggressive skua, or sea hawk. These predators fly fast and low, grab unguarded chicks, even fairly large young penguins, and, once beyond the penguin rookery, feast on their victim, sometimes two or more tearing apart the squealing chick. Often enough these thuggish birds gorge themselves to the point where they cannot take off.

As has happened on many other subantarctic islands, all types of seal have been heavily predated by man. In the mid-twentieth century Captain E.E. Hedblom of the US Navy advised: 'Hit seals between the eyes with the pick of an ice axe and then cut their throats. (For dog food, don't cut the seal's throat. Blood is good dog food.) The crab-eater seal is the tastiest, but all are edible – roast, grill or broil. Loin, tongue and heart are the tenderest muscles. Seal liver is a delicacy, but is particularly likely to be infested with parasites. The British find seal brain very good.'

We left Campbell Island, and 400 miles to the north arrived at the port of Lyttelton on New Zealand's South Island.

Oliver's wife, Rebecca, from whom he had been separated then reunited for the past few years, had grown sick with worry during the Antarctic crossing. Oliver was faced with the cruel choice of wife or Transglobe. He took the long-term option because he loved Rebecca more than his six-year-long ambition to achieve Transglobe's goals. The loss of Oliver would cause wider problems than the mere mechanics of food supplies and weights to be carried in the Arctic. Back in London the committee who represented the expedition decided that it would be irresponsible for us to attempt the northern hemisphere with a team of only two. They were solidly in favour of a third man, probably from the Royal Marines or SAS, being recruited to replace Oliver.

On arrival in Christchurch, New Zealand, I received a warning message from Anthony Preston, the ex-RAF man in charge of our London office and a volunteer staff of eight. He had discovered that an American – Walt Pedersen, one of the 1968 team that had reached the North Pole under Ralph Plaisted – was all set to sledge to the South Pole early next year. Determined to become the first man in the world to reach both poles overland, he had spent twelve years getting his act together. It looked as though he would beat us by four months, since the earliest we could hope to reach the North Pole would be April 1982. I reflected that virtually none of our Antarctic experience was applicable to our coming Arctic struggle. The two places were as alike as chalk and cheese.

In Auckland we held a trade exhibition which the New Zealand prime minister, Mr Muldoon, opened. In his speech he likened Transglobers to old English merchant adventurers. Over 22,000 visitors flooded our show.

Sir Edmund Irving, Sir Vivian Fuchs and Mike Wingate Gray, chairman and key members of our London committee, held long meetings in Auckland with Ginny, Charlie and me, but we could not agree in principle to the recruitment of a third man. I resolved to put the final decision to our patron, Prince Charles, and I explained the whole problem to him in the skipper's cabin at Sydney, where he opened our trade fair. The upshot of the various discussions was that Charlie and I should carry on alone, but Sir Vivian Fuchs rightly warned me that if things should go wrong, the blame would be entirely mine. Sadly, we said goodbye to Ollie and he returned to Britain.

On the *Benjamin Bowring*'s boat deck we gave Prince Charles three cheers and a miniature silver globe marked with our route to congratulate him on his engagement to Lady Diana Spencer. Bothie joined in the cheering, yapping aggressively until Prince Charles patted and spoke to him. While we were in Sydney, Charlie married his fiancée and Anton married Jill, our ship's cook. The *Benjamin Bowring* was becoming quite a family ship. All in all, the expedition was to witness seventeen marriages of its members, to each other or to outsiders.

From Sydney we steamed north over the Equator to Los Angeles, where President Reagan had kindly agreed to open our trade exhibition. Sadly, someone shot and wounded him just beforehand, so he sent us a message instead: 'My warmest congratulations ... Now that you are halfway through your polar circumnavigation of the earth, we welcome you to the United States ... You are attempting something which has never been done before which will take courage and dedication. The "can-do" spirit your expedition so perfectly exemplifies is still alive in the free world.'

Our final exhibition, in Vancouver, was completed on schedule, and we followed the coastline north to the mouth of the Yukon River in Alaska. If the ship had been able to continue north through the Bering Strait – between Russia's eastern tip and Alaska – she would have sailed on to the North Pole, over the top and back to England via Spitsbergen. But because the Arctic Ocean is full of moving ice, the best the *Benjamin Bowring* could do was to drop Charlie and me overboard with rubber boats in the Bering Strait and as close as she could get to the mouth of the Yukon River.

Eight years earlier we had scheduled our arrival off the Yukon for the first week of June because, in a bad year, that is the latest time that the northern rivers shed their load of ice and become navigable. All being well we would now ascend the Yukon for 1,000 miles, then descend the Mackenzie River to its mouth in the Arctic Ocean at the Eskimo settlement of Tuktoyaktuk. From there we would make a 3,000-mile dash east through the fabled Northwest Passage and north up the Canadian archipelago to Ellesmere Island and Alert, our old stamping ground. It was imperative to complete the entire boat journey from the Bering Strait to Alert within the three short summer months when the Arctic Ocean ice pack should be at its loosest. We had to reach Alert by the end of September or risk being cut off by freezing seas and 24-hour darkness.

Fewer than a dozen expeditions had ever successfully navigated this passage in either direction. Those few all used boats with protection from the elements and took an average of three years to get through due to blockage by pack ice en route.

Our ascent of the Yukon and descent of the Mackenzie rivers went to plan, and we arrived at Tuktoyaktuk harbour late in July with one month to complete the 3,500 miles of the Northwest Passage if we were to reach the far end before the sea froze. For this voyage we switched from our two 12-foot rubber boats to a single 16-foot open fibreglass boat with two outboard engines.

Worried about navigation, I visited a local barge skipper with sixteen years of experience. I was planning to navigate the passage by magnetic hand compass plus my watch and the sun. The skipper said simply, 'You are mad.'

'But I have good charts and a handmade balanced prismatic compass,' I assured him.

'Throw it away,' he muttered.

'What do you use?' I asked him.

He pointed at his sturdy barge-towing tug. 'She has everything.

She goes in the dark, out in the deep channels. Radar beacon responders, MF and DF, the works.' He shook his head dismissively. 'You must hug the coastline to escape storms, so you will hit shoals, thousands of shoals. Also you cannot go across the many deep bays for fear of wind and big waves, so you must again hug the coastline, which is like crazy pavement. You have to use more gas and take extra days. Most of the time there will be thick fog. No sun means you use your compass. Yes?'

I nodded.

He flung his hands up. 'Ah, but you cannot use a compass. Look!' He prodded his desk chart of the passage and I saw the heavily printed warning 'MAGNETIC COMPASS USELESS IN THIS AREA'. 'Too near the magnetic pole, you see. You stay here in Tuk. Have a holiday.'

I thanked him.

As I left he shouted, 'Maybe you can navigate by the wrecks of the other madmen who've tried. There's plenty of them.'

Many have tried to pass through the Northwest Passage over the last two centuries and hundreds have died in the attempt. The stories of misery and starvation, cannibalism and death, of shipwrecks caused by hidden shoals, violent storms and invading ice are legion. The down-to-earth *Encyclopaedia Britannica* is unusually descriptive:

> The hostile Arctic makes the Northwest Passage one of the world's severest maritime challenges. It is 500 miles north of the Arctic Circle and less than 1,200 miles from the North Pole ... Thick pack ice, moving at speeds up to ten miles per day, closes nearly half the Passage all the year round. Arctic water can freeze a man to death in two minutes. Frigid polar north-easterly winds blow almost constantly and can howl to hurricane force. Temperatures rise above freezing only in July and August ... Visibility is often obscured by white-outs of blowing snow ... Thick fog usually shrouds the channels during the brief summer ... There are uncharted shoals ... little is known about

> the currents and tides ... Navigation is difficult even with the most modern devices ... The compass is useless because the magnetic North Pole lies within the Passage ... The bleak featureless Arctic islands provide few distinguishing landmarks. Arctic blackouts can frustrate all communications for periods from a few hours to nearly a month.

Dr Geoffrey Hattersley-Smith, accepted British expert on the Northwest Passage and a good friend of the expedition, had written to me three years before: 'Whilst I would not doubt that this journey can be done piecemeal, I think it unrealistic to suppose that it can be done in one season. At least you would have to have phenomenal luck to do it.'

Everything that he and the encyclopaedia had warned me about turned out to be only too true. The subsequent voyage was a nightmare. It was the wettest, coldest period of my life to date, involving the most complex and stressful navigation with non-stop fear of capsize and always the worry that the sea was about to freeze over.

When our planned route between the islands of the passage was blocked by pack ice, we chose other zigzag routes and often, despite a dangerous intake of pills to try to stay awake, fell asleep at the helm, although luckily not both of us at the same time.

Every few hundred miles we would locate, usually in thick fog, one of our vital fuel dumps, often dropped by seaplane months before on some gravel promontory a hundred miles from the nearest habitation, or at a lonely Distant Early Warning (DEW) Line Station, each of which consisted of a large igloo-shaped radar dome and four radar dishes facing north towards the USSR. The whole network of 31 stations – 21 in Canada, 6 in Alaska and 4 in Greenland – was installed to give warning of any sneak attack by bombers or missiles over the top of the world.

At the remote Lady Franklin Point station, I went behind the huts at midnight and scaled two of the radar masts to hang out my radio's antenna wires and speak to Ginny in faraway Tuktoyaktuk. I noticed that the station boss was lurking close behind me. Since I had my earphones on, he need not have pussy-footed to get there. He glared at me. I smiled back politely, for he was our host and had a right to glare. I decided to close down the connection to Ginny. Perhaps I was unwittingly on a frequency that interfered with the base radio.

'With whom are you communicating?' he asked.

'With my wife.'

'Where is she?'

'In Tuktoyaktuk.'

'Do you have permission to use the radio up here?'

'Yes. On 4982 megahertz.'

I opened my bag to stack away the headphones and antenna and he moved closer to peer inside. Deciding to seize the bull by the horns, I laughed and said, 'I am British, you know. Not a spy.'

He gave me a severe and hostile look which clearly indicated that the second half of my observation was a non sequitur.

'Well,' I said, 'I'll be getting some sleep now. We must push on first thing tomorrow.' That did seem to please him.

A hundred and thirty miles to the east, one outboard gave up the ghost and failed to respond to any known remedy. We limped back thirty miles to Byron Bay DEW station, where we spent three days replacing the crown pinion gear. Then on towards the DEW station at Cambridge Bay. Wild storms lashed our passage over wide bay mouths and past forlorn capes of twisted red lava domes and fluted black pillars of cutaway bedrock. We smelled acrid chemicals and saw that a section of the cliff was on fire and glowing orange in the gloom. Sulphur deposits forever burning. And in other places we saw groups of mini-volcanoes about a hundred feet high and known locally as pingos.

I looked for places of shelter but there were none, not even a shallow cave or leaning boulder. The rain drove down from a forbidding sky. I marvelled silently at our predecessors of a century past who had ventured along this coast under sail and with blank charts. More than a hundred of Sir John Franklin's men had died in this region. Many of the features which did have names reflected the unpleasant memories of those pioneers: Cape Storm, Starvation Harbour and other evocative echoes.

For centuries the British, at the behest of the Admiralty, rich merchants or patriotic individuals, sent out explorers and sea captains who nosed around the labyrinth of islands to the north and west of Frobisher Bay. Like Frobisher, they found that the many likely-looking west-leading inlets were only coastal fjords going nowhere. There would be repeated disappointments, disappearances, shipwrecks, great suffering and major controversies, but nothing was allowed to stand in the way of the ongoing quest for the Northwest Passage and the 'quick way to Cathay'. Tantalizing clues from each returned sea captain suggested possible aims for the next voyage. Advice was also proffered by the many whaling-ship navigators operating off Newfoundland and Spitsbergen (between the seventeenth and nineteenth centuries, there were nearly 30,000 whaling voyages in that region).

Those who made it back to Britain would tell how such and such a channel was permanently blocked by ice, whereas, in reality, many of the channels do remain ice-free in summer months, if only once in five years.

After the disappointing failure of Baffin and others to find the passage in the early seventeenth century, the British sent no further ships up north for two hundred years, until in 1817, whaling skipper William Scoresby reported that Davis Strait, the channel off the west coast of Greenland, was unusually free of ice. The Napoleonic Wars had just ended, and two key London grandees, John Barrow, second secretary to the Admiralty, and Joseph Banks of the Royal Society, began a hard-hitting campaign to persuade the government to use navy ships and men to search once again for the passage and, an additional new quest, to locate the North Magnetic Pole which was vital for the establishment of new methods of accurate navigation. So, in 1818, three years after the battle of Waterloo, two ships were sent to locate the passage under captains William Parry and John Ross, whilst John Franklin was to explore north from Hudson Bay to find the magnetic pole.

These three great Arctic explorers became household names in Britain, as would Scott and Shackleton in the following century. Captain John Ross had fought naval battles on the Baltic, as he evidenced to a parliamentary body: 'I was wounded in thirteen places, both legs broken, a bayonet through my body, and five cuts in my head with a sabre.' He was as irascible and opinionated as he was brave and capable. Lieutenant John Franklin, who had also fought in the Napoleonic Wars, including at the battle of Trafalgar, was a mild-mannered and popular officer. Lieutenant William Parry, a more difficult character to pin down, became less well known than the other two, partly because of the bitter controversies that clung to Ross and the tragedy associated with Franklin.

On the 1818 expedition, after successfully exploring all Baffin Bay and the approaches to Lancaster Sound, Ross decided to turn round and head home because he reported seeing no possible ocean routes to the west. Parry and others disputed what Ross had or had not observed and the two men argued bitterly about the voyage for the rest of their lives. Parry's opinion was that Ross had turned away from the most likely route to the passage without ever giving a satisfactory reason for doing so. Franklin's separate voyage was blocked early on by impenetrable ice.

In 1819 the Admiralty sent a new expedition voyage north under Parry. By this time certain changes in Royal Navy preparations for extreme cold conditions and the avoidance of scurvy had been introduced, including portable beds in place of hammocks, warmer clothing and boots, and tinned provisions. The tin can had been invented seven years earlier, but not the tin opener, so cans had to be opened with axes.

The 1819 Parry expedition happened to coincide with an unusually loose ice year, which enabled his two ships to penetrate far west into Lancaster Sound and to survey over a thousand miles of previously unknown coastline. Then followed the first-ever wintering of a naval expedition north of the Arctic Circle. Lots of lemon juice plus daily exercise on deck and strict hygiene checks delayed the onset of scurvy. But increasingly low temperatures froze and burst many lemon juice bottles, and by the end of winter a number of scurvy cases had broken out. Blocked by ice, Parry used the brief 1820 summer to escape from the Sound and head home. He summarized this voyage: 'Though we have not completed the Northwest Passage, we have made a large hole in it.'

Meanwhile, John Franklin also set out in 1819, with three of his officers: George Back, Robert Hood and Dr John Richardson. They went up the Coppermine River and successfully surveyed hundreds of miles of virgin coastline. On the way back, running out of supplies and suffering severe blizzards, Franklin's men ate lichen and boot leather. The twelve Canadian outbackers, known as voyageurs, who accompanied Franklin's team became desperate with starvation and frostbite. One went mad, killed another and cut him up for food. Later he killed Hood, so Richardson shot him. By the time they reached safety, ten of the party had died of hypothermia, starvation or murder. The journey had taken three years in all.

William Parry (who had been promoted to commander after his highly successful 1819–20 voyage) was immediately commissioned by the Admiralty to head north for a third voyage, in 1821, with two ships, the *Hecla* and the *Fury*, to search the north-west corner of Hudson Bay where, at Repulse Bay, a 1742 navy voyage had been turned back by ice from a potential route to the passage. On this third Parry voyage, his midshipman was James Clark Ross, nephew of John Ross, who was in the nineteenth century to become Britain's greatest naval explorer.

Finding that Repulse Bay was a cul-de-sac, Parry headed east, surveyed six hundred miles of new coastline and wintered in the Foxe Basin, where friendly Inuit were camped, and then spent the next two winters of 1821 and 1822 there. No open channel to the west was entered, but the voyage was the first real close contact between the Inuit of Canada and the culture of the west. Parry's records of his studies of their way of life, both social and religious, were published in 1824 and were widely read.

Unbelievably, Parry accepted yet another northern commission in 1824, with his same two ships. This time the conditions were as unusually bad as, in 1819, they had been exceptionally good. One of the officers this time was midshipman Horatio Nelson. This expedition only surveyed sixty miles of new coastline, and the *Fury*, crushed by ice, sank in due course after all her copious stores had been safely unloaded and left on the beach. Both crews made it back home in 1825, and Parry was to command only one more such voyage when, in 1827 with James Clark Ross, he attempted to reach the North Pole by dragging boats over broken ice to reach 82°43'N, the furthest north ever reached and a record that held until the Nares expedition of 1875.

The stores left on Fury Beach saved many lives when, in 1829, the controversial John Ross with his nephew James Clark Ross as his second in command used the *Victory*, fitted with steam-powered paddle wheels as well as sail, to try again for the passage. They managed to head two hundred miles further south down Prince Regent Inlet than had Parry, but there they remained entrapped for the next three years. The younger Ross made many sledge journeys around the area, and in May 1831 he reached and established the exact position of the North Magnetic Pole.

In May 1833 the two members of the Ross family agreed to abandon the *Victory* and 'sledge' their three boats back north to Fury Beach to take on supplies. Then, boating east, they would hope to be rescued by a passing whaler. This was a reasonable hope since another winter on the trapped *Victory* would have meant certain death. The plan worked and the men were all back home by October 1833. They had survived for four years on the ice, a true Arctic survival record.

Meanwhile, remarkably resilient, Franklin, Back and Richardson had returned, after their difficult 1819 expedition, to map even more of the northern wastelands and coastline by way of the Back (or Great Fish) River. George Back, in the early 1830s, and HBC men Simpson and Dease, between 1837 and 1839, filled in the remaining gaps along the continental coastline all the way between the Back and Mackenzie rivers.

By 1845 the Admiralty had narrowed the passage search down

to locating a channel or channels heading west between the mainland's coastal waters surveyed by Franklin and the HBC men, and the more northerly channel running west from the Lancaster and Viscount Melville Sounds. The man they decided to put in charge of this search, despite being by then fat and fifty-nine years of age, was John Franklin himself, with two excellent ships – *Erebus* and *Terror* – and 134 men.

All went well at first, but bad ice conditions in Lancaster Sound and, later, off King William Island ended with both ships being crushed and all the men 'lost in thin air'. Although nobody was to learn of their fate for several years, all in fact died between 1845 and 1847, somewhere between Devon Island and King William Island. For more than two years after the last sightings (in Baffin Bay by a whaler) of Franklin's two ships, the Admiralty showed no concern. After all, the great sea captain John Ross had disappeared for four years on his passage-searching voyage, but lived to tell the tale.

In 1848 the distraught wife of Franklin (who was, in fact, his widow, though she didn't know it) offered a reward for news of his venture and goaded the Admiralty into action. James Clark Ross, the most admired of polar explorers at the time, was sent off with two ships to find Franklin. Two other vessels were to approach the passage from the west via the Bering Strait, and Franklin's old friend from the 1821 Coppermine expedition, John Richardson, was to search the coast between the mouths of the Mackenzie and Coppermine rivers. With him was a veteran traveller of the coastal region, Dr John Rae of the HBC.

Ross found that his way west was ice-blocked in Barrow Strait, so he and Lieutenant Leopold McClintock took two six-man sledges down the west coast of Somerset Island for five hundred miles. This was to be the first such sledge journey of many. Ross and McClintock followed the coast south beside Peel Sound, which they described as permanently ice-blocked, little knowing that two years earlier Franklin's two ships, finding the sound to be briefly ice-free, had sailed down it to reach the east coast of King William Island.

If only Franklin had followed the navy tradition on such voyages of leaving messages in obvious cairns saying where they intended to go, then Ross would have continued down Peel Sound. As it was, he went back to his ship and in the summer of 1849 returned to England.

The two ships sent to search from the west navigated the Bering Strait and sailed over the top of Alaska (then Russian America). A seven-hundred-mile sledge journey followed, which managed to meet up with Dr John Rae at the mouth of the Mackenzie River; the first meeting in mid-passage of searchers from either end, and, in a loose way, a considerable achievement within the overall aim of locating the passage. But there was still no sign of Franklin and his men.

The following year (1850) saw the departure of a veritable spate of Franklin searches – fifteen in that year alone – and many of the Franklin searchers would soon need rescuing themselves. Two Admiralty ships were again sent via the Bering Strait under the experienced command of Robert McClure and Richard Collinson. When McClure reached Banks Island, his ship was entrapped by ice, but he sledged on east and climbed to a high vantage point from which, with a telescope, he clearly observed the frozen waters of Viscount Melville Sound, which he knew had been reached by Parry's 1820 expedition. There was no land, only sea ice blocking the way. He, therefore, claimed success in discovering a valid sailing route for the Northwest Passage in summers when the sound was ice-free. But he failed to find Franklin.

Severe ice conditions very nearly crushed McClure's ship and imprisoned her in an inlet of Banks Island for a further two years. The men were on starvation rations, there were floggings and two men went mad, their screams echoing day and night around the decks, along which limped men with limbs black and swollen from scurvy. Thanks to a message in a cairn that McClure had left on the south side of Melville Island the year before, a sledge group from another Franklin search ship located McClure just in time.

When McClure's men eventually managed to sledge to their

rescuers' ship, the surgeon described them as follows: 'One officer subject to periods of mental aberration; one man in a state of dementia (or imbecility), his condition and appearance rendered still more pitiable from severe frostbite of the fingers; two men carried on the sledges, the one with scurvy, the other with urinary disease and phlegmonous inflammation of the leg; the remainder all more or less affected with scorbutic disease and debility.'

However, McClure's troubles were not over, for the rescue ship was herself beset for a further year, making McClure's entrapment a total of four years. Back in London in late 1854 he was promoted to captain and was knighted as the discoverer of the Northwest Passage, even though, as *The Times* adroitly commented, 'This Northwest Passage may be assumed to be open once or twice in a century during favourable circumstances for short periods.'

The ship under Captain Richard Collinson that had left England in convoy with McClure's vessel did manage to sail further east than had any other that entered the passage from the west. But they made no new discoveries and the officers were riven with dissension. Back in London some six months after McClure's return, their achievements were ignored.

One group of four ships, using a mixture of both sail and steam, was sent under veteran skippers Austin, Ommanney, Osborn and Cator. Clements Markham, who would later send Scott to Antarctica, was a midshipman on this squadron. Amongst other search expeditions at the time were a couple of navy brigs under a veteran whaling skipper, William Penny; a small schooner *Felix* under polar oldie John Ross (now in his seventies); and two American ships paid for by a New York magnate, Henry Grinnell.

In 1850 Ommanney, Penny, John Ross and others were all anchored off Beechey Island where they found graves and other evidence that Franklin had been there for a while four years earlier. But there were no clues as to where he had then headed. The search ships' crews wintered in various places and sledged all over different islands. Some sent balloons into the air which dropped messages. Arctic foxes were used like messenger pigeons with notes attached to their collars. Sledgers towing heavy loads went snow-blind, and compasses proved useless so near the magnetic pole. One diary recorded: 'The men at every step sink above their knees, and frequently deeper, in snow or water.' Many of the men were badly frostbitten, yet one group managed to travel 770 miles in 80 days and, under Doctor John Rae, amazingly long trips were achieved in record times.

In 1852 the Admiralty sent out yet another search squadron, this time with five ships under polar veteran Edward Belcher and 222 men. One ship was commanded by Leopold McClintock, who led a sledging journey of 1,400 miles in 105 days. Belcher became extremely unpopular with both men and fellow officers and was later accused of desertion when he sailed back to England, having left his four other ships trapped in the Arctic.

By the time of McClure's return in 1854, Franklin and his men had been lost for nine years, and the Admiralty announced that the officers and crews of the *Erebus* and the *Terror* were regarded as 'having died in Her Majesty's Service'. Lady Franklin was outraged at this decision, which she considered premature.

However, late in 1854 the various exploits of the many expeditions of the early 1850s were eclipsed when Doctor John Rae met up with Inuit who had found various objects that were definitely from Franklin's men and ships. Rae learnt that both *Erebus* and *Terror* had been abandoned off the coast of King William Island, and their surviving crew members had set off south on foot in a vain attempt to reach the Canadian coast. One by one they had died en route. Rae further described findings at one of the Franklin death sites: 'From the mutilated state of many of the corpses and the contents of the kettles, it is evident that our wretched countrymen had been driven to the last resource – cannibalism – as a means of prolonging existence.'

When Rae's observations were published in the London *Times*, Victorian English morals were scandalized. Charles Dickens wrote that Rae's allegations were merely based on 'the chatter of a gross handful of uncivilized people, with a domesticity of blood and blubber.' The Inuit, who he described as 'covetous, treacherous and cruel', were behind the horror, not Franklin and his men.

Rae's discoveries were about a day's march from the mouth of the Back or Great Fish River where the Inuit had found 'the corpses of some thirty persons and some graves on the continent and five dead bodies on an island near it ... Some of the bodies were in a tent or tents, others were under the boat which had been turned over to form a shelter and some lay scattered about in different directions.' Even Lady Franklin now had to accept that her husband was dead. But exactly how and where had he and the other hundred men met their deaths?

For two years her desire to answer these questions was frustrated by the government's involvement in the Crimean War, but in 1857 Captain Leopold McClintock, famous for his previous sledging journeys, agreed to take the steam yacht *Fox* on a final search voyage. McClintock, hugely successful, brought together many of the missing fragments of the Franklin mystery, showing beyond reasonable doubt that he had managed to take *Erebus* and *Terror* down the usually ice-bound Peel Sound and, when trapped off King William Island, had sledged south over that island and over the narrow channel to the mainland. This was the same sea-route (but in the opposite direction) that Charlie Burton and I, in our open whaler, would be forced to use in 1981. When McClintock returned to London, his book about his experiences was for months in greater demand than the works of Dickens or Darwin.

Long after McClintock's successful voyage in *Fox*, American interest in the Franklin saga continued. The naval surgeon, Elisha Kane, an inveterate traveller with a long-nursed desire to be first to reach the North Pole, had joined a US search for Franklin in 1850–1 and, two years later, mounted his own expedition which, heading up Davis Strait, reached further north than any previous journey. For the next two years the Kane ship remained ice-bound and, amidst much dissension and many attempts to float or sail south, the men were eventually rescued off floating ice 1,300 miles from their abandoned ship.

Kane's well-told story of his voyage inspired a newspaper editor, Charles Hall of Cincinnati, to join the Franklin search, and he set off on two expeditions. The first began in 1860, more than a dozen years after *Erebus* and *Terror* disappeared, and then in 1864–9 Hall spent five long winters in the Arctic before he finally made it to King William Island. At first he travelled with Inuit friends, but then switched to travelling with five ex-whalers. But he fell out with these men in a big way, and ended up killing one in self-defence. By the end of the 1860s Hall had lost his long fascination with teasing out the last details of the Franklin story and he switched his focus to the North Pole, announcing that this was actually 'the goal of my ambition'.

In 1871 Hall set out once again. Of his crew, he said, 'I have chosen my own men, men who will stand by me through thick and thin. Though we may be surrounded by innumerable icebergs, and though our vessel may be crushed like an eggshell, I believe they will stand by me to the last.'

By September 1871 his ship *Polaris* had managed to reach the northern tip of Ellesmere Island, a long way north of the previous record. But there was a great deal of tension and hatred amongst the crew, and Hall became suspicious, indeed paranoid, that various individuals were out to kill him. For two weeks after drinking a cup of coffee, he lay in bed, semi-paralysed and intermittently suffering dementia. He died in great pain and when his body was exhumed in 1968, the Forensic Centre in Toronto studied his fingernails and found toxic quantities of arsenic. He had clearly been poisoned. The cold and the dark can have a bad effect on the mind and the actions of normally sensible individuals.

The many Franklin searches (at least thirty-two in number) had, by the time of Lady Franklin's death in 1875, cost some £40 million in today's money, and although the exact nature of Franklin's fate was never settled, over 40,000 square miles of new territory had been surveyed in the most rugged and hostile terrain.

Charlie and I reached the DEW Line outpost at Cambridge Bay, near the southern tip of Victoria Island, on 6 August. Things were not looking good date-wise, for if we were not clear of the Northwest Passage by the end of August, the sea would be liable to freeze where not already blocked by ice.

A Northwest Passage expert, sailor and historian, John Bockstoce, had warned me, 'Be out of the passage by the end of August or you'll be in trouble.' I thought, too, of Colin Irwin, a young English sailor who, in the 1970s, had managed to sail the entire passage to this point in a specially constructed yacht. But he was blocked when sea ice closed in on Cambridge Bay from the east. He was patient and waited through two summers, but the ice never moved so he married a local Inuit girl and gave up his attempt.

I made a radio call to Ginny, who was about to fly by Twin Otter to Resolute Bay on Cornwallis Island, many hundreds of sea miles to our north, to keep in radio contact. If at any point we were swamped or lost then she would try to organize a search. Ginny would be landing to refuel at Cambridge Bay and I asked if they could take me on a reconnaissance flight to the east of Cambridge Bay. It would not take long and would give me an idea of the amount of ice around. By good luck the Twin Otter pilot was Karl Z'berg, who was booked to fly for us up in the Arctic Ocean the following year. Karl was a Swiss Canadian and reputed to be the best polar pilot of all. He agreed to help where he could, and the next afternoon landed at Cambridge Bay. Ginny, Simon and Bothie looked well, but there was a second dog, too. A black Labrador puppy even smaller than Bothie.

'What,' I asked Ginny, 'is that?'

'This is Tugaluk. Two months old and a good dog.'

'And whose is she?'

Ginny thought quickly. 'She's a wedding present for Simon.'

Simon butted in that he wasn't getting married, and even if he had been he wouldn't want Tugaluk.

'You can't keep her, Ginny, you know that, don't you?'

Ginny did. But, she explained, the puppy would have been shot if it was left as a stray in Tuktoyaktuk. 'Anyway,' she said with finality, 'Bothie has fallen in love with her. He'll probably get over it in Resolute, so I'll find a kind owner and leave her there.'

The matter was closed. Or so I thought.

I had a discussion with Karl. Charlie and I had not seen him since somewhere near the North Pole four years before when he had piloted the resupply Otter we were chartering from Bradley Air Services. If the sea to the east of Cambridge Bay was blocked with ice, we had but two alternatives: to wait, which I had no wish to do, or to skirt the mainland coast well to the south and, by adding a dog-leg of some two hundred extra miles, creep around the ice along its southern and eastern limits. Obviously, if the ice extended right up to the eastern coast of Queen Maud Gulf, even this plan would fail.

Such an extended route along a hazardous coastline with no settlements and no DEW sites would mean at least one extra fuel cache, and Karl advised the loading of three fuel drums for the reconnaissance flight. This done we took off at once, for it was getting dark. Almost a hundred and fifty sea miles south-east of Cambridge Bay, we flew over a nest of shoals and islets, one of which looked long, narrow and flat.

'Perry Island,' Karl prodded at his chart. 'It is said to be OK to land here except after recent heavy rain. If you have to come this far south, it will be on your way.' He gave me an enquiring look and I nodded. If we decided to come along this southern route, fuel left right here would be ideal. If the ice up north proved penetrable, well then, we'd go that way and someone else could use our fuel cache here if ever they found it.

Looking down at the hostile mass of islands, I found it hard to believe that anyone would want to visit, let alone live in, so desolate a region. Yet until recently there had been a village on one of these islands, complete with a shop and a mission post. As Karl circled lower, I began to appreciate that this was the very last place to choose for a boat journey. There were literally hundreds of islands, some merely rock platforms half awash, some just below the surface, and between them countless shoals punctured the sea. Moreover, the Inuit had informed me that this storm-bound coast was spattered with wrecked small boats. But however hostile, this route would provide the only alternative to a year's delay if the sea further north proved to be ice-bound.

Karl buzzed the mud island, allowing his heavy rubber wheels to touch down briefly. Then with a surge of power, rose again and, circling, inspected the wheel marks. How soggy was it? He had every reason to be careful. Too much deep mud would prevent his taking off again from the tiny strip. Six circuits and trial touchdowns later, we landed smoothly and rolled the three drums to the edge of the island. The sun had already disappeared when we left the islet with a perfectly timed take-off.

Karl skimmed over the shorter northern route: two-thirds of the sea was ivory white with ice, the rest a dusty ink. Jenny Lind Island, our fuel cache point for this route, was already cut off from the west. We needed to see no more. Either we went by the longer southern route or not at all.

I squeezed out of the cockpit and joined Ginny in the darkness of the fuselage. We promised each other that there would be no more expeditions after this. Back at Cambridge Bay, Simon and the dogs joined her and Karl and they flew away north to set up the radios at Resolute Bay.

Charlie and I, having stacked the Boston whaler with our gear and with as much fuel as was sensible, set out to cover the southerly route which I'd just flown over. Beyond the bay, the fog became dense which made navigation by eye impossible, nor was I helped by finding the shoal banks on my map blotted out by the printed words 'MAGNETIC COMPASS USELESS IN THIS AREA'. White flashes of broken water in the mist and slight changes in the colour of the ocean warned us of underwater rocks. We carried three spare propellers, but with two hundred miles of shoal water ahead, we could not afford to break off any blades too early on.

The wind rose to 30 knots, but still dense fog banks covered the islands and the mainland. It became impossible to tell which was which. I knew that I must not lose our position against the chart, since it would be extremely difficult to relocate ourselves once disorientated. We nosed into a calm bay and waited for an hour.

Briefly, a headland to the east cleared, and we set out again; navigation-wise it was a difficult day. For nine miles the coastline was flat and devoid of a single feature. I bade Charlie, at the helm, to hug it like glue or I would be unable to fix our position. We came to corridors filled with countless shoals where the sea boiled between gaunt stacks of dripping rock, and we lay off to plot a route through the obstacles before committing the whaler to running the gauntlet. Hour after hour I strained my eyes to recognize coastal features, but there were hundreds of islands of all shapes and sizes and the coastline was so heavily indented with bays, fjords and islets that the mist made it all too easy to mistake a channel for a cul-de-sac.

A great deal of luck saw us safely and accurately through 130 sea miles of this nightmare passage, but in the evening a storm came from the west and threw great rolling seas over the shoals and against the islands. Despite a strong desire to locate Karl's three-drum cache, common sense dictated shelter, and I sought a long-deserted Hudson's Bay Company hut on Perry Island some twelve miles short of the cache. We found the hut hidden around the bend of an island fjord and anchored the boat off its horseshoe beach.

For 24 hours the storm bottled us up on the island. There was rain and sleet as usual, but inside the old wooden shack we were comfortable with sleeping bags on the floor and buckets under the leaky parts of the roof. Our sodden boat-suits did not dry out, but we did. I trudged across mossy rock to the south of the island, disturbing on my way a snowy owl with a lemming in its beak, two ptarmigan and a gyrfalcon. Ollie, I thought to myself, would have been ecstatic. Quite suddenly I happened upon an Inuit village of six one-room shacks. Seal pelts, bear skins and moose antlers littered the shingle. Broken sledges and rotten fishnets lay about, but not a soul answered my calls. I fixed up the radio, but Ginny did not answer. A friendly operator from Gladman Point DEW station some two hundred miles to the north-east, and our next port of call, picked up my call and wished us good luck.

On 10 August the storm showed no signs of abating, and my patience ran out. We dodged between islands to keep away from their exposed shores, and sometimes we hitched up the outboards and waded the boat over rock beds. At noon we came to the island of our cache, but mudbanks extending from it meant leaving the boat 200 yards away and trudging through shallows with the jerry cans. Since the mud was soft and deep, our boots sank in and we were often held tight with suction, especially on our way back with full cans. Two hours later we were ready, but found that the boat, heavy with fuel, was now stuck in the mud.

As though from heaven, an Inuit in oilskins came chugging up in a long low riverboat. He spoke no English but pointed towards Perry Island. Perhaps he came from the huts I had seen and he and the others who lived there had all been out on a summer fishing trip. We fixed a line to his stern and, after many jerks with the two of us heaving knee-high in mud, we eventually unstuck the whaler. Twice more we became jammed on unseen shallows, but each time our Inuit guardian angel helped us away.

Clear of the mud channel, we again came to a maze of rock islets and shoals. The sea had calmed down and we headed east for ten hours, sometimes out of sight of land, save for ever-more isolated islands to the east and south. Since the compass was useless and the sun made no appearance, I kept my nose glued to the chart.

At dusk the wind again raced down from the north and we plunged off creaming breakers. Twice the whole heavy boat was flung into the night as great black walls of water struck us broadside.

'We'd better do that last bit again!' Charlie screamed in my ear. 'Remember, we're not allowed to fly. This is a surface voyage.'

I saw his teeth grinning in the dark, then grabbed at the handrail as another unseen surge sent us keeling madly to starboard. I began to feel that nothing could turn us over.

Not long before midnight, in the middle of a timeless, bucking nightmare, a thin moon scudded clear of the racing cloudbanks: not for long, but enough for us to spot an indent in the silhouette of the cliffs ahead. Our current progress was clearly suicidal, so I shoved my beard against Charlie's dripping hood. 'We'll go in there till dawn – but watch for rocks.'

The indent proved to be a well-sheltered inlet. Charlie steered us in without a bump and I sloshed up the beach with the painter. We erected our tent, peeled off the boat-suits and lit a wood fire. Charlie located some whisky. It is disgusting stuff I have always thought but, when you are very cold indeed, it has distinct advantages. Three hours later the bottle was all but finished. Streaks of livid orange announced the break of a new day, and the cold shapes of rock and seashore imposed themselves on our salt-stung weary eyes.

I made waking-up noises and Charlie groaned. By dint of much shouting at the sky and running on the spot, I persuaded myself that I was not only alive but could just about face the awful moment of climbing back into the clammy confines of my boat-suit. The fact that sand from the beach clung to its inside did not help, especially in the neighbourhood of my crotch, for the insides of my thighs were red raw from the long days of salty chafing.

For a further fourteen hours we weaved our weary way through innumerable gravel islands along a bewildering slalom course with north as its basic ingredient. This was now easy, since I could catch enough glimpses of the sun through the haze to orientate myself. The distant DEW dome of Gladman Point under a low black sky was a wonderful sight, and we yearned for warmth and sleep. As the station boss proffered hot black coffee, he told us that fishing parties from Gjoa Haven had been stranded by the bad weather at various points for the last five days. We could stay until the storms subsided if we liked, he said. It would be safer. The Inuit knew best: if they did not think it safe to travel, we would do well to follow their example.

The bay provided scant shelter given a storm; if we sat tight and waited for safe conditions, we would never get through before the winter ice formed. No, we would press on. It was not a question of deriding local knowledge, but purely a matter of time and distance mathematics. We picked up our fuel supplies and carried on towards Gjoa Haven, seventy miles to the east, which marked the halfway point of our Northwest Passage journey.

By evening we reached Gjoa Haven and, almost drunk with weariness, secured the whaler between two Inuit boats. This narrow bay was where Amundsen's *Gjoa* had spent two winters at the beginning of the twentieth century, during her three-year epic voyage through the passage, the first in history. From here the Norwegian reached the spot where the previous century James Clark Ross had located the North Magnetic Pole. Amundsen discovered then that the Pole had since moved some thirty miles. This discovery that the Pole moved around was a major scientific achievement.

The Inuit warned us that sea ice almost certainly blocked the Humboldt Channel and the Wellington Strait to the north. Better to call in at the last settlement before Resolute Bay, a hamlet at the head of Spence Bay fjord, and take guides. For once we set out in good weather and with no mist, and we followed the coastline of King William Island until, at Matheson Point, I took a bearing off the sun and headed across Rae Strait. For a short while in mid-crossing there was no land anywhere, then inverted mirages of the coast danced over the horizon and we made good time to the great rock-girt arm of Spence Bay, arriving late on 13 August at the isolated Inuit hamlet.

Our morale was high. From now on we would be travelling north once more. True, time was running short and soon we would meet ice, but already we were further by far than could have been achieved in a year of even average ice conditions. We were shown into a 'guest cabin' for one night and plonked our kit down in the living room. Once we had moved into our rooms, I took my spare set of maps out of Charlie's boat bag and settled back to read through the notebook which he used as a diary.

Charlie and I were both wont to read anything we came across, but an old saying goes that eavesdroppers never hear good of themselves. The same might be said of those who, on expeditions, read other people's diaries. Since, as official book writer of the expedition, I believed that, as after our polar training, I would be reading the contents of all the expedition diaries, I felt no qualms about reading Charlie's. But when I actually did so, it upset me.

When he came back, I asked him why at one point he'd said I was lost. Because, he replied, I had said so myself. Yes, I agreed, but I'd only meant it in terms of our exact position vis-à-vis two river mouths, and not as regards our overall position. But, said Charlie, he had not written that I was lost overall. He'd just made a note in his own way of what I'd said. Did I want him to stop keeping a diary? No, of course not, I replied.

It did seem to me that Charlie's laconic entry could easily be misinterpreted by an outsider who might read it, even if Charlie and I knew what it meant. But I kept such thoughts private and cursed myself for being so sensitive to criticism. Charlie was quite right: his diary saw the expedition through his eyes, and my diary through mine, and naturally and inevitably we interpreted events differently, and equally our entries could also be read in a variety of ways.

Albert Armitage, in his book on Shackleton, *Two Years in the Antarctic* (1905), is careful never to use diaries as a basis for fact. He simply sums up the character interplay between Scott, Wilson and Shackleton in general terms: 'Hardship is not always ennobling: if it produces self-sacrifice, it can equally well produce irritation and hostility. The enforced physical proximity of the three men, while they were pushing themselves to the utmost, must have had an effect on their behaviour to each other, and any latent antagonism or rivalry between the two could hardly be concealed all the time.'

Any latent antagonism or rivalry between Charlie and me was certainly not apparent when we were on the move, perhaps because our energies were fully occupied simply coping with getting to the next campsite. Only when we emerged from the lonely wastes to some warm, relaxing outpost did Charlie sometimes seem unnaturally quiet and moody. But then even after seven years spent in close proximity, Charlie was still a closed book to me. I would do well, I mused, always to remember that he was keeping his own record of what was happening, of my words and behaviour.

Two other boats left Spence Bay ahead of us. We followed in

convoy. They too were 18 feet long and outboard-powered. Included in their crews were the Spence Bay Mountie and a local Inuit hunter with an unrivalled knowledge of the region. An hour or two north of Spence Bay, the other boats turned aside and beached. We hovered offshore. What was wrong?

'There's a storm coming,' the Mountie shouted, 'a bad one. Our friends will go no further and advise you to stop here or head back to Spence Bay.'

The sky was clear and there was no more than a light breeze from the west. I told the Mountie we had better press on, and we would camp if the storm materialized. He shrugged and waved as we pulled away. Three hours later the wind had indeed risen. Storm clouds poured across the sky and, on the western horizon, a rugged run of ice edged the blackness of the sea.

'Sheep,' I shouted to Charlie, pointing at a small cream-coloured animal moving along the beach. As we approached it turned into a polar bear patrolling its patch of the coastline.

For a hundred miles we moved north through increasing signs of ice, thick banks of fog and winds of up to 60 knots. Since the coast we followed was unindented and the waves smashed its shore with mounting fury, there was nowhere we could stop. The next fuel cache was a low sand spit somewhere in Parsley Bay. With luck we would find shelter from the storm within the bay and then camp until the winds abated.

After six hours of drenching in ice-cold water, our eyes were inflamed and our fingers ached with the cold. The moment we reached the mouth of the bay, conditions altered. For the worse. The whole bay writhed with the power of the storm. Serried lines of wind-lashed breakers smashed into every shore. There was no shelter. But we could not go on, nor could we turn back. To turn broadside on to the rushing walls of water, even briefly, would be to invite immediate swamping. I squinted at the chart and noticed a stream which looped its way into the bay dead opposite the mouth. If we could but cross the two-mile reach from mouth to stream, we might find shelter.

Off Perry Island we had experienced bigger waves, but none so powerful, so steep nor so close together as these. The boat's floor was quickly awash with cans and kit floating about our feet. The wave tops completely covered the prow and smashed down into the cockpit. Most of the time visibility was nil, for as soon as we opened our eyes, a new deluge cascaded over our heads. The water streaming down the insides of our suits was far colder than it had been further south. Somehow the whaler made it through that interminable crossing. Never did two miles seem longer.

A brief gap in the pounding beach surf revealed the river's mouth. We nosed upstream, delighted at the comparative calm and the depth, for we had feared shallows. After a mile or so we moored the whaler to a piece of driftwood and struggled ashore to erect the sodden tent. The wind whipped out the tent pegs, so using our remaining full fuel cans as weights, we half fixed up the tent, brewed coffee, ate chocolate, removed our slimy suits and slept, in that order.

Next day there was no wind and the bay was smooth as a millpond. Hard to imagine how so pretty a cove could boil in such fury as it had but six short hours before. We soon found our fuel drums, cached on a nearby spit, and we continued north. For an hour we enjoyed a pallid sun, then fog closed in, dense and yellow, all about the boat and we nosed between chunks of ice and the coastline for a while before deciding to pause until we could see something.

Camping on a tiny shingle bar, we watched a herd of beluga or white whales pass through nearby shallows, flashing white and black as they rubbed old skin off their stomachs along the gravel. Belugas are not hunted commercially, but the Inuit catch them in nets and eat the fat, the meat, even the skin, which they say tastes like the white of an egg. Herds of beluga have been seen in Arctic rivers many miles from the ocean, which makes sense when their worst enemies are sharks and polar bears.

When the fog dispersed we kept going along a craggy coast with well-defined mountains and bays that made navigation a delight.

From time to time lonely bergs, grounded until the recent storm, sailed by without posing a threat until, at the end of the day, we reached the great cliffs of Limestone Island, spattered with the droppings of a million seabirds. Ahead lay Barrow Strait and, on its far side, Resolute, the only settlement on Cornwallis Island and the place where Ginny was. But the crossing was forty miles and pack ice stretched across our front from horizon to horizon.

There was little fuel left and our last cache before Resolute was another twelve miles around the island's north coast. So we edged on beneath the cliffs. Carefully, because the sea was full of chunks of half-drowned ice, from marble to man-size. We progressed down an ever-narrowing corridor between the cliffs and the pack. A strong breeze blew from the north. This worried me because the pack could shift south with the wind and close in behind us. Soon we were nudging along channels in the pack with ever-decreasing sea room.

With ten miles to go to the cache, I decided to turn back until the north wind stopped blowing. We might well reach our cache, but the chart showed that the area near it was unlikely to afford protection from invading ice. Back the way we had come by some twenty miles there was a deep inlet, Aston Bay, which looked as though it would provide cover unless a west wind blew for long enough to pour the pack back down Peel Sound and trap us in the bay.

Charlie did not look happy at the idea of turning back, but I had long ago learnt that you can't keep all the people happy all of the time. I was content to take risks if I had to, but I was damned if I would when any alternative course remained open. My mother always told me that my father respected his boss, Field Marshal Montgomery. The Field Marshal never moved forward if he could avoid it until the cards were stacked, where possible, in his favour. Neither nature nor Rommel would be likely to hand out second chances.

In a situation like this I usually avoided asking for the opinion of others. Why? Charlie probably nailed my reasoning process correctly.

He once said: 'I think Ran finds it very difficult to talk of the logistics side, for the simple reason that I will see something and say: "Well, how about doing it such and such a way?" But that might mess him up from his own thinking as to how he wants to do it . . . Then he's got another something churning around in his head, so he'd rather not listen. As a consequence he keeps it all to himself and I think it eats him away slightly.'

The fjord down which we retreated was almost ice-free and several miles deep. We eased over a shallow sandbar to the terminal bay in a wide gravel valley. Shale slopes overlooked us and water from the summer melt tinkled its way down to the fjord via several outwash gullies.

Using the tent and an oar for antenna masts, I contacted Ginny. The bay at Resolute was full of ice, she said, and added that a Japanese man and his wife with a boat equipped with sail and outboard had been waiting there for two summers to cross Barrow Strait. This was his third year, she pointed out, so I shouldn't be impatient. That kept me quiet for a few hours, but when we were still in the little bay three days later, I began to get itchy again.

Each day more ice floes appeared along our protective sandbar. Some smaller ones sneaked over it at high tide and crunched against the side of the whaler, but they were as yet too light to do much harm. Nonetheless, it would be foolish to be caught in the bay like a rat in a trap with floes pressed up solidly against our sandbar exit. On the morning of the third day a skein of new ice sheened the water all about the whaler, a sinister reminder of pending winter. In eleven days or so the remaining open sea would begin to freeze.

In a week Giles and Gerry would arrive at Resolute with the Twin Otter and would help guide us through any pack ice in our way. But a week was too long to wait and, by a lucky coincidence, an old friend of ours from the Arctic training days happened to come to Resolute for a month's pilot work. Dick de Blicquy, the most famous of Canada's Arctic bush pilots, met up with Ginny and learnt of our predicament. He agreed to guide us across the strait as soon as the weather looked right.

On the fourth morning of our stay in the fjord the wind dropped, the mist lifted and we sneaked over the ice-choked sandbar, sped round Somerset Island to our cache at Cape Anne, picked up the fuel, and within three miles had entered the pack ice. For four hours we responded to radio instructions from Dick, who circled above with Ginny and Simon in the Twin Otter. Sometimes it was necessary to push floes apart with oars and our feet; sometimes a route that looked good from above proved to be a cul-de-sac from the boat's point of view. But in the end we won through and reached the mouth of Resolute Bay two hours before fog banks poured over the cliffs of Cornwallis Island and blanketed the pack ice.

The Japanese gentleman, hearing of our arrival, treated it as a talisman and left to head south. Things were not to go too well for him, but we heard no more of his progress for a while. Tugaluk was as big as Bothie now and only happy when destroying some useful item like a mukluk or a set of vital maps.

'I thought you were going to get rid of it here,' I reminded Ginny.

'I am. Don't flap. We'll be around for at least another week and there are plenty of people here who would sell their back teeth to own such a beautiful dog.'

Within a few hours of our arrival a wind change brought pack ice back into the harbour, nearly crushing the whaler. This prevented our departure towards Alert for four critical days of mist and sleet. During this stay I received a message from our chairman in London suggesting that my route be north of Resolute to the northern end of the Wellington Channel, where there was a narrow neck of low land blocking the sea route. Here we should abandon the whaler and camp until the sea froze, and then carry on to Alert by skidoo.

In case the chairman's suggested course became necessary, I asked Ginny to check out the availability of our light inflatables with skids, which would be portable across the narrow isthmus west of the Douro Range, because they struck me as a better bet than skidoos for the conditions of ice together with water which characterise early winter. Ginny exchanged messages with Ant Preston in London who told us that Dr Hattersley-Smith, the polar-regions expert, had again stressed to our chairman 'that I have always been very sceptical about the feasibility of this journey in one season, and I told Ranulph so three years ago.'

I walked over to the Resolute meteorological research station and questioned a technician there. Could we get through the strait east of Bathurst Island? No. It was jammed solid with ice and likely to stay that way. How about going out into Lancaster Sound and up the east coast of Ellesmere Island? Again, no. Likely to be ice- and storm-bound. How about a giant detour around Devon Island and through Hell Gate to Norwegian Bay? Possible, but inadvisable, owing to the hazardous sea conditions off Devon Island's east coast. All in all, the met-man had discounted every option beyond spending the winter in Resolute.

The one thing I could not countenance was doing nothing, so I plumped for the least lethal-sounding option: a race around Devon Island for six hundred miles as soon as the ice allowed our whaler out of the harbour. Ginny was unable to contact our chairman, but she got a message through to Colonel Andrew Croft whose Arctic experience was considerable. He replied with approval for my plan.

It might seem strange that I should check such moves with the committee back in London. Surely the man on the ground knows best? This is often true, but I had never been in the Northwest Passage before, nor had Charlie, so it seemed prudent to sound out the opinions of people with experience. Having received such opinions, I felt that the final choice should rest with me. Maybe this was wrong. Charlie's view:

> Ran runs the show. He is the leader in the field but you've got to remember that he has a Committee back in England. They run the expedition. This does cause problems, as you can imagine. In the sense that if Ran wants to do something, he does it, and the board of directors, the Committee, they try and change it. I think that this is the first time Ran has had a Committee who feel that they should be organising him. This is unfortunate for him. He now feels the

strain. I can see it. Because he has to be diplomatic. He can't say, 'Well, I'm going to do this or that without telling the Committee.'

With nine hundred miles to cover in six days, there was no time for delay, yet pack ice seemed to surround us and contrary advice slid in from every quarter. The decision was mine and poor Charlie would have to suffer the consequences should my decision lead us into trouble. The journey so far had been wet, cold and bleak and we had frequently been short on sleep. Now it was getting even colder and the way ahead looked dicey. It was a tense time for all of us. No wonder Simon wrote that Charlie seemed 'overtly brash and friendly but needles underneath'.

Early on 25 August the ice moved out of the harbour and hung around a couple of miles off the coast. Before a south wind stirred to bring the pack back in again, we went in silence down to the harbour in our boat-suits and set off to the east. An American geologist, the founder of the Arctic Institute of North America, watched us leave. He wrote to Andrew Croft: 'When we were in Resolute the Fiennes group came through. They moved off in a snowstorm when the harbour ice had cleared sufficiently – but I tell you none of us would have changed places with them, sitting high without even the benefit of a windscreen.'

All that day the mist remained alongside or near to the gaunt cliff-line that we followed to the east. At the sheer cliffs of the Hotham Escarpment we left Cornwallis Island and crossed the stormy seas of Wellington Channel. Relieved to reach the shelter of the high cliffs of Devon Island, but wet and shivering, we found an inlet on the east side of an islet just off the main island. We anchored the boat and waded ashore where an old ship's bowsprit protruded from the gravel beach.

On a raised beach some way above the high-tide mark were the crumbled foundations of a small shack and, all about, the shattered remains of wooden barrels and rusty iron hoops. Beyond the bowsprit were gravestones. Some of Franklin's men had died here, but the majority had continued on to die further south. We lit a fire made from driftwood that we'd collected along our way, and sitting close to it stared out at the wild sea with its burden of ice floes, at that moment still loosely packed enough for us to be able to continue. This sea was Lancaster Sound, so long the gateway for all passage searchers, and our shelter was the site where an archaeological team had found the remains of a Franklin man whose bones showed signs of scurvy and of the cut marks usually suggestive of cannibalism.

This possibility was reinforced in 1984 and 1992 when other archaeologists dug up some of the Franklin graves both here and elsewhere. They found the corpses' clothes, skin and hair to be as good as new, with their eyes wide open and their lips frozen apart showing rotting teeth and other signs of advanced scurvy.

When knife-cut marks on many of the bones were forensically studied they were consistent with butchery by humans, not wild animals. The lead content of their bones also indicated the possibility of lead poisoning from the crudely soldered tins of meat which they were known to have used.

From this place Franklin had found Peel Sound open, and he headed down it to his entrapment and death. Just as we had found it semi-open the previous week and thanked our lucky stars.

Despite all the discoveries by the Franklin searchers, none had managed to sail through the passage and nobody did so in either direction until in 1903, in a voyage taking four years, the Norwegian Roald Amundsen got through by way of Lancaster Sound and then along the coast-hugging route that we had just used in the opposite direction in one stressful month.

The next traverse of the passage, and the first from west to east, was made between 1940 and 1942, by a motor schooner owned by the Royal Canadian Mounted Police and commanded by the Norwegian-born Constable Henry Larsen. In 1944 he took his boat the *St Roch* back through the more northerly route in 86 days.

In 1969 British Petroleum's 16,000-ton ice-strengthened oil tanker *Manhattan* became the twelfth ship to sail through the passage in order to test the validity of sending oil out from BP's

Prudhoe Bay by sea rather than by oil pipe over tundra. En route the tanker was holed by ice where her steel hull was 25 mm thick. This was not an emergency but it did suggest that the tundra route would be best.

Feeling slightly warmer, Charlie must have realized the historic atmosphere of the place, for he cut his name and the date into a slab of slate which he left on the beach. Then we shuffled back down to the boat.

In a choppy sea full of ice growlers we managed to travel 160 miles to Croker Bay. En route we crossed the mouths of many bays and looking north saw the crown of the high ice field which lies over the eastern half of Devon Island and sends its tentacles down the coastal valleys to calve into the sea fjords as icebergs. As evening closed in we moved under the cold dark shoulder of huge cliffs through an ink-black sea. There were seals and whales and many birds and, increasingly, icebergs of great height and length. At Croker Bay, as night fell on us from the ice-laden cliffs above, a storm rushed north over Lancaster Sound and caught us ten miles short of shelter. The propellers struck unseen ice with heart-stopping thuds. To be immobilized between the jostling icebergs would not be healthy.

'Monster to port!' Charlie shouted in my ear. I stared into the gloom where he pointed and saw the foaming silhouette of a giant wave strike a nearby chunk of ice. A wall of spray rose above us. Our world kicked and danced in turmoil and I strained my eyes at the rock heights to spot the indent of Dundas Harbour, once the site of a Hudson's Bay Company store, but now abandoned to the elements. I found the entry, but icebergs large and small ground together in the high swell across the bay mouth and only with a goodly slice of luck did we thread our way safely through to the haven of shallows and the wonderful sight of three little shacks by a low bar of shingle. One was almost rainproof and Charlie soon had a log fire spitting under our stewpot. For an hour we lay chatting of army days long ago in Arabia, candlelight flickering on our sodden suits hung up to dry.

East of Dundas the inland glacial mass poured ice down towards the sea: a million water-coloured chunks floated off the coastline like lethal frogspawn. Waves broke against the seaborne bergs all about us. Spray shrieked by in horizontal sheets. The storm raged along the southern coast of Devon Island all day, and from Resolute Ginny reported drifting snow and overlying ice. With but four days to the end of the month, I decided not to wait for improvement.

An hour after setting out we rounded the gaunt rocks of Cape Warrender. Waves smashed the shore in a thundering welter of surf. A course running parallel to the cliffs and 400 yards out seemed least dangerous. Several times the boat shuddered as unseen ice hit the hull or propellers. Then a shear pin went and Charlie closed down the now useless port outboard and we limped on at half power, gradually drifting nearer to the cliffs. For four miles we found nowhere to land, but we knew we must change shear pins quickly. At any moment the other propeller might strike ice and then we would be the fibreglass version of matchwood in minutes. A tiny defile with a shingle beach appeared between cliff walls. I sighed with relief. On our way in we passed several hundred beluga whales, then we nosed between madly jostling ice blocks and grounded bergs to fight through to the little beach.

Charlie grabbed my shoulder and pointed dead ahead. One of the grounded bergs on the beach at the very point selected for our landing turned out to be an adult polar bear. Perhaps the bear knew that the beluga, its natural prey, were wont to bask in the shallows off the beach. To disturb a hunting, perhaps hungry, polar bear is generally a bad idea, but we had no alternative. Unbroken cliffs stretched twenty miles to the east according to my chart.

Charlie nosed the boat in as far as he dared, and I went overboard. One of my suit leggings filled up with water to the thigh, for it had developed a tear. Holding the bow painter, I trod the slippery rocks whilst Charlie unsheathed his rifle. The bear, unfamiliar with shiny white 18-foot-long whalers, withdrew slowly and disappeared among boulders which ringed the beach.

For thirty minutes I struggled to hold the boat as steady as possible whilst Charlie worked with freezing hands to replace the shear pin and both propellers, for we discovered that they were hopelessly battered and one had a blade missing. I kept a wary eye open for the bear. As we left the beach it passed us, swimming with nose and eyes only above the water. Startled, it dived. For a second its great white behind rose skywards, then nothing.

The waves beyond the immediate lee of the cliffs were as big as any I had ever seen. For a hundred and twenty miles we bucked and rolled between heaving icebergs, impressed by the size and power of the waves. Bergs bigger than bungalows rolled about like beach balls in the 60-knot gale and I held my breath many a time as we squeezed between highly mobile ice monsters. Freezing sleet, fog and gale-force winds forced us to spend a night at Cape Sherard, but on 27 August at midday we left the coast of Devon Island and crossed Jones Sound to Ellesmere Island: an anxious journey. At Craig Harbour, under dizzy cliffs, we paused to relax beside a king berg complete with blue arched caverns. Then on and on until, feeling much like soggy bacon rind looks, we reached the deep and shadowed reaches of Grise Fiord, the only Inuit settlement on the island.

Back in Resolute, Ginny, fully aware of the dangers of Devon Island's east coast, had waited for my call for 28 hours. Simon explained in his diary: 'Ginny's face getting more introverted, frowning and bitter all day as she heard nothing.' I fixed an antenna up by two Inuit houses, threading my way through wooden stretch frames of drying harp seal pelts. Ginny's voice was faraway and faint, but I heard the happiness in it as she acknowledged our position.

The last three days of August passed by in a blur of black cliff, freezing spray and, above all, increasing ice. At the mouth to Hell Gate, escape route from Jones Sound and beneath a cliff called Cape Turnback, I decided that the conditions looked evil and the currents treacherous. We turned west and, by Devil Island, north into Cardigan Strait. Again, hours of anxiety in wind-writhed waves, but once through the strait our long detour was over. In Norwegian Bay we were once more on our original axis north from

Resolute Bay. The gamble had paid off, and still there were 48 hours in which to cover the final four hundred miles.

That evening the surface of the sea began to freeze for the first time, congealing silently and fast. We must speed on. A twenty-mile wide bay bites into Ellesmere Island to the south of Great Bear Cape, and there we again hit pack ice. Again and again we nosed up channels and leads. To no avail: the pack became more solid to seawards and impenetrable within the bay. There was nothing for it but to retreat. Again new ice covered the open sea in steadily congealing sheets. We beached in an unnamed bay and talked little that evening.

I radioed Ginny. She reported a sixty-mile belt of pack in Norwegian Bay that stretched west to Axel Heiberg Island. Our Twin Otter had still not arrived and so could not help us through the ice barrier. But an hour later Ginny came back with great news. Russ Bomberry, one of the finest bush pilots in the Arctic and a chief of the Mohawk Indians, was in Resolute Bay with his Twin Otter. He had agreed to give us two hours' 'ice flight' the next day.

The mist stayed away. The temperature dropped. I slept little that night. Only 320 miles to Tanquary Fiord, but we could be one short day too late if this last ice belt delayed us long enough to snare us in the new ice of the coming winter. At dawn we were up, teeth a-chatter, loading the whaler in readiness. At midday Russ circled overhead and we left for the ice belt.

The new ice was already thicker and filled every open lead in the pack. The young frazil ice and ice rind burgeoned like active yeast. In places the whaler could no longer plane through but meshed with it like a bumblebee in a spider's web. In the middle of the bay a light wind arose and opened channels in the ice rind. This helped. Russ ranged in wide circles north-east over the Bjorne peninsula and north-west towards the snowy peaks of Axel Heiberg Island.

Whilst he was gone we nosed about in the centre of the pack. I wondered, if Russ did not return or a fog closed in, how long it would take us to extricate ourselves from such a complex and ever-changing labyrinth. Once back Russ wasted no time; he knew the only way it could be done. To get us north to Great Bear Cape he took us west, east and even south a good deal of the time. From the air our course must have looked rather like a dish of spaghetti. Three hours later Russ dipped his wings and left us. We were clear of the close pack. The rest we could handle.

A mile or two out of the pack the steering linkage packed up. Charlie glared at it, smoked two cigarettes in contemplation of its mechanics, then fixed it in an unorthodox, but effective, fashion. We slept five hours during the next two days. For the rest we moved north through narrowing channels and travelled a hundred miles up the winding canyons of Eureka Sound to Eureka itself, an isolated camp set up by the Canadian government purely as a weather station. A strong wind kept the new ice at bay in the fjords during the night of 30 August, and the next day we began the last run north up Greely Fiord for 150 miles to Tanquary Fiord itself, a cul-de-sac deep in glacier-cut mountains.

Tiers of snow-capped peaks shaped the horizons as we snaked ever deeper into a twilit world of loneliness and silence. Wolves stared from shadowed lava beaches, but nothing moved except ourselves to sunder the mirror images of the darkened valley walls in our wash. Twelve minutes before midnight we came to the end of the fjord. The sea journey was over. Within a week the sounds behind us were all frozen.

Five great ice caps surround the head of Tanquary Fiord on Ellesmere Island, but it is possible to reach Alert, 150 miles to the north-east, by a chain of stream valleys. On our arrival at Tanquary these valleys were snow-free, but the streams themselves had frozen. There was a temptation to set out at once before the temperatures began to plummet. But this could not be, because the gravel strip and three little huts at Tanquary Camp were to form one of two bases for the Twin Otter during our coming attempt to cross the Arctic Ocean. It had been Ginny's idea to use Tanquary as an additional base to Alert. The mists in April and May were so bad at Alert, she said, that we would save weeks by having Tanquary stocked and beyond the reach of sea mists.

Ginny and Bothie had flown in the previous day by Twin Otter from Resolute. Simon and Tugaluk stayed behind to run things for the air crew. Giles and Gerry were due in a week's time with the first of the base equipment from Resolute. It would need careful sorting and repacking, for some must stay at Tanquary and some go on to Alert. This I must do before leaving. And another reason argued for delay: Charlie and I were body-weak from more than a month of inaction in a cramped boat, and in no condition for a land journey on foot.

There can be few places in the world as remote and idyllic as Tanquary Camp. I walked with Ginny along the frozen course of the creek that tumbles from Redrock Glacier. Bothie gave chase to Arctic hares. Yapping with joy, he ignored Ginny's orders to return and scampered away over moss-clad benchland unaware of his danger.

Two wolves, white like Bothie and probably attracted by his barking, loped down the hillside towards him. Ginny fired her pistol in the air. The wolves ignored her and closed the gap to Bothie. Ginny screamed. So did I. Bothie took no notice, but he lost the hare trail and turned back. The wolves stopped, gazed at us, and then moved away towards the camp. That night three adult wolves with three cubs came down to the huts. We watched them through a window. The wolf cubs looked cuddly, but we resisted the temptation to go outside and see if they liked being stroked. Arctic wolves are slightly smaller than their southerly neighbours, the timber wolves. They often prowl alone, but when hunting caribou, their main source of food, they operate in packs. Not long ago all wolves were shot on sight in the Canadian Arctic, but now only the Inuit can kill them and sell their pelts.

Charlie and I left Tanquary Fiord in mid-September each with an 80-pound backpack and a rifle, once again heading for our base at Alert. We followed a frozen stream meandering between mountains. Snowshoes were tied to our packs, but at first the frozen tundra was fine for travel in standard trekking boots. One of Charlie's feet was badly blistered with a soggy, bloody mess between the toes. With 150 miles to go and the temperature soon to plummet, this was a problem. But he did not complain. Eight miles up the stream we camped with sore backs, for we were both unfit.

No other humans ever came this way. There were no paths to follow and the scenery was majestic in every direction until, on the third day, the sunlight was shut out by canyon walls as we laboured up a narrow valley. A minor glacier tumbled down from the main Viking Ice Cap and right across our canyon. Luckily the water of many past summer floods had cut a tunnel underneath the glacier, and I stumbled in semi-darkness over frozen ice and scattered boulders as though through a railway tunnel. Emerging into daylight I waited for Charlie, but after a while I heard him shout my name. I ran back and found him squatting in the dark, blood pouring down one cheek and obscuring one eye. He had slipped and gashed his head on a rock. He felt dizzy.

I bandaged his wound and took the tent from his pack. That night his feet were in a bad way, for our boots had crashed through layers of ice crust on to the uneven rocks of the streambed for most of the day. We climbed 1,000 feet up our mountain valley, and the nights were cold in our light summer tent. Charlie's face swelled up, yellow and puffy. He limped, but kept going.

At some point the canyon opened up to a magic world – an open plain of snow-free grass patches. We passed by a group of seven musk oxen. They raised their shaggy heads to glance at us and to check that we were neither bears nor wolves, then resumed their grazing. Their mammoth-like woollen skirts brushed the ground and their stubby horns made me think of an amalgam of a Highland bull and a Disneyfied buffalo. In fact they are part of the sheep family. Charlie decided to see how close he could approach the group for a photo and, with surprising speed, all seven animals closed up into a protective circle facing outwards with their massive heads lowered defensively. Charlie retreated.

That night, by head-torchlight, I read up on the fauna and flora of Ellesmere Island in my Canada National Parks booklet. Pregnant female polar bears hibernate in snowy caves in the north of the island. Sealed over, their dens are invisible after the first snowfall.

Hibernation for them, and all other hibernators, is the way by which they survive periods of food scarcity when the calories they require to stay warm are likely to exceed those available in the area. Only pregnant female bears hibernate. They curl up, and their breathing slows down, as does their heart rate. Body temperature drops 9° and the animal starts to live off its accumulated body fat. By the time they emerge they will probably have lost half of their pre-hibernation weight.

While the expectant mothers are having a cushy hibernation, all other polar bears, foxes, lemmings and other island denizens are working hard in adverse circumstances in order to survive the winter. In principle, smaller animals lose heat more quickly than bigger ones because, for their size, they have more exposed skin and more surface area to cool off for every ounce of fat, muscle and brain tissue. They also need to burn more calories than larger animals, relatively speaking, yet they are not big enough to store much fat. Most Arctic birds simply migrate.

Musk ox and caribou (the Canadian name for reindeer) live off lichens and moss, sedges and willow, munching all day in the knowledge that, to survive the coming winter, they must build up a huge reserve of fat. They live in family herds and usually have one calf a year.

When suckling, musk ox calves creep under their mother's woolly tent-like 'aprons' for shelter. The wool of these aprons is called *qiviut* and is by far the warmest wool in the world. Compared with the wool of llamas, vicunas, alpacas, cashmere from Indian goats or mohair from African goats, *qiviut* wins if you want to purchase real warmth at a cost. It is eight times warmer than sheep's wool and noticeably softer. Native villagers in Alaska and in various parts of northern Canada buy *qiviut* yarn in cooperatives and knit pullovers, scarves, hats and neckovers. In 1981 they sold the scarves for $400, which would make them rich if only there were more musk oxen about.

In the eighteenth and nineteenth centuries, when native Canadians first used firearms, the musk ox was driven to the very edge of extinction. The US polar explorer Robert Peary killed some eight hundred musk oxen in north Greenland during his various expeditions in that region. But in 1917 the government prohibited all hunting, and the modern equivalent of the mammoth now flourishes up north.

Although generally non-aggressive, bull musk oxen can produce extremely impressive angry roars and, if provoked, especially during the rutting season, will charge at humans and are known to have injured or killed overzealous photographers.

Shaggy camels, according to fossil experts, used to roam the plains of Ellesmere Island beside the musk oxen. These beasts had a single hump and stood up to 11 feet tall. They used the hump to store fat to cope with cold winters.

Other Ellesmere natives, some of which we saw on our way north, include Arctic hares, which stay white all year round. They can smell vegetation under the snow and, with their powerful claws and lever-like teeth, they nibble at roots. Their feet are very large compared to their body weight, so they walk on snow without breaking through. A human would need to wear snowshoes ten times their foot size to achieve the same result. Living in fear of foxes, the Arctic hare always remains alert and has learnt to run along on its rear legs so that it can see above the snow level. Watching them prancing along with their long fluffy ears held high, they are the original mad hatters.

We saw no lemmings, voles or shrews, but they do all survive on this polar island, for there is food to be found in the under-snow or subnivean layer throughout the winter. Here there are beetles, spiders, fungi, fly larvae, ants and wasps. These all provide good and plentiful nourishment for the lemmings, which in turn feed foxes, owls and other predators.

Lemmings, according to my booklet, can overbreed in a given area and are then forced to migrate to search for food. Sometimes great armies of lemmings will head off in a given direction and, if water gets in the way, they will swim as far as they can. They may well die in huge numbers but, despite myths to the contrary, they don't commit wilful suicide or jump over cliffs.

Summer is short, seldom more than ten weeks, but life during that warm sunny period is made miserable for animals and humans alike by the billions of hatched mosquitoes. Inuit joke that no meat-eating person need ever starve in the mosquito season. Flowers thrive, too, and even trees, but only at ground level and only for the brief summer season. The Arctic willow spreads its branches over the ground as thick as a human thumb and a metre long, but the growth of each branch is so slow that a single tree that you might step over may well be centuries old. Dwarf versions of heather, lupin, poppy, buttercup and saxifrage provide carpets of vivid colour to a maximum growth height of six centimetres – a visual paradise in miniature made perfect by the buzz of bumblebees and the flutter of yellow polar butterflies.

Many birds enjoy the feast of mosquitoes, including snow buntings, terns, barnacle geese, ptarmigans and ravens. These birds have, in most cases, evolved modifications to cope with the cold. Their feathers are thicker and more numerous, with an underlayer of downy body feathers. Ptarmigans and snowy owls have feathered legs and feet with thick pads underneath. They also benefit from being white, not only for camouflage, but also to keep warm, since they radiate less heat and white feathers are hollower in structure and so better insulated than coloured ones.

Another animal we never saw, despite spotting many likely tracks in the snow, was the caribou. On many Canadian Arctic islands there are thousands of caribou and they have learnt to walk through snow using minimal energy by planting their front feet at a steep angle, supporting their weight in the snow on their hooves, the upper part of each foot and the dewclaw, which is a stubby growth that sticks out from their 'ankle'. Ginny learnt from a Resolute Inuit that when the great caribou herds of the Canadian Barren Lands move north on their annual migration routes, they make but a single noise – the click-click of their kneecaps. They are stalked at all times by wolf packs who feed on the weaker calves and, in the rutting season, on bulls weakened by fighting each other.

*

I lost my way in a low mist at a Y-junction of two valleys, but later found another pass which led to the Very River flood plain, where we passed by two dozen musk oxen and heard wolves crying in the night. An eerie sound which could not be accurately described as a howl. Reaching Lake Hazen, 40 miles long and 6 miles wide, we followed its northern shore with, to our left, the towering ramparts of the central ice cap. New ice was forming on the still surface of the lake as we camped beside it. Charlie was in great pain as he took his boots off his badly damaged feet. We stayed at the lake for two days to help his injuries.

I climbed up a steep hill to view the typically glaciated landscape and to plan a route for the last miles to the island's northern edge. I spoke to Ginny on the radio. She had flown in to Tanquary Fiord to set up a radio mast, and was literally surrounded at night in her prefab radio hut by white wolves. The wolves had smelt Bothie and Tugaluk and clearly decided that they would taste good. One wolf had stood on its hind legs and looked at Ginny through one of the plastic windows of the hut.

From Tanquary Fiord to Lake Hazen we had passed no single man-made object: no paths, no refuse, nothing. It was comforting to have been somewhere where humans have left no lasting mark whatsoever on their environment.

At length, with Charlie hobbling, we left the lake on snowshoes. The air was cold and clear at −10°C. To the east lay mile upon mile of rock and ice, the weird tundra polygons of Black River Vale and, fifty miles away, the frozen cliffs of Robeson Channel. The sad remains of Fort Conger, itself but fifty miles south of Alert, still stand beside the channel, mute testimony to two brave Arctic pioneers. The great American Admiral Peary tried five times to reach the North Pole, and had eight gangrenous toes cut off at Conger in 1904. Twenty years later, Lieutenant Greely, also American, experienced the hardships of an Arctic winter along the same coastline. Greely and his men ran out of food and suffered intense cold and bitter frost, disaster and slow starvation, insanity and death. To these unpleasantnesses historians have added the probability of cannibalism because the rescue party found corpses with large chunks of flesh missing. Only 7 out of Greely's 25 men survived to be rescued by the relief ship. One of these, who had lost his hands and feet through gangrene, soon died.

Despite the inhospitable terrain and the climate, humans have survived on eastern Ellesmere Island on and off for centuries. Now no one lives there, but 700 years ago Vikings are believed to have settled in the area; later Eskimos from Alaska are thought to have migrated east and colonized parts of the island before moving on into Greenland. Up to around 1950, about three hundred Eskimos lived in scattered small settlements to the north of Thule and hunted polar bear, seal, walrus and whale. Existence was harsh for all and food was scarce. Weak husky puppies were thrown to the pack as food, and old dogs were killed. Aged and infirm members of the tribe were simply left outside to die, as food was too precious to waste on non-productive members of society.

Then civilization came to Greenland and, in particular, to Thule and the surrounding region. Drink and venereal diseases were introduced for the first time, along with refrigerators, skidoos and outboard motors. Many of the young preferred to gain a technical education in Denmark, rather than follow the traditional ways of life.

On 21 September the temperature dropped to –18°C. We came to a featureless plain, so I began to use the compass with care as the North Magnetic Pole was now a long way to our south. The needle was sluggish but seemed to settle with some consistency. I followed a magnetic bearing of 130° and ignored the temptation to take easier-looking routes which veered off this course. Ice hid all pools, and we crossed the 3-mile-long Lake Turnabout without even knowing it, for the snow cover had made it invisible. Musk oxen snorted and stamped as we loomed up through the freezing fog.

Visibility was poor again the next day and distinguishing landmarks were nil. My dead reckoning might be way out, but without proof either way, I carried on up and down the valleys until I came across the prints of musk oxen climbing a narrow defile up one side of the valley system. We reached the foot of the Boulder Hills at 2,200 feet and camped beside a frozen gully. Here there was no water, so we melted snow, a process wasteful on cooker fuel.

For three long days we plodded through deep snowfields with temperatures at −20°C. The stillness was immense. No musk oxen now. Nothing and no one. On 23 September we camped at the foot of the great Eugenie Glacier, its well-formed snout armed with layers of glistening teeth, stalagmites from a previous summer's brief melt. Mist rolled over the plateau from the east, but now the very rim of the Grant Ice Cap brushed our left flank and, spurred on by the increasing cold, we limped at last to the northern tip of the plateau.

There were many steep snow banks to climb up or slither down. In awe we laboured beneath the towering icefalls of Mount Wood where twin glaciers tumbled two thoussand feet down to a lonely lake. Here everything had a contorted, temporary look. Gigantic blocks of ice, scarred and smudged with alluvial muck, and blackened walls of ice reared up like monster waves frozen in the act of crashing against some puny dam. In the wary hush of this place where no birds sang, some new and cataclysmic upheaval seemed imminent. Craning my neck up to ease the pain of the sledge harness, the sky-high icefalls appeared to teeter from their summits.

Thankful to leave, I sought a tiny stream outlet from the lake, and we stumbled by good luck into a corridor, some ten yards wide, between two boulder outcrops. This narrow rock-girt passage immediately descended, in curves and steps, to the west-north-west. There could be no doubt we were in the upper canyon of the Grant River, a winding ravine that falls for thirty miles to the sea. Once in it there was no further need to navigate, there being no branch-off valleys. The only place to camp was on the river ice. All game followed the river, too, and myriad little hoofprints of fox, hare, lemming, caribou and wolf dented the snowdrifts all about.

The metal spikes of our snowshoes, long since blunted by rock and slate, no longer gripped the sheet ice. Every few minutes evil language echoed off the narrow canyon walls as one or other of us slipped and crashed over on to the rocks. When we switched to snowshoes, they often smashed through the ice and dropped two or three feet down to the streambed.

The canyon kinked and snaked, was blocked with high black boulders and once even seemed to climb. But this must have been an illusion. One night was spent in a bottleneck some twelve feet wide between high black walls. Our tent stood suspended on ice above a neat round pool.

On 26 September, towards noon, the riverbed plunged thirty feet down a frozen waterfall. From the top of this cleft we looked out at the Arctic Ocean where an inlet, Black Cliffs Bay, edged in to meet the mouth of our river valley. A jagged vista of contorted pack ice stretched away to the polar horizon. Travelling along the edge of the frozen sea, we came by dusk to Alert, to the four little huts that we knew so well, the most northern habitation on earth.

We had travelled around the polar axis of the world for 314° of latitude in 750 days. Only 46° to go. Looking north at the chaotic ice rubble, thirty feet high in places, there was no doubt in my mind: the hardest nut was yet to be cracked.

Chapter Eight

Once again we would spend the long dark polar months further north than any other human being.

For five days before our arrival at the Alert huts, Ginny had slaved away to make them habitable, for no one had wintered there since we ourselves had done so back in January 1977. The main shack was a garage just big enough to take two Land Rovers. This was to be used for our skidoos, all outdoor stores and, in one half, the generators which Charlie would have to run now that Ol was absent.

We arrived during autumn when the temperature hovered around –20°C, a few hours of sunlight still graced each day and life was a delight. It was a far cry from the first bitter January night we spent at Alert back in 1977, when Oliver had written that the huts were 'deplorable'. There was then no heater and it was impossible to get warm. Two days later, after settling in a bit, he added: 'Have now had time to take in the environment. It is pitch black most of the time and even the moon has pissed off for two weeks. Apparently, it gets light on 2 March. Everything and anything freezes solid. Tins, toothpaste, food, apples, paper, pens, metal, engines, human flesh. My hands are already a great problem.'

This time, soon after we arrived, Major Reg Warkentin, in charge of the main camp two miles to the south, called on us by snow caterpillar. Later on a Roman Catholic padre held a Thanksgiving Service for our safe arrival in Alert, and he congratulated us on joining the community of the most northerly men on earth: the nearest manned base is Eureka, which is three hundred miles to the south. There is no possibility of visitors by sea or land, nor, when the weather is bad, by air. The battered remains of a transport aircraft and the nine graves of its occupants rested close to our huts, a mute testimony to the hazards of reaching Alert.

The fact that Alert is Canadian, not American or Russian, goes back to the days of Martin Frobisher and John Davis in the sixteenth century. Frobisher discovered a 'very great gulfe', now Hudson Strait, which is the passage to the inland sea named Hudson Bay at the heart of Canada. In the seventeenth century, this was opened up by British sailors and merchants, mainly from the Hudson's Bay Company.

The form of politics and the choice of language in Canada today are largely due to the early explorations of Martin Frobisher and to the lack of explorers from other countries heading into the region at the time. British sovereignty over Arctic Canada was passed to the new nation of Canada in 1870, including outlying terrain such as Ellesmere Island in 1880.

By the 1870s the British government was disillusioned with the idea of a commercially viable Northwest Passage since, after eventually locating a potential way through it, at great cost in lives and money, it was obvious that no quick route was available over the top of North America. So the prime minister, Disraeli, was urged by a committee on which sat many of the veteran Franklin searchers, including Collinson, Rae, Back, Osborn and Markham, to ignore the passage but send voyages of purely scientific value as far north as possible. The public took this to mean that a Union Jack would be planted on top of the world. The North Pole took over from the Northwest Passage as the next national quest – or, at least, the 'Furthest North'.

Another ex-Franklin searcher, George Nares, was to command two ships – *Alert* and *Discovery* – to head north up to Baffin Bay and hopefully beyond. The man with whom Nares had sledged years before, Leopold McClintock, was the chief adviser on equipment, so 55 Greenland huskies were taken. Nares left Portsmouth in 1875 and found remarkably clear seas between Canada and Greenland all the way up the Kennedy Channel to Hall Basin below the black cliffs of Lady Franklin Bay. His wintering site on the bay's low beach, was later to become better known as Fort Conger.

Leaving *Discovery* in Hall Basin, Nares took *Alert* on northwards where no ship had been before and into Lincoln Bay, where huge icebergs jostled on the very rim of the polar ocean. Nares now inched his ship north-west around the north-eastern tip of Ellesmere Island and into a small bay, Discovery Harbour, where he could winter, not very far from the place where, in 1982, Ginny, Charlie and I were waiting for our own pole attempt.

At first, scurvy was kept at bay, for some local game was shot, but an overall lack of fresh food made frost wounds slow to heal. Rae's suggestion of building igloos was never taken up, and tents and bedding became damp and heavy with frozen breath that increasingly lined the material and entered the sleeping bags.

In the spring Nares sent his men sledging north in exactly the same McClintock-inspired manner that Nares himself had championed years before, but the conditions then were far less difficult than the great walls of broken sea ice, often thirty feet high, that they now had to deal with in the polar sea proper. Unfortunately, the McClintock navy faction on the advisory committee had proved more influential than the Rae HBC faction, so heavy boat-sledges and clothes of European design were favoured over Rae's light sleds and Eskimo clothing. Only one man had taken snowshoes with him and he had suffered derision until the first Nares sledging journey over the polar pack ice, where soft snow in deep drifts lay over a chaos of broken ice blocks of all shapes and sizes.

Without skis or snowshoes, manhauling was a nightmare. Sledge loads averaged out at 216 pounds per man, which turned out to be unmovable without relaying and thus doubling the distance to be covered and the time taken. The sledgers sank to their knees, sweated, and then, in damp clothes, suffered from frostbite.

Attempts at using their dogs to pull sledges ended in farce as inexperienced sailors tried to handle unruly snarling teams and tangled traces.

Led by Albert Markham, the sledge group, made up of 21 men and 3 officers, returned from that first journey with a third of their number incapacitated, and many fingers and toes were amputated to avoid gangrene. But they did obtain the Furthest North and they did lay out depots to help the planned main journeys to come. On 3 April 1876, at −36°C, three separate sledge groups left *Alert*, one to explore Ellesmere Island under Pelham Aldrich and the others to head north under Markham. Scurvy symptoms attacked within days and men had to be carried on already heavy sledges. Nonetheless, despite getting nowhere near the North Pole, Nares (unlike Hall and Kane) brought back valuable records of geological, astronomical and botanical observations which were later published in more than forty major science journals. Aldrich's charts of the northern Ellesmere coast were the only ones in existence for half a century until aerial photography was pioneered.

Politically, there was every reason why what is now Canada could very easily have been first explored by the Americans for, after all, the land to the immediate north of the existing US border would naturally be highly desirable to them. And had their explorers been the first to arrive there, they, and not the faraway British, would have claimed the land. Equally, the Russian empire, which already owned all of Alaska (until 1867 when they sold it to the Americans), could have sent one or more of their own great polar explorers east to claim at least the northern areas of the Canadian archipelago. As it was, the Nares expedition successfully claimed all land to the south of Alert as British, and therefore, a few years later, Canadian territory. Scurvy-ridden and inefficient sledgers though they were, they ensured Canada's future status.

The Admiralty, post-Nares, turned their attention away from the North Pole and left discoveries beyond the Ellesmere Island coast and the far north of Greenland to the great American explorers in the closing years of the nineteenth century.

Lieutenant Adolphus Greely of the US Navy was sent north with twenty-five men in 1881. He established a base at Fort Conger and successfully reached 83°24′N, within four hundred miles of the pole, before having to turn back. They had broken Markham's record by 4 miles. However, two summers passed without a relief ship arriving to pick up the Greely team. One relief ship failed to break through the ice and a second vessel was crushed and sank. When nothing was heard from Greely for two years, Winfield Scott Schley of the US Navy was sent to locate him, once a suitable ship was found. The Americans reminded the British that, not so long ago, they had salvaged the Admiralty's lost ship *Resolute* and had handed her back. So now Greely was given Nares' ship *Alert* by the British. Two other ships were also purchased and all three left New York in April 1884.

Schley wrote to Mrs Greely assuring her of his every effort to find her husband. His three ships searched hard, as did eight US whaling captains, encouraged by the government's offer of $25,000 payable to anyone who could save Greely. The search covered the whole likely area from Lady Franklin Bay in the north to Cape Sabine in the south. Eventually messages were found in cairns indicating that Greely was somewhere close to Cape Sabine on the coast opposite and not far north of the modern Thule Air Base. By this time, and bearing in mind the known amount of food supplies that Greely had originally taken, it was likely that he would be dead.

In fact Greely's men had managed to stay alive for quite a while on a varied diet which included old leather boots, broth of boiled oily sailcloth, beetles, shoe laces, bird droppings and thousands of sea fleas bred on the decaying flesh of a dead crew member. And finally, at least two of the men had surreptitiously cut chunks of flesh from their dead colleagues' bodies. When Greely caught one man stealing from their dwindling food store, he shot him through the head. The men died one by one. Some contemplated suicide. Many were badly frostbitten. Most died of starvation and hypothermia.

When Schley eventually located the sagging Greely death tent and had it cut open, he described what he saw: 'It was a sight of horror.

On one side, close to the opening, with his head toward the outside, lay what was apparently a dead man. His jaw had dropped, his eyes were open, but fixed and glassy, his limbs were motionless. On the opposite side was a poor fellow, alive to be sure, but without hands or feet, and with a spoon tied to the stump of his right arm.'

Another survivor, and there were seven, wore a skullcap and a filthy dressing gown. His joints were swollen, but his body was skeletal. He was black with filth and feverish. This was Greely, whose only words were, 'Did what I came to do – beat the best record.' Then he fell back exhausted. The Americans had beaten the British.

The survivors were taken by stretcher to Schley's ship. One was operated on to amputate his feet, but he soon died. *The New York Times*, after initially celebrating the record achieved and the rescue, soon fell back to digging up stories from the survivors, especially of Greely's shooting of the food thief and of cannibalism.

Americans were as shocked to hear that their heroes ate each other as the British had been thirty years before. Large strips of meat had, it turned out, been sliced from six of the dead bodies, all of which were brought back to the States. The doctor was suspected because the flesh cuts were neatly performed. He, too, had died so, if he was guilty, it hadn't done him much good. The *Times* nicknamed the expedition 'The Shame of the Nation', but Greely's reputation survived intact when it became known that he had beaten the dreaded scurvy by the correct use of pemmican soused in lemon juice plus fresh musk ox meat when available. Also that his scientific results were impeccable and valuable.

He lived, amazingly, to see his ninetieth birthday and became the very first American sailor to enlist as a ranker and retire as a general. He was a founding member of the National Geographic Society and held many other prestigious positions, including boss of the US Weather Bureau. In this last job in 1888 he announced to the public that 'a cold wave is indicated'. He was right, and in the blizzard that duly arrived, temperatures dropped 55° in eight hours, not including wind chill. In the white-out that followed, some two hundred and fifty people died from hypothermia or frostbite, many of them children.

In 1888 the great Norwegian explorer, Fridtjof Nansen, managed to ski right across the Greenland ice cap, and this fact greatly inspired Robert Peary, a young US Navy civil engineer who had long harboured an obsessive desire to be a polar explorer and had already tried to cross Greenland the year before Nansen's success. He wrote to his doting mother: 'Remember, mother, I must have fame.'

In 1891, with his wife Jo on board, he sailed to north Greenland, aiming to cross it and also to verify if it was just a large island or a southerly extension of some great Arctic continent. To ascertain this, he would need to find and chart a northern coastline. Among his team were his personal black manservant, Matthew Henson, and Dr Frederick Cook, later to become a bitter polar rival. During various trips into the Greenland interior in 1892 and 1894, Peary made the first crossing of the northern Greenland ice cap and discovered many new features where no white man had ever been.

He usually based himself at Etah, where he considered himself to be an avuncular benefactor of the many Eskimos he used to support his expeditions. He had children by a local teenager, as did his manservant. However, his wife Jo had also produced a baby daughter, Marie, and when she heard that her husband wished to stay in the north into 1895, but without her, she was devastated.

The media had by then latched on to Peary in a big way, but not all the publicity was favourable to his image. Various team members from his Greenland journeys had grown to dislike him, and said so. One biographer wrote, 'Many in Peary's command used to return hating him in a way that murder couldn't gratify.'

By the time Jo sent a relief ship, the money for which she had raised by giving public lectures, Peary had achieved nothing new since 1893, but he did manage to transport three great meteorites from their Cape York resting place, despite knowing them to be the most sacred of totems to the local Eskimos. He needed tokens of achievement, and if they couldn't include the pole then he would find something else to excite the media back home. So in 1897 he exhumed the bodies of five Eskimos with whom he had previously hunted, loaded them into barrels and sold them to the American Museum of Natural History.

In 1897 up to 10,000 people a day came to see the six live Inuit who Peary also brought back from Etah, north of Thule, and to observe the world's largest meteorite, thanks to the great explorer. The museum put the Eskimos up in their basement, but by the following spring five of the six were dead from pneumonia. Two of the bodies were dissected, labelled and mounted for display in the museum. Displaying indigenous people in museums would be considered abhorrent today, but in the late nineteenth century it was commonplace. Jo later sold the meteorite to the Museum for $40,000.

In 1898, on his way north again but halted by ice in the depths of winter, Peary heard that Otto Sverdrup, a well-known Norwegian explorer, was also in the area and, Peary suspected, ready to try for the pole. So, to forestall the Norwegian, he set out to trek over the ice north to Fort Conger at a highly dangerous time of the year. As a result he nearly died close to where most of Adolphus Greely's men had perished in 1881. Many months later Peary was to comment that he thought Greely's behaviour in abandoning his Conger base was 'a blot on the record of Arctic exploration'. Admiral Greely, by then a man of considerable influence, became a hostile detractor of Peary.

Whilst at Fort Conger, Matt Henson cut away Peary's boots when he said that his legs felt 'wooden'. Both legs were found to be bloodless to the knees. Several of his toes came away with the boots and the doctor had to amputate the stumps without anaesthetic. 'A few toes aren't much to give to achieve the Pole,' Peary said to Henson. The trip to Conger had proved worthless, and Peary was carried by sledge back to his ship, where more rotten toes were cut away. Back in the USA, Jo, pining for her always absent husband, had a second daughter who, aged seven months, died of cholera.

In May 1900 Peary managed, despite his foot problems, to reach the very northern tip of Greenland and proved that it was just an island. Jo and her surviving daughter Marie decided to join Peary up north that year, but their ship was caught by ice and severe storms. One of the Eskimo women on board, a teenager called Aleqasina, had a baby which she innocently explained to Jo had been fathered by Peary. Jo wrote to her husband, 'To think she has been in your arms, has received your caresses, has heard your love-cries, I could die at the thought.' Aleqasina fell ill on the ship and Jo had to nurse her. She recovered and years later had three more children, one of whom was fathered by the incorrigible Peary!

In May 1901 the weather between Fort Conger and the ship cleared and Peary made the journey to Jo's benighted ship. Somehow Jo, as always, forgave her errant and so often absent husband, but instead of going back to the States with her, Peary stayed on for yet another northern journey. His obsession was fuelled further in 1902 when he heard that Umberto Cagni, a captain in the Italian navy, had beaten the previous northerly record set by Nansen, having reached within 237 miles of the pole. 'Next time,' Peary told Henson, 'I'll smash that all to bits.'

Back in New York in 1903, Peary managed to gain an important ally to support a further attempt: President Theodore Roosevelt himself. The great explorer was promoted to commander, awarded various medals and voted president of the American Geographical Society. At this time, however, Captain Robert Scott was thought to be about to claim the South Pole for Britain, and somebody somewhere might yet steal the North Pole from the United States, or rather Robert Peary. There was no question: he must try again. Roosevelt agreed.

Peary focused entirely on his preparations, ignoring his wife and daughter to the extent that Jo wrote to him in 1905: 'I am terribly disappointed and I think we might as well call the whole thing off. The sooner we make up our minds that we must each go our own way the better it will be for us.' Nonetheless the ever-faithful and forgiving Jo was there at the dockside later that year, smiling and waving as the latest Peary polar voyage left America in a ship sensibly named *Roosevelt*. This time Peary's furthest north was 87°6′N, only 174 tantalizing miles from the pole.

Stateside once more in 1906, he learnt that a one-time ship's mate of his, Doctor Frederick Cook, a fairly well-known climber and polar adventurer, was already in the Arctic and all set for a pole attempt using the very dogs and Eskimos from Etah that Peary always took on his own polar attempts. Peary was, understandably, enraged and could not get back north quickly enough. When *Roosevelt* reached Etah in 1908, Cook was already on his way back to the States via Europe, but had not yet made any announcement about the results of his pole attempt.

Peary had, by the time of his last polar journey of 1909, evolved an excellent method of travel involving a support group of over two hundred huskies and fifty Etah Eskimos who blazed a trail north (zigzagging to avoid the worst pressure ridges and open leads) along which they built igloo camps and left food dumps. As the expedition crept further from land, the number of dogs and men became less, a pyramid system such as would be copied in decades to come for attempts to ascend Everest.

At a camp named after Peary's old sea captain friend and co-sledger, Robert Bartlett, Peary went ahead with only his loyal manservant, Matt Henson, and four Eskimos. Bartlett was, of course, disappointed to be left behind at this key moment after many years of supporting Peary. To this day many 'polar watchers' believe that Peary calculated that the glory of reaching the pole would be the greater without other white men to share the spotlight. Also, should he fail to actually reach 90°N, that fact would be less likely to leak out if only Henson and the Eskimos were witnesses to his navigation.

From the moment Peary left Bartlett behind, the daily distances at which his pole group advanced north increased in a truly remarkable manner. This would later cause critics' eyebrows to raise. The progress rate was, in fact, nearly three times faster than his previous average speed, which Peary put down to much longer travel days in near perfect ice and weather conditions. On 6 April 1909 Peary recorded: 'The Pole at last. The prize of three centuries, my dream and ambition for twenty-three years. *Mine* at last.'

As Peary made his way back south over the next four months, Cook reached a telegraph station and was able to announce to the world that he and three Eskimos had reached the North Pole on 21 April 1908. This was on 2 September 1909. A few days later Peary announced his own success and denounced Cook as a fraud.

Public opinion soon divided between Cook and Peary supporters. Of the two men's claims, neither could be undisputedly proved, but Cook's were soon discredited and he was forever labelled as a 'deliberate swindler'. Peary's travel log and navigational notes were checked and verified by the National Geographic Society, he received many more medals and international accolades, and was promoted to rear admiral. He summarized his claim with the words, 'The discovery of the North Pole on the 6th of April 1909, by the last expedition of the Peary Arctic Club, means that the splendid frozen jewel of the North, for which through centuries men of every nation have struggled and suffered and died, is won at last, and is to be worn for ever by the Stars and Stripes.'

During the last ten years of Peary's life he suffered from pernicious anaemia. He died in 1920. Jo survived him by thirty-five years, during which she continued to fight his corner against the ever-present doubters of his North Pole claim. Some sixty years after Peary's death, the controversy was still going strong, and Peary's loyal supporters at the National Geographic Society commissioned my old friend Wally Herbert to write an assessment of Peary's North Pole diary. They had decided that Wally, as an expert navigator and highly successful Arctic explorer with dog-driving skills and many Etah Inuit friends, including Peary's grandson, would be the ideal person to verify Peary's claims once and for all.

Wally, a long-time admirer of Peary, took on the job, went to Washington and corresponded with Peary's family who were helpful and clearly expected that Wally would back Peary's claims. Sadly for Wally, he came up with a great many navigational errors, discrepancies and important unanswered questions. The pages covering some of the most critical dates of the Peary journey were left blank or were inserted into the main log as loose sheets. One of these was the note Peary wrote when he claimed to have reached the pole, including the date. Key longitude records and details of daily mileage covered were also missing.

Always an honest, upfront person, Wally realized that his duty was to state his findings, not just in a paper to the Peary-supporting National Geographic Society, but to the world at large in a book. This took him four long years of meticulous research and a degree of stress that resulted in two heart attacks. When the book, *The Noose of Laurels*, was published in 1989, Wally was attacked by both Peary and Cook supporters. The Peary family were not hostile, but others all over the world poured vitriolic criticism on Wally and his family, including making personal attacks. Wally survived an emergency quadruple heart bypass operation, but in November 1993 his younger daughter, Pascale, died in an accident.

My wife Ginny and I invited Wally and his family to our Exmoor home that Christmas. We could see the deep wounds that they were suffering. Deservedly, but thirty-one years after leading the first complete crossing of the entire Arctic Ocean, Wally was knighted by the Queen. But the Peary issue never went away.

In 2005 a British polar traveller, Tom Avery, decided to find out whether, with dog teams and replica Peary sleds, a group of four men along with an accomplished Canadian dog-driver, Matty McNair, could reach the pole using the Peary route in the same time – 37 days – as he claimed the journey had taken him in 1909. Avery took trouble when planning his expedition to check out other people's views on the project, but it was clear that when it came to the old commander, emotions still ran deep.

In 2009 Avery's book about his expedition was published under the title *To the End of the Earth*, and subtitled *The Race to Solve Polar Exploration's Greatest Mystery*. Avery was naturally surprised that his book and the press conferences that preceded it were met, in his words, 'with the same kind of scepticism that had greeted Peary on his return to America ninety-six years earlier ... We will never know for sure who was the first to the Pole. It's a matter for people to form their own opinion, based on the evidence available. But as I said at the press conference on our return to the UK and in all the interviews I have given since, I believe that we have shown that Peary could have done it.'

One man whose great plans to be first to the North Pole were smashed on hearing the claims of Cook and Peary was Norwegian explorer Roald Amundsen. He immediately switched his focus to the South Pole and said of Peary, 'I know Peary reached the Pole. The reason I know it is I know Peary.'

Ginny, Charlie and I settled into our huts on the northern edge of Ellesmere Island some sixty-one years after Peary's death. Our only companions were the two dogs: Bothie and the Inuit black dog Tugaluk.

In midwinter our camp was rocked by successive storms. I had to lash the roof of our hut down with cables and ropes. Outside, after one storm gave way to a calm moonlit night, I went out to the nearby edge of the frozen sea of Alert Bay and, looking north, saw black open water to the horizon. I checked the thermometers in our beehive screen. Minus 4°C. Such warmth so late in the year did not bode well for our future travel plans. We needed a cold hard winter to make the sea ice grow thick and solid. By mid-December, in one of the coldest winters ever recorded in Britain with temperatures on the usually mild south coast of −18°C, we were basking at Alert at a mere −28°C.

I spent long hours each day in the garage preparing every item for the coming journey: weighing, greasing, modifying and packing. I checked pistols and rifles after leaving them loaded outside for a couple of days. I mock-loaded the 8-foot 6-inch steel sledges, as well as the fibreglass manhaul pulks. Since the smaller steel sledges had performed so well in 1977, I had made no alterations to them, despite the problems with the larger versions in Antarctica. I cut up and redesigned aluminium bridges with which to cross frozen sea leads.

I checked my hand compass for variation when used on the skidoo and off it, with engine running and switched off, held in my left hand wearing a quartz-powered watch and in the right hand above metal-spiked snowshoes. Snow clearance and fuel drum work took time, too, and served to keep me fit. Charlie tried to rest to help his feet recover when he was not giving the generators their weekly service.

Whilst we worked slowly at our preparations, four other groups announced their intention of reaching the North Pole in the spring. A French team intended to travel with skidoos from eastern Greenland to the pole and thence to Svalbard. A group of Spaniards aimed to sledge from Svalbard to the pole, and three Russians held a press conference in Montreal to announce a plan to cross from Siberia via the pole to Canada. All these schemes were due to begin in a mere nine weeks' time, for the first of March is the optimum start date. Not until Christmas-time did we learn of a five-man Norwegian team: a Canadian Eskimo and three Norwegians, under the leadership of Ragnar Thorseth, Norway's best-known contemporary explorer. The Christmas Canadian Hercules brought mail to Alert, which included some news cuttings about a month old sent by Ant Preston. A Norwegian paper, *Aftenposten*, in early November printed:

RACE TOWARDS NORTH POLE

> Ragnar Thorseth who aims to lead the first Norwegian expedition across the ice to the North Pole, will be in competition with several foreign expeditions.
>
> Simultaneously with Thorseth, British, French and Russian expeditions will also set out for the Pole. 'We aim to win the race and arrive first,' Thorseth says. 'It is only fun with a little competition. We'll be going nearly parallel to the British and French and on a collision course with the Russians, but we aim to reach the Pole first. There is only one time to make a start and that is the beginning of March. Earlier it is too dark and later the Spring thaw starts.'

The next cutting, from the *Svalbardposten* in late November, added a new ingredient:

> The Scott-Amundsen duel looks as if it is going to be repeated in the New Year. It will of course be at the other end of the world but will be, as before, Norwegian and English expeditions in a race to a Pole. As far as we know, the English expedition is aiming to leave from the same place as Thorseth. The leader of the English is a lord who is very well-equipped. It is rumoured that on a recent North Pole attempt he took prostitutes with him so that the hardships would not be too severe. Scott had horses with him on his tragic South Pole expedition. The question now is whether prostitutes will bring better luck to the expedition team than horses.

In mid-December the *News of the World* pricked up its ears and announced:

> ARCTIC TEAM BLASTS SEX SLUR
>
> Members of the Arctic expedition sponsored by Prince Charles are furious at allegations that they are taking good-time girls with them. The claims are made in a Norwegian paper under a banner headline 'Lord to North Pole with Prostitutes'. The Lord is Sir Ranulph Fiennes who is leading the expedition. A Norwegian expedition with the same aims will depart at the same time and the allegations are part of a dirty tricks campaign to stir up hostility between the two teams.
>
> Robin Buzza, the British team's representative in Spitsbergen, said the allegations were 'a load of old codswallop'. After Buzza complained, the relevant editor printed an apology saying he had been given wrong information. But he added, 'Competition does exist and the race is starting long before they hit the ice.'

As the old year faded I walked to the end of the isthmus over wet, ill-formed snow. Forty mile an hour gusts blew from the south, but the temperature remained around −16°C. I listened. From beyond the great angular inshore ice chunks, whose sinister silhouettes could be seen in the semi-darkness of the moonlit noon, came a rushing sound as though gravel was pouring from a great height on to concrete. In a while my eyes grew more accustomed to the darkness and I perceived wide rashes of black sea not far beyond the coastal rubble. Then followed sounds of muted struggle, muffled thuds and the splintering crash of ruptured floes as wind countered tide. I thought of climbing over the immediate ice blocks to get a better look, but an old saying flashed through my mind, 'Sufficient unto the day is the evil thereof'. I retired to the protection of the huts.

In mid-January, three short weeks before we must set out on to the sea's creeping crust, the news from the local met station was bad. The bay ice was only 87 centimetres thick, thinner than that of any previous January on record, the average being 105 centimetres.

The true coldness, that crackles the nose and ears, congeals the blood in fingers and toes like rapid-setting glue and fixes the sea ice slowly but surely into a precarious platform to the pole, finally came. Better late than never. A whole host of tasks could now be done which I had left for the advent of the cold. The tent must be erected on the bay ice, and the naphtha heater tested for fumes. I bedded down in the tent that night with Ginny. The ice about us spat, cracked and boomed as the floes contracted.

Up at the camp that week they recorded −51°C with a 10-knot breeze, and fixed safety lines between the huts. In our kitchen we sat and ate wearing duvets, boots and woolly caps, for the hut was really a metal-sided caravan and the cardboard slats I had taped to the walls provided scant insulation. But our morale was now high for the sea ice was surely growing out there. And it might not be too late.

Ginny's mouth swelled up from a poisoned gum. Soon her cheek was also swollen, but we gave her penicillin pills and it subsided. She received a message from Peter Jenkins at Sheffield University

Space Physics Department which delighted her: the initial results of her long hard hours at Ryvingen had been analysed, and they showed a recording quality even better than those obtained by the professionals at the British Antarctic Survey base at Halley Bay.

Charlie's feet had slowly recovered and we began to take daily exercise together. He ran through the details of skidoo servicing and repairs with me. The vehicles were precisely the same, apart from having different carburettors, as the ones we had used in 1977. I took him up on the hillside with a theodolite to shoot some stars. Each evening I practised Morse with a key and a recorded tape prepared by Ginny.

Back in London our sponsors, the *Observer* newspaper, held a reception for the rest of the media at which the editor, Donald Trelford, made it clear that he wished for no monopoly in covering the news of our progress. Prince Charles, who presided at this reception, radioed through to Ginny and mentioned that he had heard rumours of a race with the Norwegians.

'No racing,' he told me.

'No, sir,' I replied, 'we will not race.'

But suddenly I remembered how he loved a race, whether briefly during polo matches or out on hazardous four-man cross-country steeplechases, and I knew that he would not object to our indulging in a little healthy competition in a quiet way. I determined that whatever the Russians, French and Spanish might do, we must not let the Norwegians complete the Arctic Ocean crossing before us, even if they were to reach the pole first. In a small way it would be nice to avenge Scott's much-heralded defeat at the hands of Amundsen three-quarters of a century ago.

The rest of January stayed cool for us. It now took longer for Ginny to knock up our meals. Although the larder was in the centre of the kitchen and well insulated, she had to use a hammer to batter frozen soup out of bowls stored there, and place tins of fruit into boiling water to thaw them out in time for lunch. Raw eggs emerged from their shells like golf balls, although they did not bounce quite as well due to their shape.

To offset my mania for an open window at night, Ginny began to use a hot-water bottle under her duvet. One night a fox outside our room barked us awake, and Ginny found her bottle frozen solid by her feet. But none of us minded these little manifestations of the cold: it was all in a good cause. We remembered with much mirth our fear of the cold when we first came to Alert in 1977. How in our greenhorn state we were wont to touch metal without mitts on, a mistake not usually repeated since uncovered flesh sticks fast to metal and, if torn away, leaves the skin behind, burning the hand just as though it had touched a flame.

On 29 January I saw clearly for the first time the aurora borealis: not just an electric flicker on a summer night such as is common in the Scottish Highlands, but the full brilliant display of green and white curtains evolving from one marvellous pattern to another and fading away only after an hour of, for me, almost hypnotic fascination. Fridtjof Nansen wrote of one such display in 1895: 'The glowing fire-masses had divided into glistening, many-coloured bands which were writhing and twisting across the sky, both in the south and north ... an endless phantasmagoria of sparkling colour, surpassing anything that one can dream.'

Despite keeping our eyes open in the hope of seeing the so-called Novaya Zemlya effect, first noted in 1597 by Willem Barents, we never spotted it. This consists of a mirage involving refraction of the sun's rays which makes the sun visible above the horizon when, in fact, sunrise occurs many minutes later, thus making for two sunrises on the same day.

With no moon and an average temperature of –41°C, a succession of crisp clear nights provided some good navigation practice, my favourite target stars being Regulus, Arcturus and Vega, all too bright and easily located to be mistaken for other nearby bodies when pinpointed in my theodolite's narrow field of view. I recorded the precise second at which one star moved across the horizontal line in the centre of my theodolite's eyepiece, and then did the same for two others. After which I computed backbearings from all three which should then enable me to work out my own position on the surface of the earth. Very simple in normal conditions, but doing this in the dark and cold had become no easier, despite my previous Arctic and Antarctic experiences.

The same problems still bedevilled my efforts: the vertical and horizontal bubbles in the alcohol moved sluggishly and insensitively, with slow lurches to left or right because of the cold, so it took me some time to get them to settle centrally to ensure that the theodolite was correctly set; my mouth and nose dribbled involuntarily because of the cold, so ice formed from my bottom lip to where my balaclava fitted into my wolfskin parka. This set hard and stopped my neck moving, preventing me looking upwards; my eyelashes stuck to the metal of the scope, despite a chamois leather covering over the eyepiece itself, and my nose felt as though it was succumbing to the first symptoms of frostnip. If I breathed anywhere near the eyepiece, it froze instantly and I had to extricate a gloved finger from my inner mitten to rub the lens. Other difficulties centred round the small eyepiece used to view the instrument's graticule scales.

What would have taken me twenty-five minutes to accomplish in England, here took well over an hour: the cold frustrated each of us whenever we tried to complete the simplest task. After each practice session with my theodolite, I would return to the warm hut to thaw out myself and my clothes, leaving the instrument outside to avoid condensation. I thought how much simpler a sextant would be. Wally Herbert, however, who was adept with both instruments, had counselled us strongly against the less accurate sextant. And I often wondered about my ability to keep track of our position in the drifting floes of the Arctic Ocean. So long as the sun was out there should be no problem, but given too many foggy days . . . I would shrug off such thoughts at this point.

By the last day of January I needed to make up my mind exactly when we would set out to cross the whole ocean and reach faraway Spitsbergen. To reach this decision I thought of the overall problem, of those who had tried before us and of our own failure in 1977 when we had tried to travel as far as the pole, less than half the distance which faced us this time. We had failed convincingly. Then, four of us had left in early March but the cold had caught out Geoff, eight of whose fingers were frostbitten. So, three of us had set out again in mid-March. After fifty unpleasant days, we'd found ourselves 160 miles short of the pole and surrounded by a sea of moving slush-ice too thin to travel over.

This time we must get further sooner. To be precise, we must reach the Pole by mid-April at the latest. Once in its vicinity we would be out of the grip of the Beaufort Gyral, which floats ice backwards towards Alert, and into the pack ice of the Transpolar Drift, which heads over the top of the world and down towards Greenland and Svalbard. Beyond the Pole, for some two thousand miles of floating travel, we could expect to move wherever the by then fractured pack might take us. Hopefully the *Benjy B* would be able to penetrate the pack along its southern fringe and so remove us somewhere in the region of Spitsbergen without getting herself crushed.

Could such a journey be made in one Arctic summer season? Impossible to predict, since it had never been done before. Wally Herbert, the only man to have crossed the Arctic Ocean, had taken two seasons. Back in England at the time, he commented to our film team:

> I think the big physical problem of crossing polar pack ice is that, at least initially, you travel in very cold weather and, in order to get to your destination before the ice breaks up, you have to put in a lot of travelling time, which means being exposed to temperatures of –45° to –50°, for up to fifteen hours a day. Now –45° is not very cold by Northern Canadian standards, but if you are exposed to it for that length of time and you have to knock your way through pressure ridges and across open leads, then it is a big strain. At the times when you really need to push hard, it is going to be twilight, or even dark. It is going to be a lot colder and you will be travelling a lot longer across moving ice which can swallow you up at any time or which physically needs a lot of effort to knock down. So you might be burning up in the region of 7,500 calories a day. That is pretty high going.

Our own north-polar adviser, Andrew Croft, said, 'You will not be able to start for the North Pole, without excessive tribulation and breakages, until late February. That will be the time to start.'

Charles Kuralt, writing about the four-man Plaisted group, the only men to have reached the North Pole without dog teams, said, 'There is only a short span of time, mid-March to mid-May, when man can safely walk on the Arctic ice. Earlier in the year darkness and severe cold can make travel hazardous. Later the rising sun turns the ocean snow cover to mush and high winds break the ice pack into thousands of individual floes.'

Back in 1977 our final start date had been 14 March. Now I decided to cut this by a month, to 14 February, and then to subtract a further week for good measure and unforeseen teething troubles. I would aim to start in the dark in the first week of February. What worried me most was the likelihood that one or other of us might get frostbite in the dark. The only way of avoiding amputation of a frostbitten limb would be evacuation to an intensive care hospital with the right equipment. Until sun-up in early March, this would be totally out of the question, since even an efficient ski plane like our Twin Otter, with a brilliant pilot such as Karl Z'berg, could not land on the Arctic pack ice in pitch-blackness. Nonetheless I continued to aim for 7 February.

Three things occurred during the last week of January to frustrate this arrangement: the Twin Otter sustained damage to an aileron in its hangar at Farnborough; Gerry Nicholson began to suffer severe abdominal pains which were diagnosed as a hiatus hernia; and half of one of my teeth fell out one evening, followed by its neighbour the next morning. Inside the resulting cavities were black rotten places, and the nerve ends were bare.

The weekly Alert–Thule Hercules left that morning and would be returning to Alert on 9 February, three days before our Twin Otter should arrive, so I caught it in order to visit the young Danish dentist at Thule. He spent one and a half hours in my mouth and fixed me up with two 'new' teeth.

Whilst waiting for my return Hercules, a US Army colonel took me around the missile-warning centre. 'All kinds of things here have been screwed up because of this warm weather,' he told me. 'Normally we have a drivable ice "road" across the bay. It saves a long detour. But this year the ice is only three feet thick, instead of the normal six or seven feet. So no road. Usually the whole bay is solid in October. This winter she only began to freeze in late November.'

On my return flight to Alert, the navigator let me sit beside him in the cockpit as he pointed down at the sea just off the coastline. 'Those areas of darker shading,' he shouted in my ear, 'they're either open water or freshly formed ice.' I digested this unhealthy news and grinned back in a sickly fashion.

Karl now informed us that he could not arrive in Alert until the 15th, but that he would be bringing Simon with him in the Twin Otter to replace the ill Gerry. Rather than wait five days, I decided to set out within 48 hours, as soon as the sledges were packed. Laden trials the next day indicated that the loads were too heavy, so we were delayed until the 13th. My diary for that day records: 'Poor Ginny has a sharp and persistent headache which really stuns her. This is despite four of her special pills in the last twenty-four hours. She's really down-and-out and tired tonight and looks miserable. I hate the thought of leaving her.'

The night before we left, a radio message came from Wally Herbert in the form of a rhyme:

With my very best wishes for the final dawn
I send tips to help win the fight:
Beware of the calm that follows the storm
And the floes that go bump in the night.

Never trust ice that appears to be dead,
And if you want peace of mind,
Steer well clear of the bear up ahead
And cover that bear behind.

I left Ginny a file of details on camp logistics to give Simon. Included was a note suggesting, should anything happen to Charlie and me, that he and another long-term member of our support team, David Mason, should carry on from where we left off. Simon would as usual be working with Ginny and David, when he arrived, running Tanquary Fiord.

The weather was clear as Charlie and I left Alert to cross the Arctic Ocean via the North Pole: we drove open, heavily laden ski-doos, each of which towed a sledge laden with 600 pounds of camping equipment, fuel, spares and gear. The thermometer indicated −45°C and the prevailing wind brought this down to the actual temperature of −90°C, so we were well muffled up in our full Antarctic sledging gear. For four hours, shortly after midday, there would be enough twilight for a man with a touch of experience and common sense to travel by.

The camp commanding officer and six others came down to see us off, their hand torches darting about below haloes of freezing breath. They had been good to us. I said but a quick goodbye then to Ginny. We had spent the previous night in our hut closing our minds bit by bit to reality. Over the years we had found it better that way. The wrench of leaving her was perhaps worse than in Antarctica, for we both knew that the southern crossing would prove to have been a rose garden when compared with the journey ahead.

As I jerked my sledge away and headed out of the pool of light between the huts, I saw Ginny crouch by the dogs and look up at the passage of darkness by which we had left. I kept the memory in my head like a photograph, as a squirrel will keep a last nut for the winter ahead.

Chapter Nine

Using the brief hours of twilight and the memory of our previous journey along the same coastline five short years before, we made good speed and no mistakes. There was nothing clever about this, for simple familiarity makes light of even the worst conditions, whereas the ignorant can founder at the easiest fence.

The second morning, in Patterson Bay, we spotted the round paw marks of a bear. Bears are known to range this coastline when there is open water where they can fish. Some years ago two scientists had been dropped by helicopter for research work, not far west of our location. Both had been badly mauled. We checked our individual weapons and kept them close to hand.

The ice pressure against the shoreline was in places heavier and higher up the beaches than previously. In others it was clear going, where before there had been walls of rubble. With great caution we skirted between high cliffs to landward and great walls of sea-ice blocks until we reached a steep slope down which we lowered the sledges bit by bit. It was dark by the time we camped along the rim of James Ross Bay.

On 15 February we sneaked through a defile between mountains on the Parry peninsula and descended to Sail Harbour, surrounded by snowfields on every side. New snow lay soft and deep in this bay and the going was slow. The hills fell away on either flank to reveal a view of frozen wonder, Clements Markham Inlet, a giant sea loch ten miles wide at its mouth and penetrating deep into the interior mountains. Although the sky was dark enough to see the major stars, the air was clear all the way to the looming bulk of Mount Foster, the western sentinel of this wild fjord. We camped eighteen kilometres west of the fjord in bitter cold. So easy to make a little mistake in the darkness, to allow the creeping nip to stay that little bit too long in a finger or a toe.

Of the rare and time-scattered expeditions to travel west along this coast, some were never seen again. As recently as 1936 Kruger, leader of the German Arctic Expedition, was lost along the coastline further west with two companions. No trace of them was ever found. In 1983 David Hempleman-Adams, an experienced mountaineer, was to set out from this same coast on 10 March, well after sun-up, but was soon evacuated back to his base, saying, 'These last nine days were the hardest in my life. I am physically, mentally and psychologically marked by them.' Yet he had climbed the notorious Eiger, which was to me, at that time, an unthinkable challenge.

Late on 16 February I spotted the food and fuel cache Giles had left well south of our route over the Cape Aldrich Ice Shelf. We spent an hour there replenishing and repacking, then camped a short distance to the north: it was dark and –46°C.

Next day we set out early. The coast steamed with the brown murk of frost-smoke, a sure sign of open water in the vicinity; at a guess, the coastal tide creek had opened up during the night. Open water in the depths of winter, long before sunrise and at a point of maximum coastal pressure, was ominous. Skirting the steaming slits, I kept as near to land as possible when rubble fields forced me out on to the sea ice. Every few minutes I turned in the seat to check that Charlie never faltered, never fell out of sight for long. Between the encroaching walls of pressure ice from the sea and the tumbling glaciers which descended from Mount Cooper Key there was a narrow corridor, in places merely ten yards wide. Into this we crawled, for there was no other way west.

To our right frozen waves of snow lay shoulder high where, five years before, I had seen pellucid green blocks, piled layer on layer to a height of twelve metres, a testimony to the great driving and cutting power of the pack ice. We had no trouble in the gloomy corridor and emerged at the foot of a steep snow slope just short of Cape Columbia. This we ascended to its summit, and I spent a while observing the immediate area since, any time now, I must find a route north on to the sea ice.

The black slab of Cape Columbia stood out to the south, the site of Monzino's base camp for his 1970 dash to the Pole, and still littered with the remains of his camp. The Italian count, a millionaire and professional explorer, had set out with 150 dogs, 13 Eskimos and 7 others. After a week or two, half of the Eskimos, a Dane and a Canadian returned separately. There was much disappointment and dissent. But, with the daily help of a spotter aircraft and a C-130 Hercules transport plane, Monzino made his goal. Asked if he would do the journey again, he shook his head vehemently, saying, 'Too much; too much of everything. Too much danger. Too much cold.'

A short distance west of Cape Columbia the rolling white layers of the Ward Hunt Ice Shelf thrust north into the sea for over ten miles. The ice shelf was made up of thicknesses of sea ice forming off the coast and attaching themselves, in most places still afloat, to the original coastline. Each year the shelf grew upwards because seawater with a low saline content froze to its lower surface at the same time as summer meltwater from inland refroze to its upper surface.

As with all Arctic ice, the ice shelf was subject to immense strain and could fracture without warning. In 1961 massive calving from the Ward Hunt Ice Shelf reduced its area by some 600 square kilometres. The resulting islands floated away both to the east and to the west and a subsequent aerial study of their float-routes suggested that Cape Columbia lay at the spot where westerly and easterly currents separated. This makes it the best start point for anyone wishing to travel north, as the poleward route is not powerfully influenced by the pull of either current.

Large chunks of pressure ice were piled in places to a height of forty feet. They formed a wall between snowfield and frozen ocean, but in places there were narrow gaps. We descended the hill and slithered down a ramp after some easy axe work to bridge a 20-foot void and – we were at sea. Already we had covered a hundred miles or more towards our goal, albeit on a somewhat devious route, but we had managed to set out many days earlier than any of our predecessors. On 17 February, two weeks before sun-up, we camped for the first time on sea ice.

As we erected our tent three hundred yards out from the coast on the edge of a seemingly limitless field of impenetrable icy rubble I pressed one mitt to the raw end of my nose, and felt a moment of dread for what was to come and memories of what had passed last time we tried to pit our wits against the power of the Arctic Ocean.

As a result of our 1977 failure to reach the North Pole, I had this time planned a pessimistic schedule, which allowed for initial progress of only half a mile per day. During the first day's twilit labour, we fell short of this scheduled distance, but only just, for we cleared 800 yards of rubble. The 'motorway' we axed and shovelled was exactly the width of a skidoo and zigzagged between ice walls and isolated boulders.

During the next six months there were many times when we felt truly at the end of our tether, but not once did we consider giving up. The thought of facing the crew of the *Benjy B* having failed was not something I could even contemplate. Would it have been more sensible, more responsible, to have given up? Who can say? As will be seen, even our Arctic experts were to counsel evacuation, and with good cause. In those first twilit days, however, we did not think of anything but the next few yards of slow and frozen toil.

According to Wally Herbert, we would have to travel 825 miles in order to cover the 474 miles beeline distance to the pole – a 75 per cent detour factor. Wally – and nobody knew better than he for nobody else had ever crossed the Arctic Ocean – said that we were unlikely to succeed unless we reached the Pole before 17 April. With this date in mind we could afford only minimal delays. At that time no man had ever reached the North Pole without resupply by air. Wally's support came from Canadian Air Force C-130 Hercules aircraft. If our own lifeline, the Twin Otter, was out of action for any reason at any time, it could critically delay our progress.

On 19 February we axed our way north with a 15-knot breeze and temperature of −42°C. By the end of the twilight hours a further 200 yards were hacked away, and I decided to bring the skidoos up the 1,000 prepared yards from our first coastal campsite. Despite the work we had done, there was a great deal of pushing and pulling, bouncing and sweating in order to persuade the skidoos and sledges to move over our rough-hewn motorway. The sweat turned to ice particles inside our underwear as soon as we stopped. I broke off half a fingernail, but felt no pain as the finger was cold.

Like me, Charlie weighed 185 pounds, so between us we could, by using our weight jointly and sensibly, shift the 800-pound laden skidoos and 600-pound laden sledges bit by bit over each new blockage. But progress was hardly the word for it: we were like a couple of geriatric snails on a Sunday outing. Luckily the visibility remained passable during the hours of twilight, so we did not lose track of our hard-wrought motorway.

Much damage was done to the skidoos, since there was sometimes no way of negotiating the 'cleared' route other than at full pelt, rebounding off walls and iron-hard ice rocks. Just short of the roadhead my drive axle snapped. That did it. I decided to switch to manpower and abandon the skidoos.

The previous winter in Alert, preparing for just such a switch, I'd tested out two 8-foot-long fibreglass manhaul sledges and lightweight survival gear to go with them. That night I asked Ginny to get this manhaul equipment to us the next day in the Twin Otter. We would try to find a flat place where Karl might drop the kit without smashing it. In the tent I wrote out lists of small items that we would also need. Although we lay in a dark deep freeze, there was enough light to see by from a polythene bag hanging on a string from the tent's apex. The bag was filled with luminous beads called Betalights, which threw out a green and restful, if somewhat satanic, light.

Because the art of landing a ski plane in the dark on tiny Arctic ice floes with pressure ridges on all sides is a skill possessed by only a handful of brave pilots, we were lucky to have one such man backing our Arctic crossing – Karl Z'berg, a Swiss Canadian. He landed in the twilight with incredible precision, unloaded our two man-sledges and light gear, shook our hands and took off.

So, on 22 February, in semi-darkness, we began the long haul. I thought of Wally Herbert's words: 'There can be few forms of polar misery more physically exhausting than hacking a route through pressure ice when it is cold and there is scarcely enough twilight to see the joke.' After eight hours, our underwear, socks, face masks and jackets were soaking wet or frozen, depending on which part of the body they covered and on whether we were hauling or resting at the time. Each load weighed 190 pounds.

The new North Face tent was only 9 pounds, compared with our 100-pound Antarctic tent, and was difficult to keep 'warm'. Small and igloo-shaped, there was little room for drying clothes other than on a suspended net from which the drips fell on to us, our bags and the evening stew. It was never possible to dry clothes out but, with a bit of effort, they could be improved from wet to damp.

Our eyes stung when the cooker was burning but never as badly as during 1977, since we burnt clean naphtha at all times, never petrol. There was the occasional fire alarm resulting from refilling the cooker tank inside the tent, as some fuel invariably spilt and ignited, but this was usually quickly doused with a sleeping bag. I was forever putting sticky tape over holes burnt in my bag, and our beards were usually dusted with feathers.

For four long days of twilit gloom we hauled, sweated and froze over the endless rubble. I suffered from the problem which you get in warmer climes through sitting on hot radiators or wet grass, and this made the constant vicious tugging at my harness an altogether unpleasant experience. Charlie's legs and back were also displeased with life. But by the end of the four days we had completed eleven long miles. That doesn't sound very impressive unless you have seen pressure rubble for yourself and travelled through it in the dark and in temperatures of around –40°C. The previous year a team of four sturdy Canadians set out for the North Pole from the same spot as we had done, but with the benefit of sunlight. After five miles they were evacuated, one with bad frostbite. They were well trained and sensible, but their luck was out.

Sheer exhaustion overcame any fear of bears most of the time, but I often mused about the best action to take if attacked, remembering the words of a friendly Greenlander in Thule: 'The old bears, going blind, die slowly of starvation as they roam the pack ice, less and less able to find a meal. But they retain their scent for hot-blooded animals, and a human will suffice if they happen to smell one.' I kept my pistol readily available on the pulk at all times.

We struggled to part ourselves from the mountains, but they seemed to move with us. The day when we could no longer see them would mean much to both of us. We longed for some visible sign of progress. We tried to avoid stopping in rubble fields. How stupid to be caught napping by a sudden storm. Yet it was often tempting to camp wearily on a small slab in a field of rubble liable to instant crack-up and massive fracturing. Often, exhausted and sore, I gave in to my weakness and we camped in just such fragile places in full knowledge of the danger.

The safest sleeping places were chunks of consolidated pack ice where many floes were frozen together. They were never completely flat but, if made up of older multi-year floes which had somehow survived disintegration for several summers, they proliferated with well-rounded hummocks polished by years of wind and sun. You could cut away chunks from the yellow-white hummocks on these old floes and find, on melting them, that the water was salt-free, or as near as made no difference.

On 3 March, despite a slight lowering in the temperature, our world took on a new rosy glow as the blood-red ball of the sun slid briefly along the rim of the frozen sea. The sun was, of course, our number one enemy. Its ultraviolet rays would soon begin their deadly work upon the ocean's skin, eating at the sea ice, melting the thinner sections until, in a few weeks' time, our progress would be at the whim of the winds and currents which control the loosely packed ice floes on which we travelled. Nonetheless, after four months of darkness, the sun was, for a while, a welcome friend.

On 4 March at 3 a.m. Ginny's alarm went off and she climbed off her bunk to listen in for us, as was her wont. By then a field telephone had been rigged between her room and the Canadian camp two miles to the south. Just before 4 a.m. its bell jangled. It was the duty watchman. 'I think there is a fire somewhere by your huts,' he said. 'I can see flames down at your place.' Ginny thanked him, and looking out of her own frosty window she saw an orange glow coming from the garage. The dogs sensed something was amiss. The big black Tugaluk cowered under Ginny's table and little Bothie put up a strident yapping.

Ginny, forgetting the temperature, which was −40°C, rushed across to the garage and tried to pull back the main sliding door. 'It was just one big fireball inside,' she said later, 'with smoke issuing from all the seams in the walls and flames filling the windows. I shouted "FIRE!", but nobody heard me. I moved round to the rear end of the hut where there were eight 45-gallon drums of gasoline stacked beside the wall. We had once tried to remove them, but they had been there for many years and were frozen deep into the ice.'

The garage was a mass of flames from end to end. The scientific gear, including a valuable seismometer, was already destroyed, as were machines, spare parts, rations and all the items I had modified during the winter, including ladders to see us safely over porridge ice and open canals nearer to the Pole. Ginny used four fire extinguishers, but she might as well have spat into Hell.

As she watched, the eight drums of gasoline exploded, and soon fusillades of rocket flares and FN 7.62 mm bullets further enlivened the scene. Within an hour of the fire's peak, we later learned, American signals interceptors picked up Soviet messages to the effect that a fire had been spotted at Alert. If Ginny had not been told by a watchful Canadian, the Russians would have known about the fire before she did. We will probably never know the cause of the fire. Simon believed that it was likely to be something to do with the electrical wiring.

There was an unforeseen side effect. The expedition had managed to cross Antarctica in 66 days and navigate the entire Northwest Passage in four weeks without causing a ripple of interest in Britain or anywhere else. Suddenly, newspapers and television screens all over the world mentioned us: 'Conflagration at Polar Base' and 'Polar Expedition in Flames'. After the night of the fire every action that we took, and one or two that we didn't, became news from London to Sydney, from Cape Town to Vancouver.

But out on the ice we had other things to think about when Ginny told us that absolutely everything, the result of seven years of painstaking sponsor-getting and equipment-testing, was burnt. We had food for eight days, so we tried to close our minds to the disaster at Alert and concentrate on the job of immediate concern, that of haulage over the next few miles or, to be precise, the next few painful yards.

As our resistance lowered imperceptibly day by day, the effects of the unremitting cold began to tell and our pace began to slacken. I found the worst of it was the trail-breaking, the sinking of each snowshoe at every step into the deep soft snow on the floes and the still deeper traps of hidden holes between ice blocks. My legs ached and the pain of the piles made life difficult to enjoy. Our shoulders were chafed from the day-long tug of the sledge traces. My nose, red-raw at the nostrils for two weeks now, had become frostnipped on its bridge. This too now lacked skin and bled as the rough and frozen material of my face mask rubbed across it.

We failed to solve the face-mask problem to our satisfaction. Heavy breathing and the continuous involuntary dribble from nose and mouth resulted in a plaster cast of ice around the neck, to which my beard froze solid. I could not wipe my nose to stop this happening since, being raw, it preferred not to be wiped. By night we thawed out the armour-plated face masks above the cooker, where they soaked up the smell of our rehydrating meal. So every day we slogged along breathing in the aroma of yesterday's supper.

This was frustrating since we ate nothing at all by day, being unable to force food through the little mouth hole in our masks and unwilling to open up the masks once they were frozen into position for the day. Attempts at reaffixing a frozen but disturbed face mask usually failed to prevent frostnip to nose, forehead or cheeks. So daytime snacks were out.

The worst troubles at night also concerned the face. Generally speaking, polar travel would be quite pleasant if one didn't have to breathe. If you try to snuggle down inside your sleeping bag, tying up the drawstrings above your head, then your breath forms a thick rime of frost all around your head, particles of which fall down your neck or settle on your face and in your ears. If, on the other hand, you leave a hole at the top of the bag just big enough to frame your nose and mouth and then manage to keep them in that position through the sleeping hours, your nose grows very painful as soon as the temperature descends to around −40°C, which it does once the last of the cooker's heat fades away.

By 7 March, on which day I was thirty-eight years old, we had lived and hauled for three weeks at temperatures much colder than a deep freeze and with winds usually above 15 knots. Both of us now knew why people do not venture out on sea ice in these latitudes before the coming of March. It had taken a lot out of us; perhaps too much. Charlie said of those days:

> Instead of drinking something like six pints a day, which we needed, we were only getting about two pints, so we suffered from dehydration. As you get dehydrated you get weaker. If you are out for a long period of time and don't stop to recuperate, you get weaker and weaker, until you simply can't even pick up an axe ... You start hammering away and after about five minutes you collapse and gag and don't know what to do with yourself. You start to suck ice and snow. I can remember times when Ran and I couldn't pick the axe up any more. We were absolutely shattered; so tired. We dragged our way back, hardly raising our feet off the snow and crawled into the tent and went to sleep like

dead mutton. But there is always the light at the end of the tunnel, and this is what you've got to think about the whole time you're killing yourself.

Late on 8 March, in a brief gap between snowstorms, Karl found us in a flat but narrow 'alleyway'. He managed to land and offloaded two skidoos – not the Elans we wanted, since they had been burnt, but a slightly heavier model called a Citation, also made by Bombardier.

Manhauling, we had averaged six to seven miles per day and we had covered over a hundred miles of the worst sort of pressure ridging. Now, with skidoos, we reverted to one mile on the 9th and two on the 10th. Admittedly, there was non-stop white-out and high winds, but that was not unusual. The problem was the old one: skidoos, unlike dogs and manhauled sledges, simply will not negotiate small heaps of rubble, let alone walls of ice blocks. So the days passed in endless hauling and pushing, bogging down and overturning, with inevitable breakdown delays. And all to little avail in terms of progress.

Charlie's back became most uncomfortable from the strain of dragging the 400-pound machines up rubble walls. This was alarming: we needed a sprained back like we needed a pain in the backside.

All about our floe one foggy night, as the wind steadied at around 40 knots from the west, came the sound of roaring water. The pack was on the move, but there was no knowing in which direction. It was easy to worry yourself sick inside the tiny tent. At times the wind tore away the windward side of the flysheet. I shovelled a wall of snow around us and double-pegged the guy ropes, but each new crack and boom from outside made my ears prick up and my skin crawl slightly down my back.

Four days of wind, acting upon sea ice far less compacted than it would be after an average winter, caused widespread fracturing over thousands of square miles and there were vast regions of open water where, for at least another two months, the ice should have remained solid. Fortunately, we were not able to see a satellite photograph of our overall predicament.

Open canals began to proliferate and widen. Soon there was a spider's web of these canals cunningly concealed by the poor light and the newly fallen snow. From time to time I turned to check the whereabouts of Charlie in the twilit murk. This I did once too often and narrowly missed a wide canal zigzagging across my front.

No sooner did I come clear of this cutting than a divergent channel with 4-foot-high banks barred my new course. Again I swerved. This time too late. Skidoo and sledge skidded into the trough, flinging me towards the far bank. My legs broke through the snow's crust and water filled my boots, but my chest was against the further wall and I scrambled out.

The skidoo was beyond my reach and already settling fast like a cow caught in a quagmire. Within minutes it was gone, its 900-pound laden weight pointing down at the black ocean floor far below. Slowly the steel sledge tilted, despite the air trapped between items inside the sledge boxes. The front of the sledge was just within reach and I grabbed at a lashing strap. With a twist around my leather mitt, the strap could not slip.

I shouted for Charlie. He was twenty yards away, unaware of my problem and unable to hear me above the noise of his skidoo. I could not stand up to attract his attention, but did so with my free hand while lying down. Charlie saw this and came up at once. 'She's going down!' I shouted somewhat unnecessarily. 'Try to save the tent.'

The tent was in a rear-mounted box. Each box had a separate lashing strap and, since the sledge had already been briefly immersed in saltwater ditches that day, the straps were covered with a sheen of hard ice. Charlie found that he could only just reach the rear of the sledge, and with thick mitts could not unlash the straps which held the tent box. So he took his mitts off, a thing we do very rarely indeed outside our tent, and began to work at the frozen strap. As he did so, the sledge settled slowly but surely and my arm began to feel stretched to its limit. I could not hold on much longer. My body, laid out on the ice bank, was slowly pulled over the edge.

With my free hand I opened the second box and pulled out the radio and search beacon. Charlie could not get at the tent, but he loosened the lashing of another box and retrieved my theodolite. He also removed a bundle of tent rods tied separately to the sledge. But by then one of his hands had lost all feeling and my own arm could take nothing more.

'I'm letting go,' I warned him, and did so. If my arms had been measured just then and turned out to have been of equal length, I would not have believed it. Within a minute the sledge had silently disappeared. The tent went with it.

The temperature fell back to −40°C during the night. Two of us could in no way fit into Charlie's sleeping bag, but it came with an outer waterproof cover and an inner cloth liner, both of which Charlie gave me, and this kept some of the cold at bay. There was much chattering of teeth that night, and halfway through it I made us a cup of coffee. Charlie's face, staring at me in the dim light from a candle balanced between us, looked skull-like.

'You look half dead,' I told him.

'Thanks. You don't look too healthy yourself.'

I had made a stupid mistake, and we both knew it. In my zeal to press north whatever the conditions, I had lost precious equipment and, very nearly, some of Charlie's fingers.

At midnight, with my little radio none the worse for its brief immersion, I called Ginny on our emergency night schedule. As usual she was listening and picked up my faint call sign through the permanent crackle, static and plethora of Morse signals. She sounded calm but concerned when I told her of our situation. Since all our replacement gear was destroyed in the fire, I feared there would be a bad delay. But, Ginny said, the sledge Ollie had always used with its standard load had been in the snow clearing outside the garage. She promised to get it, the camp runabout skidoo, and a tent belonging to our film crew to us as soon as possible. If I sank that, she said, there would be nothing else; even our skis had been burnt.

As soon as the weather cleared Karl set out, and half a mile from the site of my accident he found a clearing where he landed . . . just.

I cannot imagine many other pilots even considering such a site. On his way back to Ellesmere Island, Karl warned us that the ice was now horribly broken. He reported: 'Whole areas of open sea.'

On 16 March we woke to find a 40-knot wind battering the tent and showering the layer of frost from the inside of our flysheet on to our faces and into our bag openings, where it promptly melted. In semi-white-out we nosed north. There was no sign of the sun, so I applied an error of some 92° to my compass bearing and hoped for the best. The temperature had shot up to −6°C, a sinister sign and unprecedented so early in the year. By evening, the conditions resembled a lily pond with ourselves hopping from one floating leaf to another. The powerful west wind fortunately ensured that most ice chunks touched each other at some point. If they did not, we retraced our route and tried a new one. There was inevitably a great deal of west–east travel involved as we zigzagged north, and much axing of ice blocks to make bridges.

The wind rose to 55 knots as we set up the tent, and the sound of shattering ice vied with the roar of the elements. We both knew that small isolated floes are highly susceptible to crack up, not only when larger neighbours weighing millions of tons began to nip them, but simply because of lateral wave action bending and straining the natural flaws in the ice. Sleep avoided me for much of that noisy night.

All day on 17 March we remained cut off and a new crack opened up some twenty yards from the tent. Although this happened soundlessly, we both felt the sudden temperature change as warmer air emanated from the unzipped sea beside us. The temperature lowered a touch to −26°C and the wind held at 52 knots. The main lead to the north was now a wind-whipped river some forty feet across. To sleep in such conditions might not be difficult for people with no imagination at all, but for less fortunate souls a sleeping pill would be the only way to catch up on much-needed rest.

The noise and the vibrations were truly spectacular once the ice began to move. We refrained from taking pills only because of their daytime after-effects on our state of alertness. The fracture and pressure sounds were many and varied, but the most awe-inspiring were the booming and crunching type. Like the pipes and drums of an approaching enemy horde, the distant rumble and crack of invading ice floes that grew louder and closer hour by hour was difficult to ignore.

Next morning the wind dropped, as did the temperature, to –36°C. At 7 a.m. I scouted around our floe and found a narrow junction point at its southern extremity. There was a deal of grinding and whining at this point and much flaking off of ice from our side of the touchpoint. An hour later we were packed and, with a little axe work, managed to manoeuvre the sleds across the moving junction of the floes. Only a few miles to the north we entered a miasma of brown gloom, a certain sign of open water, and soon afterwards we stopped before a sea of dirty sludge that moved across our front. In the mist we could see no limit to this marsh.

After a reconnaissance flight around us, Karl reported: 'The ice is very rotten and much in motion. I am sure that the ice group are stuck for a week or more until the ice can settle and refreeze. They are in a trap. To their east, north and west there are high ridges and open water all around. I can see only one way out. They must retrace their tracks for half a mile and then go west for one and a half miles, where I can see some ice bridges. Then they can try to go north. If they miss any part of my prescribed track, there is no way out.'

Ginny made contact with a pilot operating out of Cape Nord in north-east Greenland, the area we must float past sometime during the next six months. At this time of the year it should be mostly solid pack ice. He reported: 'No ice older than second-year floes, and all the younger ice, appears thin, weak and broken up. Even three hundred miles north of here the sea is like a watery mosaic.'

That night Ginny said, 'When I look to the north of the camp here, I should see an expanse of unbroken ice. All I see is open water to the horizon.'

From our camp by the sludge marsh we went out on long

journeys on foot, taking with us weapons and axes. The first two trips led us through much impressive scenery and evidence of wide upheaval. I thanked God that we had not been camped anywhere in this region during the recent high winds. It was as though the floes had been shaken through a great sieve and dropped back into the sea like croutons into chilled consommé. A most unpleasant region to travel through, even on foot.

We retreated to the tent and I took down detailed advice from Karl following his recent overflight. His route was complex, but we followed it even though it meant filling in two 20-foot-deep ditches which took us four hours, during which time the blocks about the ditches shifted a good deal, causing us some fright. But we stuck to it, and after fourteen hours' travel had progressed six miles to the north before a new lead stopped us.

Karl later wrote: 'I was very, very curious if they could make my route, and I must say in that respect Ran is an excellent navigator because next morning Ginny told me that they had made it out of the ice jungle and were some miles north of it.'

My diary entry ran:

> We have come nine miles along Karl's suggested route today to 84°42′. Only 318 miles to the Pole. Another thousand or so on the other side, but that is not even worth contemplating yet ...
>
> My chin was numb when I came in and lit the cooker. Must have pulled my frozen face mask off too hard. When thawing it out and picking the ice bits from around the mouthpiece, I found a one inch diameter tuft of my beard complete with skin implanted in the bloody ice. It took a while to remove this from the wool. Where the skin has come away there is now an open patch of raw flesh the size of a large coin. In a while my chin warmed up and began to bleed. Now it is just weeping liquid ...
>
> Tonight we've had a fire. Charlie restarted the cooker, but a leak around the pump caused flames all over the safety blanket and on the tent floor. We chucked the flaming cooker out of the tent in case the tank decided to explode, then we beat out the

flames. Now we are using the spare cooker and patching up the holes in our bags with black cloth cut from a marker flag . . .

Charlie's leg went through the ice into the water today as we tried to pull out a sledge jammed in a moving trench. Dead on –40°C all day and wind steady from the north-west bang into our eyes. All the world is misty. We've been out here well over a month and I cannot wear goggles on the move; they mist up and navigation becomes impossible. I just can't spot that vital best travel-line through the murk which is the key to success or failure. At midday, clouds of black steam rose up right across the northern horizon. There is no noise, just the steam. I find it impressive and a touch uncanny. The equinoctial tides may well be shifting the sea and so fracturing the ice.

Have just finished trying to patch up my chin. The raw place is now down to the bone; I can see it in the mirror of my compass. I look a disgusting sight. Charlie confirmed this . . .'

On 22 March, fearing that our days of drifting had taken us too far east into the looser conditions above the outflow channel west of Greenland, I steered 15° to the west of north. That night I slept not at all as my chin throbbed like a tom-tom. Not having any more antibiotic cream, I applied the cream I used for my haemorrhoids. Charlie found this highly amusing. 'He's got piles on his chin,' he shrieked with mirth. It was lucky that we shared a weird sense of humour.

I still have a tape recording of a strange conversation that we had in the tent about Charlie's toe. Typical of many of our discussions, it was as though our brains were in neutral.

'Very strange,' Charlie observed. 'Right at the end. My feet are dead. No feeling. Very strange.'

'Can you feel that there's no feeling?'

'I can feel there's no feeling.'

'What sort of feeling is it?'

'No feeling.'

'Yes, I know the feeling.'

During the night of 28 March we awoke sweating inside our damp bags. The atmosphere was oppressive and there was deathly silence. I thought briefly of a line from Wally's doggerel: 'Beware the calm that follows the storm.' As I moved outside in the morning I knew at once that something unusual was happening. Our rubble-strewn paddock was entirely surrounded by mottled marshes of steaming sludge. The light of the sun, a sickly yellow, appeared to flutter and fade from minute to minute. Neither of us spoke as we raised camp and tightened the lashings of our sledges. To the north-east a brown-skinned lake disappeared into the gloom.

There followed five hours of hell. By rights we should not have tried to travel. Our route was about as straight as a pig's tail and went where the perils of the moment dictated. To stop would mean to sink. For a thousand yards we moved over this first lake, which was in reality more like a wide river, with a sludge wash spreading out in front of our slow advance. The brown-skinned lane ended in open water which hissed with curling vapour on both sides of us. A solitary floe chunk with one low edge gave us brief respite. From it we listened for signs of what lay ahead in the yellow murk.

A soft squeaking and grinding emanated from nowhere in particular. Satan's private cauldron could hardly have produced as evil an aspect. Often that morning we lost sight of each other in the fog. Sometimes we moved on foot to scout a route, Charlie waiting on some bump suspended in the marsh halfway from the skidoos and shouting to guide me back. We were frightened lest a new fracturing cut us off from the sledges. If that happened we could not expect to live for long. By noon we were weary with apprehension, since the marsh, for all we knew, stretched on for many miles. Then the mist grew less dense, and in a while, thank God, it cleared away altogether and fourteen miles of solid ice rewarded our morning's efforts. We had reached 87°02′N, within nine miles of our furthest north in 1977 and forty days earlier in the season.

If our aim had been solely to reach the North Pole, we could perhaps have felt confident. As it was we had at least nearly reached the polar convergence, where the prevailing currents would alter.

Once past it, we would be out of the Beaufort Gyral, the current that flows in a giant clockwise circle between the Pole and the top of Canada. For a while we would be in a sort of no-man's-land where floes might or might not find themselves shoved back into the gyral. But within a few miles of the Geographical Pole we would enter the Transpolar Drift proper, which heads over the Pole from the coast of eastern Siberia and down towards Greenland. Where these two currents meet and diverge there is, of course, corresponding surface disturbance which, in places, tears floes apart, in others jumbles them together. We believed this highly mobile belt to be at around 88°N, 120 miles short of the Pole.

For three days we struggled on with some good old floes, many breakdowns and two nasties – occasions when a sledge sank into a lead and its skidoo became jammed in the sludge. So long as both of us were close by when this happened, we could usually tow the stricken units out frontwards or backwards. But there were many near squeaks. Not good for the nerves.

At 87°48′N we were stopped by the most massive wall I had ever seen in the Arctic. Not in height but in sheer bulk. First a 10–12-foot-wide moat, fortunately frozen, then a sheer-sided 20–30-foot-high buttress a hundred yards in depth. Then a jagged rubble belt ending in another rampart which almost twinned its parallel neighbour. There was no causeway over this barrier and no detour round it, so we fashioned a devious zigzag route over it, and four hours later bounced down the far side to eighteen miles of better going and no leads of any consequence.

Throughout the day black shadows along the line of the horizon, similar to rainstorms seen on steppe-lands, helped me steer clear of open water. A helmsman in polar seas knows by ice blink, a portion of brightness in an otherwise dark ocean sky, just where ahead he will find floes. Conversely, black smoke, known as steam fog or frost smoke, tells the ice-bound pilot where he may find an escape route from the pack. The steam comes from cold air striking warmer water: it is the rapid and visible discharge of moisture and heat into the atmosphere.

We tried to speed up our progress, and next day managed 21 miles despite open canals, wide rubble fields and much axe work. We were operating well together and the magic of knowing we were north of 88° worked wonders. My diary noted:

> 8 April: Crossed sixty-two sludge cracks today and two major ridge features. But the bit is between our teeth. Twenty-one miles done and no more than thirty-one to the Pole . . .

> 9 April: Charlie's sledge swam for twenty yards today but the breaking nilas never quite caught up with his skidoo. This area is a dreadful mess.

Suddenly, some twenty miles short of the Pole, the ocean's surface improved and remained almost unbroken with hardly an obstacle in sight. At midday on 10 April a theodolite sighting put us at 60°W. Our local noon was at 1630 hours Greenwich Mean Time (GMT). The last miles to the Pole were flat with three narrow leads that caused no problems. I checked the miles away with care after the noon sunshot, not wishing to overshoot the top of the world. We arrived there at 2320 GMT and I contacted Ginny at 0215 GMT on Easter Day 1982. I had to think for a while when laying out the antenna to point due south towards her since every direction now was due south. The temperature was −31°C. We were the first men in history to have travelled over the earth's surface to both poles.

Chapter Ten

Following our arrival at the North Pole, the *Daily Mail* commented: 'On the anniversary, almost to the day, of Robert Falcon Scott's tragic death in Antarctica in 1912, there is something very satisfying about Englishmen beating Norwegians at the other end of the globe.'

Our journey to the Pole had been dogged by a Norwegian group, but they never caught us up. When Scott reached the South Pole, the Norwegians had been and gone and left a tent there. But if and when the Norwegians reached the Pole behind us, they would find no trace of our having been there, for the ice floes move for ever over the top of the world.

We still had over a thousand miles to go to reach any possible rendezvous point with the rest of our team on the *Benjy B*, at that moment still docked in Southampton. We could not count our chickens, and I remembered a famous old Viking saying: 'Praise no day until evening, no wife until buried, no sword until tested, no maid until bedded, no ice until crossed.'

Fifty-one years before we reached the North Pole, the Australian adventurer Hubert Wilkins tried to reach the Pole in a decommissioned First World War submarine. He failed, and it was not until the Soviet Union's space success with Sputnik in 1957 that the USA was goaded into gaining a counter-trophy and sent the world's first nuclear submarine *Nautilus* to try for the Pole. On her third attempt, after being thwarted by shallows in the Chukchi Sea, she crossed the Arctic Ocean via the Pole, taking only four days for the nearly 2,000-mile voyage. Since then, literally hundreds of submarines from the USA, Britain and the Soviet Union have passed under the polar ice.

From the North Pole all directions are south, and I decided to travel by night and sleep by day. That way the sun would be behind us and would throw the shadow of my body ahead of the skidoo, allowing me to use it as a sundial and so dispense with a compass for much of the time. Also there would be less glare and more perspective. Our new 'day' time was hardly welcomed by the rest of the team back at Alert, since it seriously curtailed their daily sleep quota. For them, our travel hours were from 2 p.m. until 2 a.m., with a radio safety schedule at 5 a.m.

I like operating on simple schedules based on solid information, but for the next phase of our journey I had none. I wanted to travel across the Arctic to a place where the *Benjy B* could reach us, by a route with the thickest ice. Where exactly should we aim in this mild, warm year? Which way would be safest?

Uncertainty as to the best course for us was continuing in London. The chairman, and one or two others, counselled an attempt to reach the coast of north-east Greenland and then to sledge over the ice cap to some part of the coast which the *Benjy B* might reach. But Andrew Croft disagreed and suggested that we keep to my original plan to head east towards the northern coast of Spitsbergen. Although I trusted Andrew Croft, I feared the current signs of an unusually early break-up. At Cape Nord, the lonely Danish military outpost at the northern end of Greenland, an American meteorologist had announced that the pack ice was more broken north of Fram Strait than at any time in the last thirty-seven years since the first observations had begun.

This being so, I was equally shy of heading too far west or too far east. It seemed safer to stay halfway between Greenland and Spitsbergen, almost on the Greenwich Meridian, where the southerly current was thought to be strongest. So I made up my mind to consider historical evidence rather than current opinions.

Only two expeditions in history had travelled south from the

Pole in this region, and neither could be treated as a safe yardstick from which to draw conclusions applicable to our own route. The weather alters radically year by year, and anyway the other two expeditions were evacuated from extremely hazardous sea-ice conditions in a manner not available to ourselves.

In 1937, near the end of May, Ivan Papanin was deposited by ski-plane at the North Pole with three companions and a prefabricated hut and they drifted slowly south down the east coast of Greenland in the succeeding winter darkness. They had chosen a multi-year floe of size and solidity, but by mid-February it had all but disintegrated. At this point three Russian icebreakers, sent by Stalin, crashed through the ice pack to rescue the stranded men just west of Jan Meyen Island. We had no icebreakers at our disposal, nor could we expect the might of the British navy to be sent to our rescue. Mrs Thatcher, in the year of the Falklands conflict, was not in the business of helping lame ducks.

I had all my hopes pinned on the *Benjy B*, but I knew that she could not penetrate pack ice in the way that an icebreaker could. The only way that she might reach us was through the skill and spirit of skipper and crew acting in unison, with Karl as their eyes in daylight and summer conditions. Such conditions exist only for five or six weeks in an average year, from late July until late September, so we must reach at least 81° of latitude north, and preferably well east of the Greenwich Meridian, by that period, otherwise even the best endeavours of the *Benjy B* would be to no avail. For the ship to linger after the end of the short Arctic summer would be to invite disaster upon herself.

Apart from Papanin and his crew, the only other men to have travelled south from the North Pole on this side of the world were the four members of Wally Herbert's 1968 team. With some forty huskies, they left the Pole on 7 April, but by late May had been cut off from their goal, a landfall on the Svalbard coast, by the ice break-up. However, two of the team managed to scramble on to a tiny island some twenty miles north of Svalbard to retrieve some granite rock symbolic of their success. In increasingly broken mush, they floated west to a rendezvous with HMS *Endurance*, an ice-patrol vessel of the Royal Navy, whose helicopters managed to uplift men and dogs to the safety of the mother ship.

Our skidoos could not cope with mush ice and open water because, unlike dogs, they were not amphibious. The *Benjy B* could not penetrate pack ice as well as the far larger HMS *Endurance*, nor did she possess any helicopters. Therefore, it would be foolish for me to attempt to follow Wally Herbert's route, even assuming that the 1982 break-up was to be in late May, as it had been in 1969.

I decided to steer a central course. The Greek philosopher Cleobis had a lifelong dictum: 'The middle course is best.' This seemed to fit the bill for me, too. We would head south under our own steam at a speed comparable to Wally Herbert's, whilst the temperatures remained reasonably low and the pack relatively stable. But once local conditions deteriorated to the point where I considered a break-up imminent, then I would search for a floe as solid as Papanin's on which to float south towards the best pick-up point, somewhere close to the Greenwich Meridian and not too far west or east of it. This way we might reach the *Benjy B*'s limit-of-penetration point before winter darkness and new ice forced her out of the Arctic. No man had crossed the Arctic Ocean in one summer season before, but given a few more weeks of solid ice and skilful handling of the old *Benjy B*, we might conceivably make it.

For four nights of travel from the Pole, surface conditions were better than ever before, the weather was warm and pleasant, never below –28°C, and, despite signs of recent upheavals, there was no open water to be seen. We averaged 22 miles of southerly sea travel each night without pushing the pace.

During the night of 22 April, I noticed the prints of an Arctic fox at 88°N, many hundreds of miles from the nearest land. Although there were no bear prints in evidence, it was safe to assume that the fox could only have survived so far from the source of any natural prey, such as hares, by shadowing a bear and feeding off its left-overs. Bears have been spotted by air only a few miles from the pole itself.

That day we made 31 miles in 14 hours, probably our best night's travel. Over the next three nights of 24, 20 and 20 miles respectively, conditions slowly deteriorated. There were many regions of ridges, and rubble as bad as any to be found off the Ellesmere Island coast.

From 88°N down to 86°N was a continued decline. Rubble fields became more frequent, with many more open-water leads. Potential airstrip floes were correspondingly rare. I had grown accustomed to keeping an eye open at all times for airstrip potential. In the Arctic no one could tell when a flat floe of at least 24 inches thickness, the minimum needed for a Twin Otter landing might not become a life-saving necessity. Through the nights of 20 and 21 April, for forty miles there had been no potential strip of any sort. The pack ice was far too broken and, for huge areas, too thin. Nothing I saw in all that time could have served us for a floating platform on which to head south.

The temperature was by now in the –20°Cs and rising daily. It was no longer necessary to wear a face mask. By rights we could count on four more weeks until break-up, given normal conditions. But this was no normal year and I became daily more wary as the weather grew more balmy. For the first time I felt that there would be no great problem should one fall through the ice when on foot patrol. As long as it was possible to clamber out, frostbite would no longer be a risk. Open water, pools and leads began to occur many times each mile, with no signs of new ice forming over them.

This was no time for indecision. The ultraviolet rays of the summer sun were daily weakening the cohesion of the floes. Over 70 per cent of the Arctic Ocean's mobile ice finds its way annually down the ice motorway between Greenland and Spitsbergen, jostling and fracturing, floe against floe, on the way south. Only by quickly locating a big chunky ice platform for our floating base could we hope to survive such a risk-ridden, unpredictable ride.

The whole area looked ready to go. Several times, approaching grey sludge, I sank into waterlogged ice which had appeared to be firm. Along the side of one narrow canal, I tripped and fell headlong. The hand holding my axe shot out to ward off a heavy fall, and it disappeared through the surface, as did my arm up to the elbow and, somehow, one leg up to the knee. I was partially soaked, but the snow-covered sludge held my overall weight.

Seven miles later seawater cut us off in all directions, so we camped. The wind still blew at 30 knots with the temperature steady at −13°C. Chunks of ice floating across pools and along canals all seemed to be heading east. In the tent I told Charlie that I would start searching for a floe suitable for a long float south. For three days no sunshot had been possible, but a rough estimate put us at 86°10′N.

Charlie did not argue strongly that we should not stop. He acknowledged that the decision was mine, but wished to dissociate himself from it. I could see his point of view. After so many weeks out on the ice, the one thing that we both wanted was to get the hell off it as soon as possible. Indeed, to risk stopping so early and so far north must have seemed like wilful masochism to him.

'But Charlie,' I argued, 'adopting a float mode is not something you can do at a moment's notice because there are, as we have seen for the last fifty miles, very few suitable floes on which to float. I, too, would like to carry on further before floating, but the choice we face is either stopping after the break-up signs have become apparent, as you suggest, in which case it is more than likely that no suitable floe will be attainable and we will be in the position of "foolish virgins" being wise too late in the day. Or I can risk accusations of overcaution and try to find a reasonably safe floe whilst it is still possible to get to one.'

After thirty-eight years of behaving like a bull in a china shop, deriding the canny and the cautious, I had decided to join their ranks. Whether it was the right decision was, of course, quite another matter. The outcome of starting to float too soon from too far north might make us end up well short of the ice edge and out of reach of the *Benjy B* when the new winter ice formed in September or October. If so, fingers would point fairly and squarely at me for 'chickening out'.

It was clear that nobody else wanted us to stop yet. The decision had to be mine alone, and I could see that the popular course all round would be to 'bash on'. But Ginny and I had each put ten years of our lives into this expedition and we were at last on the home straight. The current was now with us. My natural instinct to hurry on conflicted with an inner intuition to be careful; an intuition developed over fifteen years of expeditions. Of course, it was one thing to decide to float but quite another to locate a suitable floe.

Dangerously weak surfaces during the last week of April ended with us stranded on a sizeable old floe surrounded by open water and sludge, and we were imprisoned for six days. On the sixth night I reread the notes I had kept on the 1938 Papanin float. I noted in my diary: 'If we float from here at Papanin's rate, we will reach 80°N 8°W by 15 August.' This would be a reasonable date and place for the *Benjy B* to reach us in, hopefully, loose summer ice. One week later Karl flew over with Ginny on her way to Cape Nord to ensure that she was in radio signal reach of us. Simon, also on board, told us the good news that our ice floe had floated south for 44 miles, despite strong contrary winds over the past three weeks.

That day at Longyearbyen in Spitsbergen, the *Benjy B* with Anton Bowring and his crew arrived, eager to push north into the ice to locate us on our ever-diminishing ice floe. Meanwhile, I thought of other Arctic drifters and their fate.

A Canadian anthropologist, Vilhjalmur Stefansson, a great believer in living off the land as Nansen had done, persuaded the Canadian government in 1913 to finance his plans to explore the unknown regions between Alaska and the North Pole and, if he found land there, to annex it for Canada.

As skipper of his ship *Karluk*, Stefansson chose Captain Bob Bartlett, who had taken Peary north on the *Roosevelt* and accompanied him part-way on his final Pole bid. Bartlett had retired to the whaling fleet, but gladly accepted the *Karluk* mission. A mixture of men from very different backgrounds made up the *Karluk* crew, including five Inuit, two geologists, a botanist, a zoologist, two topographers, an oceanographer, a surgeon and a Scottish meteorologist, William McKinlay, who in 1976 finally told the disturbing story of his *Karluk* experience. He believed that his leader Stefansson, who received the top accolades from the National Geographic Society, from Peary and from Greely, was indeed a successful anthropologist, a great survivor in the wild, and an accomplished spin doctor, but that the *Karluk* expedition from which he made his name was badly planned, organized and led.

Soon after rounding Point Barrow, the *Karluk* was gripped by the powerful north-west coastal current, which had for years sucked in and crushed a great many whalers. This was definitely not part of the Stefansson plan, and McKinlay, until then a great admirer of their famous leader, like other young members of the crew, began to have his doubts. Captain Bartlett, and no one could navigate ice better than he, struggled to pull his ship back to the east. But he wrote of the ice that gripped *Karluk*: 'Seldom a foot thick, the *Roosevelt* could have ploughed through it, but the *Karluk* was powerless to do so.'

After three months of drift, but still quite close to the Alaskan coast, Stefansson took five men with him to go, ostensibly, on a ten-day hunt to keep the crew in meat. Bartlett was to lay out beacons to help the hunters back to the ship. But a storm broke up the ice between ship and shore and blew *Karluk* west at thirty miles per day, away from expedition leader Stefansson.

Whilst the *Karluk* drifted ever west towards the Siberian coast, Stefansson began a five-year study of Eskimo life and hunting skills in the islands north of Canada. He discovered no great lands nor minerals to annex to Canada, and two of his men perished whilst trying to resupply him. Meanwhile, millions died, including hundreds of thousands of Canadians fighting in the Great War.

On 10 January a jagged chunk of ice ripped through the hull of the *Karluk* and seawater poured into the engine room. Captain Bartlett gave the order to abandon ship. All stores were hauled on to the nearest flat ice block. The following morning the *Karluk* disappeared under the ice, watched by 22 men, 1 woman, 2 children, 16 dogs and a cat.

Bartlett led the way, painfully slowly and with various separate sledge groups, to the barren shores of Wrangel Island. Then, in mid-March, he and one Inuit set out on a remarkable journey to arrange a rescue ship. Crossing to the Siberian mainland, to the Chukotka coast, they sledged hundreds of miles east and eventually found a ship which took them to Alaska and a telegraph station. Meanwhile, on Wrangel Island, sun-blindness and starvation were soon the order of the day. One man shot his tent mate through the eye, and by the time rescue came in September 1914 only twelve of the original crew were still alive.

When Stefansson's book of the *Karluk* expedition came out, it put the blame on many of the characters involved, but none on himself. In 1921 he organized another expedition, based on Wrangel Island. All but one of its members died there. McKinlay, in 1976, wrote that all the horrors of the Great War in which he later fought never eclipsed the memories of his year of Arctic hell.

Americans really did take over from the British in terms of North Pole travel efforts in the last part of the nineteenth century. But the Russian, Ferdinand von Wrangel, had been the first to discover a huge polynya, or open polar sea zone, off north-east Siberia back in the 1820s. This new geographical anomaly was taken by the American hydrographer, Silas Bent, and the German geographer, August Petermann, to indicate a potential gateway of warm open water which was described as a 'thermometric gateway' to the North Pole.

The *New York Herald* owner, James Gordon Bennett, knew that nothing sold newspapers as well as polar stories and other extreme expeditions. He had, for instance, commissioned Henry Morton Stanley to search for the long-lost Dr David Livingstone in central Africa. A search for this new ocean gateway to the pole must have seemed like another good potential scoop. So Bennett enthused and sponsored Lieutenant George Washington DeLong, who had made a name as a determined explorer during an 1873 search for the missing Charles Hall.

Bennett bought what he felt was a suitable vessel for DeLong and christened it *Jeanette* after his sister. The US Navy provided a crew of four officers and twenty-three sailors. At the time nobody had reached to within 400 nautical miles of the pole, and Bennett was happy when the US Navy commissioned DeLong with various scientific research tasks, plus the hope of discovery of a polar continent in the central Arctic Ocean.

They set off in 1879 and, at St Michael in the Bering Strait, the place where Charlie Burton and I began our Yukon River journey, DeLong's ship took on board forty dogs and their handlers. They then headed north through the strait, where they very soon hit ice, and their oceanographers squashed all ideas of a 'thermometric gateway' to the North Pole.

Gripped by the pack ice, the *Jeanette* spent the next twenty-one months drifting in various directions until in June 1881 she was crushed and sank in a few hours. Thirty-three men with sledge boats slogged south and fourteen eventually made it to the Siberian mainland. DeLong was not among them. Three years later a band of Inuit found equipment marked *Jeanette* floating on ice off south-west Greenland; clear evidence of a drift current of 1,500 miles per year.

The Norwegian explorer Nansen's reaction was to design an ice-proof ship, *Fram*, which he drifted over the top of the world between 1893 and 1896. When the ship's most northerly drift point was reached, Nansen and one colleague skied northwards as far as they could to achieve the existing world record for the furthest north. Their remarkably daring journey was completed without loss of life, as were other voyages through the Northwest Passage by fellow Scandinavians A.E. Nordenskjöld in 1878, and Roald Amundsen in 1903–6. Amundsen spent two years en route based in Gjoa Haven where he was involved with research projects and proved at that time that the magnetic poles do not stay still.

The last of the great polar drifters was Wally Herbert with three co-dog-drivers in 1968. His route from the Alaskan coast to the pole, and then, like our own in 1982, south towards Spitsbergen, included a long winter drift over the top of the world.

*

Back on the ice floe, we had been twelve days in the tent. Despite the continued white-out, the surface of the floe was becoming slushy. Signs of last year's melt pools, shiny green patches, were daily more in evidence as the actual snow cover decreased. Radiation from solar rays was gnawing at our precarious floating platform and eating it from under us. Wally Herbert wrote: 'There is no surface more unstable nor any desert more mistily lit than the Arctic ice pack in the month of May.'

On the night of 11 May, and without a sound, our floe unzipped five hundred yards to the east of our tent. This was not, as far as I could determine, along the seam of an old ridge or any other fault line. Initially the size of half a football field, our territory was now suddenly a third smaller than it had been the previous day. Bending over the new canal, I saw that our floe appeared to be some twenty feet deep, one-ninth of which, as I knew from my schooldays, was above the waterline.

Early in the morning, after three months without seeing a bird or an animal, a single faint cheep awoke me. Peeping out of the tent flap, and once my eyes were accustomed to the glare, I spotted a snow bunting, the size of a robin redbreast, perched on a ration box. Somehow I felt full of hope and optimism. The bunting soon departed into the damp mist, God knows to where.

On 17 May Ginny reported that the *Benjy B* was stuck firmly inside Longyearbyen fjord because of a wind change. This same roaring southerly pushed us back north towards the Pole and caused new fractures and a second major split right through the floe, which effectively halved our original 'safe' area. By the end of the month we were well behind my float schedule.

Each day I walked around the floe's perimeter. There were no signs of bears so I took only a pistol. Although I lost sight of the tent after a few yards, there was no chance of getting lost for I could always retrace my own prints, and anyway there was now open water all around our floe, in places up to forty yards wide, edged with huge upright slabs.

On 1 June Charlie plucked three grey hairs out of my mop. 'Poor old man,' he said. 'Getting past it.' I reminded him that he was a year older than me and that his bald patch had doubled in size since we left Greenwich. He checked his diary and discovered that this was the one-thousandth day of the expedition.

It seemed as though we had been on that floe for aeons, but strangely we weren't bored. A conversation about even the simplest matter seemed to take for ever. That evening I remember we had a fifteen-minute discussion about how and why the word for a bundle of sticks, faggots, had become an insulting term of reference to gay men. Charlie's face and hands were by now black with carbon deposits from the cooker fumes. Our beards were wild and tangled and our clothes ragged. But the sores of our earlier travels were mostly healed.

My diary of that time reads:

> Strong westerlies on 6 June and average temperatures of minus 3°C. Non-stop fog. Last night our floe was blown against its easterly neighbour. Where they met, a fifteen-foot high wall of ice fragments has reared up. It is thirty metres long, noisy and spews up new blocks as you watch. I am bailing out the water from the tent floor every other day now. Communications are awkward to Ginny: she has a blackout to England and to the ship, and the Danes cannot raise anyone. I get through to her only with Morse, and then only on 9002 megahertz on the brief up-surges of that frequency.
>
> We have been on the floe fifty days and nights, but not a bear yet. On my evening walks it is too wet now to use snowshoes, so I wear waders and take ski sticks for balance ...
>
> Ginny says that David Mason's brother was on board the Royal Navy ship *Sir Galahad* in the Falkland Islands war last week when it was bombed and set on fire. Many of the crew were killed or mutilated in the resulting furnace, but Mason junior escaped unhurt.

One thing was certain: sooner or later polar bears would find us, for their sense of smell was legendary. Eskimos say that they can smell a seal from twenty miles away. We had with us Canadian and Norwegian pamphlets which told us about the polar bear, stressing its great size and weight. Large males could weigh over half a ton, be 8 feet long and tower to 12 feet tall when erect. Yet for all their size, they could glide over the ice with fluid grace and thunder along at 35 m.p.h. They were said to be able to kill a 500-pound seal with a single blow of the paw, and might attack a man, if they felt threatened or were hungry, with supple leaps.

In 1977 a group of Austrians with children camped at Magdalene fjord in Svalbard. A polar bear wandered into the camp and snuffled at a tent. The man inside unzipped the door flap and the bear seized him by the shoulder and dragged him down to the sea and on to an ice floe, where it slowly ate him in front of the other Austrians who did not possess firearms.

I was in my sleeping bag one evening when I heard snuffling sounds beside my head, which was up against the single canvas skin of the tent. The noise went away in a moment or two, but shortly afterwards and close to the gap between our tents, a ration box began to make scraping noises. Donning waders and jacket over my long johns and vest, I grabbed my camera and revolver and peeked with great care out of the door flap.

A large polar bear stepped out from behind the tent. Its front legs were across the guy ropes some three yards in front of us. It licked its lips and impressed me with the length of its long black tongue. The official warning notes came back to me: 'Do not allow polar bears to get close.' There was not much we could do about that. Without remembering to focus or adjust the shutter speed, I took a couple of photographs, hoping not to irritate the great beast with the clicks. The bear eyed us up and down for a while, then slowly walked away. Like a poodle that barks ferociously once a bulldog has left its immediate vicinity, I began to shout, 'Shove off,' at our visitor when it was well clear of the camp.

Next time we were not so lucky. Again, the bear moved about by the tent for a while before we were sure that we had another visitor, not just gusts of wind disturbing things. When we emerged, armed, the bear was very close. We shouted at it and I fired my revolver over its head. All this was studiously ignored. Charlie's .357 rifle was bolt-action and at the time he had only two bullets. I had plenty of ammunition, but my Ruger .44 magnum revolver had been ridiculed by some Canadians as inadequate for effectively stopping an aggressive bear, so I had little confidence in it.

For ten minutes the bear padded about us in a half-circle between our ration boxes, whilst we shouted abuse in three languages, clashed our pots together and sent revolver bullets past its ears. After fifteen minutes Charlie lay down on a sledge and took careful aim. I stood behind and to one side and fired off a parachute illuminating flare. The rocket blasted by Charlie's head and struck the snow in front of the bear, fizzing brilliantly. This was also ignored, and the bear crouched down in the snow facing us, waggling its rear end slightly in the manner of a cat stalking a mouse. It began to approach us.

'If it comes within thirty yards over that snow dip, I'll fire one shot at it,' I whispered to Charlie.

The bear, a beautiful-looking creature, continued to advance and I aimed the pistol at one of its front legs. The shot went low, through the foreleg and probably close to the paw. The bear stopped abruptly, as though stung by a bee, hesitated for a moment, and then moved off sideways and away. There was no sign of a limp, but splashes of blood marked its spoor. We followed it to the end of our floe, where it jumped into the sea and swam across to another floe.

Would it have been better to have killed the animal? A dead bear lying beside our camp, or even floating in a nearby lead, might attract other visitors. Or should I have left it alone? Exactly how close should one allow a bear to get? To my mind, no closer than you feel is the distance where, if it does charge, you can shoot it dead with your available firepower before it can reach you. A single raking scratch from the paw of even a dying bear is to be avoided at all costs, especially by individuals who cannot be evacuated by any means.

*

In 2011 in Svalbard, a good friend of mine, Spike Reid, was one of two leaders of a group of thirteen students, mostly in their late teens. He described how a polar bear attack happened as they camped on the edge of a glacier in Spitsbergen.

> It was early in the morning and we were collectively asleep. Our team was camped on the edge of the Von Post Glacier. It was the beginning of a great adventure, and we planned to hike unsupported high up across glaciers to a mountain for the rest of the expedition. We hadn't set a night watch as we thought it to be a low risk location. As part of our evening preparations and in order to stave off the risk of a polar bear attack, we had erected a perimeter defence around us. Somehow a polar bear got through our defences without firing the flares.
>
> Then it attacked. The first thing we knew was when my co-leader Andy and I heard shouting. We leapt from our sleeping bags and found that a starving bear had torn into the tent where Horatio Chapple and two other team members, Scott and Patrick, were sleeping. We left our tent through opposite flaps and I took the rifle. The first thing I saw was a huge polar bear, metres away. It was towering over a young man, who I later learned to be Horatio, a superb man and team member, who had been dragged from his tent.
>
> I quickly cocked the rifle, aimed carefully at the bear and squeezed the trigger. Nothing happened. The rifle didn't fire. I cocked it again and it spat the unfired round out. I repeated the attempt to shoot the bear, then tried repeatedly until the magazine was empty, but with no luck. Four bullets lay on the dusty ground by my feet, the bear was still attacking and I had not yet succeeded in shooting it. It turned then from Horatio towards me and charged. It threw me to the ground and I could not fight it off. It swiped me several times with its mighty paws and then bit hard into my head. I distinctly remember hearing loud cracking noises.
>
> Luckily, Andy, the other team leader, was there, and he saved my life. As the rifle lay close to both the bear and to me, and as

we had no other gun, he resorted to throwing rocks at the beast until it stopped attacking me. For all his labours, the bear then turned on him, viciously attacking his head and jaw.

Without mercy, the bear returned to Horatio's body. Quickly, it spotted Matt, another member of the team, who had grabbed the rifle and tried to get some more rounds into it in a valiant attempt to end this nightmare. The bear chased Matt around the tent, but he skilfully outwitted the animal. Four of the team slipped out of the back of their tents and started to escape from the camp and the attack. Others hid in their tents, for there was nothing they could do without a loaded rifle.

Patrick and Scott were keeping a low profile in the remains of their destroyed tent, but the bear found them there. It attacked Patrick in his sleeping bag, breaking his arm and hitting his face. With the huge animal less than a metre from him, Scott tried to escape. He ran with the bear close on his heels, and it attacked him, badly wounding his head and jaw.

Eventually I was able to get up after the attack. I reloaded the rifle swiftly with a round I recovered from the ground. Seeing me standing, the bear came towards me again. It charged and, just in time, I fired the rifle. I shot it in the head and it fell to the ground in the middle of the camp, a metre or two from me. The attack had ended at last, but with the terrible loss of a good young man.

The bear was dead and the team rallied to keep the injured members alive. The four of us had all suffered facial trauma, and I found out later that Andy and I were in a critical state. This meant that the team had no designated leaders. Rosie, one of the youngest in the team, took it upon herself, with Matt's help, to raise the alarm and get things in order.

Even though most members of the team were no older than seventeen, they were exceptional that morning. Andy and I would certainly have died without their care, and we are both forever indebted. Furthermore, I would not be alive without Andy's brave attempt to get the bear off me and away from the camp. None of this will ever be forgotten.

The loss of such a good team member in the attack will always be with me. Horatio aspired to be a doctor, and he would have made a great expedition medic. I don't think I will ever get over the loss of that wonderful young man.

We were evacuated very swiftly to Longyearbyen and then to Tromsø on mainland Norway where the closest hospital was – 1,000 km from the scene of the attack. The nightmare was finally over, but this is just the start of my story and in that hospital began a very long road to recovery.

As the weeks on our floe lengthened into months and as great cracks split across its surface, a goodly number of bears wandered across our floe, and eighteen came up close to our camp. Each one seemed to react differently to our scare tactics. Their visits kept us from being bored. So, too, did the shrinking nature of our floe. Any noise outside the tents had us listening intently. There were many false alarms. One night I awoke in a gale, and amongst the plethora of wind noises, I heard a rhythmic scuffling that I was certain must be a bear. It turned out to be merely the sound of my heartbeat against the canvas earflaps of my nightcap!

Based now at the isolated Nord Station, base of the Danish Sirius Patrol, high up the north-east coast of Greenland, Ginny was having great difficulty with communication, partly due to Soviet jamming and partly to the changing weather. She tried every trick in the book: frequency hopping, intricate tuning and antenna changing. Much of the interference was a speciality of the polar regions and in the auroral zone, not the normal mush that ham operators around the world have to deal with.

As in lower latitudes, radio waves passing through the polar ionosphere are distorted and the spoken message carried on them can become hopelessly garbled. By using CW (Morse) messages, we could still operate because they remain intelligible on a narrower bandwidth. But from time to time the polar ionosphere reflects noises which do not trouble lower latitudes and these noises often correlate with disturbances in the earth's magnetic field. The disturbances can result from strong outbursts in the sun's activities or ionospheric storms. The behaviour of the aurora and of cosmic rays can also lead to communication problems.

In the last week of June Ginny told us that the *Benjy B* had reached the southern rim of the pack ice. I took an altitude shot of the sun and confirmed that our floe had reached a point not far from the marginal ice zone, the ice pulverization area in Fram Strait. Two million square miles of the Arctic Ocean are covered by pack ice and one third of this load is disgorged every year through Fram Strait, which acts as a giant drainage plughole. In a week or two our already disintegrating floe would enter this bottleneck, where the speed of the surface currents increases by as much as 100 per cent and the fragmenting ice burden is rushed south at an incredible 30 kilometres per day. The *Arctic Pilot* warns ships about the specific dangers caused by the Fram Strait ice:

> The Greenland Sea pack ice is in general unnavigable. In the northern part the pack may be up to six and a half feet thick. As a result of pressure due to wind or current, the pack ice may be hummocked to a height of twenty-five, or even thirty, feet. Typical forms of damage to vessels by the ice are the breaking of propeller blades, rudders and steering gear, damage to stern and plating causing leaks in the forepart of the vessel and the crushing of the hull. Also due to ice pressure is the buckling of plating and the tearing out of rivets, causing seams to open and leak.

On 10 July, our seventieth day on the floe, my sunshot put us at 82°S, 408 miles from the pole.

At around that time, a complete chunk of some two acres across broke away from our south-east corner. Our next-door floe rose up and over one sector of ours, over a 40-yard front, and 80 per cent of our floe was covered in slush, which varied from 18 inches to 7 feet deep. Over the following week new ridge walls rose up daily with a good deal of noise where we struck against our neighbours.

Off our sea-side edges, the wind whipped up wavelets on the black water lakes where regattas of broken fragments sailed by before the wind. All around us the ice was bare of snow cover, so that weak seams now showed up clearly like varicose veins. Day after day there was no sign of the sun, and the low-hung sky reflected the dark blotches of great expanses of open water to the south and north of our floating raft.

There was no room after a while for a single large tent, so we pitched two small tents side by side. We could not stand up because the 'floors' of axed ice were uneven and daily became more sodden with snowmelt, which also made sitting down impractical. So we lay in our sleeping bags raised up on ration boxes to keep out the damp and the cold. We never washed as there was no point.

By the end of July our ship had twice turned back to Spitsbergen after vain attempts to penetrate the pack ice to our south.

Each day Charlie, trained three years before at the Scott Polar Research Institute, measured the snow depth of our floe as an average of ten separate probes well away from the nearest pressure ridge. Once the snow turned to slush and then to puddles of water on top of the overall ice floor, Charlie's probes told the depth of the puddles, which reached their deepest in late July and then drained partially away via brine drainage channels down to the sea. Charlie's logged records of the entire crossing were studied by Britain's top oceanographer Dr Peter Wadhams, who later explained the importance of such studies to me.

He told me that not much of the ocean's heat makes its way through ice cover and into the atmosphere, but when, especially in the short Arctic summer, the ice floes separate, a considerable heat exchange takes place between sea and atmosphere. As the ice cover diminishes, so an increasing majority of solar radiation incident on the ocean is absorbed into the water, which increases the heat in the whole ocean/atmosphere balance. Fairly small climate changes in polar regions could easily trigger major, possibly catastrophic, raising of ocean levels.

Often our floe would float free of all those surrounding it, save when a strong wind blew it briefly against another, causing much peripheral damage. At times I woke suddenly and listened intently. Was it a bear close by or a new upheaval around the floe? As an answer, more often than not came the plunging roar of many tons of ice breaking off our floe-rim, followed by echoes as miniature tidal waves broke against the far side of the leads.

The noise of the wind and the surf sound of the sea was now joined by a gurgle of drainage, for the melt pools had eaten away a network of sluices from pool to pool and finally off the floe into the sea. In the water all about us huge floating chunks jostled, and humpback whales, surfacing with much resonant splashing, swam back and forth, rather like dolphins except for their Moby Dick tails. Often they would snort like horses, and by night their unearthly music floated clear over the misty ice fields, sometimes like the eerie howl of wolves, at other times more like some soulful Mississippi dirge.

The diaries of whalers told of homesick men believing that their loved ones were trying to communicate some message, maybe the birth of a child or the death of a relative, when they heard the ghostly whale songs echo through the wooden hulls of their ships while lying in their hammocks. Scientists have recorded the song of a single whale lasting over eighteen hours.

Whaling in the Arctic, as elsewhere, quickly devastated the numbers of many species, but every now and again the whalers suffered too. In the Greenland Sea in 1777 one whaling fleet was trapped in ice and 26 boats were sunk. Including the crews of rescue ships who were also sunk, over three hundred men died that summer. Nonetheless, demand for whale extracts increased so that by the 1840s over a thousand ships, mostly American, plied the waves with ten thousand professional whalers.

Between 1800 and 1880 American records show a cull of 193,000 right whales, so named because they were easy to catch. They floated well when dead, and they yielded plenty of blubber oil and high-grade whalebone for corsets and skirt-hoops. Once right whales were extinct, sperm whales, whose heads contained a type of wax ideal for candle-making, became a favourite prey. Sperm whales could dive down to 1,000 metres and more to feed on deep-water squid, which they consumed in great quantity. One single sperm whale's gut, when opened, was found to contain over 18,000 squid beaks.

Another popular target was the bowhead whale, which grows up to 60 feet long and has blubber layers up to 2 feet thick. This blubber is more than just insulation, for it helps the whale to float. Despite the blubber layer, bowheads in the Arctic lose about 10,000 calories a day to the cold, so in order to acquire enough fat, a single whale will need a hundred tons of food a year just to stay warm and another hundred to live, move and breed.

Blue whales, the largest living mammals, need 4 tons of krill daily. In certain Antarctic waters krill (a Norwegian word for whale food) mass in giant swarms estimated at up to 2½ million tons, and because they swim body to body and synchronized like Chinese infantry this makes feeding easy for the whales.

Sadly, there are very few big blues left in today's oceans. In the 1930–1 season alone, 31,000 were slaughtered.

Whales have to breathe air, so survival under ice is a risky business, even though they can manage to swim over a mile, if they have to, between surfacings.

Our floe passed over the favourite latitude of two specialist Arctic whale species – the unicorn whale, or narwhal, and the small white beluga whale, both of which rely on frequent open leads in the pack for breathing.

Although we never saw one, there were also ringed seals that live all over the Arctic, and even at the Pole in winter. To survive the cold, in addition to their blubber, they are armed with a coat of super-warm fur. Sea otters, also numerous in far northern waters, have no blubber but are compensated by having a jacket of hair which is thicker than that of any other animal in the world.

As the weeks and months on our ever-smaller floe rushed by, we grew increasingly apprehensive, for in the last days of July the melt pools all around us and the floor slush in the tents began to freeze. The sun hovered imperceptibly lower each day.

The problem was obvious. The ship had already tried twice to smash a way north to reach us whilst the sea ice was still summer-loose. Both attempts had failed and the members of our committee in London were extremely worried. They had to answer the frequent media and sponsors' queries as to what would happen if we were still on the floe when winter made it impossible for any ship or aircraft to reach us. Not only would the two of us stand a high risk of drowning, but ten years of huge effort, planning, sponsorship and hard unpaid work by all involved would end in failure at the very last obstacle.

The committee grew daily more nervous and their state of mind was not improved when, on the ship's second foray, ice cracked a major weld in the stern of the ship's hull. Our captain at the time, also a member of our ship committee, was Tom Woodfield, a veteran skipper of British Antarctic Survey ships. In the words of Anton Bowring, 'Tom is at the controls and hurling the ship at six to seven feet thick floes ... but the ice is more solid and further to the south than on our last attempt.'

At about this time, two of our main sponsors flew over Fram Strait and, back in London, they warned the committee that, to put it mildly, things were looking bad. They counselled an attempt by Karl to land the Twin Otter immediately, to evacuate us whilst our floe was perhaps still sufficiently long and unfractured. Ginny, therefore, received a message to arrange the evacuation, but her communications had problems just then and by the time she felt able to pass the message on to me, our floe was definitely unsuitable for any ski plane to land on.

Anton and all the ship's crew supported a third bid to reach us. Tom Woodfield, back in London, advised the committee that such an attempt must wait for prevailing winds hopefully to loosen the pack ice. Skipper Les Davis was now at the helm.

On 27 July a bear reached our tent without our hearing a thing. A powerful wind had blown up and the roar of the surf drowned all sound but the crash of ice segments breaking from our floe-rim. All night on 28 July I slept little, listening to the rumbling explosions from the sea – as though elephants were belly-flopping off skyscrapers. Our floe was daily decreasing in size.

On 29 July Charlie warned me that the bare seams in the floe between our lavatory shelter and the tents were widening, as were those between his tent and the nearest part of the melt lake. We had now been on the floe for 95 days and our entry into the fracture zone was imminent. Les decided to sail at once to the edge of the pack and, at the first sign of it loosening up, to fight north towards us. So, on the first day of August, our seventh month on the sea ice, the *Benjy B* slipped into the low mist. Shortly beforehand Ginny, certain at last that she could communicate with our floe from the ship or from Longyearbyen, had left Nord Station and the kindly Danes. Now she too was on board.

Late in the evening of 1 August, I heard Anton speaking intermittently to Simon. The ship was 49 miles from our last reported position and was moving slowly through medium pack and thick fog. Progress between the larger floes was hampered by wedges of ice small enough to be pushed under the bows but too tough to break. They had to be nudged aside and swept past by the draw of water from the propeller, a frustrating business that took considerable skill from the bridge. In fits and starts, with many detours, the *Benjy B* moved through an ever-changing and ill-lit icescape, occasionally startling seals and bears and minke whales and gradually gnawing away at the edges of the floes that barred her progress. 'The shuddering and grinding of the hull,' wrote Anton, 'is a constant accompaniment; the lurch as we strike each new floe often throws us off our feet.'

Many of the crew spent long hours on deck in foul-weather gear peering into the gloom and clinging to the rails. A cautious and expectant mood of optimism slowly surfaced. Late on the afternoon of 2 August, the fog rolled away from the *Benjy B* and Karl took off from Longyearbyen at once. After circling for a while, he began to talk Les Davis through the labyrinth of broken floes and, with great skill, guided the ship to a jagged 12-mile lead heading north-west towards our floe.

At that time the crew noticed ominous signs of a wind change and, within the hour, a southerly breeze had picked up. Any stronger and the pack would begin to close about the ship, which was now deep inside the marginal ice zone, too deep to escape if the floes concertinaed. Throughout that long night the whole crew willed the ship north, yard by yard, and despite much battering and many a retreat, the *Benjy B* squeezed through.

At 9 a.m. on 3 August I made contact with Ginny. She sounded tired but excited, and said, 'We are seventeen miles south of your last reported position and jammed solid.'

I shouted the news to Charlie. We must be ready to leave by canoe as soon as possible. Both of us hoped that somehow the *Benjy B* would smash a way through right up to us. For us, even half a mile of travel from our floe might prove disastrous, for everything was in motion about us. Great floating blocks colliding in the channels and belts of porridge ice marauding the open sea lanes. At noon I shot the sun and sent our position to Anton: 80°43.8′N, 01°00′W. The ship was to our south-east. To reach it we must move over the sodden surface of the racing pack for some twelve nautical miles and cross the Greenwich Meridian en route.

At 2 p.m. on our 99th day adrift, we stowed 300 pounds of gear, rations and our glaciological records into the two aluminium canoes and trudged away from our bedraggled camp. I had a compass bearing to the ship at the time we set out: the longer we took to reach her the more this would alter. The wind was a stiff 12 knots as we paddled across the first choppy lead.

The wooden ski attachments for hauling the heavily laden canoes over floes broke off within the first hour. After that we simply dragged the naked hulls over the rough ice and prayed that they would not wear through. As we arrived at each successive pool, river or lake, we lowered the canoes off the crumbling ice banks with care. We had lain in our sleeping bags with scant exercise for so long that the strain of the haul was considerable. Charlie was nearly sick with the effort. Every so often I filled my water bottle from a melt pool and we both drank deep.

At one stage a swamp of porridge ice and floating fragments barred our way. Once into it, we were committed. That hour we progressed only 400 yards. But normally, spotting such marsh zones well ahead by clambering up the high ridges, we took long circuitous detours to avoid their hazards. Melt pools several feet deep were no problem. We simply waded through them hauling on our two ropes. Trying to negotiate a spinning mass of ice islands in a wide lake, I looked back to check that Charlie was following, just in time to see two high blocks crunch together. The impact sent a surge of water after my canoe. Fortunately Charlie had not yet entered the moving corridor and so avoided being flattened.

Our hands and feet were wet and numb, but at 7 p.m., climbing a low ridge to scout ahead, I saw two matchsticks upon the broken horizon along the line of my bearing. I blinked and they were gone. Then I saw them again: the distant masts of the *Benjy B*.

I cannot describe the joy of that second. I found tears smarting at my eyes and I yelled aloud to Charlie. He was out of earshot, but I waved like a madman and he must have known. I think that was the single most wonderful and satisfying moment of my life. Until then I could never bring myself to accept that success was within our grasp. But now I knew, and I felt the strength of ten men in my veins. I knelt down on that little ridge and thanked God.

For three hours we heaved and tugged, paddled and sweated. Sometimes we lost sight of her briefly, but always, when again we saw her, she was a little bit bigger. Shortly before midnight on 3 August, Kiwi engineer Jimmy Young, up in the crow's nest with binoculars, shouted down to the bridge, 'I see them! I see them!'

On the bridge, gazing into the low wan sun, one by one the crew identified amongst the heaving mass of whiteness the two dark figures that they had dropped off so long ago at the mouth of the Yukon River on the far side of the Arctic Ocean. Down below decks First Officer John Parsloe, another Kiwi, was just turning in to his bunk when Terry, the bosun, rushed down the gangway shouting, 'Up! Up! The boys are home.' At 0014 hours on 4 August at 80°31′N 00°59′W, we climbed on board.

Each one of us retained the image of that moment on our ship amongst the floes. We would never forget. At that moment we shared something no one could take from us, a warm sense of comradeship between us all: Swiss and American, Indian and South African, British, Irish and New Zealander.

Ginny was standing by a cargo hatch. Between us we had spent twenty years of our lives to reach this point. I watched her small, tired face beginning to relax. She smiled and I knew what she was thinking. Our impossible dream was over. The circle was complete.

Chapter Eleven

> The Arctic trails have their secret tales
> That would make your blood run cold
>
> ROBERT SERVICE, *FROM* 'THE CREMATION OF SAM McGEE' (1907)

As the less comfortable memories of the Transglobe Expedition faded, I found myself thinking of new polar challenges which wouldn't take Ginny and me seven years to organize.

We tried to make a living from lecturing to corporate conferences, but times were hard until, in 1984, one of the chief sponsors of the Transglobe Expedition, Dr Armand Hammer, the founder and boss of Occidental Oil, phoned me at 2 a.m. one night from his HQ in Los Angeles. He offered me a job as his personal gofer (American for general lackey) in Europe, and I accepted with alacrity. Part of the deal was that I should stay self-employed and could take up to three months' unpaid leave each year if expedition work came up. Dr Hammer, one-time friend of Lenin, was eighty-seven years old at the time and I stayed with him for eight years until he died and his successor sacked me.

With spare money for the first time in our lives, Ginny and I bought an abandoned farmhouse with no electricity or other facilities in the middle of the Exmoor National Park. A narrow, half-mile-long bridleway was the only access route, known as the

Drift Road because, as we discovered during our first winter there, snow on the lane drifted up to eight feet high between its banks. At such times, Ginny would get to the village shop, a mile or so away, using a small sledge and with help up the hill from Tugaluk. Bothie was no help at all. He just yapped.

I made a basic living by giving corporate lectures at conferences, many of them abroad, and I tried to keep fit by jogging in various, often weird, locations.

In Canada I was hit on the nose by a hailstone, although the weather was not especially cold at the time. I had never seen any hailstones bigger than standard Sussex ones and I was shocked by the size of the stones that day in Alberta. I cowered for some minutes under a bush until the brief storm had passed.

I later discovered that an individual stone has been measured at 8 inches in diameter and 1.93 pounds in weight. This one fell in Dakota. During one storm at an airbase in Kandahar, three Afghans were killed by hailstones and millions of dollars-worth of damage was caused to RAF Tornado jets, helicopters and drones. A hailstone cracked a cockpit window in 1977 in Georgia, causing a forced landing on a road and 68 deaths. And a hailstorm in Ottery St Mary in Devon caused six-foot drifts that buried cars and blocked drains and there was subsequent flooding caused by melting ice.

Looking into the mechanisms of hailstorms, which I have never experienced in the polar regions, I found that they have little to do with the ground temperature. Hail begins as water droplets in thunderstorm clouds where much of the cloud is below freezing and there are strong updraughts. These blow the frozen droplets, at speeds of up to 110 m.p.h., high into the parent storm cloud, where they increase in size until their weight overcomes the updraught and they drop to the ground.

In addition to jogging between lectures, I worked for Dr Hammer and helped Ginny slowly build up a herd of pedigree Aberdeen Angus cows on Exmoor. This often involved walking her best bull around arenas at agricultural shows wearing a long white coat, tweed cap and Aberdeen Angus Society tie.

No expeditions were planned until, one day, Ollie Shepard, still married to the lady whose threats of divorce had taken him away from Transglobe, phoned us with the proposal that we walk or ski to the North Pole without outside support. Sooner or later, Ollie said, somebody would do this and, knowing how best to goad me, he added that the somebody was likely to be Norwegian.

I had been trying to quash my intermittent inner urges to 'go polar' once more because I was past the age at which Ginny and I felt such trips were suitable. We had been concentrating on preparing an archaeological search journey in the Omani desert. I surrendered to what the North Pole claimant Dr Frederick Cook once called 'the voice of the Arctic, the taste for the icy response of the polar sea. Something keeps calling, calling, until you can stand it no more and return, spell-drawn by the magic of the North.'

In the winter of 1985 Ginny flew on a scientific mission which landed briefly at the northern tip of Ward Hunt Island, a few miles from where Charlie and I had set out to cross the Arctic Ocean in 1982. There she visited the skeletal steel ribs of a deserted hut once used during the brief polar summers by Canadian scientists. Its canvas walls had long since been ripped away by the wind, so she measured its dimensions and, back home, ordered up a tailor-made canvas cover with ground ties – a great deal simpler than the four bespoke cardboard houses she had designed and in which we had lived through the Antarctic winter of 1979–80.

British Aerospace designed our sledges in the shape of legless bathtubs, so that they could 'swim' if necessary. Made of light Kevlar, their dimensions were fixed initially by the simple process of wrapping up 90 days-worth of cooker fuel and rations in chicken wire shaped like a long sausage. Ginny set up a radio base at our Exmoor home, running it off the Lister generator which was, at that time, our only source of domestic electricity.

Ollie and I had agreed, from our many shared years of polar experience, that we would be better off keeping the pole attempt to just the two of us. A third, younger, stronger individual would be nice, but we knew of nobody that we could trust and who fitted the job other than Charlie, and he was by then employed by a security business. So Ollie and I agreed to go it alone and by manhaul.

One problem caused by the extreme nature of Arctic hazards is the narrowing of choice when looking for suitable travel companions. I received many letters from aspiring polar explorers, but the risks involved in taking an unknown quantity to the Arctic Ocean were too great to even consider. So, wherever possible, I took only those who had a known history of survival on polar journeys in winter. This was, in principle, unfair on young hopefuls, for it caused a chicken-and-egg situation where those needing polar experience would find it difficult to make the break.

To manhaul over polar pack ice involves many hours of great exertion, often dragging more than 300 pounds deadweight. You sweat like pigs, despite outside temperatures of around −50°C. When you stop for breath, the sweat turns to ice in your underwear. Little people, however bold in outlook and determined of spirit, are simply not built to manoeuvre heavy weights. So you need men, not women, of hefty stature and with good pulling power; carthorses not fine racers.

On our flight to the north we were grounded by bad weather in Eureka, a remote weather station on Ellesmere Island. Also stranded there was Will Steger, a well-known American explorer who, like Wally Herbert, specialized in dog-sledging.

He asked me about Antarctica and we studied my old Transglobe map of that continent. He was keen on a route that ran down the very longest axis of Antarctica and he intended to use dogs. At the time that we met he was bound for a point some twenty miles west of Ward Hunt Island from where his team of 8 men and 50 dogs were about to set out for the pole. I wished him luck, both North and South.

On reaching our Ward Hunt base we fixed Ginny's bespoke canvas cover over the old skeletal framework, producing a cosy weatherproof camp in an hour. We then set up scientific recording gear, sledged through the darkness to measure ablation on a floating island of ice and carried out exhaustive tests of prototype sledging gear in temperatures below −50°C over fields of fissured ice blocks up to twenty feet in height. On a number of occasions we became separated many miles from our base, and twice I feared for Ollie's life when he failed to return to Ward Hunt Island during long and fierce blizzards that came without warning.

So long as we held a demonstrable chance of being the first to reach the North Pole without support, I could be confident of finding a sponsor, but neither Ollie nor I were happy with our winter trials. The sledges, when laden with enough food and fuel for ninety days' travel, weighed 460 pounds each. Our progress rate with these loads was one mile in three hours, which meant that we would never reach the Pole, 425 nautical miles to the north, in ninety days. So we played with mathematics. Could the journey be done in forty-five days, giving us less horrendous loads, but in only half the time? There seemed no obvious answer.

In mid-November we packed up the base, making it snowproof by applying heated cloth-tape to even the tiniest of holes in the canvas walls and sealing the chimney and vents. Then we placed tins of kerosene-soaked rags at intervals along the plateau to the east of our hut, ready to provide an illuminated runway. Karl Z'berg, the Transglobe Arctic pilot, managed the hazardous, ill-lit landing, and three days later we were back in London.

There followed three months in which to modify our sledges and equipment in response to the lessons we had learnt at Ward Hunt. We must be back there by first sun-up on 3 March 1986.

The smallest points had to be covered. For example, on the Transglobe journey Ollie, Charlie and I had, north and south, carried a large pyramid tent when using skidoos, but we now needed to change to a much lighter model for manhaul travel. The type of two-man geodesic tent that we chose was erected by inserting four 10-foot-long jointed alloy poles into the tent's four tubular sleeves. At temperatures below about −30°C the long elastics inside the jointed poles lost all their elasticity, which made it extremely difficult to join any pole up into its full length. So we made up 10-foot-long carrier tubes for the four poles, plus a spare, so that they could survive rough sledge journeys without ever being disjointed. This was an apparently unimportant detail, but, in fact, a key part of our kit preparations.

The time passed as a blur, for I had a backlog of Occidental work for Dr Hammer and wanted to spend as much time as possible on Exmoor with Ginny. The farmhouse was almost a mile from the next neighbour. The winter months had been lonely, sometimes frightening, for Ginny. There had been disturbances in the night, and only the company of Bothie, Tugaluk and her puppies had kept Ginny from going back to London. For weeks cold weather had cut her off without access to the nearest village road, without electricity when the ancient generator refused to start, and often without water, except from the stream, when the pipes froze.

We arrived back at Ward Hunt Island late in February 1986, together with Laurence Howell, a member of the Transglobal team and his wife Morag. A few days later a Twin Otter brought in the French manhauler Jean-Louis Etienne. We agreed to show him the best route through the chaotic pack ice that forms a high wall just north of the Ward Hunt Ice Shelf. Although this is in continuous motion and sometimes gives way to many miles of open sea, there had been little change since our trials there the previous winter and we soon found the best passage through the tortuous fields of ice. We shook hands with the diminutive doctor and watched him disappear into the moonlit icescape. Not long after, his Argos rescue beacon stopped working and he came back to our hut where Laurence managed to repair the unit. In the few days of his initial foray to the north, Jean-Louis's sleeping bag had increased in weight, due to frozen body moisture, from 12 pounds to 28 pounds. We thawed it out on a line in the hut, and I remembered that, in 1902, Scott's man Cherry-Garrard's sleeping bag weighed 18 pounds at the start of his six-week winter journey and 45 pounds at the end.

'I wish we had sledges like his,' Ollie commented, as we again waved Jean-Louis off. The French sledge weighed 12 pounds and its load 80 pounds. Our own 450-pound loads included 70 pounds of bare sledge. Jean-Louis would be resupplied by air every eighth day and his sledge would be replaced whenever it was damaged, so he could afford to travel light. He happened to meet up with Will Steger's dog teams on the way to the Pole, and the two men, unlike many rival pole-seekers, hit it off so well that they later joined forces on a great transantarctica dog journey along the route that Will and I had discussed back in Eureka.

As the Steger dogs and Jean-Louis slowly battled their separate ways north, each vital day after sun-up found us still floundering about the ice shelf in fruitless experiments with our giant loads. Even the superior design of our new sledges did little to improve our snail-like performance. We pared down equipment to a bare minimum, even shaving the Teflon runners with Stanley knives. All to no avail. The blow came by radio in late March. Ollie Shepard received an ultimatum from his London employers, Beefeater Gin. Either he returned within four weeks or he lost his job. With a wife and a home to look after, the latter course was no option. So, with great reluctance, he signalled for a Twin Otter to come north by the end of the month.

Back home Ginny set about finding a replacement for Ollie. Since she had no time to go through a selection process for a suitable character with manhauling ability, she had to find someone with an existing proven polar record. Dr Mike Stroud was one of only four Britons at that time who fitted the bill, having recently returned from an epic South Pole manhaul expedition. Mike responded to Ginny's call, obtained leave from Guy's Hospital and arrived at Ward Hunt Island four days later. That was the beginning of a quarter of a century working together on polar and other projects.

A few days later the outline of Ward Hunt Island gradually disappeared behind us. Travel through polar pack ice is not merely a matter of brawn and the correct equipment. The greatest bonus is experience, which brings an awareness of the ever-changing ice conditions, where to avoid, where easy corridors might best be sought, how to detect zones of open water before reaching them, what colour and thickness of wet ice can safely be crossed even though it screeches and bends at every step. Such knowledge can save hours, even days, and it is the greatest single factor in the success or otherwise of any expedition, save only for the matter of luck.

Each of us towed a load of 380 pounds. Since our expedition was, above all else, unsupported, to request any aid at all was to admit failure. At the time, no man had reached the North Pole without support, and the world record stood at 98 nautical miles following the near-fatal journey of the Simpsons and Roger Tufft in 1968. Subsequent attempts, such as those of David Hempleman-Adams and Clive Johnson in the 1980s, had ended in failure and frostbite less than fifty miles from the Arctic ice-pack.

An exact physical parallel of the task involved would be to drag two heavy six-foot-tall men, tied together, through sand dunes for 425 nautical miles. The terrain includes some two thousand walls of ice rubble up to twenty-five feet high, regions of rotten ice that break up and overturn as you try to negotiate them with your hefty sledge, and zones of open water, sometimes as far as the eye can see, which are often laden with treacherous shuga ice of porridge-like consistency. Add to these obstacles a temperature that is often lower than a deep freeze and a northerly wind that cuts into exposed skin like a bayonet, and it was no wonder that, despite intense international competition, the challenge had yet to be met.

Mike and I met nobody on our journey, and although we achieved a northerly record for unsupported manhaul travel, we came to an abrupt halt due to an error that I made early on. This is best described in Mike's words:

> On just the third day out of Canada, descending from a pressure ridge, Ran's sledge had broken through thin ice and taken him in with it. He had disappeared for a few seconds, and I thought I had lost him, but then he had popped up and struggled out, shivering as he shook the water off.
>
> It was at that moment that I saw his toughness for myself. He made no comment about falling through, or about being cold. He just said, 'Let's get out of here. We need to find a place to camp and wring out my clothing.' It had been unsafe to stop where we

were; the ice was too thin and unstable, moving, cracking and grinding. There was no possibility of stopping immediately and it was over forty minutes before we came to a safe floe.

By the time we had put up shelter, lit the stove, and were ready to remove his boots, they were frozen on. We had needed to set about them with a knife, and inside there were chalky-white areas to confirm our fears. His foot was badly frostbitten. Even then Ran had no thought of pulling out. He had just asked me to treat it as best I could.

The little toe on his right foot, and the area of skin adjacent to it, had been deeply frozen, and a couple of weeks later part of the toe had come off in his sock. By that time, we had used up most of our antibiotics in an attempt to prevent infection, and with only a few days' supplies left, we had been forced to call for our aircraft. It turned out to be the right decision. On the day of the pick-up, his whole foot became a cellulitic mess.

Back in Britain, a 3-inch-square skin patch was cut away from my thigh and grafted on to the damaged area of the missing chunk of toe and foot.

Some months earlier Canadian magazine *Maclean's* had stated that none of my polar expeditions had 'scientific value'. So we opened a libel case against them, since such a statement was likely to harm our chances of future sponsorship. Both Sir Vivian Fuchs and Mike Stroud appeared as witnesses and gave evidence of their past involvement in our scientific research programmes. The jury of twelve, after the two-day hearing, unanimously awarded us £100,000 and a full apology. *Maclean's* appealed, and the award was reduced to £10,000, but that was a fortune to us and they had to pay all the very considerable court costs.

In 1988, with top radio operators Laurence and Morag Howell based on Ward Hunt Island, we made a second unsupported attempt on the North Pole, but were met with a terrible year for huge ridges, wide open water leads and successive storms with high winds that smashed up floe against floe. Facing facts and eager not to spend our sponsors' money on a no-hoper, we made a third attempt in 1989, and when that fell short of our 1986 record, we agreed to attack the North Pole from the other side of the world.

Gorbachev had recently announced glasnost, so I took advantage of the Soviet Union's newly welcoming attitude to Westerners and wrote to ask if I could lead the first non-Soviet polar expedition from Siberia. I located a famous Russian polar explorer, Dr Dmitry Shparo, Hero of the Soviet Union and holder of the Order of Lenin, and he kindly agreed to organize all aspects of a polar journey from Cape Arkticheskiy on the Siberian coast in the spring of 1990. He warned me that one Colonel Vladimir Chukov of the Soviet Special Forces was about to try the same journey with an eight-man army team.

Dmitry proved to be a highly efficient organizer and he knew his way through the complex web of Soviet permits. I once spent eight hours with him at Moscow's Sheremetyevo Airport just to get one .44 magnum revolver into Russia. He had led some amazing expeditions including, back in 1979, the first journey from Eurasia to the North Pole. His team had used manhaul and skis with minimal air support.

Mike and I trained extremely hard in the summer of 1989. By then Mike was head of Army Personnel Research at the Royal Aircraft Establishment in Farnborough. In an experimental chamber in the RAF Institute of Aviation Medicine we underwent various body analysis tests. Our bodies both proved to be remarkably resistant to cooling. A two-hour immersion in a cool tank designed to lower the core temperature of most men of normal build produced a report that my 'resistance was extreme with core temperature actually *rising* slightly during the course of the immersion.'

In the spring of 1990 Morag and Laurence Howell, our radio communications team, joined Dmitry, Mike and me on a Soviet Air Force flight from Moscow to the Siberian mining towns of Vorkuta and Norilsk.

The winter in Norilsk lasts eight months, with extreme low temperatures and months of 24-hour darkness. Joseph Stalin used the place as part of his Siberian web of gulag prisons in the 1930s and, on his death in the 1950s, it became a secretive and key part of the Soviet Union's great military-industrial complex producing precious metals. Today, it is Russia's biggest single source of industrial pollution. The ground is so rich in nickel that it provides 20 per cent of global production, along with 3 per cent of global copper, 10 per cent of global cobalt, 17 per cent of global platinum and 46 per cent of global palladium. Also produced in key amounts are iridium, ruthenium and gold.

From Norilsk we flew on north to Sredniy in the Sedov district, where we stayed in a scientific camp with eighty or ninety contractors. This was a highly classified part of the then USSR where only a year earlier, before Gorbachev's advances towards democracy, we would never have been allowed. The station was the Soviet equivalent of a Distant Early Warning (DEW) base in Canada.

Two heavy lorries drove us for three hours along a snow track to the remote station of Golomiany. One of the six inmates, whilst checking a generator outside, had recently been killed and partially eaten by a bear, and the cook at the base showed us photographs of the poor man's mauled body lying in the snow outside the main hut. The camp huskies had subsequently frightened the bear away, but one still had a long livid scar along her back, inflicted during her brave fight to ward off the bear.

None of the five remaining staff spoke English, but they explained through our interpreter that we were to be their guests that night at a dinner they wished to hold for us, for we were the very first foreigners to visit Golomiany 'since the days of the Czar'. Two days later an ex-Afghan gunship helicopter flew us a hundred miles to Cape Arkticheskiy, the most northern point of land in Novaya Zemlya.

We flew over vast areas of tundra and boreal forest. This was, however, no pristine wilderness. The Kola Peninsula in the Murmansk region has a population nearly twice that of Alaska and almost a quarter of all the inhabitants of the Arctic.

Industry and resultant pollution are on a grand scale. Under the

Czars and their Marxist successors elaborate gulag systems were introduced and these provided free labour for mining the rich minerals of the region. Long-distance pipelines, tundra roads and summer seaports were constructed in the most remote places.

From early days the Soviet authorities saw the Arctic Ocean to their north as their territory and a potential source of great wealth, as was already the case with the land just south of the coast, where the smelting of copper, nickel and cobalt was carried out. These ores are rich in sulphur, and most of the smelter plants do not scrub the sulphur dioxide from the resulting emissions. Just three smelters on the Kola Peninsula emit some 220,000 tons of sulphur into the atmosphere annually, and the plant in Norilsk, where we landed to refuel, emits over 1 million tons each year, which is the largest single source of man-made sulphur dioxide in the world and responsible for over 1 per cent of total global emissions.

Man-made pollution from Norilsk and other industrial centres is adversely affecting the climate of the northern hemisphere. This pollution of air clarity is known as Arctic haze. When the Arctic air is clear, one can see up to 120 miles through the atmosphere. When the haze is heavy this distance is reduced to 18 miles or less. Pilots first noticed this in springtime despite good weather conditions. Add to this haze the many mining operations, the dumping of mining waste, oil spills and nuclear waste storage, and you get deep pollution of forests, vegetation and of the soil itself. Ecologists describe such damaged lands as 'technogenic barrens'.

Most of the friendly workers, miners and soldiers that we met whilst in Vorkuta, Norilsk and other isolated bases further north were proud of their work in the extreme climate of their Siberian motherland. Norilsk artists, we learned, hold ice-sculpting contests, drink at ice bars, get married in ice chapels, teach ice-sculpting to tourists, and were even talking about building an ice hotel, like ones already in existence in Quebec, Finland, Sweden and Norway. And they all love the fact that they hold the world record for climate extremes, with the village of Verkhoyansk having achieved a high of +37°C as well as a low of –68°C.

On the other side of the Soviet Union, far to the west, Russia's 'Mother Winter' has long been her most trusty defence against invaders, and Russians all know from their schooldays what happens to those who dare attack their homeland. Napoleon's all-conquering armies reached Moscow in triumph in 1812 but, on the arrival of winter, were soon in chaotic retreat. Like Hitler's soldiers a century later, they suffered frozen limbs and died in their hundreds of thousands leaving long trails of frozen corpses along the tundra way.

From Cape Arkticheskiy, after Dmitry and his chartered helicopter had waved us goodbye, we set our hand compass due north, loaded our rifle and started hauling our 300-pound amphibious sledges over the coastal ice-rubble belt. All along this Siberian coastline the prevailing current rushes its burden of ice at faster-than-walking pace in a generally easterly direction, only briefly halting when the ice gets jammed against some promontory. We had to find just such a transitory jamming point and use it to transfer from land out on to the moving sea ice, then hurry north to reach a lesser drift zone where the local current would head north to help us on our subsequent six-hundred-mile trip to the pole.

We were the first foreign expedition to take advantage of Gorbachev's perestroika and glasnost, but Soviet polar expeditions with the same unsupported aim as ours had recently attempted the journey. The great Italian mountaineer Reinhold Messner and his brother had bad luck when they made the key land-to-sea transition at Arkticheskiy and, threatened by polar bears, were swept away by a band of chaotic breaking floes. They were lucky and managed to escape by helicopter, but the same year an experienced French woman, Dominick Arduin, disappeared, presumed drowned, within days of leaving the coastline at Arkticheskiy.

I had problems with my hands soon after Mike and I set out and I was unable to keep a detailed diary, but from Mike's it was clear that the Russian route did not provide a panacea for northerly polar travel. I use extracts from Mike's notes to describe our experiences that summer, both in the tent and on the move.

While Ran searched for items by touch, I tried to complete my dressing with fingers that were blistered, raw and stiff. Frostbite numbs only when deep enough to kill the tissues. More superficial damage is exquisitely tender, and it is only with burning needles in the fingertips that one appreciates the force required to pull on thick socks . . .

I heard Ran cough impatiently. He had finished the packing and was waiting to take down the tent. By now the cold had seeped through his clothing, chilling his body core and hurting his hands and feet. I swept the hoar frost from walls and roof and joined him outside. We completed the preparations and were ready. I hated this place, I hated Ran, and I hated myself.

We tried to set off quickly in order to warm up, but we couldn't push chilled muscles. It wasn't just the cold that impaired them; we had eaten nowhere near enough to allow them to recover from the previous day's exertion. To operate fully, muscles require a rich supply of glucose from the store within them, and given our poor level of intake, this was depleted from the outset. As a result, glucose manufactured from other tissues of the body had to be drawn in through the blood and each day we were literally consuming ourselves. Our legs felt as if they had just completed a marathon.

We both began to accept that we would run out of food and fuel before we could make the pole. We had, by the end of April, broken all previous unsupported records by many miles. Some 89 miles from the North Pole, Mike recorded:

Although the realisation had been slow to dawn, we both knew that the end was imminent. We had been in decline for weeks and only the perseverance of the other kept us going. Staggering across the endless sea ice, driven by a desperation not to give up so close to our goal, we were the embodiment of frailty. I was weakened by 450 miles of wading through knee-deep snow, following the breakage of my ski binding in the first week, and Ran was in great pain from a deep blister, turned ulcer, that was eroding his heel. For a couple of weeks he had also been losing his vision and now he was nearly blind. He stumbled after my vague outline, cursing as he tripped over every unseen obstacle.

For the moment, however, all our problems were overshadowed by the pain in our near frozen fingers. This happened every morning as packing needed some dexterity. You simply couldn't do up straps wearing inner gloves and two pairs of mitts. Strangely, the fingers were now numb as well as painful. With sensation lost from the bloodless skin, the pain arose from joints and tendons within. Hands curled up inside the mitts felt totally alien, as if frozen sausages had been left in the glove. It would be half an hour before they thawed. Then they would burn fiercely as the blood returned, and new blisters would form where the tissues had turned to ice.

... We felt close, linked by a camaraderie that had grown through the hardships we had endured, a feeling of unified suffering and achievement.

Mike summarized our last day of travel:

Ran was shaking me by the shoulder. He said, 'Mike, unless the wind has changed, you are off course, it's blowing over my left shoulder.'

I checked the compass. Near South – entirely the wrong direction. Stupid of me, just losing concentration. But why couldn't I see properly and why were my legs like jelly?

'Shorry, I wassh dray deaming.'

The words were slurred and inarticulate. Ran knew what it meant. He put down his pack and started unpacking the tent. As he said later, it was like the drunk leading the blind and he realised that it was far too dangerous to go on. I had been hypoglycaemic again. Now was the time to call for removal with the satellite beacon.

We had carefully arranged for this eventuality, whether from the pole itself or en route. Morag and Laurence liaised with Dmitry, and the helicopter from a Soviet-manned ice-island base located our beacon and took us to their ice floe three hundred miles away. Soon after arrival there, I suffered a kidney stone attack in the tent where the Russians had quartered us. Mike plied me with painkillers and, a week later, we returned to Moscow where the Soviet Komsomol president gave us medals and Dmitry Shparo confirmed that we had made the longest and fastest unsupported journey in the Arctic to date.

Whilst awaiting our flight back to Britain, Mike and I were both surprised to find that neither of us could see very clearly, nor could we focus on anything more than a few yards away. Mike later wrote:

> Back in Britain, the mystery was to be explained. It had been known for decades that, with nothing to look at, the eye will focus at about one metre in front of it, and this effect had been implicated in a number of aircraft accidents. Pilots looking out through the window into a cloudless sky become accommodated and focused on a point shortly in front of their face without realising that they can no longer see clearly at a distance. When another aircraft appears in front of them, they take no evasive action to avoid a mid-air collision.
>
> Of course, pilots turn and look round their cockpits every few moments and land at an airport within a few hours. We had spent weeks of travel looking at precisely nothing, and now our eyes had become so used to fixing on that near point that they had lost the ability to do much else. The muscles that controlled the focusing system had become weak with disuse and it would be a fortnight before we could see properly again. It was the first time that anything like it had been reported in the annals of ophthalmology, and my guess is that there won't be many similar reports in the future.

Not long after our return home, we learnt what rival North Polers had been up to on the North American side of the Arctic. A Canadian team had retired with frostbite from their attempt after two weeks. Separate Norwegian and Soviet attempts had both received air contact due to injury or death of team members en route, thus compromising their unsupported status. This the Soviet team had accepted with good grace. The Norwegians, however, had not. Their leader, Erling Kagge, disputed our record and claimed the ultimate unsupported North Pole challenge for his team.

Back in London, after a kidney stone operation, I joined Ginny on an archaeology expedition in Oman, and so had to turn down an invitation from the Royal Geographical Society (RGS) to confront the leader of the recent Norwegian polar expedition in front of a ticket-paying 700-strong audience. Mike agreed to represent us. He recorded the occasion:

> In Kagge's opinion, the injury and evacuation of the third member of their team was irrelevant ... I pointed out that Ran and I don't fully agree with this interpretation. Muttering and murmuring followed and, to my right, a small group jeered.
>
> The Royal Geographical Society was not used to dissension – at least, not since the days of Burton and Speke and their arguments over the source of the Nile. I flinched, but carried on ...
>
> 'Both Ran and I agree that they made a magnificent journey and, obviously, they honestly believe it was unsupported. However, we think that they have failed to appreciate that they did receive support.'
>
> More murmurings from the audience. There was one call of 'Must we listen to this?' But it was not the majority. Most people were quiet and listening intently. I got the impression that I was to be given a fair hearing.
>
> 'Erling and his two companions set off to walk to the North Pole, as we did, unsupported. But, after ten days, Geir was injured and had to be evacuated. This entailed Erling and Børge waiting four days for the plane to arrive and during that time they

admit that they consumed Geir's food rather than the supplies they carried themselves. As a result, they benefited in a number of different ways. Firstly, during the earliest, coldest and hardest part of the journey, a third man helped move the general equipment. Secondly, they effectively ate extra food and had a free rest. It may have been after only ten days, but that extra food went into their body stores which would have already been depleted. It helped them later and, in terms of resupply, was just as effective as putting food on their sledges . . .

'Thirdly . . . when they planned their expedition they planned for three men. The limiting factor on any of these trips is the weight one believes one can pull. Within that limit, one takes as many days' food and fuel as possible. Erling calculated this to be sixty-five days, but if he planned for two men in the first place, he would have taken less. When the third member of the team dropped out after ten days, Erling and Borge went on with fifty-five days of food. They considered that that was fair enough, but they were fooling themselves. When they reached the Pole with no food, they should have realised that without Geir's help they might never have got there. If we had had that much assistance, we might also have reached that goal.

'Finally, many of you will have heard of the Russian, Colonel Chukov. Last year, he and his men reached the pole, but a number of his party had been forced to drop out. He also claimed, at first, that his journey was unsupported, but when it was pointed out that – for similar reasons to those I have just expressed – he and his companions had received help, he withdrew his claim.

I paused. There was silence.

'Ladies and gentlemen, if a team climbed Everest without oxygen, except for just a little on the way, their claim would not be accepted. This Norwegian team may well have been successful if the third man had not been injured, but he was, and as a result they were even more unlucky than we were. They completed a magnificent journey, but not an unsupported one. I believe that they are sincere in their interpretation of their trip, but they are wrong. If they are not, Colonel Chukov made the first unsupported journey to the North Pole last year. Thank you.'

After the confrontation, Mike and Erling shook hands and had dinner with the RGS president. During the ensuing conversation, Kagge mentioned that he was planning an unsupported Antarctic crossing. At this point, Mike later wrote, 'I tried to keep my expression bland because Ran and I were already making plans for the same journey in 1992/93. The last thing I wanted was a race.'

One of Britain's great polar travellers and a dog-driving expert, a worthy successor to Wally Herbert, was Geoff Somers. He told Mike after the RGS event what he thought of Kagge's claim. 'He's talking rubbish. You don't even need logical arguments. Unsupported trips just don't involve visits from aircraft.' Another old friend and veteran polar expedition leader, Pen Hadow, wrote of the definition of 'unsupported':

> 'Without resupply' requires that you do not have any food or fuel or equipment brought in to you, but it leaves open the question of whether anything from video tapes and redundant equipment to injured or exhausted team members can be taken out by aircraft. Amateur polar travellers or adventurers don't necessarily appreciate or even care about such distinctions, but there is a serious point underlying them. If someone is seriously injured then obviously no one would argue against flying them out, but in my view the expedition cannot be considered unsupported unless the remaining team members return to the starting point and begin again.
>
> The reason is obvious; a team member may have suffered a genuine injury, but equally he might merely have fallen out with the team leader, or been used in the same way as a pacemaker in a long-distance race, or a Sherpa on Everest – someone to do the donkey work and then step aside to let others reach the goal. There is no way of proving that it wasn't the plan all along to lose that spare person once he's done his job of carrying your supplies

> for you. Taking it to its logical extreme, once the principle is breached, there is nothing to stop someone from using human mules to sledge-haul his supplies almost all the way to the Pole.

Over thirty years of cold expeditions have made me respect the rugged, dogged and practical abilities of our Norwegian rivals, such as Ragnar Thorseth in the 1970s, Erling Kagge in the 1990s and, subsequently Børge Ousland.

The great Norwegian leader of the pioneering Norwegian-British-Swedish Antarctic Expedition of the 1950s, John Giaever, wrote: 'It is a good rule for Norwegian diplomats in the realm of polar exploration to keep well away from British preserves. One may be quite sure that the British, for their part, will not meddle with the Norwegians.'

Our Antarctic expedition plan that Mike had alluded to was the brainchild of Charlie Burton and Ollie Shepard. I had received instructions to meet them in the map room of the Royal Geographical Society without delay when I came to London to have my kidney stone removed. I arrived to find both of them poring over a large Antarctic map (more aptly described as a sheet of white paper). A decade had passed since the three of us had completed the longest and first one-team-only crossing of the Antarctic continent. Now they were suggesting that we do it again, but without any form of outside support.

'Since neither dogs nor machines can make it,' I assured Charlie, 'humans on foot certainly can't. Amundsen proved that dogs out-perform humans trying to manhaul.'

'Rubbish!' Charlie shouted. 'Scott was absolutely right in favouring manpower to be the most efficient method, and we will prove it.'

Their idea was that I should organize and plan the trip with Ginny as base leader and radio operator. I agreed to their proposal on the condition that Mike could be the fourth member of our team. All went well for a while but, some months later, Charlie's health deteriorated and Ollie's business life became hectic, so they decided to handle the organizational side of the project.

Mike saw the plan as being worthwhile, not only as a chance at a major polar record but also, from his professional point of view, the opportunity for unique research in his own specialist medical field, studying the effects of different diets on physical performance and body composition. When his friends asked why on earth he should keep subjecting himself to physically unpleasant experiences, Mike would produce the well-worn dictum of Wally Herbert: 'Those who need to ask such a question will never understand the answer, while others who *feel* the answer will never need to ask.'

By the end of the expedition I would be just a year short of fifty, so it might be my last chance at a major cold challenge. And Mike, at 38, was not exactly a spring chicken, either.

Chapter Twelve

Chris Brasher, one of the team who first achieved the 4-minute mile and later founded the London Marathon, found me a sponsor for the Unsupported Antarctic Crossing Expedition in the form of The Pentland Group, who had recently sold Reebok to the Americans.

The period of the Antarctic summer during which we could hope to travel weather-wise across the frozen continent was a maximum of 108 days, and since the total distance from coast to coast was 1,700 miles, we would have to manhaul an average of 16 miles a day with no rest days.

Mike worked hard on designing field rations that would give us sufficient energy to pull all the food and cooker fuel involved. He agreed with Charlie Burton that Captain Scott, despite subsequent criticism, was correct in believing that manpower, not dog, pony or machine power, was by far the most efficient hauling method when measured as distance covered for weight of fuel carried. He observed:

> Everyone assumes that it is possible to go farther with dog teams or motorised vehicles pulling sledges full of fuel. They are quite mistaken. Dogs could never pull loads great enough to see them over anywhere near, for example, the distance from the coast to the Pole, unless you involve dog eating dog, as Amundsen did. Tracked vehicles, skidoos, whatever forms of motorised transport could never pull their own fuel so far. Only men dragging their

loads behind them could possess enough drive and determination to have any chance of success.

Mike designed our sledge rations at 5,500 calories each per day. This compared with Captain Scott's rations of 4,500 calories daily, and his surviving team members lost an average of only 20 pounds. Since a 15 per cent loss of body weight should not weaken a person's strength, Mike reckoned that this should suffice for our crossing.

We estimated that the traverse might be feasible if we could physically manage to manhaul a total weight of 485 pounds each. Captain Scott's team, after reaching the South Pole, hauled 190 pounds each. Their stronger ponies managed 580 pounds each, the weaker ones 400 pounds and the two dog teams 1,570 pounds between all twenty dogs. On their first sledge trip across the flat Ross Ice Shelf, Scott, Wilson and Shackleton each hauled 175 pounds, and in the 1990s the world's greatest mountaineer, Reinhold Messner from Italy, wrote of his Antarctic crossing attempt: 'Two hundred and sixty four pounds is a load for a horse, not a man.'

Our loads constituted by far the heaviest one-man sledge loads of any recorded expedition. Our main worry was not merely the sheer physical work, but also the heavy footprint the sledges would bring to bear on the thin snow crusts over crevasses. I weighed 98 kilograms and would be hauling 219 kilograms.

Much of the route we intended to follow to the South Pole was unknown, but then all human experience in Antarctica has been relatively recent. The coast of the continent was first seen only in 1820, the first landing was made within a year, and the first major penetration of the land mass was in 1908. The whole coastline was not charted until 1976, nor the outline of the land beneath the ice until 1980.

To reach the Atlantic coast of Antarctica we would first have to travel for some two hundred miles over the Filchner Ice Shelf, a floating ice sheet often badly crevassed. Whether we were to attempt to cross Antarctica including its attached floating ice shelves or merely the continental land mass was not a major distinction as far as either our sponsors or the media were concerned. The ice shelves alter annually in terms of their size as their seaward edges constantly fracture and float out to sea. To exist at all they require an annual mean air temperature of below –6°C and air temperatures where even the warmest month is sub-zero.

Since the days of our Transglobe Expedition, the Foreign Office Polar Regions Unit had softened their attitude to my intermittent requests for their permission. Their recent boss, Dr John Heap, later the director of the Scott Polar Research Institute, had even given his written approval of the scientific results of our past polar journeys. The polar desk was not alone in their reluctance to give approval to civilian expeditions in Antarctica. Every country with science bases on the continent had agreed on a set of rules that all would adhere to.

During the Second World War the Germans sent aircraft to drop steel swastikas on to prominent Antarctic features. Chile and Argentina in the early 1940s had sent forces to harass British bases on the Antarctic peninsula, and with the advent of the Cold War in 1948, the USA did all it could to exclude the USSR from any involvement in Antarctica. To this end, they proposed a cosy legislating condominium to consist of the eight countries having historical connections with the continent: themselves, Australia, Argentina, Chile, Great Britain, France, New Zealand and Norway. This, for various reasons, did not work out. Then, in 1950 the Soviet Union, citing the 'discovery' of Antarctica by their man von Bellingshausen in 1820, asserted that any future talks about shared Antarctic sovereignty must include them.

For a decade or so, at the height of the Cold War, discussions on the topic were heated and no generally acceptable way forward was found. The solution came in 1950 from an international grouping of scientists to whom the Poles were critical simply because the Earth's magnetic lines converged there. In order to determine Earth–Sun interactions, the pre-eminent geophysicist of the day,

Sydney Chapman, and other key physicists needed to measure solar activity in the ionosphere along magnetic lines that meet in the polar regions. So, on an ostensibly apolitical basis, an Antarctic Treaty was signed in 1959 which included the first multinational arms treaty to be agreed since the Second World War. This covered all land and ocean to the south of 60°S, some 10 per cent of the earth's surface. Importantly, the USA and USSR both agreed to make no territorial claims in this designated area.

There followed an indecent rush by many countries to at least achieve squatters rights and thus have a say in future Antarctic conferences by setting up a national base on the continent. By 1991 thirty-nine nations had built a base or bases, mostly on or near to the coastline. Even Greenpeace, keen to be a consultative member of the treaty, built a base (right next door to one of Captain Scott's old huts).

From Puntas Arenas near the tip of South America, Mike and I flew a thousand miles over Antarctica's great inland plateau to reach the start point of our traverse attempt, the northern edge of Berkner Island. That same day our erstwhile Norwegian 'rival', Erling Kagge, set out from further round the same coastline, but his plans involved a solo journey to the South Pole rather than a traverse of the entire continent. Although I failed to keep a precise diary, I have used excerpts from Mike's to describe what was, at the time, probably the coldest experience of my life.

After our ski plane had dropped us off, we loaded the sledges, adjusted the manhaul harnesses about our stomachs and shoulders, and I lent against the traces with my then 210-pound weight, but my near half-ton sledge did not budge. I spotted an 8-inch rut across the front of the runners and pulled again, this time with my left shoulder only. The sledge moved grudgingly forward. The thought of having to haul this massive load for another hour or another mile, never mind to the South Pole and beyond, was appalling.

In every direction there was nothing but mirage shimmer and the great white glare of Antarctica.

After five and a half hours it was time to halt, for we had been awake for 24 hours since leaving Punta Arenas. For navigation purposes, we had to keep to a carefully timed daily schedule. I intended to use my watch and body shadow to establish direction all the way to the Pole, and that meant keeping the sun due north at local midday. There were, I reasoned, only another 1,696 miles to cover, and since we had rations for a hundred days, there was yet time to find a way of increasing the daily average to 16 miles. There must be absolutely no rest days or we would fail. Mike wrote:

> Even straining to the maximum, neither of us could do more than creep forward very slowly, and despite all our training before departure, we couldn't sustain it. Every few hundred yards we would have to stop and rest, allowing our burning thigh muscles to clear the toxic substances that accumulate when over-worked. After four hours of struggling – sweating in a temperature of –20°C – we had managed to move only a couple of miles. By that time exhaustion had forced us to stop and make camp ...
>
> By the end of two weeks we had travelled about 150 miles. This was not at all bad for the start of an expedition with such heavy weights, but we were acutely aware that for overall success we would have to average some 17 miles per day. There would be a lot to make up. On Day 14 we reached the point at which we had no choice but to turn and head for the mainland. To travel any farther along the coast of the island would be to go too far west. I have to admit that the thought of casting out on to the open ice shelf frightened me.
>
> My fears were well founded. When we left Berkner Island behind, our route took us across what appeared to be a featureless flat white plain. Yet, as I led the way about fifty yards in front of Ran, there was a sudden muffled bang and ahead of me a plume of snow crystals rose into the air as if someone had triggered a small explosion. Then there came a long deep rumbling, felt as much as heard, and ten yards in front of me apparently solid ground began to open. Slowly, and then with increasing

momentum, a black zigzag crack split the white surface, widening as the edges fell in upon themselves. Within moments, it had become a ten yard wide deep fissure exactly where I would have walked and, as I watched, it steadily extended for about forty yards in either direction. For several seconds after it had appeared, I could still feel through my feet the rumbling of the huge ice blocks as they tumbled and dropped into the very heart of the shelf . . .

Where else around me did these hidden chasms lie? Which way would take us safely out of here? Although everywhere looked smooth, with no sign that the ground was hollow, similar chasms lay all around and no route was safe. As soon as I turned to head parallel to the newly opened rift, there was another muffled rumbling and another crack unzipped. This time it was back beyond Ran, in an area that we had both just crossed. Then there was another, and another, and our smooth plain became a heaving nightmare. We roped up, both now terrified. The ground was alive and blue gaping mouths opened before us, behind us, around us. On one occasion, as we made our way forward one step at a time, probing the snow with hard stabs of the ski sticks, a canyon appeared between us, and I turned to see my tracks fragmenting and crashing into a void spanned by our pathetically thin rope. These crevasses were so big that they could have taken us both at once, and all were invisible before they opened.

I couldn't understand why they were there. Crevasses normally occur where glacial ice flows over a convexity so that the surface is stressed and breaks. Here, out on the ice shelf, there seemed to be no good reason for them, although I guessed that there was some submarine cause, perhaps a rise in the sea floor hundreds of feet below us. But without any visible sign of their origin, we could take no obvious course to get away from them, and all we could do was doggedly press on, heading south and praying that the disruption was localised. Fortunately it was. After two hours – beyond doubt the most frightening of our lives – the cracking came to an end and slowly our fears began to settle as we set out across a now quiet flat white plain, following a compass bearing for landfall.

Neither of us had previous experience of using wind-powered equipment such as kites or parasails, but we had been given two parachutes and had spent an hour in South America listening to a USA polar team explaining the theory of wind support when manhauling. Our first attempts were disastrous, often creating, in Mike's words, 'a tangled disaster of strings, sledge and ski bindings plus a risk of frostbite as we tried to undo the mess with thinly gloved or bare hands.'

> ... On one occasion I had seen Ran, just ahead of me, fall to the left of a long open crack. Further to the left, the ground looked quite firm, and so I had steered that way and carried on. What I failed to realise was that he had not fallen over by chance. Hidden by a rise, the crevasse actually extended to either side of him, and he had thrown himself over to avoid going into it. He tried to warn me as I approached, but I was going far too fast, and both I and my sledge were pulled into the gaping chasm.
>
> I was very lucky to survive. Instead of falling freely, I was partially held up by my sail and, even more fortunately, I went into the crack where it turned a tight bend, just at the point where blowing snow accumulated to build a delicate arch of drift. Instead of plummeting into bottomless darkness, I dropped only twenty feet on to a snow bridge – winded but unhurt. The next moment I was terrified. Crevasse walls rose almost vertically above me and to either side, just a few feet away blackness beckoned. The bridge was clearly frail, and it took considerable effort to quell my fear and to unload the sledge one ration, one fuel bottle, one piece of equipment at a time. Each of them had to be thrown up to Ran on the edge twenty feet above before finally the sledge was empty. Then, with the aid of a rope, I gratefully climbed out. It had been a narrow escape.

I remembered a journalist telling me, as we left England, 'Of course it isn't the same nowadays as it was eighty years ago. Now you have all the trappings of the technical age. The sense of adventure and the dangers are gone.' I tried to think what technical items I carried on my sledge which might stop me descending into a crevasse or help me out once I was down one.

Crevasses are today, just as in the time of Scott and Mawson, the chief threat to Antarctic travellers, and the danger has not lessened one iota over the intervening years. This does not stop ignorant media reporters (who have never travelled through crevasse fields), nor old buffs (who have, but regard their own heyday in the 1930s, 1940s or 1950s as being the end of the heroic era of no gadgetry) from denouncing polar travellers of today as cosseted joyriders who have but to press a red knob to receive instant rescue from all predicaments.

Many of the crevasses were over a hundred feet wide with sagging bridges. The weakest point was not, as might be expected, in the centre, but along the fault line where the bridge was joined to the crevasse wall's lip. In the most dangerous cases the whole bridge had already descended a few feet down into the maw before catching on some unseen temporary 'stopper'. New snow had then partially filled the resulting gap.

Hauling the sledges down on to such teetering bridges presented no great physical task since gravity was on our side. If the bridge held, under our initial weight, we pulled onwards over the centre span. At this point the going became singularly off-putting because, in order to manhaul our monster loads up the far side of the disintegrating bridge, maximum downwards pressure with skis and sticks must be applied at its weakest point. There were moments of sickening apprehension as our straining ski sticks plunged through the crust, or part of a sledge lurched backwards, its prow or stern having broken through.

For three days foul weather closed in on the ice shelf. Exposed skin was frostnipped. Crotch-rot developed on the inside of our thighs and I suffered a resurgence of haemorrhoids despite having had deep injections in London. My back and shoulders continued to complain through the long hours. Harnesses, skis and skins needed frequent repairs, but the repair materials were not limitless. Like everything else, they had been cut down to the bare minimum.

On Friday, 13 November I began to aim west of south, but a rash of great holes kept us out on the shelf. Mike wrote: 'The crevasses seem to be everywhere ... Today I fell through. It was a vertical-sided chasm. My ski was pressed against one side. My arm and shoulder on the other. I could see no bottom at all, just blue-grey going to black.' From time to time we were sufficiently scared by near escapes into fixing safety ropes to our waists, but this was a last resort since the rear person is forever treading on the rope, which then jerks the navigator off balance and provides yet another general embuggeration factor at a time when toleration levels are low.

My crotch-rot reached the stage where both scrotum and inner thighs were raw and uncomfortable, despite the daily application of Canestan powder. My cotton boxer shorts (which I wore under a pair of thin wickaway long johns and some army baggy cotton trousers) were continually rucking up and exacerbating the raw patches.

Fifteen miles above us, a hole in the ozone layer opened up at this time of the year (and was at its worst in November). It allowed dangerous levels of ultraviolet rays to descend unfiltered to Antarctica and southerly lands like Australasia and Patagonia. Although a senior scientist at the British Antarctic Survey, Joseph Farman, had discovered and announced the alarming existence of damage to Earth's vital shield, his findings about the ozone layer, as far back as 1977, were derided by NASA.

In 1985 a highly frustrated Farman went public with his dire warning that a hole the size of the USA was opening every Antarctic summer, allowing lethal levels of ultraviolet rays to enter our atmosphere which increased the incidence of cancers, damaged sea life and weakened immune systems. This gap was then found to be widening, and another was discovered over the Arctic. By 1988 the ozone shield had thinned by 5 per cent, and by the early 1990s

South Pole-released balloons showed that, at 11 miles up, ozone density had dropped from a norm of 2,000 parts per billion to only 15 parts per billion.

Since we were travelling directly under the ozone hole's epicentre at the worst time of the year, it made sense to protect our skin from direct sunlight, but this proved impossible. Heaving our great loads by way of dog harnesses, our ribcages were compressed as we advanced and, breathing heavily at every step, we could not cover our mouths with air-constricting materials. We also needed to breathe without fogging our goggles, so the sun shone day after day on our lips and noses. Perhaps Mike protected himself the better with suncream, or merely manhauled in a more hunched position, shading his face. Whatever the reason, my lips deteriorated rapidly from burns and my nose swelled into a bulbous blister. When we scooped our evening meal from the communal cookpot, my spoon would invariably contain dribbles of the blood which welled out of the deep cracks in my blistered lips.

The scabs always grew together overnight, and when I woke the act of tearing my lips apart (in order to speak and drink) opened up all the raw places. Breakfast consisted of porridge oats in a gravy of blood. Mike recorded:

> Antarctica is a terrible place for ultraviolet radiation. It rapidly burns sensitive areas, and our lips soon became blistered, cracked and sore. I had my share of this problem, but Ran's was far worse. As well as burning areas directly, ultraviolet light can also reactivate the virus responsible for cold sores. This lies dormant in susceptible individuals, and Ran had had such sores in the past. Now they returned with a vengeance, and his lips became ravaged and swollen, a mass of open ulcers that wept constantly. In the evening, as we ate directly out of a shared cooking pot, they would bleed into the food – something that I found quite distasteful. Overnight his lips would stick together so that in the morning he had to ease them apart with a finger before he could speak, or even smile.

Mike gave me three different lip balms, but none of them seemed to help the deep ultraviolet burns. My diary reads: 'Agony from shoulder blades and hips. Bottom lip now like raw blubber. Crotch bad and lower back twinges. Mike cooked excellent spaghetti. His willy is apparently frostbitten and blistered.'

I found myself thinking that many of my aches and pains were mainly due to age. Shackleton, I recalled, had died at my exact age. Whilst lancing my foot in a gangrenous area one evening, Mike said, 'To be attempting this journey when you're approaching fifty is quite extraordinary.' I remembered the words of Dr Phillip Law, head of Australia's Antarctic services, when selecting men for Antarctica. 'Our standards of fitness are very high. It is unusual for a man past forty years to possess the necessary physical drive and energy we require.'

My energy levels were indeed seriously low and falling. Mentally I kept thinking that there were hundreds of miles ahead of us and the worst of it was yet to come, including the 10,000-foot climb described by Dr Charles Swithinbank, our route adviser, as 'bone-crushing toil'. Mike wrote:

> The friction from the ice was far greater than we had expected. Even though our sledges were equipped with runners of the best non-stick materials, the slipperiness of the ice and snow was minimal. Even at low altitude and far from the pole, the temperature was often down to –30°C, which is too cold for the downward pressure of the sledge to cause the usual surface melting that provides a slippery mixture of ice and water under the runners. It was more like dragging huge loads over sand, and we struggled to make about one and a half miles per hour. That meant pulling for between ten and twelve hours a day to make even reasonable progress. Twenty days passed on the ice shelf before we met the edge of the land itself.
>
> Once we reached land, we began the long climb up towards the Polar plateau, an ascent of more than 10,000 feet. The hard slog rapidly changed to bone-crushing toil. To our dismay, we

found that we would haul our loads uphill all day, only to lose all of the height gained in just a few minutes of dropping into some valley that crossed our path. It was very disheartening. Adding to our misery, the winds blew constantly from the high plateau straight into our faces. We battled with white-outs that lasted for up to five days, seeing nothing and being pushed back by the force of the storms. The winds also carved huge dunes of snow and rock-hard ice ridges, known as sastrugi, around and over which we had to wind. As we climbed, it became steadily colder. Our pace grew slower and slower until we could no longer make even one mile per hour.

Mike was finding that his ongoing and meticulous research into the unusual stresses which our bodies were going through was paying dividends. The process of muscle cannibalization once body fat reserves were gone was one of his chief study areas, as was the behaviour of our cholesterol levels. He noted:

> An extreme example of the effects of exercise on fat metabolism was to be seen in the blood samples taken from Ran and myself during our Antarctic crossing. We ate a very high fat diet during our walk in order to minimise the weight of the sledges we dragged, and the fat source used was mainly butter. Our food was not only high in total fat, but very high in saturates. The World Health Organization recommends that you eat a diet containing no more than 30–35 per cent fat, of which the larger proportion should be unsaturated. Our Antarctic rations contained 57 per cent fat, and that was as a proportion of a diet containing more than twice the normal adult consumption. The result was an intake of more than four times the saturated fat normally considered wise, yet our total cholesterol stayed at healthy levels and the good HDL type went up while the bad LDL went down. The message was clear. If you exercise enough, the fat gets used for the purpose that nature intended.

I never ceased to admire Mike's dedication to his research work. However sick he happened to be feeling at the time, he would never skimp the tiniest detail of his science schedule. At certain set times in the tent, he produced two small bottles from his science pack and we each drank the contents, which consisted of very expensive water. It contained very high concentrations of heavy isotopes of hydrogen and oxygen, both of which are stable and so remain in heavy form indefinitely without radioactive decay.

He explained the purpose: 'This stuff is deuterium and is made up of heavy hydrogen and O_{18}. Like atomic heavy water, but non-radioactive. Each bottleful costs hundreds of pounds, so don't spill any.'

'So what good does heavy water do us?'

'None at all. It just gets mixed up with all the other water in our bodies which we will slowly rid ourselves of and I will slowly collect. The O_{18} will come out partially in the form of carbon dioxide. We will burn everything up sooner or later, but the O_{18} disappears first. I can use the differing disappearance rates revealed by analysis of our urine samples to measure our daily energy expenditure.'

The results of the first thirty days of the isotope study showed that when we made the ascent to the plateau, the isotopes gave daily energy expenditures of 10,670 calories in myself and 11,650 in Mike. They confirmed the highest maintained energy expenditures ever documented – values that must lie close to the physiological limit. This was 5,500 calories more than we were eating – a deficit equivalent to total starvation while running a couple of marathons a day.

As Mike pointed out, we were infinitely better off than generations of previous polar explorers who, in addition to our slow starvation, suffered from the horror of scurvy. Even in the twentieth century, Scott was unsure of its precise cause. After a 1902 outbreak amongst his team, he described the onset of the sickness as 'an inflamed, swollen condition of the gums ... spots appear on the legs and pain is felt in old wounds and bruises; later, from a slight oedema, the legs and then the arms, swell to a great size and become blackened behind the joints.'

The French explorer Cartier, searching for the Northwest Passage, commented on scurvy symptoms, for which he found an apparent cure from the bark and leaves of the Northern white cedar tree:

> The said unknown sickness began to spread itself amongst us after the strangest sort that ever was either heard or seen, insomuch as some did lose all their strength, and could not stand on their feet, then did their legs swell and their sinews shrink. Others also had all their skins spotted with spots of blood of a purple colour: then did it ascend up to their ankles, knees, thighs, shoulders, arms and neck: their mouths became stinking, their gums so rotten that all the flesh did fall off, even to the roots of the teeth, which did also all fall out.

There were a number of conflicting scurvy theories in Scott's diary; vitamins had not yet been discovered, and even the famous Fridtjof Nansen was under the delusion that scurvy came from tainted tinned foods. British polar exploration was entwined with the Royal Navy, many of whose early voyages and later boat-sledge forays ended with mass scurvy deaths. Successive expedition leaders failed, despite many meetings over the years with the Inuit, who survive on a wholly fresh meat diet with no fresh fruit or vegetables, to put two and two together. And other countries' navies were equally stricken.

In 1497 Vasco de Gama's history-making voyage from Portugal to India and back included the abandonment of two of his four ships and the death by scurvy of two-thirds of all his men. In 1519 Magellan's greatest voyage set out with five ships and 265 men, but returned to Spain with only one ship and 18 men. Even in 1593 Sir Richard Hawkins was none the wiser as to how to avoid scurvy, which he described as 'the plague of the sea'. Eighty years later, the physician to Charles II, Gideon Harvey, wasted his time dividing different scurvy forms into mouth scurvy, acid scurvy, stomach scurvy, land scurvy and sea scurvy. He also believed that babies developed scurvy from being kissed by scurvy-ridden parents.

Our own scurvy protection was in the form of little Vitamin C pills, which kept us clear of the sickness even though our rations were made up of 57 per cent animal fat in the shape of ghee butter.

One big mistake that we made early on was to jettison our main items of warm clothing, our bulky duvet parkas, because there was simply no room to stow them and, desperate to make our loads more stable, we decided that we could keep a reasonable level of warmth by either manhauling, which kept our metabolisms pumping out heat to the extent that we sweated at −30°C or, the very moment we stopped hauling, to speedily erect and enter our tent. This worked for over half the journey until high altitude and approaching winter made us bitterly regret our lack of any truly warm gear.

We found navigation a tiring task and so switched the lead every hour, handing over the magnetic compass. We never spoke throughout the day unless some unusual happening warranted conversation. If you did ask a question, you could be sure that the answer would be, 'What?' Sound travels more slowly through cold rather than warm air, and snow muffles sound. Our ears were muffled by at least two balaclavas plus our jacket hood, and every movement of frosted clothing or of skis on crusty snow made hearing difficult.

The navigator on a clear day would check that the compass needle was swinging true, despite the alcohol, thickened by the cold, making the movement of the needle sluggish. Usually some glint or shadow well ahead would then serve as a reference point to aim at in order to avoid constantly rechecking with the compass. In overcast weather, or worse in a white-out, finding any reference point anywhere was nigh impossible. Scott mentioned this problem:

> It is difficult to describe the trying nature of this work; for hours one plods on, ever searching for some more definite sign. Sometimes the eye picks up a shade on the surface or a cloud slightly lighter or darker than its surroundings; they may occur at any angle and have often to be kept in the corner of the eye. Frequently, there comes a minute or two of absolute confusion,

> when one may be going in any direction ... It can scarcely be imagined how tiring this is or how trying to the eyes.

Additional clues as to direction could be gained from feeling the direction of the prevailing wind and from noting the directional pattern of sastrugi ridges which were formed by the dominant winds. One of Scott's men, Charles Wright, leading a team in a white-out wrote: 'I turned a complete (half) circle and came back to meet our own tracks on a dreadful day with no horizon, no wind, no sastrugi or drift to help the navigator.'

Mike and I had different tendencies as to our inbuilt directional impulse during such conditions. I would tend to head off all over the place, whereas Mike would always veer off to the right as though in response to some unseen magnetic force.

Much easier than using the compass, whenever the sun was out, was simply to glance at the position of your body's shadow and at the local time on your watch. Since the sun is due north at local midday, you have only to walk on your shadow at that time to be heading due south. As the sun traverses the horizon at a rate of 15° an hour, when your watch shows one o'clock, you simply walk at 15° to your shadow, at three o'clock you walk at 45° to your shadow, and at six o'clock your shadow is directly over your shoulder. To use this method, it is best to set out each morning so that midday on your local meridian is close to the middle of your planned travel hours.

Each evening I would, in the tent, check our position on our GPS, extremely thankful that technology had invented it and remembering the misery of using my theodolite or sextant during the 1979–80 Antarctic sector of the Transglobe Expedition.

In early December the gradient began to increase in severity. There were times when our skis slipped backwards at every step and the only way upwards was to tack at 45° to the slope, adding a deal of extra distance to the whole. On the interminable, grinding ascents there was little to be done but grit your teeth together and force any images of the future or of distance ahead out of your thoughts.

When periods of no wind coincided with a cloudless sky, the sun beat down through the ozone hole and we grew so hot that we stripped to our vests. Sweat dribbled into our eyes. Our unwashed hair and bodies itched and emitted a powerful stench. The sweat-salt stung my crotch sores and the renewed assault from ultraviolet burns further damaged my lips, from which blood and pus leaked into the chin cover of my face mask.

Mike announced that an abscess on one of his heels was so swollen that he had decided to operate. I watched with intense admiration as he gave himself two deep injections of Xylocaine anaesthetic and then plunged a scalpel blade deep into the swelling with diagonally crossed incisions. Pus poured out of the wounds and the swelling visibly decreased. Mike then bandaged up his heel and packed away his medical kit. I am not sure whether or not he felt faint, but I certainly did.

Most of the plasters over our blisters and crotch-rot were not changed daily. They became semi-permanent fixtures because plasters, like everything else, were in short supply. This state of affairs sometimes caused sores to deteriorate, and after thirty days my right foot began to hurt when travelling. I removed the bandage one evening and noticed that a two-inch area was soggy and swollen. Mike incised the area with a half-inch slit and relieved the pain immediately. I rubbed haemorrhoid cream, of which Mike had a plentiful supply, into the foot slit (and also on to my raw lips) before replastering the foot. By now there were nine separate bandaged areas on my feet. Mike had applied Granuflex pressure-sore pads to his blisters and swore by the results, which seemed to have miraculously cured some of his worst sores. I tried one, but found it too bulky for my relatively tight-fitting plastic boots.

Over the next three days we climbed to 5,000 feet above sea level with constant Force Eight winds in our faces. The following day brought our first true white-out along with uneven sastrugi and heavy crust snowdrifts, through which the sledges ploughed only with the most determined haulage.

For twenty years, largely in the Arctic, I had navigated in the worst of glare-ice, month after month, without eye protection. But in Siberia this stupidity, born of frustration with misted goggles, had caught up with me and the best London ophthalmic surgeon had warned me that I would risk blindness if I ever again subjected my retinas to further overdoses of blue and ultraviolet light. Frightened, I no longer gave in to the temptation to tear off misted goggles, but I fully sympathised when Mike did so.

Under true white-out conditions it is quite possible for people to walk off cliffs, and for aircraft to 'land' by mistake. Some individuals are physically sickened by white-out travel and, that morning, Mike complained of feeling 'disturbed and totally disorientated' when he removed his jacket hood to prevent his goggles misting. As a result he kept his hood up, his goggles became unwearable and, in an especially bad sastrugi field, he removed them for a period of two hours. Towards noon the clouds shifted and a slight horizon was visible. This enabled us to hold our bearing by simply crossing successive sastrugi trenches at an angle of 70°.

When we camped, after a memorably nasty ten hours lurching over unseen obstacles, crossing ski tips and crashing into invisible trenches, I found that both my cheeks were burning and inflamed by UV rays. A mole on one cheek was especially tender. I had exposed my cheeks to help demist my goggles, but it had been a mistake. The cheeks were later to blister because the burn conditions had been so bad.

Mike's eyes, even though he wore goggles for all but two hours throughout the day, were also damaged. Soon after we camped he developed snow-blindness symptoms. It was only the mildest of attacks, but enough to have him lying back in considerable pain. We carried a bottle of amethocaine eye drops and these provided Mike with exquisite relief for about an hour, after which he would wake in renewed pain and apply further drops.

Since our overall speed and rate of progress for the first forty days had been slightly better than for any previous Antarctic man-hauling journey on record, our pace should not, theoretically, have caused dissension. But we were both under increasing strain and our bodies, under the stress of slow starvation combined with enormous energy expenditure, were altering chemically. Subsequent analysis of our blood samples was to show that our whole enzyme system, everything that controlled our absorption of fat, was changing and we were getting levels of gut hormones twice as high as had been previously known to science. We were adapting to our high-fat rations in a way hitherto unrecognized. Furthermore, we were losing muscle and weight from our hearts as well as from our body mass. During this period of the steep climb to the Pole and beyond we were losing muscle fast. On the 51st day of the journey, Mike recorded: 'Last night I weighed us. Ran has lost 40 pounds and me 30 pounds. Twenty per cent of our body weight.'

Although we did not know it, I learned later that the relatively low air pressure near to the poles markedly increases the effect of altitude on humans. Circulating polar winds form a vortex which lowers the pressure at the Pole and has the effect of rendering its effective elevation as over 10,000 feet during the brief summer season: 8,500 feet here produced the same conditions as 11,500 feet on, say, Mount Everest.

At 11,500 feet the thinness of the air and the consequent lack of oxygen causes many people to suffer from altitude sickness, with shortness of breath, dizziness, even nausea and confusion. One of Scott's men collapsed from altitude sickness at 9,000 feet; and although ten dogs hauled Amundsen's sledge, he found 'it was hard to work and breathing was an effort.' Keeping up the body's demand for oxygen at high altitudes increases heart and respiration rates.

Even on a day doing nothing at the Pole, your calorie requirement goes up from 300 to 500 calories. Food is less easily processed and metabolized at altitude, especially the fat which made up over half of our rations. Breathlessness, gasping for air and, at night, waking short of breath are all likely to be experienced at the pole.

Given the low air pressure, our strict daily allowance of cooker fuel allowed us, at best, half a gallon of liquid, from melting snow, to drink a day. Even had we remained stationary without exertion at this altitude, we would be badly dehydrated. The correct intake of liquids for bodies in our circumstances should have been a minimum of a gallon and a half each daily. But we were breathing heavily as we hauled and, at 10,000 feet taking more frequent breaths than usual, the greater carbon dioxide flow was making our blood more alkaline to which altered state our kidneys were fighting to adjust, and they function best only when they have adequate water. What with the dry polar air and our increased breath rate, we were losing body moisture at a great rate and becoming badly dehydrated.

In addition to the effects on our bodies of altitude and dehydration, there were differences in our physiques, as between any two individuals. Scott observed that 'Oates's nose is always on the point of being frostbitten', but that 'Bowers is wonderful ... I have never seen anyone so unaffected by the cold.' One of Scott's men, Apsley Cherry-Garrard, pondered the difference between manhaulers big and small. 'I do not believe,' he wrote, 'that this is a life for such [big] men who are expected to pull their weight and to support and drive a larger "machine" than their companions, and at the same time to eat no extra food ... It is clear that the heaviest man will feel the deficiency sooner and more severely than others who are smaller than he.'

Cherry-Garrard, commenting on the fact that Seaman Evans, the biggest of Scott's five-man polar team, was the first to die, wrote: 'Evans must have had a most terrible time. I think it is clear from the diaries that he had suffered very greatly without complaint.' Medical studies today suggest that Evans, who weighed around 200 pounds in normal times, would have needed, in such cold conditions, some 400 calories a day more than a 150-pound co-manhauler, without which he would have lost more weight. For my part, I kept thinking, 'I'm bigger than Mike. I should have more food.'

Mike and I experienced cuttingly cold winds in the week before we came to the pole. Some twenty miles from our goal we emerged from our tent into especially cold conditions with a strong steady headwind. The wind-chill factor, which expresses what the temperature feels like when coupled with the existing wind speed, hovered around –80°C.

The conception of such a factor is credited to the famous US polar pioneer, Paul Siple, who suggested it based on a simple graph which could be key to military clothing in cold weather warfare and was, therefore, kept as a military secret until the end of the Second World War. Additional to the wind and the still-air temperature must be added humidity in the shape of fog, since moisture in the air removes body heat quicker than does dry air. This three-factor measurement produces what polar met-men call the 'relative outdoor temperature'.

Titbits of polar statistics, some more useful than others, include the formula that the relative values of Fahrenheit and Celsius cross over and meet at –40°. Will Steger's group always knew when the still-air temperature dropped to –60°C because their sponsored Colgate toothpaste then froze solid.

Breaking camp and loading the sledges was always a tricky job wearing clumsy mitts, balaclavas and goggles. If a strap was frozen in a harness buckle or a main zip jammed, mittened fingers could often prove useless to sort out the problem. Then the temptation to un-mitt was considerable but best withstood at –80°C wind chill.

That morning is one Mike will never forget. He recorded: 'When I started moving, I felt much colder than usual. My hands in particular, with only gloves and thin mitts on, became increasingly numb . . . I curled my fingers into my palms in an attempt to restore the circulation . . . my fingers would be frostbitten if I didn't do something soon.' Mike needed his thickest mitts, the type I knew as elephant mitts. He had them stowed at the most accessible part of his sledge. His diary reads:

> Survival in the cold is an art and anticipating problems is very much the key. But although my mitts were instantly available, I could not get them on my frozen fingers. I couldn't grasp with one hand the cuff of the other to pull it up. To make matters worse,

although numb and dead to touch on the surface, my fingers felt unbearably painful inside. I found myself whimpering like a dog ... Ran, who started out behind me, came up to help, but even with his tugging on the cuffs, I still could not get my inert hands inside. As the minutes slipped by the situation became desperate. We were now both losing the function in our hands and getting rapidly colder. It prompted Ran to make an almost ultimate sacrifice. He took off his own still supple mitts and gave them to me, struggling to get his large hands into my stiff cold ones. Then he urged me to get moving again. It was a wonderful gesture.

Although my hands soon felt better, the stop had taken ten minutes and I was now deeply chilled. I wanted to step up the pace, to get warmer, but could scarcely move my sledge. My muscles had cooled to the point where they no longer functioned properly. Unable to move fast, I could not generate enough heat to match my further losses. I was getting colder and colder, and before long I realised that I had to stop again. I needed more insulation on my body as well, in what had become a full Polar storm.

The only other garment I had was a fleece jacket. It would be tricky to get it on, especially as it needed to go under my windproof, before I became truly hypothermic. The dressing would also need some dexterity, which meant taking off my gloves again. Once I removed my gloves it was only moments before my fingers would not obey commands. This time it was the zips on the jackets that defeated them and failed to move. I was dismayed to see the tips of each digit turning chalky white and I could almost feel the ice crystals forming inside them. I began to panic. I was stuck, half-dressed, with literally freezing fingers when Ran caught up once more.

With his help, I managed to get my two jackets on and then to force my pitiful hands back inside the mitts, but the stop took another ten minutes, during which my body cooled further. I had reached a point too deep in a downward spiral, and as we set off again, my thinking began to fade. Although I kept on hauling for another half-hour or so, it was never fast enough to generate

> much heat. I steadily became colder still and more withdrawn until finally I began to wander from our course.

Mike's problems had made my own hands unworkable, in terms of trying to de-fog my goggles, and the only feature I could see in the near white-out was Mike's indistinct silhouette eight yards ahead of me. His tracks were invisible and I came to an abrupt halt as my ski tips struck the rear of his sledge. Normally when he halted to announce that it was my turn to navigate, he would shout the word 'Time' loud enough for me to hear above the screech of my ski sticks. There had been no shout and, as I came alongside to detach the compass from Mike's chest harness, I noticed something unaccountably different about his behaviour.

My standard practice, having clipped the compass to my own chest-strap, was to move a few yards ahead of him and check the correct bearing before setting off for my next ninety-minute session. It was not my habit ever to look back, except in a zone of crevasses or other hazards, and if, on this occasion, I had followed my normal procedure, Mike would certainly have died. As it was, some aspect of Mike's stance, perhaps just a total lack of movement, alerted my subconscious and, removing my near-useless goggles, I peered at his face. I could not focus for a while as the cold wind whipped at my tear ducts and Mike's face gave me no clues through his goggles and balaclava. Ice spikes poked horizontally from his chin as from a grotesque clown's mask. 'Are you OK, Mike?' I screamed at him, and struck him on the shoulder. There was no response at all and his head seemed to loll.

I remembered seeing him once before in this state, somewhere in the Siberian Arctic, and realized that he was about to succumb to hypothermia. Because my fingers were numb and a steady Force Seven wind made things awkward, I spent several minutes unpacking and erecting the tent. When the inner tent was up I shouted to Mike to go inside and start the cooker whilst I fixed up the flysheet. A couple of minutes later I found that Mike was still kneeling in the snow and staring vacantly into space.

I hustled him through the door flap and, unpacking his sledge, threw his mat and bag inside. Once the cooker was going, Mike began to remove his clothes as though in a trance. He said nothing, but accepted a mug of tepid soup from the Thermos. He slept for an hour and when he awoke spent some time staring at the tent ceiling. His memory, which had entirely gone as far as the last few hours were concerned, gradually returned. I made him two cups of tea and he ate two of his chocolate bars. Mike wrote of this experience:

> In many ways I was lucky to survive. If Ran had been out in front when I started running into difficulties, I would have been struggling with the gloves and the jacket alone. Inevitably I would have become more deeply hypothermic and probably wandered off and collapsed. Motionless on the Antarctic plateau, my survival time would have been a few minutes at most. By the time Ran realised that I wasn't behind him, his tracks back to mine would have been blown to oblivion.

Mike and I had, years previously, agreed to wear clothing that was as light and breathable as possible when manhauling extreme loads, even in extremely cold conditions. We would, in theory, cope with the cold by working hard whenever not in our tent. This was, Mike wrote:

> . . . a policy that worked well while we were of normal weight, but it began to go wrong as we lost more and more. In fairly thin clothing – equivalent to normal office clothing in Britain – more than half of your insulation comes from the layer of fat beneath your skin. Ours was rapidly disappearing. At the same time, while we towed less, we could never stop moving for long. In each of our twelve-hour days, we stopped only twice for short five-minute breaks.
>
> In any case, I am not convinced that thin garments were the only cause of my hypothermia. Although my symptoms were

typical of severe cooling, my recovery in the tent was rather too fast for that. Perhaps I was also suffering from a low blood sugar – a condition known as hypoglycaemia – which can stop the temperature controller in the brain from doing its job properly. During our Antarctic journey, eating the high fat diet and working hard enough to consume our glucose stores, we had good reason to end up with low sugars.

Analysis of our samples showed that our blood glucose had been low from the very first day, in fact at the bottom of the normal range. During the last thirty days of the expedition they appeared to be impossible. On one occasion Ran had a level of 0.2 millimoles, while I had one of just 0.3. In ordinary circumstances, these would be fatal, for it is thought that the brain cannot survive without a reasonable amount of glucose for fuel. It seems that we must have adapted in some way to cope with the situation.

The day after Mike's bad experience the wind dropped, the mists cleared and we carried on. Towards the evening I screamed at Mike, 'Look ahead. Over there. There's a thing!' For the first time in over seven hundred miles a man-made object was visible in the snow. We had a two-part wager between us. Whoever spotted the first sign of the Pole would get a free hamburger snack and, for sighting the South Pole itself, a free 'slap-up' lunch. The thing turned out to be a half-buried meteorological balloon, and its presence was a definite boost to morale.

At 7 p.m., glancing ahead as I topped a slow rise, I thought I saw movement. Removing my goggles and squinting to focus, I could just make out a series of dark, blurred objects: five or six black marbles dancing on the shimmer of the southern horizon.

I turned back and shouted to Mike. It was a rare moment of sheer elation. The journey was far from over, but we had dragged to the Pole just enough stores to allow us to cross the continent and survive. If our luck held.

The American polar base, known as Amundsen–Scott South Pole

Station, was ten miles from the point where we first glimpsed its buildings. A series of rising steppes kept hiding the site but, after seven hours of hauling, on 16 January we topped the final rise and came to the first of many isolated science domes at 1700 hours Greenwich Mean Time, on the 81st anniversary of Scott's sad arrival there.

Imagine that your father died in the course of a remarkable achievement and that all the world was then treated to a best-selling book and a world-popular nine-hour documentary film series attacking his well-deserved reputation for efficiency and bravery with a pack of derogatory lies. This is what happened in 1979 to the great naturalist Sir Peter Scott, whose late father was Captain Robert Falcon Scott of Antarctica fame.

The historic facts are simple. Scott set out in 1910 to reach the South Pole and, through his team of top scientists, to learn a great deal about a hitherto unknown part of the world. He was not planning to race any rival since, to the best of his knowledge, no rival existed. In 1902 he had been the first man to penetrate the unknown land of Antarctica and the first to discover that it was a true continent. His two expeditions, including the one on which he died, produced more scientific research results than all the other Antarctic expeditions of the first half of the twentieth century.

The story of the Norwegian explorer Roald Amundsen, who reached the South Pole a few weeks before Scott, is filled with polar drama. After achieving world fame by his successful drift through the Northwest Passage in the *Gjoa*, he determined to be first to reach the North Pole by copying Nansen's *Fram* drift, but from a different start point. He was always ready to adopt alternative methods. For a while, for instance, he seriously considered having sledges towed by teams of polar bears.

He persuaded the Norwegian Parliament to give him a hefty grant and Nansen to lend him the *Fram*.

Just as he was about to set out north, he heard, to his intense frustration, that the two Americans, Peary and Cook, had both made claims to have reached the North Pole the previous summer. A touch later it became clear that Cook's claim, made on 2 September 1909, was considered fraudulent. Having spent a memorably miserable winter in Antarctica with Cook some years earlier, Amundsen said, 'Whatever Cook may have done or not done, the Cook who did them was not the Dr Cook I knew as a young man. Some physical misfortune must have overtaken him to change his personality, for which he was not responsible.' When Peary made his own pole claim only a few days later and rubbished Cook's, Amundsen wrote, 'Peary's behaviour fills me with the deepest anger and I want to proclaim publicly that Dr Cook is the most reliable Arctic traveller I know, and it is simply unreasonable to doubt him and believe Peary.' He was later to change his mind.

Since his North Pole plan was apparently now pointless, due to Peary's claimed priority there, Amundsen secretly decided that he would go south instead in order to capture priority for that other pole which, if he could hoodwink everyone, he could just about manage to pull off without Scott's team learning of his intention until it was too late to switch from their existing plan for a sedate science-based polar trip to a race against ski experts and fast dog teams. With consummate guile, Amundsen succeeded in his grand deception plan, fooling his government, his generous mentor Nansen and, until the last minute, even his own team of expert skiers and dog drivers.

In September 1910, by which time he knew Scott was in Australia and would have no chance at all to recruit the correct men and dogs for a race, Amundsen sent Scott a blunt telegram: 'Beg leave to inform you *Fram* proceeding Antarctic. Amundsen'. On the same day, only three hours before he set sail from the island of Madeira with 19 men, including the best cross-country skiers in the world, and 97 of the best sledge-dogs, he summoned his team to tell them that they were to go south not north! He gave his only confidant in Norway, his brother Leon, letters of apology for his deceitful behaviour, to be handed in due course to Nansen and to the King of Norway.

His voyage south went well and he landed at the Bay of Whales which, as a start point for a race, was sixty miles closer to the South Pole than was Scott's base at McMurdo Sound. Amundsen was lucky. The Bay of Whales was not, as he had assumed, safely attached to land. At any time his camp there and the *Fram* could have broken away from the ice shelf and faced disaster.

The Norwegian set out at once to drop food and fuel dumps en route to the south, but one of their subsequent depot-laying journeys was at a time of year when conditions were far too cold. One of the men nearly died, many were frostbitten, dogs were lost and a minor mutiny broke out. Amundsen stamped on it with his accustomed ruthlessness.

He is generally considered to have been a meticulous planner, and yet he forgot to take to Antarctica several vital items, including a single snow shovel and, even more serious, key pages to his only copy of the navigation tables for the period. However, his quotient of Lady Luck was bountiful for, on setting out for the pole with his best five dog drivers, he happened upon a glacial arm, which he named Axel Heiberg, that led straight and true to the South Pole.

Three hundred miles short of the bottom of the world, the Norwegians made camp at the upper reaches of their glacier, where they killed 24 of their dogs to feed to the rest. Soon after, Amundsen forgot to pack the team's crampons, which caused great difficulty in areas of hard ice. But again their luck held and they survived bad crevassing zones.

Above the Axel Heiberg they made a beeline for the Pole and, once there, spent a great deal of time and care establishing its exact position so that, unlike Peary and Cook up north, they could be certain of their prize. Believing that the British would arrive any day, Amundsen left a small black tent and certain other items at the pole before heading back to the coast to tell the world of their success. Their journey had achieved a great world record, but it was virtually devoid of scientific value.

Although Amundsen's two main 'mutineers' had been left behind at the Bay of Whales, there was much bad feeling within the small team on the way back to their base. And this despite the euphoria of their success. Amundsen proved to be an arrogant and short-fused leader, and one key member of his polar team, Hassel, later wrote after being rebuked for snoring in the tent, 'That's OK by me, but things can be said in several ways. Mr A always chooses the nastiest and most haughty one ... One might think the man has a screw loose. He has many times in the last few days actually initiated quarrels, an extraordinary stand for a governor and leader for whom peace and good camaraderie should be the main target.'

For the last week of the expedition Amundsen and his chief ski expert, Helmer Hanssen, did not speak to each other at all following an argument about the dogs, and Amundsen never forgave Hjalmar Johansen for his angry remarks about the Boss's poor leadership following the 'too early' depot-laying and its resulting frostbitten men. When the team's great success was celebrated back home in Norway, Johansen went to the centre of Oslo and committed suicide – a sad result of his time with Amundsen.

Awards poured in from all over the world, and Amundsen gave lectures everywhere that counted, including to the Royal Geographical Society in London, at the end of which their president, Lord Curzon, gave a speech which Amundsen took as a public insult. He wrote that 'by and large the British are a race of very bad losers.'

Scott himself cannot be accurately described as a bad loser, although he and his team were, of course, bitterly disappointed on manhauling all the way to the pole to find that they had been beaten to their goal. In Scott's heartfelt words, 'Great God! This is an awful place for us to have laboured to it without the reward of priority.' But bad losers they were not. The plain-speaking and observant Birdie Bowers wrote in a note for later posting to his mother, 'I am awfully sorry for Captain Scott who has taken the blow very well indeed.' Dr Edward Wilson recorded about Amundsen's victory: 'We are agreed that he can claim prior right to the Pole itself. He has beaten us in so far as he made a race of it. We have done what we came for ...'

As for Amundsen's own victorious team, when they later heard that Scott's men had made the longer route to the South Pole dragging their own sledges, their best skier exclaimed, 'It is no disparagement of Amundsen and the rest of us when I say that Scott's achievement far exceeded ours. Just imagine what it meant for Scott and the others to drag their sleds themselves. We started with 52 dogs and came back with eleven, and many of these wore themselves out on the journey. What shall we say of Scott and his comrades who were their own dogs? Anyone with any experience will take off his hat to Scott's achievement. I do not believe men ever have shown such endurance at any time, nor do I believe there ever will be men to equal it.'

It is indeed ironic that after all the centuries of British polar exploration, with all the allied suffering and death, neither pole was reached first by a Briton. In 1982 Charlie Burton and I did our best to even up the overall record by achieving the first surface circumnavigation through both poles, thereby being the first people to reach both poles and to traverse both polar ice caps from end to end. To date, such a journey has never been repeated by any route.

Susan Solomon, an American atmospheric scientist with fourteen years' experience of studying Antarctic weather patterns, has written a book in which she compares the known weather data of 1912 with automated met-records meticulously collected from weather stations all along Scott's Barrier route between 1950 and 2000. This data can now be accessed, through the Internet Archive, at the University of Wisconsin–Madison. It shows with cold, hard data that rogue weather played havoc with Scott's group, whilst Amundsen had, by sheer luck, chosen a route to the South Pole which the Gods smiled upon and experienced fine Antarctic weather out and back. To quote Susan Solomon in *The Coldest March* (2001), describing the unusual weather event that so delayed Scott's poleward journey in early December 1911:

> A wet warm blizzard of such extended duration with winds in excess of fifty miles per hour has not yet been observed in eight

years of December data at one nearby automated weather station, or in fourteen years of December data at another. The longest and windiest storm recorded by modern instruments in this region of the Barrier occurred in December of 1995. It lasted about two days and displayed peak winds of about forty miles per hour. But Scott and his men were tent bound while their blizzard dumped heavy snow for four full days, 5–8 December 1911, and they estimated the wind speed at up to eighty miles per hour. Scott and his men were the victims of bad luck in this exceptionally severe and prolonged storm, which must have been due to a tongue of warm wet air from the ocean that pushed unusually far across the Barrier.

The case of the storm of December 1911 reflects not the skills of the two leaders in dealing with the weather, but rather their fortunes in geographic placement. If the same storm had occurred three weeks earlier, both teams would have been equally pinned down.

Solomon then switched her meticulous research to the weather records affecting the epic homeward journey of Scott and his men:

In the last month of their lives, nature dealt them a crushing blow in the form of conditions that can now be shown to be far colder than normal, and therefore radically different from those they quite sensibly expected to find. In simple terms, Scott and his men did everything right regarding the weather but were exceedingly unlucky. I will make the case that they were killed not primarily by human error but by this unfortunate and unpredictable turn of meteorological events.

Daily minimum temperatures were a bitter debilitating 10–20°F colder that what can now be shown to be typical based on many years of observations in this region ... As decade after decade passed, the legend of Scott's mistakes flourished. But interest in the meteorology of the remote Antarctic also mounted, and scientific curiosity resulted in the installation of a network of automated weather stations around the coldest continent on earth beginning in the 1980s. The meteorological observations obtained for the sake of science as a party of men [Scott's group] struggled for their very survival, took on a new and startling meaning as they were compared to the data points routinely and impassively collected over the passing years by the machines. The scientific data showed that the three key weeks from 27 February to 19 March 1912, during which Scott's party fell farther and farther behind the daily distances that they had to achieve in order to survive, were far colder than normal. The new information points not to errors made by men, but toward the capriciousness of nature as a stunningly decisive blow to the survival of Scott, Bowers, Wilson and Oates.

On the return leg of their journey, they had expected the wind to blow from the south as a blessed aid to progress, but the coldest temperatures are associated with windless conditions. The world-class meteorologist, Dr George Simpson, later wrote, 'There can be no doubt that the weather played a predominating part in the disaster, and . . . was the immediate cause of the final catastrophe.' He asserted that 'the Barrier could be traversed many times without again encountering such low temperatures so early in the year.' He added that 'the polar party would probably have survived in nine years out of ten, but struck the unlucky tenth one.' In a more normal year, with greatly reduced chances of frostbite, helpful winds to whisk their burden along, and a considerably kinder snow surface, surely their fates would have been different.

Mike and I arrived at the South Pole ravenously hungry. We put up our tent, drank tea and ate one of our precious chocolate bars. Then, eighty minutes later, we moved on once I had sorted out in which direction to head – even my GPS was confused.

The polar site had vastly altered in the twelve short years since my last visit. Strangely shaped installations on jack-up steel legs reared monstrously in every direction from the main central feature, the black-roofed dome, in which overwintering scientists live and work. Constructed over an area of two square miles, the site no longer resembled the moonscape of my memory with its small huddle of earth stations. We were now confronted by a film-set vista as of a long-deserted industrial estate, littered with oil drums, pipes, construction materials and many thousands of large wooden crates.

A mile beyond the Pole we entered a region of snowquakes. Without warning I heard a crashing roar and felt an instant of extreme panic as the solid snow surface under my feet dropped away. When snow builds up into a patch of wind crust several inches thick, whether as big as a sports arena or merely room-sized, the pressure of even a dog's paw can be enough to trigger a sudden collapse of the whole suspended mass. The drop is never more than a few inches, but is enough to petrify the ignorant passer-by and to spark off thunderous sound waves for several seconds.

By the time we made camp in thick mist, we had hauled over ten miles despite the delay at the Pole. I cut my last Mars bar in half and we silently savoured the exquisite taste for a minute of luxury by way of self-congratulation for reaching the South Pole.

I was worried by our body weight figures. I had weighed in that afternoon at 11½ stone (161 pounds) and Mike at 9½ stone (133 pounds). We had each lost some 25 per cent of our body weight, in my case 49 pounds, and Mike now forecast that I would probably lose a further 21 pounds over the next thirty days. Neither of us could afford this sort of weight loss, since the colder temperatures now setting in with the imminent onslaught of winter would cut right into our body cores. Normally our body fat would have provided natural thermic protection, but we were already devoid of fat and, especially in Mike's case, vulnerable to hypothermia.

All our previous sufferings were as nothing compared with the days which followed our arrival at the Pole. Much of this was my fault for underestimating the extreme cold at 11,000 feet above sea level and the effect it would have on our battered bodies. I should have obtained and packed much more protective clothing and I should not have suggested abandoning our down jackets and outer sleeping bags. We were now suffering for these mistakes, and the immediate future looked grim.

Only now, beyond the Pole, were we discovering the true meaning of cold. Our conditions, in terms of body deterioration, slow starvation, inadequate clothing, wind-chill temperature, altitude and even the day of the year, exactly matched those of Scott and his four companions as they came away from the Pole. Dr Wilson, Scott's friend, wrote: 'Thin air, low pressure and oxygen deficiency reach a point, at about 10,000 feet, above which even well-fed, fit humans will be affected by altitude "sickness". It is best not to exert yourself but, if you must, you will find every movement is an effort. The pulse rate races away, and to breathe is to gasp as your lungs and heart fight to pump oxygen around the body.'

We learned from Morag that our long-time Norwegian 'rival', Erling Kagge, had reached the pole a week before us and had been airlifted out. The Norwegian press talked of his 'winning the race', but our sledge loads were twice as heavy as his and our journey was twice as long, so our morale was not too badly dented by this misleading piece of media spin.

Not far beyond the pole, Mike wrote: 'We were weakening fast . . . On a day of deep, deep cold and as the end of the fifth long hour approached, I began feeling utterly fatigued – not the same old tiredness that we had been feeling throughout the expedition, but a new sensation, as though running on empty.'

Chapter Thirteen

Eternity is white, not black

Our ailments began to slow us down. With a sterilized scalpel Mike lanced my infected foot in several places, releasing quantities of surface poison. That side of my foot was now death-white, spongy and hypersensitive. Even inside our tent, with the cooker rehydrating the spaghetti, it was intensely cold. I forced myself to take down my trousers in order to apply haemorrhoid cream to various places, including the raw regions of my crotch, scabbed lips, nose and chin.

'I don't believe it,' Mike exclaimed, staring at my legs. 'You can't pull anything with those. They're Belsen-like.'

The following day was purgatory. Mike wrote:

> Cold is an understatement ... it became very unpleasant indeed and I nearly blew it by delaying putting on my outer jacket in the morning. I suffered both general cold and severely cold hands as a result.
>
> A desperately cold day, perhaps minus 40°C with a stiff wind that kept us deeply chilled, despite wearing all our clothing and going as best we could. My hands were very bad and, after each pee, they took thirty minutes to recover. Even then they would still be weak, which led to further problems at the next pee – a vicious circle.

My own diary was beginning to lapse into a mere record of impressions. 'New kind of chisel-hard hoar frost in sudden patches. It is now horribly body-cold. I feel as though naked. At halts I have to clasp my arms around my torso and jump and sing or swear. We have run out of glue for our skins. Every six days now the average temperature drops two degrees.'

Two explosive attacks of diarrhoea involved taking my trousers down and squatting clear of my skis. This reopened my haemorrhoids, which in turn made leg movement a misery. Since the wind-chill factor was around –85°C, I pulled my trousers back with alacrity and without careful attention to detail. This soiled my trousers and mitts, but the excrement quickly froze solid and was then easily knocked off.

The following day Mike diagnosed possible 'deep-seated infection in the foot bone' and put me on metronidazole and flucloxacillin. Unfortunately, we were running short of these antibiotics, which seemed the most effective. The cold in the afternoon and evening was so penetrating that it had the excellent effect of taking my mind off my feet.

Our current sorry state had largely been caused by the long weeks of calorie deficiency. As Mike put it, 'Our calorie *deficit* has been the equivalent of the total *input* of a normal person. It is exactly as though a normal person had eaten nothing, I repeat nothing, all this time. After several weeks they would get weak and desperately hungry. In fact they would starve. We *are* slowly starving.'

At noon Mike discovered that both his ski sticks had somehow fallen off his sledge. He had already scanned his back-track, but could see nothing. We could have wasted the rest of the day searching to no avail, so I gave Mike one of my sticks and suggested we try to progress with one each. But even on flat stretches we found it exceptionally difficult to progress with only half our previous thrusting power. Working at only half-thrust, I began to freeze and was forced to step up the pace. Mike's legs were shorter than mine, plus he was suffering from a twisted ankle, and he needed two sticks more than I did. Every time I stopped to await him I became colder until my body shook as though with the ague. I would have given anything for more clothes, or even some newspaper or straw to stuff under my jacket and trousers. I considered cutting up the remaining polythene ration bags and stitching them to the inside of my jacket.

Our hauling was now ridiculously slow, and especially painful for whichever foot corresponded with the stick-wielding arm. I became so cold that my feet went numb. In something of a panic, I could think of no answer but to stop early; but that was taboo, a sign of likely failure. For thirty minutes we advanced through less than ideal wind-chill conditions, but Mike's speed gradually decreased to a crawl and his head began to loll with exhaustion. I spoke to him and his response was blurred. I grew frightened. He was clearly heading for hypothermia again. Some twenty-five minutes before stop time I erected the tent and made hot tea, which tasted exceptionally good.

Our bodily condition was becoming highly suspect. I was not in the business of leading suicide expeditions. We were approaching the edge of our ability to cope safely with very extreme conditions, and this was, we both knew, because we were starving.

Precision in our navigational accuracy after the Pole became far more important because serious, if not lethal, results could be caused by even a minor error. On the way down to the Pole, even a very vague bearing, like marking the position of a slow-moving cloud, could suffice to keep us heading in the general direction of south. There was, after all, only one possible 'due south' that we could aim for. Now, travelling away from the pole, there were 360 'due norths' to choose from. This was confusing, even to the GPS. Mike wrote:

> The device relied upon estimating its own position from the positions of several satellites, receiving signals from them and cross-checking the information. Because we were still so close to the Pole, longitude information was especially vulnerable to error.

After all, at the Pole itself, one position corresponded to all possible longitudes. The machine wasn't built to be intelligent. It could not understand why it was being told slightly different values and frequently decided that it could give us only the simple message – ERROR.

The instrument, once it had settled, did give us our exact location, but for direction we relied on the sun's position vis-à-vis our watch time. Mike's diary explains:

Many of the days were bright and sunny and I would start off leading, heading for the north, guided by my shadow. In order to use our shadows for navigation, and to prevent the low sun from shining directly in our eyes, we always moved with the sun behind us.

Before the Pole, this had meant walking during the local geographic daytime, with the sun in the east as we started, our backs to the north in the middle of our day, and to the west, on our right, when we stopped. This had allowed us to head southwards, using our watches and avoiding the need for endless consultations of the compass, which was slow to settle so close to the magnetic Pole.

Now that we had passed the geographic Pole, all this had changed. Local daytime would have seen us walking into the sun, since, in a single stride as we passed the Pole and without a change in direction, we had moved from walking south in the western hemisphere to walking north in the eastern.

We had effectively switched from day to night and, perhaps even more strangely, changed from one date to the next. The result was that our morning start now corresponded to local evening, and when we set off I walked with the sun to the west.

As we crept towards the edge of the great inland plateau and approached the mountain range, through the valleys of which we must descend 10,000 feet to sea level, I constantly checked the compass, whether the sun was out or not, for I knew that we would need great accuracy in order to enter the Mill Glacier, the start of the long and lethal descent from the plateau down to the Pacific coast, by a relatively crevasse-free route. The slightest deviation could lead us into vast fissure fields, as unstable as any in the world. From now on success would depend entirely on selecting the correct tortuous pathway between man-killer crevasse fields. This entailed the use of watches that were 100 per cent accurate timekeepers, and not affected by the cold.

Timekeeping in extreme conditions is inherently fraught with complications. Before the days of English watchmaker John Harrison's H4, a super-precise marine chronometer, seafarers had no means by which to determine their longitudinal position accurately. This problem stemmed from the temperature and pressure fluctuations at sea. In climates of extreme cold, a timekeeper can, quite literally, freeze up, regardless of whether its movement is powered mechanically, by a battery or using solar energy.

Approximately 98 per cent of conventional watches are powered by quartz movement, which is to say that they are not mechanical watches. Batteries are famous for losing their potential energy as temperatures drop, and so using a battery-powered watch on a polar expedition is counterproductive. The solar panel on a solar-powered quartz watch is equally impractical as extreme cold rapidly increases the chances of the panel cracking.

The answer, therefore, lies in the use of mechanical timekeepers. They, too, have a unique set of problems. The oil that keeps the metal wheels and escapement mechanism lubricated tends to get thick and thereby loses its viscosity, causing the watch to slow down dramatically or 'lose time'. However, unlike those of their quartz counterparts, the problems found in mechanical watches can be overcome with some ingenuity. Watches destined for polar regions can be specially modified to withstand extremes of temperature. For example, Rolex makes the Explorer II, a watch that can, on request, be equipped with a special lubricant that ensures that the watch is reliable in temperatures of down to –90°C.

Kobold Watch Company in the USA goes a step further with their explorer's model, the Polar Surveyor Chronograph. It, too, features this special lubricant, but it also comes in a case made of aerospace-grade titanium. This metal found its way into the watch industry in the 1980s and is infinitely better in the cold as its thermal conductivity is considerably lower than that of stainless steel. So if one's exposed skin were to touch such a titanium watch, the chances are that it wouldn't stick to the surface of the watch.

Most professional-grade wristwatches are equipped with rotating bezels which allow the user to take an additional time measurement, such as elapsed time. All too often these bezels get stuck permanently in extremely cold conditions. Ice builds up beneath the bezel's rail and click-spring mechanism, causing it to freeze. Kobold found a solution by using small ceramic ball bearings that are impervious to this type of problem. Four of these ball bearings ensure that the bezel spins as intended and clicks into place at the user's discretion. So Mike and I used Rolex or Kobold watches with confidence in the −50°Cs.

We were both grateful to be escaping, as we believed, from the unbearable cold of the high plateau, but we were apprehensive of the 9,000-foot labyrinth below. The massive bastion of the Transantarctic Mountains, which effectively dams a mile-deep ocean of ice, is 2,000 miles long and 200 miles wide. When the moving sea of inland ice, descending from the polar plateau, laps against the upper flanks of this range, even 6,000-foot-high peaks seem vulnerable to the surging forces of ice which have drowned two-thirds of their rock mass. The scale of rock and ice is massive, the pent-up power of nature threatening the jumble of gigantic tributary glaciers, contorted icefalls and deep hidden valleys more grandiose than anywhere on earth.

Many thousands of great glaciers have forced a path through this range, tearing away mountainsides and burying anything and everything in their wake. Of all these glaciers the Beardmore is king, the second-biggest glacier in the world and twice the size of Alaska's Malaspina, which held the Number Two slot until Shackleton discovered and named the Beardmore in 1908. At some point after we began to negotiate the Beardmore's long descent, I felt ever colder for no reason that I could identify, far colder than at any time in my life.

Mike, always keen to look on the bright side if there was one, pointed out that we were at least beginning to lose height, and with it many of the invidious and debilitating effects of altitude. He wrote:

> At altitude, one of the worst effects was that you wanted to pee a lot, and one of the prerequisites of peeing was that you had to take your mitts off to undo zips. While you stood there for just those few seconds, your fingers became painful and then useless, and when you had finished, you couldn't get your mitts on again. For some reason you also couldn't finish peeing successfully. All men recognise the 'last drip down the leg' phenomenon, but here it was the last half cupful. I constantly had that horrible feeling of warm wetness down the leg that quickly turned to ice. Later, in the tent, the urine-soaked clothing irritated the skin, and stank. Mind you, after a couple of months without washing, we stank anyway and lived with it.

I had studied the recorded comments of the two predecessor groups to have sledged down the Beardmore. The record from Scott's team in 1912 included, 'Falling into crevasses every minute' and 'Huge chasms, closely packed and most difficult to cross.'

Their geologist, Edward Wilson, found time to do a side trip on to a rock face and came away with samples of coal and 'beautifully traced leaves in layers'. These fossils later joined with others, garnered by Scott's other sledge teams, as evidence that the continent of Antarctica had once been a great deal warmer.

Wilson wrote of the Beardmore's crevasses: 'They were constantly giving way as we crossed them one by one on the rope. We never unroped the whole time as they were everywhere and not a sign of them until one of us went in and saw blue depths below to any extent you like.'

Another of the team wrote: 'The chief safeguard, however, is the sledge itself, which is twelve feet long and, being some way behind the men hauling it, acts as an anchor to the sledger who goes through the surface. Down he goes with a sickening fall, but the harness holds him and he swings round, helpless but safe, until his companions can get him out ... Time after time there comes that hideous fall; the moment's fear that the harness will not hold.'

Will Steger, the American dog-sledger and leader of many successful polar journeys, commenting on attempts such as ours to cross Antarctica by manhaul, wrote:

> If anyone can accomplish the manhaul, Messner (and partner Arved Fuchs, a veteran German polar explorer) probably can. The first man to successfully climb all of the world's fourteen tallest peaks, each taller than twenty-six thousand feet, he is held in high esteem by mountaineers around the globe. At forty-five, he has led quite an adventuresome life. He lives in a castle outside Juva, Italy; has lost two of his brothers in mountain climbing accidents, as well as eight of his toes to frostbite; and has documented his travails in two dozen books. He has more high altitude experience than any climber alive. But by tackling the flat plains of Antarctica he has entered a new realm. His plan to ski from the edge of the Ronne/Filchner Ice Shelf to McMurdo in 120 days will take all the stamina he and Fuchs can muster. It will also demand a great deal of luck ...

The secret of Reinhold Messner's epic mountain climbs had always been his ability to travel light. In Antarctica this approach has severe limitations, due to the great distances involved and the unavoidable need for plenty of food and fuel. Messner and Fuchs used aircraft to resupply them, but they completed their journey and descended the Beardmore Glacier, as we were about to.

Messner wrote: 'I had difficulty in pulling the sledge with its initial weight of 80 kilos. I had to strain in my harness like a horse on dry drift snow in order to progress. It didn't feel good.' We had set out with initial weights of 200 kilograms and our loads were still well over 80 kilograms by the time we reached the Beardmore.

Both Reinhold and I had been given a specific route down the Beardmore which was designed by Charles Swithinbank to avoid the worst crevasse fields. Reinhold must have taken a wrong turn at some point, for despite his unparalleled experience in glacier ice-falls, he soon became lost in a maze of huge interlocked crevasses. At one point he wrote: 'The hardest and most dangerous day so far. For the most part we move between and over gigantic crevasses. We have to overcome an icefall which looks like the Khumbu Glacier on Mount Everest.' And later: 'We go two miles to get one mile north. From above we have no view of the route. We try to reach the middle of the Beardmore by crossing side streams. We go three hours with crampons on bare ice and come to a widely shattered icefall marked on no map. We get stuck. We go back. In part the crevasses are so big one could put a church inside.'

Of these conditions, Scott's man Cherry-Garrard wrote: 'I cannot describe the maze we got into and the hair breadth escapes we have had to pass through today. Fathomless pits fell away on each side too numerous to think of. Often and often we saw openings where it was possible to drop in the biggest ship afloat and lose her.' So it was with Mike and me on our 88th day but, unlike Cherry-Garrard, we had no crampons or pointed sticks to help grip the ice as we crept along slanting, slippery crater rims and knife-edge ridges between deep, dark craters.

Mike wrote: 'The crevasses were huge and the combination of icy surfaces, slopes and changes in direction totally knackered me.' Mike was especially at risk since, although I had lost more weight, he was still the lighter of the two of us and so more prone to succumb to the nerve-racking behaviour of our sledges. At moments when, with dizzy drops on both sides and virtually no traction, we traversed slanting gangplanks of ice, our sledges would sometimes slip sickeningly sideways and their weight, heavier than our own bodyweight, would try to tear us from our precarious foothold. In one hidden hole, small but deep, I fell at a time when I was unclipped from my harness. Only the fact that one of my ski sticks jammed between the two walls saved my life.

We had to choose with care where we camped, and preferably on level snow platforms away from ice and, when near either rocky flank of the glacier, away from zones of obvious rockfall from the cliffs above. We ensured that our tent was pegged down with our longest ice screws and tied to our nearby sledges because when gusts of katabatic wind struck, they could and did whip away standard tent pegs in seconds. Mike's diary:

> The wind came from the cold air of the plateau behind us. Flowing over those broad weirs of ice that marked the edge, it accelerated as it began to drop rapidly and was then channelled by the mountain massifs to become faster still before it screamed through the ice-carved valleys, carrying all before it. The wind was the cause of the bare blue-ice on which we walked, blasting it clean and racing onwards laden with snow and ice. Our clothing was laughable in the face of such a katabatic gale. That icy wind cut through to the skin with no hindrance. It was as if we were naked, and it hurt. It hurt from the start to the finish of each day.

My Australian guidebook describes these winds well:

> Another problem unique to Antarctica are the katabatic winds, which can reach 305 kilometres per hour. On top of a plateau, you don't have to worry about them, as their impetus is purely gravitational. When the temperatures change, warm air travels upwards and cold air takes its place. But if this temperature difference occurs where the land is dropping from high mountains down into valleys – a descent of 2,740 metres in 160 kilometres isn't uncommon in Antarctica – the winds can whip from gentle to 160 kilometres per hour in just a few minutes.

By following Swithinbank's suggested route with great care and frequent compass checks, Mike and I avoided many of the worst crevasse fields described by Scott and Messner, and a few days down the great glacier we came to a point where the Beardmore widens to 30 miles from wall to wall, and in the centre has relatively few crevasses. Here an unusually gentle breeze allowed us, for the first time during the descent, to try the parachutes. They worked well, but the wind took us far to the west of the comparative safety of the Swithinbank route and slap into an area of massive crevassing just east of a rocky feature known as the Wedge Face, somewhere between 172° and 173° west of Greenwich.

I knew that we were heading for trouble, but the deadly effect of the cold, made worse by the very act of keeping my arms raised to control the parachute lines and the resulting lack of circulation, had a deadening effect on my thought processes. Zombie-like, I just kept on thinking, 'We must use this breeze while it lasts no matter where it takes us.'

After one bout of wind-sailing, Mike recorded:

> We found ourselves falling and being dragged over rough ground at tremendous speeds. Our sledges turned over and were ripped along upside down. After becoming tangled in the rigging, we were numb with cold and my fingers became frostbitten, blistered and were weeping pus. In addition, I was hobbled by a fractured ankle. Ran, too, had problems with his feet. A graft from a previous frost injury had broken down early in the journey and the pain he had suffered ever since hurt him more than ever now.

Although Mike and I both took our skis off from time to time, especially after being reduced to only one ski stick each, for most of the time we depended upon the glide of our skis to ease every step that we took. On days when this vital glide factor was absent, our lives were made miserable, and as winter advanced our skis glided less and less.

Skis have been around for quite a while, if not actual knowledge of the physics of gliding. Laplanders are reputed to have followed their reindeer herds on skis some 4,000 years ago, and the word ski comes from the Scandinavian word 'skith' or 'stick'. A thirteenth-century map, known as the Hereford Mappa Mundi, shows Earth as a circular disc with Jerusalem at the centre, and the Garden of Eden as well as Noah's Ark in precise geographical locations, and includes a man holding a long stick and wearing long flat boards on both his feet. This is the first known drawing of skis, apart from Stone Age carvings on cave walls.

Scott's men knew none of this, but they did work out that both warmer and colder temperatures affected the performance of the runners of their skis and their sledge runners. The ideal glide temperature, they found, was –9°C, and at about –29°C the glide action disappeared, to be replaced as it got colder by more and more drag. Scott wrote on a –32°C day: 'Very minute crystals . . . absolutely spoil the surface; we had heavy dragging during the last hour in spite of the light load and full sail.'

The prevailing temperature decides how easily a thin film of liquid water will form under a runner, as its very movement over snow causes friction and, therefore, heat. It is also generally believed that, at –30°C, the snow becomes too cold to melt under a ski, so it ceases to glide and starts to drag. Additionally, it is likely that the molecules of frozen water on the snow's surface, whilst still frozen, are not as tightly bound to the layer of crystals immediately beneath them, so they provide less grip for a ski. Inuit in the Arctic had long ago showed me how to encourage a fixed layer of ice to form on runners, one method being to urinate on them. But, like commercial ski waxes, such treatments only work in moderately cold conditions.

The lower stretches of the Beardmore were impressive. Nothing else lived here, nor ever had since the dinosaurs of Gondwanaland. No birds or beasts or the least bacteria survived. There was only the deep roar of massive avalanches, the shriek and grind of splitting rock, the groan of shifting ice, and the music, soft or fierce, of the winds from a thousand valleys, moving to and fro across the eternal silence. I do not remember ever feeling so deeply chilled. Not ever.

The wind roared against the cliffs in Force Eight strength, and donning my skis I found it possible to body-sail over lakes of wind-scoured blue-ice. The wind struck my back with enough power to move me, sledge and all, with the blessed bonus of less boot action and a corresponding reduction in foot pain. My arms became numb with cold, since they were no longer pumping with the rhythm of the ski stick.

Antarctica is by far the coldest place on earth, with still-air temperatures of –88°C. In such temperatures mercury turns to solid metal, tin falls apart into granules, the flame of a candle becomes hooded by a wax helmet, and a carelessly dropped steel tube is liable to shatter like broken glass. I have met people who come from Canada or Minnesota and they laugh, 'Oh, I was working at –60°C last year. It was easy.' As like as not these polar veterans experienced their cold wearing adequate clothing, with full stomachs, healthy and about to return to a nice warm bed.

For humans in Antarctica the danger is chiefly the wind. Each knot of wind has the effect on human skin of a drop of one degree in temperature. We, like Scott, found ourselves starving, freezing and in danger of falling into crevasses without hope of rescue. The wind knifed through me and I found my body chattering beyond control with violent shivering seizures. The ever-nagging pain from my feet disappeared, at least from my awareness, with this utterly new experience, which had not even accompanied previous Arctic soakings and the subsequent waiting, sodden, with clothes turning solid. At least my core resistance had on those occasions been in fighting form. We were now experiencing the coldest 'skin' temperatures of the expedition. This was the worst of conditions.

As the elevation drops and air warms, gusting katabatics are wont to grow stronger. Tents are ripped into shreds by katabatic gusts, and I knew we must find a camp spot somehow protected from the full blast that polished this blue-ice canyon. Rounding a bend in the cliff-wall I spotted, through the blowing snow, a sudden steep descent of several hundred feet. I retraced my northward trail and headed straight for the rock face, in the hope of finding some nook of protection for the night. Small rocks began to litter the ice floor, and these increased in size until we were clambering between boulders, manoeuvring the sledges with care for they tended to jam.

Battered by katabatic blasts, but afforded some shelter by the boulders, we made camp working carefully together to avoid the tent being torn from our grasp as, with our near lifeless fingers, we tried to push the rods into the sleeves of the billowing cotton dome. With considerable relief we crawled into the tent. This was the first of our nights on half-rations. For some reason I remember it as the only night when I smelled a powerful aroma of stale body odour in the tent. Whether the stench was mine or Mike's I am unsure. We never washed in three months.

Mike's hands had gradually deteriorated since his mitt problems just before the Pole, and they now looked quite impressive, for three of the main finger blisters had burst, the dead skin falling away to reveal raw stumps like red sausages. He continued to handle our evening cooking and turned down my offer to help (my fingers were in good shape). What pained him most, it seemed, was the removal of his mitts, for their wool sometimes stuck to the raw finger flesh.

On reaching the great crevasse field beside the black cliffs of the Wedge Face, and knowing that neither Scott nor Messner, or any other group, had ever attempted to cross it, I looked for a way around it. There was no visible alternative but to turn back and complete a ten-mile loop, maybe more, to circumvent the unknown nature of the crevassed zone ahead. Perhaps because of my cold-affected mindset, I simply couldn't face turning back into a strong headwind, and so we carried on into the turbulent mess dead ahead. Mike wrote:

> Slowly we climbed towards the middle of the disturbance. We came to a region of total anarchy. The ice was split in all directions and it seemed as if more of the area was occupied by black voids than by white surface. Furthermore, most of the surface consisted of the wind-blasted blue glass, with just a few patches

of soft snow which formed into crevasse bridges. It made things very difficult. It would have been suicidal to cross the bridges without skis, yet elsewhere they skittered sideways on the glassy surfaces which funnelled towards the deep canyons. Worse, the sledges had a mind of their own, slewing to one side at the least opportunity and doing their best to drag us to destruction. It was terrifying. At any time it seemed as if one could slip, fall or be pulled over, and nothing would have stopped one from disappearing through the gaping mouths, down into the dark black throats.

We made our way through like men in a maze, wandering back and forth, seeking bridges strong enough to bear us, and turning aside from chasms too large to cross. Our course meandered so much, and it would have been so cold if we delayed, that neither of us suggested using a rope. We just took our chances and looked for the routes that seemed strong. We both moved as fast as we could.

When we emerged from the crevasse field, we had travelled in extreme cold conditions for twelve hours non-stop. We camped, exhausted but relieved. Mike wrote: 'Only two days from crossing the continent. Amazing thought.'

At this point we had travelled hundreds of miles further than any of our unsupported predecessors, including Scott's men, but we were near the end of our tether. Mike's diary:

I looked at Ran's feet. They were a ghastly sight. The right foot was deformed by the swelling at the base of the little toe, a product of two months of inflammation and infection, and some of the other toes were blackened and blistered. The left was far worse. Where once had been his toes, there were now black, fluid-filled bags, so grotesquely swollen that they merged into one. From them oozed a vile dark liquid that smelt dreadful, despite the cold . . .

[He looked] old, thin and haggard. Perched upon his bony buttocks, his long legs stretched in front of him were worse than mine, and they ended in those horribly damaged feet. His face was ravaged, almost ancient, and hooded lids covered eyes that were somehow dulled. His features were puffed and doughy, and his lips were still scabbed and broken in places. The frost had left its mark. His ears were blistered and beneath one eye was a raw patch where he's pulled off glasses while they were still frozen on. His hair, thinning a little before we started, is now falling out in tufts.

Only one more obstacle lay between us and the coast of Antarctica where the ice of the Beardmore flowed into the floating Ross Ice Shelf. This was the chaotic ice trench between land and sea, and Charles Swithinbank had given me a meticulous set of compass bearings, based on the Gateway route originally pioneered by Shackleton in 1908, in order to pass through this disturbance.

Some forty miles out on the sea ice and on the 95th day of our journey, we made a radio call to Morag asking her to send our chartered Twin Otter to remove us from the ice. Mike wrote from his perch on the sea ice of the Pacific Ocean:

> While Ran made the radio call for our pick-up, I went and stood outside. Our tent was pitched in the middle of a huge white plain. To the south, a thin line ran back from where I stood to disappear beyond the horizon, towards mountains and wind-sluiced valleys. There it ran back up the glacier and then due south to the Pole. It continued on – straight for the rest of the plateau, and dropped tortuously through valleys, dunes and sastrugi to the ice shelf on the far side and so to the Atlantic coast. It was the longest, unbroken track that any man had ever made.

All attempts for a century, whether by Norwegians, Soviets or Americans, to cross the continent unaided and using snow-machines or dog teams had failed miserably. In hauling our own loads across this area, greater in mass by far than the United States, we have shown that manpower can, indeed, be superior to dog-power and, in doing so, have partly exonerated Scott's much-abused theories on the matter.

The 1993 *Guinness Book of Records* states: 'The longest totally self-supporting polar sledge journey ever made and the first totally unsupported crossing of the Antarctic landmass were achieved by R. Fiennes and M. Stroud. They covered a distance of 2,170 km (1,350 miles).'

Of the tangible results of Mike's meticulous scientific work, Dr John Heap, the director of the Scott Polar Research Institute in Cambridge, wrote:

> When Ran Fiennes and Mike Stroud were about to be picked off the ice after the Antarctic crossing, I had a call from a gentleman of the press saying that he had been asked by his editor to write a piece about the expedition. In a bored voice he asserted, 'It doesn't really amount to anything, does it?' 'Have you,' I asked him, 'personally, by your own efforts, contributed millions of pounds to medical research, and have you, yourself, taken part in a human physiological experiment requiring you to tread on and off a machine five million times in one hundred days in temperatures which would kill you if you stopped?' Only if he had done these things, I suggested, would he have a right to make a judgement about what the expedition amounted to. He hadn't.
>
> Ran has never sought to justify his expeditions on the basis of questing for knowledge, but he has, nevertheless, contributed greatly to science in the polar regions. While asking the general public, through his books, to have regard to the adventurous tales they unfold, he has quietly ensured that good scientific use is made of wherever his expeditions happen to be, taking advantage of whatever phenomena were before them. In these days of scientific teams involved in large scale scientific programmes, such serendipitous research is a rarity indeed; but nonetheless valuable for that.
>
> Much as Ran might consider himself to be in the steps of

adventurers like Roald Amundsen, these volumes of scientific results place him more in the scientific tradition of Captain Scott. But, unlike a Shackleton, he had the good sense and judgement to survive to tell the tale – sometimes only just!

Chapter Fourteen

For a year after Antarctica I helped Ginny on the farm and wrote books, but in 1995 I heard from Morag and Laurence Howell that Børge Ousland, a colleague of Erling Kagge and an ex-member of the Norwegian Navy special forces, was planning to cross Antarctica solo and supported only by windsail in the following year. Børge had wind-skied to the South Pole in the record time of only 44 days. This was like a racehorse trouncing the previous best performance of carthorses. He was thirty-four years old and at the peak of his ability.

Solo travel has never appealed to me. Half the fun of an expedition is the planning of it and, as with old soldiers, the shared memories afterwards. Photos and video footage, vital to lecture and book income after an expedition, are also less interesting if only one person is involved. Nonetheless, to cross Antarctica solo and unsupported was a tempting idea, and even better if done before rather than after Børge.

Mike and Morag discussed the challenge and agreed to help with preparations. At fifty-two years of age, I needed to keep fit and I trained with Mike and three others for the 1995 Eco-Challenge race in the Canadian Rockies. Morag agreed to accompany me to Antarctica as base and communications boss as, by then, Ginny was full-time into farming on Exmoor.

Morag had studied Børge's success and she advised me to learn how to use one of the high-tech kites that had so revolutionized polar travel. A kitemaker in Wales made me a kite, and James

Dyson, of vacuum-cleaner fame, agreed to sponsor the expedition, provided it raised funds for his favourite charity, Breakthrough Breast Cancer. Outside his Wiltshire factory a kite-expert Dyson employee gave me my first lesson, but the kite flew over a tree and some power lines to land in a road where it was run over by a Volvo.

I spent the next eleven months involved in competitive team racing, and one newspaper described me as 'the fittest 52 year old in Britain'. I made do with a total of two days attempting to learn the complex art of kite-flying. This was a bad mistake.

We flew to Punta Arenas in Chile, where blizzards kept us – and Børge's team – waiting for two weeks. There were two other groups also going for the solo traverse: a giant of a man, Marek Kaminski, thirty-three, a Pole who had the previous year become the first person to ski to both poles in a single year; and a Korean, as small in stature as Børge and Marek were big.

A British team arrived in Punta also bound for Antarctica, and one member, Clive Johnson, showed me an impressive wind-assistance device called a parawing. This was far easier to use than my kite and, Johnson discovered, was the same model that Ousland and Kaminski had both used so successfully the previous year. Trials, in a field by the main Punta graveyard, soon proved the parawing to be infinitely superior to the kite. I tried to obtain one, but the weather at Patriot Hills improved and we flew on to Antarctica the next day, so I had to stick with the kite.

Our four expeditions were all dropped off at various well-separated spots on the Atlantic coast of the continent, and all set out within a few hours of each other.

I said a quick farewell to Morag and the crew of the ski plane, set my compass for 165°, which was due south, and hauled hard at my 495-pound load containing supplies for 110 days.

I did not fancy my chances of beating the other three men unless there was a shortage of wind or a generous helping of injuries to the others, which, in Antarctica, was always possible. Anyway, it was nice to be back in Antarctica with a competitive task, Morag on the other end of the radio, and rations plus medical pack carefully planned by Mike. Charity-wise, Dyson planned to raise £1 million for the breast cancer clinic on the back of the expedition.

The clothing I wore was the result of experience obtained from previous manhaul trips. Antarctica is a very dry place where less than an inch of rain occurs annually, like the central Sahara desert, so there is no need to carry standard waterproof outer clothing. But the effort of manhauling, even at low temperatures, produces moisture through sweat and heavy breathing into a balaclava. Clothes do, therefore, get wet from the inside, so my long-term clothing sponsors had designed many of my garments, including down jackets, socks, mitts and also sleeping bags with an inner vapour-barrier lining to hinder body moisture saturation. This vapour-barrier material loses its advantage in extreme cold because its microscopic pores, large enough to let water vapour through, but not liquid, are ineffective once water vapour freezes.

Because my hooded sledge jacket, the main item of warmth (not normally worn when actually manhauling) had this vapour-barrier lining, it was stuffed with duck down which, despite the advent of modern artificial insulation materials, remains by far the warmest material for its weight factor, but only so long as it stays dry. None of my clothing was woollen, since artificial fleece absorbs less moisture and artificial materials provide more insulation-effective underwear than cotton.

My mitts had artificial fleece pads on their backs on which to wipe my constantly running nose before the ice dribble formed into what polar jargon describes as snotsicles. I always wore a balaclava over my head and usually, unless sweating, my fur-rimmed jacket hood as well. This fur rim is traditionally of wolverine fur, which is the least likely to ice up with the moisture from expelled breath. Mike's dictum was:

> When you are well wrapped up in cold conditions, as much as ninety per cent of your remaining heat losses can come from your scalp, and so putting on or taking off a hat can change thermal

> equilibrium substantially. Without the problems of fiddling with buttons or zips, you can regulate your overall comfort and may even influence thermal balance in distant parts of the body. If you have cold hands, you should put on your hat.

Big ski goggles with nose protection snouts needed to be close-fitting to avoid breath quickly fogging up their lenses. My ski sticks were designed to be shorter than usual, so that my hands would remain lower than my heart when manhauling and I would, therefore, be less likely to suffer from loss of blood circulation.

Our four solo expeditions set out from their respective start points just as a blizzard descended from the high plateau and roared down to the coastline. I stayed in my wildly flapping tent, having pegged it down, not with standard ice pegs but with my skis, sticks and ice axe, plus an anchor line to my sledge.

This blizzard nearly killed Marek Kaminski, as I later learnt. He decided to travel despite the adverse conditions, but he had bad luck. Briefly detached from his sledge and kite, he was struck on the head when the kite unexpectedly took off, sledge and all. When he recovered his wits in conditions of blizzard and white-out, he realized his extreme and immediate danger of exposure: no tent, no cooker, no food, no radio. Luckily, he saw a bloodstain in the snow in the direction that the sledge had disappeared. So, on a compass bearing, he stumbled off into the gloom and, sometime later, to his huge relief, found his sledge jammed against a sastrugi ridge which had halted its rapid progress towards the pole.

The whole business of super-powerful polar blizzards along the coastline beneath high ice caps, whether in Antarctica or Greenland, has always been a high risk and annoyance factor to the few humans who base themselves there. Antarctica's katabatic winds have been clocked at over 200 m.p.h. and, at Thule in Greenland, at 208 m.p.h. Scott's man Cherry-Garrard described his first experience of a katabatic blow: 'Outside there is raging chaos ... Fight your way a few steps from the tent and it will be gone. Lose your sense of direction and there is nothing to guide you back.'

The katabatics which rampage across Antarctica are conceived in the womb of the polar winter as freezing air builds up on the lofty interior plateau. The katabatics begin when this cold dense air spills down the contours of the ice cap into the deep mountain valleys, gathering velocity as they roar down the glaciers to the ice shelves below.

Will Steger noted that in the calm cold conditions that often follow a severe katabatic, the cooling winds can cause ice crystals to form, and Russian resupply aircraft on their way to and from the Vostok base could be heard by his team a good five minutes before they arrived overhead, such was the clarity of sound in the super-cool air. And that long after the aircraft had passed by, he could still smell kerosene on the ice crystals of the post-katabatic air.

Despite my initial sledge load weighing 485 pounds, exactly as it had been for our continental traverse two years before, I found the day-to-day manhauling definitely easier. This I put down to the improvement of equipment, such as the skins under my skis. Previously Mike and I frequently had to adjust and re-glue the skins, but now, new glues ensured that they never came unstuck, so I avoided getting cold fingers.

My communication equipment was smaller, lighter and far more efficient than ever before. Morag now had Inmarsat gear, on which she daily conversed with her husband Laurence back in Scotland, and he told her the latest exact location of Børge and sometimes of Marek. So in the tent each night I was able to compare my speed of advance with theirs. By pressing a button on my GPS I could instantly know where I was without the cold, laborious task of mounting a theodolite or sextant to shoot the altitude of the sun or some star. Times were certainly changing.

I have found it difficult to stop trying for polar records. It is a sort of addiction which seems to have affected quite a few individuals, and Shackleton was probably one such. Only eighty years ago, and in living memory, he plotted his grand design. He called it his 'last great expedition'. His previous obsession, to be first to either pole, had been rendered obsolete by others. He was noted as saying: 'With

Amundsen's success, only one great Antarctic journeying remains – the crossing of the South Polar Continent, from sea to sea.'

At the time, he and his wife Emily, who in 1911 had their third child, were not happy. He was not a good businessman and could be aggressively argumentative. In London he spent hours in his club, hired taxis for days of merely visiting friends and paid, in Emily's opinion, too much attention to certain other women.

Slowly but surely he put together the necessary sponsorship for his expedition. His route plan was simple but highly ambitious. With a team of five polar veterans, he would land his ship *Endurance* somewhere along the coast of the notoriously ice-riven Weddell Sea. Then sledge to the South Pole over a totally unknown route. Thence, reversing Scott's polar route down the Beardmore, he knew he would run out of food. So the other half of his team in his second ship *Aurora*, bought from the Australian explorer Douglas Mawson, would, by the time he reached the Beardmore's bottom, have dropped off food and fuel dumps all the way to McMurdo Sound. He called this other team the Ross Sea Party.

The year 1914 was not a good time for male Britons to go adventuring as too many were heading for the trenches. Shackleton, who had a heart condition, had repeatedly tried to be posted to the front but had always been turned down. In August the British government announced general mobilization for the First World War, and Shackleton pledged his ships and men to the service of king and country. Both Churchill, First Lord of the Admiralty, and the King told Shackleton to go ahead with the expedition. So *Endurance* left Liverpool the following month and Shackleton wrote a letter to Emily which must, to her, have seemed as cold as Antarctica.

> ... for some time past we have not seen eye to eye and that the fault lies with me ... I wonder if you know me really: I am not worth much consideration if I were really known and I have shown you that or rather tried to show it to you, only you think differently, don't you? ... I have tried to look at things [from] your point of view as well as mine and all to no purpose: and I

> go round in a circle ... I am just good as an explorer and nothing else, I am hard also and damnably persistent when I want anything: altogether a generally unpleasing character: I love the fight and when things [are] easy I hate it though when things are wrong I get worried ... Now I am on my own work I will be better and more at peace and I don't think I will ever go on a long expedition again.

On reaching the Weddell Sea in February 1915 the *Endurance* ran into heavy pack ice, which in due course set hard as concrete about her, and eight months later crushed and sank her, a thousand miles from the nearest inhabited island. To put it mildly, Shackleton then made the best of a bad job. He and his twenty-seven shipmates managed to survive five months of manhauling three lifeboats over shifting drifting ice floes until, on reaching open water, they battled huge seas to reach the barren shores of Elephant Island.

Knowing that he and his men would die there if no rescue came, Shackleton and five others navigated eight hundred miles of the wildest seas in the world in one of the lifeboats and reached South Georgia where, after a three-day scramble over high glaciers, they arrived at a whaling station. With great support from the Chilean government and after four separate attempts to reach ice-bound Elephant Island, Shackleton eventually rescued the men he had left there nearly five months before. The *Endurance* expedition had clearly been a failure, since it never set foot on Antarctica, but Shackleton turned it into an internationally acclaimed saga of human survival against all odds.

A disgruntled Falklander wrote in the *Magellan Times* in 1916, ''E oughter 'ave been at the war long ago instead of messing about on icebergs.' And there were, as always with professional media critics, a few rumbles along the lines of Stephanie Barczewski's recent comment: 'Shackleton had no business going off on a frivolous expedition to a useless frozen wasteland at a time of national crisis.' But for the most part, the legend of Shackleton as an icon of superb leadership was firmly established.

In the early 1990s Sir Vivian Fuchs, who in the 1950s successfully completed Shackleton's planned traverse, told me that in his considered opinion the sinking of the *Endurance* had been a blessing in disguise, since it precluded a far worse ending to the whole project.

Many polar-history enthusiasts today praise Shackleton above all because, in dire straits, he 'never lost a man'. But this is true only if you ignore the other half of his expedition, the Ross Sea Party, who are often forgotten. It was their vital job to place resupply dumps from McMurdo to the base of the Beardmore. If they failed to do this, they knew that Shackleton's planned traverse would also fail, due to starvation on the Ross Ice Shelf.

Their ship *Aurora* landed ten men, including the skipper Aeneas Mackintosh, the heir to the chieftainship of the Mackintosh clan, at McMurdo Sound, but was badly damaged by ice whilst still unloading vital stores and only just made it back to New Zealand. Although it was thought that there was plenty of food for the ten men to survive and to complete their mission because they could raid the supplies left in Scott's hut, there was evidence of considerable distress because of poor management and preparation.

Polar veteran Ernest Joyce who frequently fell out with Mackintosh, openly vented his anger at those in the expedition's London office who had packed the gear for the sledging work. Less than half the necessary clothing had been included. Joyce stated: 'I will one day interview the person responsible for this disgraceful omission.' The initial poor planning and organization was to lead to considerable suffering over the next two years, and even in 1928 the polar historian Dr Hugh Mill agreed that it might be best not to publish certain aspects of the story. 'The full tale,' he wrote, 'had better remain unpublished for some time to come.'

Despite their lack of equipment, the stranded men scrounged enough gear to manhaul nearly two thousand miles to achieve their mission for Shackleton, but in ignorance of the fact that their sufferings, which were great, were utterly pointless since *Endurance* was already at the bottom of the Weddell Sea. The advent of efficient radio communications a few years later would have prevented a tragedy, for one man died of scurvy and two, including Mackintosh, were lost on fractured ice floes.

In 1917 the *Aurora*, under the veteran polar skipper John Davis, finally rescued the Ross Sea Party survivors, and Davis, who had seen many men ravaged by polar travels, observed that, 'Their great physical suffering went deeper than their appearance. Their speech was jerky, at times semi-hysterical, almost unintelligible ... these events had rendered these hapless individuals as unlike ordinary human beings as any I have ever met. The Antarctic had given them the full treatment.'

Shackleton's men had no kites, but on my fourth day of solo travel over Berkner Island the northerly blizzard fell away to be replaced by a strong breeze from the sea, so I decided to try out my kite. The idea was to hold its control lines with both hands and ski along harnessed to my heavy sledge. Several times gusts slammed the sledge into the back of my legs and I collapsed in a welter of skis, sticks and tangled ropes. One high-speed crash gave me a painful ankle and smashed ski tip. I bandaged both with industrial tape.

This was the learning process. Necessity is the mother of invention and, for the first time, I began to develop the kiting knack. To my enormous delight, I learned to catch the wind and hold it, but only in the direction the wind dictated. That night, to my amazement, the GPS told me that I had advanced 117 miles to the south, my personal record for a day's polar travel without machine aid.

On 18 November I made weak contact with Morag. She told me that over two days I had gained nearly 30 miles to Ousland's 21 miles. The following day, however, saw the arrival of a steady east wind which enabled Ousland to use his parawing and cover a staggering 99 miles in two days. His skill enabled him to use winds from the west and east to propel him southwards. If only I could do likewise. I swore at my folly for not discovering parawings before it was too late to obtain one.

Throughout 21 and 22 November there was no wind, only white-out, and both Ousland and I manhauled due south. He managed 19 miles, I completed 19.3, despite my extra hundred pounds of load. Not exactly catching him up, but a good sign for the five-hundred-mile plateau ahead, where manhauling should come into its own due to the head winds that prevailed there.

Every evening I attended to my developing crotch-rot with Canestan powder and applied lengths of industrial sticky tape to raw areas. My back and hips were sore, but not as painful as on previous journeys because my harness designers had developed an effective new padding system. For the first time on a heavy polar manhaul journey, life was truly bearable.

The sun provided no relief. It burst through the white-out one day and I was immediately too hot. I continued stripped to my underwear, but any bare strip of skin quickly burned purple because the ozone hole was at its worst at that time of year. I fashioned some headwear from a ration bag, and this covered my neck and shoulders like the flap of a kepi. A day later the white-out returned, but I still managed eleven hours of non-stop manhauling. I was well ahead of schedule.

From Berkner Island the ice shelf was flat and easy until, on reaching the coastline, a sudden ascent known as Frost Spur rose dead ahead. To me, a dedicated no-climber, the spur appeared as a crevassed and seemingly impassable barrier, an ice-sheathed cliff rising to the abrupt blue-sky horizon high above. As a vertigo sufferer since my early twenties, I would not have relished the ascent with a light rucksack on my back, let alone a sledge-load still weighing about 470 pounds.

Black clouds along the eastern horizon promised further bad weather. I began to haul myself up the icy incline, but repeatedly slid backwards. Exhausted, I pitched the tent and decided to split my sledge-load into four. If I could make my first ascent while sunlight still bathed the wall of the spur, showing me the best route, I could then descend again, eat and sleep, and complete three more climbs the next day.

Only fifty feet up my hands were already cold, and the ice wall was about to switch from brilliant sunlight to deep shadow when I was seized by vertigo. Shaking my head to break its mesmeric

Mike Stroud in 1987 skirting a patch of nilas ice

Oliver Shepard. Too wide to jump across?

Charlie Burton patrols one edge of the floe on which he and Ran Fiennes floated hundreds of miles south from the North Pole

A curious polar bear beside the ship when beset in Arctic pack ice in 1982

Charlie Burton and Ran Fiennes during their dash through the Northwest Passage by open boat in 1981 when the ice conditions were open. Often they were not

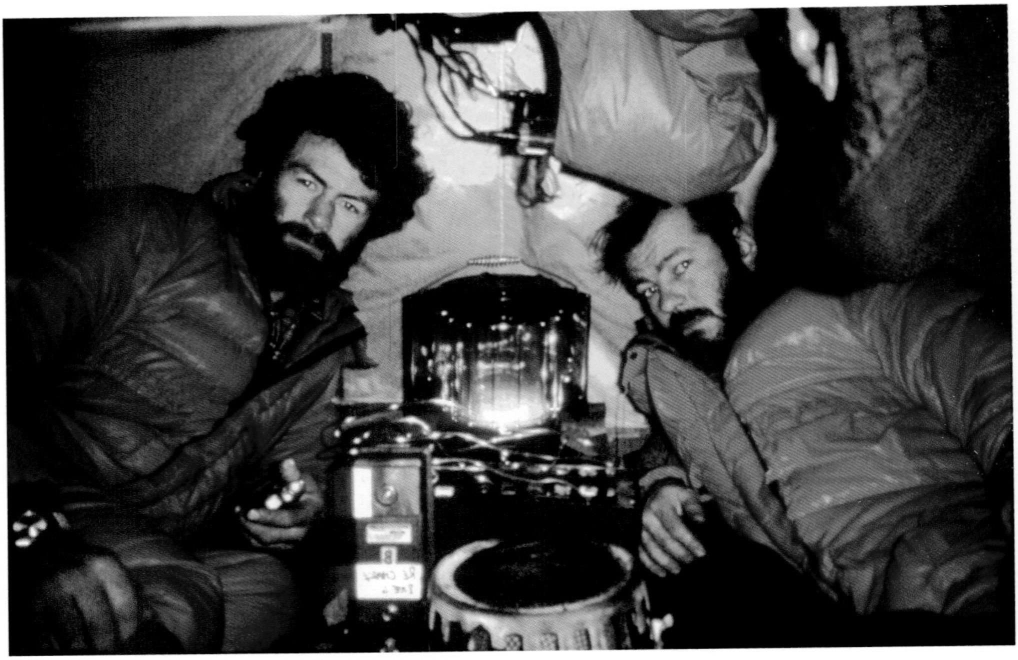

Ran Fiennes (left) and Charlie Burton taking it easy in the large polar tent

Charlie Burton exiting from one of the Ryvingen cardboard huts in 1980

Simon Grimes erecting the cardboard polar hut designed by Ginny Fiennes and Tri-Wall in 1978

Ran Fiennes and the contents of one sledge load for an Antarctic crossing attempt

Oliver Shepard preparing ration packs at the hut on Ward Hunt Island in 1985

The larder tunnel which was used for eight months during the Antarctic winter of 1979/80

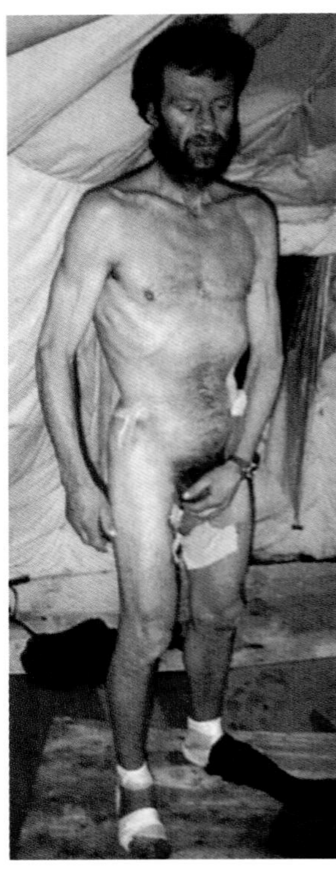

Ran Fiennes skeletal and sore after a polar journey

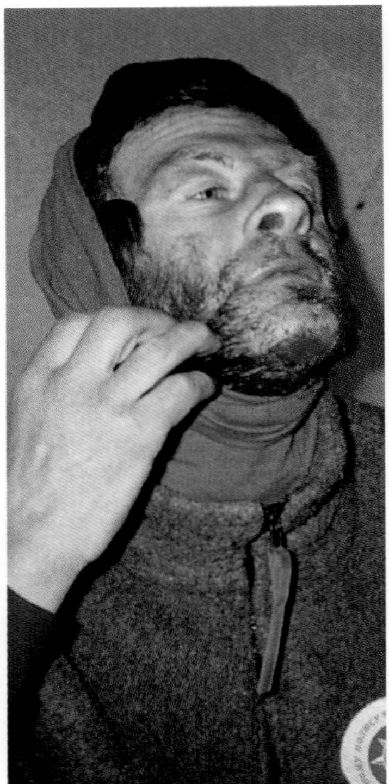

A common polar sore when ice forms below the chin from nose dribble. Taking a balaclava off can rip skin and beard from the chin

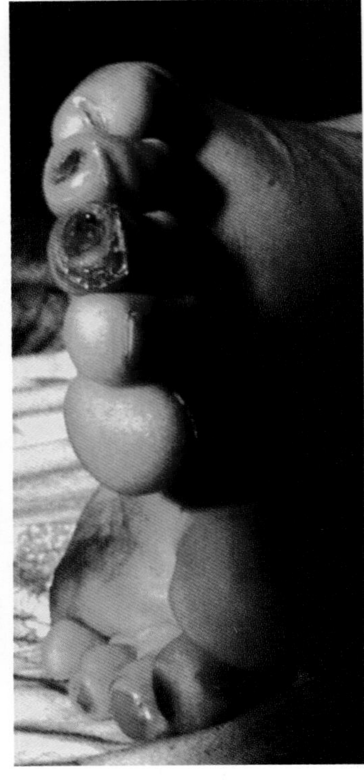

Ran's feet in Antarctica. Toe damage is common when manually hauling extreme loads by sledge

Ran Fiennes' self-surgery on frostbitten finger ends

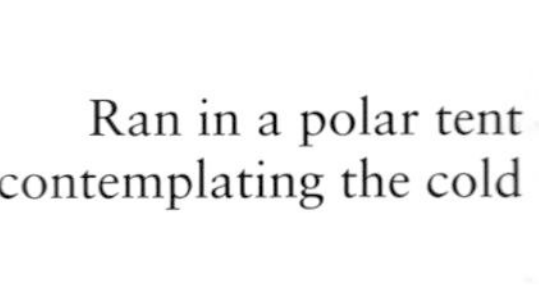

Ran in a polar tent contemplating the cold

The first recorded game of cricket at the South Pole. Bothie fielding at silly mid-on

Ryvingen Mountain at rear. Bothie is worried by a pair of vertical frozen jeans with no occupant

Transglobe team member Dave Hicks meeting a vocal local on arrival in Antarctica in 1979

One of the tracked Land Rovers tows its sea-going platform onto land ice from the sea in the Bering Strait

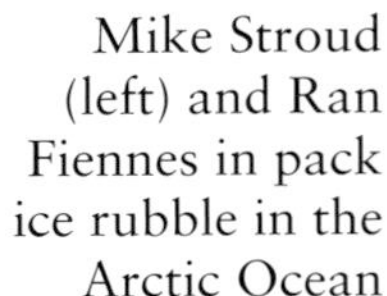

Mike Stroud (left) and Ran Fiennes in pack ice rubble in the Arctic Ocean

The most gentle incline on the entire ascent of the Eiger's North Face, the final summit slope (from which Ran nearly sent Ian Parnell to his doom)

spell, I gingerly retrieved my ice hammer from its sledge bag and started to pick my way up the frozen face of the spur. It was four hours before I reached the top and cached my first load. Here, in a wide expanse of nothingness, I stacked the rations and marked the pile of bags with a single ski. The journey back down to the tent took just forty minutes and, with relief, I cooked my rehydrated spaghetti bolognese and drank two pints of tea.

Ten minutes after I had fallen asleep a series of katabatic wind blasts struck the tent. This went on for an hour before I realized that I must move or the tent would be damaged. In a quarter of a century of travel, I had never encountered winds of such ferocious aggression. Sleep was out of the question during the brief lulls between each fresh blast. I dismantled the tent in seconds and lashed all my gear to a fixed ice screw.

I climbed the spur again, though several times the winds blew me from my fragile holds. Once I slipped thirty feet or more, desperately trying to dig the hammer's pick into the face. Gulping air, I rested shivering against the ice with the sledge dangling below me until I could resume my snail-like ascent.

The third ascent was the worst because I took a wrong route in the poor visibility and headed too far east. That meant that I had to climb twice as high to reach the rock-lined upper rim of the spur. With the clouds to the east now obscuring the escarpment, I immediately made a fourth ascent, but was too tired to manage two 25-pound ration bags. So I had to descend a fourth time to retrieve them.

The final and fifth climb, with the 50-pound load over my shoulders and no sledge, was easier. However, the storm clouds from the east reached the top of the spur before I did. Light snow began to fall and I could find no trace of my equipment cache or my previous tracks. I grew cold as the sweat of the climb froze on my skin. I knew that the twenty days' supply of bagged rations over my shoulders would do me little good if I failed to find the cache.

I prayed hard and an hour later I stumbled on the dump. Such moments of relief almost make these journeys worthwhile. Hearing the news of winning a lottery jackpot could not even approach the sheer happiness of that instant when I found my cache above Frost Spur.

Although I could not actually see the Antarctic plateau – in fact, I could see no feature at all in any direction – I knew that I had reached the gateway to the Pole. The dangers of the ice shelf and the escarpment were behind me. For the next seventy miles there would be crevasses and wicked moraines (masses of ice debris that formed difficult barriers), but after that there was nothing but the vast open plain of the polar plateau.

Morag's radio call on the last day of November told me that I was a hundred miles ahead of Kaminski and the Korean and slowly catching Børge. By the twentieth day of my journey I was already ten days ahead of my previous crossing. Not because of faster man-hauling, but entirely due to the single day of southerly kiting. Then on 2 December my growing optimism was dashed. Ousland had used his wonderful skill at parawing control of flank-winds to travel 134 miles in only four days. Ahead of me stretched the Jaburg Glacier and the heavily crevassed snowfields. This was one of the most wild and beautiful places in Antarctica and, in parts, one of the most dangerous.

I had seldom travelled alone before, except on SAS selection courses in the Brecon Beacons long ago. I believe solo journeys in remote places are irresponsible, and now two minor niggles chased me. Firstly, anybody can fall into a crevasse. In the smaller fissures, you can get jammed in a smooth ice bottleneck as the crevasse narrows. The warmth of your body will cause you to slide downwards and become wedged until you die. With a second person carrying safety ropes, there is a chance of rescue. Secondly, hypothermia can strike any polar traveller. It happened to Mike only two days short of reaching the South Pole. Had he been alone, he would certainly have died. Quite a reasonable way to go, if you think about it, but another reason why I believe solo trips to be irresponsible.

Being more fearful of crevasses than ever in the past when travelling with a companion, I would come to an abrupt, shocked halt whenever a sudden subsidence of the snow beneath my skis was announced by a low rumbling roar as of tons of gravel being dropped from a high crane. One of Scott's scientists described his first experience of such a snowquake: 'Every now and then a shiver would shake the surface and we could hear the eerie wave of sound expanding like a ripple all around. Sometimes one could see the whole snow surface sinking slightly, and at first the effect was very unpleasant.' This phenomenon seems to occur in certain regions in certain conditions. Snow, which has built up in a layer several inches thick and may cover an area as large as a football field, suddenly collapses from its own weight on to the layer of air below.

For ten hours a day I headed south and climbed slowly, for there was no usable wind. When the sun was out, sweat poured down my face, and my forehead and the back of my neck were seared. The ultraviolet light pouring through the ozone hole was far more noticeable than on my journey with Mike Stroud in 1993. I saw tricks of light caused by minute ice crystals glittering in the sunshine and forming, or so I thought, glowing pillars and haloes of rainbow delight. I remembered how I had wholeheartedly agreed with Will Steger, who, during his great Antarctic traverse of 1989, had read the story of a short visit to Antarctica by wilderness writer Barry Lopez. Steger wrote:

> Lopez's romantic, vivid descriptions of Antarctica are getting on my nerves. My concern is that I am not capturing Antarctica and its romance properly. Lopez's view seems fresh, flowery and evocative by comparison to my own descriptions. For him everything was new; his advantage in such a short stay was that his mind and descriptive powers were not bludgeoned by the monotony and remoteness that is the real Antarctica. I understand; it is easy to step off a tourist plane for a few days and conjure up images that paint Antarctica as a kind of cold paradise. Many days now I see it as quite the opposite.

I did not feel lonely, although I had been expecting to. Nor did I feel subdued by the great silence all about me because the smallest movement was amplified by that very overall silence so that I could, at night, hear my breath in my nose, my clothes rustle, my balaclava rub, and my watch tick. And, when not in my sleeping bag there was always the rush of my sled runners, skis and sticks or the roar of the cooker.

Shackleton wrote of his loneliness and quoted Coleridge: 'Alone, alone, all, all alone, Alone on a wide, wide sea!' He talked also of being 'truly at the world's end', at 'the birthplace of the clouds'. Scott recorded: 'The scene about us is the same as we have seen for many a day, and shall see for many a day to come – a scene so wildly and awfully desolate that it cannot fail to impress one with gloomy thoughts.'

My own gloomy thoughts, when I had them, were mainly concerned with exactly what I would do should I fall into a crevasse. Over the years I had done so, but always when roped up to, or at least close by, another human. Anybody can fall into a crevasse, for most of these natural hazards are so well snow-bridged as to be invisible to even the most practised eye.

To me, an even greater tale of survival against all the odds than that of Shackleton and his men was the incredible solo journey of Douglas Mawson in 1912, the year of Scott's death. The same company that sponsored me with the *Benjamin Bowring* in 1978, Bowring Brothers, had provided Scott with the *Terra Nova* and Mawson with the *Aurora*.

Mawson, born in Yorkshire, was taken to Australia aged two, became a successful geologist and explorer and turned down invitations to join the main expeditions of both Shackleton and Scott. He did, however, as part of the 1907–9 Shackleton expedition, achieve the first ascent of Mount Erebus and the attainment of the South Magnetic Pole.

In 1911 he mounted his own expedition to investigate and survey the great quadrant of Antarctica lying adjacent to Australia. He split his team into groups who would explore and map the coastal areas to the west of the region visited by Scott and Shackleton. They would keep in touch with each other by short wave radio. In

November 1912, seven separate groups set out from their coastal base with Mawson leading his own team of three sledges each pulled by ten dogs. His companions were a 22-year-old British officer, Lieutenant Belgrave Ninnis, and a Swiss doctor, Xavier Mertz. Their task was to survey King George V Land.

For five weeks, moving over three hundred miles of badly crevassed coastline, they collected geological samples and mapped the terrain. Then, crossing what is now known as Ninnis Glacier, disaster struck when Ninnis, his dog team and sledge broke through a crevasse bridge and plunged some two hundred feet. Mawson and Mertz were unable to retrieve anything. By bad luck, all the food for the dogs, all but seven days' rations for the two survivors and most of the survival gear, including their tent, had been on the Ninnis sledge because they had believed that the rear sledge would be the safest. With three hundred miles of the most treacherous coastal terrain to traverse to get back to their base, and in that part of Antarctica which is riven all year round by the strongest of blizzards, their immediate future looked grim.

They replaced the tent with some canvas propped up on their three-legged theodolite tripod and, when they ran out of food, they killed their huskies one by one and ate them. The remaining dogs were soon so thin they provided little sustenance, but bones and guts were fed to those yet to be killed. Ravenous as they were, Mertz and Mawson devoured every edible scrap, including the livers. Inuit hunters had long ago learnt that Vitamin A in the livers of seals, walruses, polar bears and huskies is poisonous to man. Unaware of this, the two men continued to eat the liver as their skin turned yellow and peeled off in layers. They were violently sick and often dizzy. Their hair and their nails fell out.

Mertz began to go mad and, despite their desperate need to keep moving whenever the weather allowed, he would refuse to budge from his wet sleeping bag and became increasingly violent. When he tried to destroy their vital makeshift tent, Mawson had to physically restrain him. Towards the end, Mertz bit off the end of one of his own frostbitten fingers. Mawson tried to tow Mertz on the sledge, but could only manage a snail's pace and Mertz grew rapidly core-cold. So to his intense frustration, Mawson had to watch his own survival chances diminish as, tent-bound, he watched his mad companion die.

By the time Mawson buried Mertz, he was himself emaciated. Wherever his skin had peeled away, these raw places were soon rubbed into open wounds. One morning, taking off his socks, he found that the sole of one foot had come away as a single footprint-shaped cast. Using lanolin cream on the raw underneath of his foot, he then strapped the skin sole back on with a bandage and whatever spare socks he had prior to donning his boots.

His solo journey back to his base remains, to my mind, a miracle of human will to survive against all odds. He broke through crevasse after crevasse, saved only by the 14-foot knotted rope with which he towed his sledge. Boils broke out on his face and body. He was a walking skeleton by the time he came to the high ground somewhere above the base. With no crampons, he found that he could not descend the sheer wind-scoured ice to reach safety. He survived three further days and nights of blizzard and drifting snow in a snow cave, all the while fashioning makeshift crampons from bits and pieces.

To avoid a year's entrapment, his ship, the *Aurora*, had been forced to leave for Australia only a few hours before Mawson, just alive, limped back into his base, and was joyously welcomed by the five men who had stayed behind to search for him. When, a year later, and still suffering from his appalling experiences, he and his men were returned to Australia, they had added more to the maps of Antarctica than anyone else of their time. His team had explored and mapped some two thousand miles of the unknown coastline of Earth's last unmapped continent and added a huge amount of data to our scientific knowledge of the frozen continent.

Crevasses had crippled Mawson's team and pack ice had done for Shackleton, but three weeks out on my own traverse attempt I felt optimistic. I was halfway to the pole and, thanks to the kite, 125 miles ahead of the point that Mike and I had reached in the same time in 1993. On my 25th day, however, I was sick a few minutes after eating my breakfast gruel. I felt faint and started out four hours behind schedule on a fine sunny day, neither too hot nor too cold. In six hours I manhauled six miles despite a long, steep climb. The improved surface continued, but I felt queasy and took two Imodium tablets.

Behind me the deep tracks of my runners disappeared to the north, where countless mountain peaks shimmered as though floating on waves of air. Ahead lay only a blue sky and the gently sloping snowfields leading without further obstruction to the South Pole.

To my surprise, I was violently sick again after eating my evening meal, a delicious mixture of ghee milk fat with rehydrated shepherd's pie and Smash. I stared at the results on the tent floor and wondered how I could recycle the mess, since I had towed that ration for four hundred miles and it represented energy for ten miles of further manhauling. I informed Morag that night that I had been sick, but was uncertain why, since I did not have diarrhoea. She told me to call her at any time if the symptoms persisted so that she could relay advice from the camp doctor.

Two hours later the first cramps attacked my gut and I recognized at once the symptoms of a kidney stone blockage. I lit my cooker and heated water. I would flush the bloody thing out of my system. Drown it with water. The pains were impressive. Groaning and talking aloud, I wrenched open the medical pack that Mike had meticulously prepared in the knowledge of my previous kidney stone attack in 1990. On that occasion we were stationary at a Soviet science station on a remote ice floe, so Mike had borrowed drugs from a Russian medic. I gulped down morphine-substitute tablets, two Buscopan anti-pain pills and inserted a Voltarol suppository for quick pain relief. Within half an hour the initial pains, which I think I can safely describe as excruciating, had dulled to a background throb. But the relief did not last.

For six hours, every hour on the hour, I tried to call Morag. However, atmospheric disturbances prevented any communication until the next morning. The weather was excellent. I yearned to be on my way. Since I was eating nothing and using fuel only to heat snow for water, rather than to heat the tent, I was not technically reducing my overall chances of success, but Ousland was ahead of me and widening the distance. Kaminski and the Koreans were creeping up from behind. But there was no way I could carry on until I had shifted the stone from my urinary tract.

When I finally made brief contact with Morag, the lady doctor at her camp – a former flying medic from north-west Australia – advised me to take painkillers every six hours and drink lots of water. For 24 hours, possibly the least enjoyable period I can remember ever having spent, I writhed about in the tent. I took more painkillers than the doctor had advised and drank a great deal of water, but the stone failed to shift and the pains from my lower stomach, back and sides stayed with me.

At 11 a.m. on 27 December I decided that the danger of irreparable damage to my kidneys, as well as the risk of running out of painkillers, was too great a price to pay for the chance of being first to cross Antarctica solo. I pulled the pin of my emergency beacon which, a few hours later, informed a satellite signal watcher in England, who called Morag, who in turn alerted the Twin Otter ski-plane crew at Patriot Hills as to my exact position.

Nine hours later, with the fine weather beginning to change, the Twin Otter landed by my tent. Throughout the flight back to Patriot Hills, the Australian doctor fed morphine into my blood system through a drip. I was soon completely stoned and in wonderful, painless bliss. Morag called my medical insurers, who advised immediate evacuation to a clinic in Punta Arenas. The weather, miraculously, held just long enough for me to fly on a scheduled Hercules flight to Punta.

After an exhaustive series of X-rays, an enema and fluid injections, the surgeon sent a report to my insurers, who advised that, should I return to Antarctica, as I hoped, they could not cover any further stone-related costs. Although the stone had shifted once the morphine had relaxed my nervous system, the condition could return at any time. Any future evacuation flight would cost over

£100,000. With enormous reluctance, I accepted the end of the expedition.

Ousland went on to cross Antarctica in an amazing 55 days, managing to sail for well over three-quarters of the entire distance, avoiding the drudge and the toil of manhauling. On his arrival at Scott Base my signal was the first to congratulate him. Kaminski and the Koreans reached the pole too late to continue onwards.

Using wind assistance with kites or parawings that can use winds from 180° is very different from the use of following-wind devices, such as the parachutes or dinghy sails used by Amundsen, Shackleton, Scott and, in 1993, by Mike Stroud and me with singular lack of success. Had my kidneys behaved themselves, I am sure Ousland would still have beaten me across Antarctica, but I am also sure that I would have maintained my lead on the others. My big mistake was to concentrate on manhaul fitness rather than becoming a wind-assistance expert like Ousland. Businesses that do not move with the times get left behind.

Dyson raised £1.7 million through the expedition and helped set up Europe's first dedicated breast cancer research centre. If I had completed the journey, the sum raised would have been a good deal more.

Chapter Fifteen

The roar of winds, and waves, the crush of ice

JAMES THOMSON, *FROM* 'WINTER' (1726)

In 1999, together with top Russian polar explorer, Dr Dmitri Shparo, and his friend, Canadian Professor Gordon 'Sockeye' Thomas, I agreed to organize a journey by vehicle around the world's land mass from the most westerly point in the Republic of Ireland, 23,000 miles through Europe, Russia and Canada to the eastern tip of Newfoundland. The terrain would mostly be in very cold regions, but all three of us had long specialized in cold projects.

The toughest all-terrain vehicle available in the world was the basic Land Rover, but it was a car, not a boat, and would need to be taught to swim because four major water obstacles were an unavoidable part of the journey: the Irish and English Channels, the Bering Straits and the Strait of Belle Isle between Canada's mainland and Newfoundland. The last of these watery hurdles was not far north of Nova Scotia's Bay of Fundy, which has a tidal rise and fall of 45 feet.

Land Rover sponsored the expedition and helped modify two of their vehicles into amphibians. Using bespoke catamaran-shaped pontoon skids with outboard engines powered and steered by the drivers in their cabs, we were eventually able to drive at sea in relatively rough conditions, as well as tow the skid units over snow or ice.

After many trials off the UK coast, Land Rover chartered a cargo flight for all our gear to an Inuit village called Prince of Wales on the Alaskan coast of the Bering Straits. The plan was to train there for two summer months, both in the ice-strewn strait and over the high mountains just inland of the village. To succeed in completing the expedition we would need to know that we could 'swim' in up to Force Seven ocean conditions and drive through remote virgin mountain valleys, despite snow drifts.

We based our team of six in the garage shack of an American technician named Big Dan, who lived in Prince of Wales village with his Inuit wife and children. The villagers were all friendly, many had huskies and some pegged sealskins and polar-bear pelts on to screens outside their houses near the sea front. Temperatures in this part of the sub-Arctic between winter and summer can differ by up to 180°. Although snowfall is light most winters, the extreme cold until mid-May means that the ground remains well snow-covered for most of the year. On a clear day, Big Dan's wife told us, you could see Russia, some forty-five miles across the strait. Dan joked that that was only possible after a good deal of whisky, but Prince of Wales certainly is at the narrowest point between the USSR, as it then was, and the USA.

The area is indelibly linked with the history of human endeavour to penetrate the cold dark northern lands. Without this ice-bound channel into the Arctic Ocean there would be no Northwest, or Northeast, Passage. To the north of the strait lies the Chukchi Sea, and to the south the Bering Sea. This low-lying area between Asia and America, known to geologists as Beringia, was sometimes covered, as today, by seawater, and at other times, depending on the current state of various Ice Ages, it was dry land which formed a bridge for humans and animals to transit from continent to continent.

The fact that Alaska was, until fairly recently, an eastern outpost colony of the Czars, and later the Commissars (known in my schooldays as the Commy Czars), was initially due to the value of furs. Russian armies, as early as 1582, crossed the Ural Mountains to colonize Siberia for the fine sable furs which they knew came from the far north. As the fur-bearing animals were killed off, so the colonizing process moved ever further east and north, reaching the great Lena River in the 1620s. Trappers and hunters on the Arctic coast then used the various northern rivers to penetrate new unexploited territories until, at length, all Siberia was colonized.

The most easterly coastal tribes of the Chukchi Peninsula and the Kolyma River region proved the most difficult to subject, as was experienced by the first Russian explorer to pass through the Bering Strait, Semen Dezhnev, in 1648. His expedition was made up of 90 men in seven ships, five of which were lost and the crews killed by the Chukchi. When his last two ships were wrecked, Dezhnev and 25 of his men survived, set up a thriving fur trade and, years later, made it back home.

The story of Dezhnev's voyage, when it was recounted in Moscow, reopened an interest in the potential of a Northeast Passage for Russian trade with China and sparked off the great journeys of the 1730s by Vitus Bering, which eventually crossed the Bering Straits, and halfway across discovered the Diamede Islands. He also postulated, although fog prevented him actually seeing the American coast, that Asia and America were not connected by land. Bering died of scurvy and exposure with most of his men after his ship was wrecked in 1741. Within a few years of his discoveries of the islands off Alaska, Russians had made contact with Alaskan Eskimos and were trading all the way down to San Francisco.

Thirty years after Bering's death, by which time Czarist Russia had successfully claimed all of Alaska, Britain's naval power had blossomed and in 1778 her own great explorer, Captain James Cook, was sent to find the Northwest Passage to China. By meticulously charting Alaska's coastline, Cook proved that Asia and America really were, as Bering had suggested, completely separate lands. He was backed up by George Vancouver in 1792, who told the Admiralty that the only transcontinental route from west to east across the newly formed United States or Canada was, as pioneered by Alexander Mackenzie, overland and by rivers and not via some icy seaway in the far north.

Various expeditions had tried crossing the Bering Straits on foot, but despite the short distance – about twice that of the English Channel – strong currents constantly fracture the ice cover so that it is rare to be able to travel across on solid ice. However, the year before we arrived at Prince of Wales my friend Dmitri Shparo and his son Matvey completed the first modern crossing of the Bering Straits on skis.

Our forays out among the floes and bergs with the vehicles on their pontoon skids, often in high winds and choppy seas, grew gradually more bold, by night as well as in daylight. Whilst our base commander, Andrew 'Mac' Mackenney, and our three Land Rover mechanics continued to progress with sea trials in all weathers and all ice conditions, Sockeye Thomas and I plotted a route to get our vehicles across Canada once the Russian sector and strait crossing were complete, hopefully the following summer.

From Prince of Wales we would have to cross the inland Alaskan mountains to the former gold rush boomtown of Nome, but there was no vehicle track nor, for hundreds of miles on the far side of Nome, was there any obvious route. So we chartered a small bush aircraft and overflew the rugged terrain involved. On advice from the bush pilot, we studied the route of the big annual dog race, the Iditarod Trail, a rough trail prepared annually by snowmobile volunteers between Nome and, 675 miles away, the south Alaskan towns of Kaltag and Ruby. The race was first organized by a couple of dog enthusiasts in 1973, and it had since become globally famous. The route is part based on a once-vital freight trail between Nome and Anchorage, and it is also called the Coldest Race in the World.

Often forgotten is the week-long panic in Nome back in January 1925, when there were no snowmobiles, no winter-practical aircraft and the last ship of the short Nome summer had departed back to the closest major port, Seattle, 2,400 miles away. At that time messages from Nome to the outside world went via radio, telegraph or submarine cable. Unfortunately, the constant grinding of ice over the seabed frequently broke the cable, telegraph wires often succumbed to blizzards and radio to solar flares.

About a week after the town became cut off for the year, the town doctor, Curtis Welch, was treating an Eskimo girl for a sore throat. She died overnight and two other Eskimo children with similar symptoms died soon after. Welch carefully inspected the mouth of a fourth suffering child and found bloody tonsil ulcers. He began to fear an outbreak of diphtheria. The small supply of anti-toxin serum that he held was old, and although he had ordered a resupply the previous summer, it had never arrived.

Diphtheria bacteria cause the initial throat ulcers to thicken, scab and become so large that the windpipe is blocked and the victim slowly suffocates. Children under ten are the most likely to die and, prior to the availability of the anti-toxin, whole communities would die of what, in Europe, was known as 'the plague of the throat'. Attempts with forceps to tear out the lesions and scabs simply left raw surfaces in the throat and caused great pain. The diphtheria bacteria are hypercontagious, airborne by a single cough or the touch of a carrier, and can remain active lurking on a table, a book or a tap for weeks awaiting the fatal touch of the next victim.

Welch sent emergency appeals to the Alaskan government for a supply of anti-toxin, and soon the 'impending Alaskan disaster' was front-page news all over North America. The only feasible way to get the serum to Nome was by dog-team relay. Sixty years before, the USA had bought Alaska from Russia but had not then given the Alaskans their statehood, so all decisions had to be made in Washington. This caused delay, but eventually a sufficient amount of serum was located and sent to the accessible Alaskan town of Nenana. A number of top dog-sledgers volunteered to make the hazardous runs along the 674 miles of hostile terrain to Nome, including 208 miles along the coastline of the Bering Sea which traversed river deltas, lagoons and known blizzard zones. Forested mountain trails were treacherous by night with boulder-strewn slopes and many awkward, icy inclines.

By bad luck, the winter of 1925 in Alaska was the coldest on record for twenty years. The dog-mushers at the time were well aware that sustained exertion of their prized dogs in such low temperatures was likely to cause what they called 'lung scorching', a canine version of pulmonary haemorrhage. The dog breathes in air at −50°C and the blood vessels in its lung sacs burst. As the lungs fill with blood, the dog either dies from lack of oxygen or by, literally, drowning in its own blood.

Through the courage, endurance and skill of the teams, men and dogs, mass deaths were eventually avoided in Nome, and what became known as the Serum Run passed into local history.

After our overflight of the dog trail, Sockeye agreed that this would be our own best route, providing that we could train our Land Rovers, now adept at 'swimming', to drive through deep snowdrifts on steep mountain inclines.

To keep fit whilst the sea trials went on, we sledged along the coastline of the Lopp Lagoon. Sockeye, proud of his lifetime of extensive wilderness travel in North America, was a mine of information. Alaskan grizzly bears, he said, frequented the area and did not normally mate with their polar cousins. When they did, however, it was anybody's guess whether future generations would come out brown or white, but, either way, they were likely to be huge, weighing in at around sixteen hundred pounds and living over thirty years.

Sockeye called himself a cryophile, a lover of all things cold, and said that he envied me my polar travels. When not indulging in his hobby of cattle-roping and bronco-riding at rodeos, his favourite holiday away from his home, not far from Vancouver, was to tramp in the wildest, coldest, loneliest parts of Canada's far north. The ice-laden sea that we walked beside was, Sockeye said, as full of colourful life as a Nome bordello in gold rush days. He had camped on islands in the Gulf of Alaska and watched great herds of walrus displaying, the sunlight flashing off their impressive tusks. Their main food, of which they consume some forty-five kilograms a day, is shellfish which grow in profusion in cold Alaskan waters. Fish that survive in the dark, cold depths of polar seas use body fluids like vehicle antifreeze and, in the polar tundra which we were walking over, various insects, worms and springtails can likewise survive all-year-round polar cold with temperatures down to −38°C.

The tundra, Sockeye enthused, was to him a place of beauty, simplicity and solitude, where he could more easily muse about the beginnings of time and space and the meaning of life. He raged against the Alaskan Department of Transport who had tried to bulldoze a road over hundreds of miles of tundra from Fairbanks to the great oil base at Prudhoe Bay, traversing virgin terrain. The bulldozers' blades had cut away the surface layer, which melts briefly in summer, and had scraped off the hard permafrost layer beneath. This initially produced an excellent winter road, but the following summer the newly exposed permafrost, sand glued together with ice, melted into a long straight boggy scar unusable by vehicles and an ever-deepening eyesore for posterity.

Sockeye had seen bison bodies, dead for thousands of years but perfectly preserved by permafrost. Almost 20 per cent of the land on earth, excluding glaciated areas, is underlain by permafrost, which includes 'dry' permafrost that is frozen but does not contain ice. Submarine permafrost can be up to 100 metres deep. In parts of Siberia permafrost has been measured to reach down to 1,500 metres, but in summer, even there, the surface will thaw to form bogs, lakes and sodden vegetation which in uneven terrain will actively flow over the unthawed surface below and can transport rocks over many miles. A known example of this in the USA is a single rocky feature moved over seven kilometres and weighing more than 13,000 tons.

Some thirty miles north of where we camped on our first night out was the border of the Bering Land Bridge National Preserve, an area, like the rest of historic Beringia, where Arctic steppe terrain, once covered by shrubs and trees, had become treeless, so that the Eskimos who lived along this coast in sod houses could only prop up their roofs with whale bones or driftwood found on the local beach. In the same way as the various effects of altitude control the treeline of different tree types on mountains, so the cold controls where trees can grow in the Arctic and sub-Arctic.

In those Arctic regions where trees do grow, the abrasion and the weight of blown snow can mould them into weird shapes like 'flags', where all upwind branches have been snow-abraded, or 'mopheads', where only branches above the level of blown ground snow can survive. Many thousands of kilos of snow piled up in a tree can cause its roots to tear out, whereupon branches evolve, as on certain firs, which all point downwards so that snow slides off and cannot settle.

We camped where the Pinguk River reached the sea and lay awake after a meal of warm baked beans. To the background squeal and grind of ice floes along the beach, Sockeye, a one-time professor of advanced mathematics, gave me a crude rundown on some ways in which humans have made practical good use of the cold. He tried to explain to me the concept of Absolute Zero, which in simplistic terms I thought of as the coldest temperature that could be reached assuming that there was such a limit. This is deemed to be –273.15 Celsius or –459.67° Fahrenheit, at which point the thermal energy of matter vanishes. I asked Sockeye to explain this in plain English.

'In plain Canadian,' he said, 'I will give you the A to Zee of temperature measurement.' Then he went on to explain. Daniel Fahrenheit, a German glass-blower whose surname has been immortalized by his temperature scale, developed the mercury thermometer in the early 1700s with his 'zero' set at the coldest temperature he was able to achieve in his shop. His scale used 96 degrees, which he measured by putting his thermometer in his mouth to acquire 'the heat of a healthy man'. Water on his Fahrenheit scale was found to boil at 212°F and to freeze at 32°F, which neatly left 180°, or half a circle, between the two extremes. Two decades later, Swede Anders Celsius invented his Celsius scale with his 0°C point that of freezing water and his 100°C point that of boiling water. Fast-forward a century and the Briton, Lord Kelvin, came up with his own scale based on Celsius but with his zero point set at the lowest known temperature, 459° below zero Fahrenheit, just above which helium liquefies. Lastly, Sockeye pointed out, was what he considered the unprofessional measurement of 'degrees of frost'. 'These used a scale on which one degree of frost equalled one degree below freezing on the Fahrenheit scale.'

Having neatly summarized temperature measurement alternatives, Sockeye then launched into thermodynamics and quantum mechanical zero-point energy measurements, at which point I felt my eyes beginning to glaze over.

The first to aim for Absolute Zero was a Scottish professor, William Cullen, in 1748 who wrote of his experiments under the sexy title: 'Of the Cold produced by Evaporating Fluids and some other Means of Producing Cold'. Long before Cullen, humans had learned to keep meat fresh with snow and ice. Eskimos, Egyptians and the Chinese had for two thousand years left evidence of doing so, as had the Romans and Greeks in their villas.

In the 1830s an experimenter, Jacob Perkins, developed an insulated box in which liquid was allowed to vaporize inside a tube, a process that absorbed heat and made the inside of the box cooler. The chemicals variously used as the stimulants for this vaporization included ammonia, sulphur dioxide and carbon dioxide, all of which could and did kill householders when things went wrong and poison gases leaked out. The discovery of Freon, a stable, non-toxic refrigerant, led to safer and ever more efficient refrigerators and freezers.

The advent of such coolants put an end to the business of ice merchants like Frederic Tudor, the Massachusetts 'Ice King', who grew rich by creating a demand for iced drinks as part of the glamour of tropical holidays in the Caribbean. He then satisfied this demand by shipping out ice collected from American ponds in winter to insulated 'ice storage houses' that he built for the end-users.

Ship-towed icebergs certainly could, in theory, help countries with a shortage of drinking water. They are definitely big enough. Soviet sailors in 1965 measured a berg at 87 miles long and 2,700 square miles in area. One great berg 25 × 45 miles in size dislodged a second chunk 13 × 36 miles, and the larger of the two alone contained sufficient drinking water for all California's needs for many years. But the cost of towing such bergs to Los Angeles, or indeed to water-hungry Arab countries, has to date prevented any commerce in 'iceberg water' starting up.

A study of past Nobel Prize winners, Sockeye noted, showed that 'cold-seekers' were well regarded down the years. The 1940s Nobel list included the inventor of a cooling system described as adiabatic demagnetization; in the 1990s a prize was awarded to a team who developed a laser-based cooling system; and in 2001 a prize went to a team working with rubidium atoms. A future prize would, in Sockeye's opinion, be awarded to the inventors of what he described as cryoablation, which uses super-cooled needles to freeze cancer tumours. Since all body cells mostly consist of water, the process is likely to stand a good chance of success.

Of far less use to the human race, but of great interest to cryophile Sockeye, were the recent advances in the science of cryonics, or the freezing of live organs for temporary storage. A cat's brain was frozen for seven months by a professor in the 1960s, and then, although not exactly revived to the point where it meowed, it did at least show brief evidence of active brain waves. That same decade saw the opening of a commercial facility where a human body (or just a body part) could be submersed in liquid nitrogen immediately after death. Then, years later when some medical breakthrough became available, it could be thawed out and, in principle, cured of whatever originally caused death.

The business that now looks after this frozen cryonic store, Alcor, also freezes poodles and other much-loved pets, but not all cryonics professors are confident of successful revival results. One Dr Arthur Rowe is quoted as saying, 'Believing cryonics could reanimate somebody who has been frozen is like believing that you can turn a hamburger back into a cow.'

'Nonetheless,' Sockeye pointed out, 'it must make dying easier simply knowing that you might be able to come back in a while and check up on your loved ones.' I could think of scenarios where such reappearances should be avoided at all costs.

Other businesses to whom, as Sockeye put it, 'Cold is cool', included those who pay healthy donors to sell human eggs or sperm which are then frozen in liquid nitrogen at –320°F and then offered worldwide for purchase at competitive prices.

On a different tack, Sockeye confessed to being an enthusiastic cold-swimmer. A lover of Scandinavia and all things Scandinavian, he affirmed that winter swimming was highly popular in the lands of the midnight sun. Most people, apparently, just dip briefly into cold water after a sauna or at the local pool, but others compete in winter swimming races, the first Winter Swimming World Championships having been held in Helsinki. Today, a burgeoning health business, based on cold-water immersion, thrives and promises a great many possible benefits, including increased blood circulation, relief of back, neck and shoulder pains, reduction of depression, insomnia, asthma, and even rheumatoid arthritis.

The Swedish company Icebar by Icehotel franchises the concept of ice bars in various cities, including London, Stockholm and Oslo. The London venue's advertisement reads, 'Enjoy the exhilarating −5°C experience of Icebar by Icehotel, the UK's only permanent bar made of ice, before warming up in the contrasting warmth of our restaurant'. The Oslo venue includes the use of freezing conference rooms and ice-sculpting lessons. The original ice bar, set up in Swedish Lapp countryside by the wild Torne River, serves drinks in glasses made of ice to people who have been dancing on a floor of snow. Lapland also offers nights in a snow hotel in comfortable glass-roofed igloos with all-ice furniture, and honeymoon suites with high-quality thermal sleeping bags and motorized revolving beds from which you can gaze up at the Northern Lights, when not otherwise occupied.

After Sockeye and I sledged back to Dan's hut, all six of us set out to cross the York Mountain range that blocks the way between Prince of Wales and Nome. Instead of using winter tyres to cope with the six-foot-deep snowdrifts and steep slopes, our Land Rover technicians, Charles, Gill and Granville, fixed triangular linked tracks to each hub, thereby transforming the vehicles into miniature bulldozers. This worked better than our wildest dreams could have imagined, and we seldom had to use the long winch hawsers that we had ready.

On returning to Britain, we gave a video presentation to the Land

Rover sponsors and made our final preparations through Sockeye in Canada and Dmitri in Moscow. Two months before we were due to depart, BMW purchased Land Rover and removed our entire budget overnight.

As with all expeditions, you often spend years in the planning and the organizing and nobody pays you during this period. You hope for success, but always need to remember that if you are trying to do what has not been done before then your chances are slim. So there is no point in wallowing in self-pity when things don't work out. The problem in the year of our Alaska trials was that Ginny and I were in dire need of income, and we depended largely on my books to keep going.

Early in 1999 my publisher agreed to pay a very fair amount for the story of another polar journey: this time attempting the direct route from the Canadian coast to the North Pole, solo and without support, one of the few remaining polar challenges still to be achieved.

Mac Mackenney, our base camp boss in Alaska, agreed to handle communications from Resolute Bay with help from Morag Howell, who was working at the time as base manager at Resolute for the Twin Otter charter company First Air. He weighed all the gear that I would need for an 85-day journey, and the total, 510 pounds, was divided between two amphibious sledges, each to be pulled separately. At that time the use of an immersion suit to swim between floes had not been tried out.

On 17 February 2000 I flew with our old friend and expert polar pilot, Karl Z'berg, from Transglobe days twenty years before, to Ward Hunt Island, where he landed me and the sledges in the dark on a flat stretch of the ice shelf. We unloaded, and clasped hands. Then Karl was off. The little plane's winking lights disappeared back south and left me alone.

The sun would not arrive here for another three weeks, and then for only thirty minutes a day. This did not matter, for I planned to travel by available starlight and moonlight plus a lithium-powered head torch. I took a bearing to geographical north. The compass needle pointed to magnetic north, three hundred miles west of Resolute Bay and six hundred miles south of my position. I had to set a magnetic lay-off of 98°, then wait a minute for the needle to settle in the less than normal viscosity of its alcohol-filled housing. I could not use the North Star as a marker because it was almost directly overhead. Nor, pulling a sledge, could I use my GPS position-finder for direction.

The clothing policy I had evolved over twenty-eight years of polar expeditions was based on non-stop movement and light, breathable clothes. Any halt, however brief, could lead to hypothermia. Once my metabolism was up and running, pumping blood furiously to my extremities, I took off my duck-down duvet and stuffed it in the sledge next to my vacuum flask and 12-bore pump-action shotgun. Now I was wearing only a thin wickaway vest and long johns under a black jacket and trousers made of 100 per cent Ventile cotton. Cotton is not windproof so body heat is not sealed in. Alas, no modern clothing, such as Gore-Tex, is completely breathable so, when pulling excessive loads over difficult terrain, the manhauler perspires. The sweat turns to ice inside the clothing and can quickly lead to hypothermia. Cotton is still the best compromise, provided you keep your blood running fast, except when in your tent and sleeping bag.

In seven hours of hard manhauling I had reached the wall of broken ice blocks where the ice shelf's edge meets the sea. Once both sledges were there I erected the tent in six minutes and started the cooker in four. Life was good. My .44 magnum revolver lay beside the radio as on so many past expeditions. Just as joggers run along the edges of lakes, so polar bears patrol the sea edge and I was camped along their trail line. Not a good choice, but I was tired.

Over the years I had heard many stories about polar bears and had had close encounters with several, but never when I was alone. I knew that they always attacked the last person in line, and on North Pole journeys everyone advances in file, not line abreast, because of the extra effort required to break trail. So, as leader, I liked to travel up front, giving the weapon to the person at the back.

Travelling alone on the Arctic sea ice for the first time, I spent more time than usual thinking about the bears.

Dogs have far better scenting abilities than most civilized humans. Wolves can smell an injured caribou from almost half a mile away, and polar bears can smell their prey from twenty miles, even in windless conditions. This includes the scent of an injured human. Their vision is good at night and, very sensibly bearing in mind that in summer their hunting environment is often in conditions of harsh glare, their eyes are smaller than human eyes.

Size-wise they are the biggest predator on earth. Their back is twice the size of that of a large lion or tiger, and an average male weighs half a ton, with paws at least a foot in width. Standing up they can measure over 11 feet tall. Using both front paws they can lift an adult beluga whale, far heavier than themselves, clear out of the water, and their neck muscles make Muhammad Ali's look skinny. Like the famous Kiwi rugby player, Jonah Lomu, they combine body mass with a remarkable sprinting speed of up to 35 m.p.h. on land and 6 m.p.h. when swimming. They can stay underwater for two minutes and can swim non-stop for a recorded distance of a hundred miles.

Their menu is mainly seal meat, and since they can only catch seals in areas where there is pack ice, no sea ice means no seal hunting. So in July when there is no ice in the more southerly parts of the Arctic, three months of summer scrounging is necessary. They will then wander hundreds of miles feeding on berries, pouncing on lemmings, patrolling cliff bottoms to catch fallen chicks and locate eider duck eggs, kill the occasional caribou, human or musk ox. They may even stoop to grazing on patches of sedge grass, just like docile cattle. For choice, however, they favour seals and can easily wolf down 150 pounds at one sitting, killing an adult seal at a rate of about one every four days.

The breath and general body odour of all seals is almost as foul as that of the arch-stinker, the elephant seal, so their favourite resting places, even when they are temporarily absent, give off a powerful odour which tells bears exactly where they are likely to reappear. So a hunting bear will find the seal's breathing hole, called an aglu by the Inuit (who also kill seals at such aglus), and wait there knowing that a seal must surface every twenty minutes for air. The Inuit say that the bears, which are all white like ice apart from their nose, will push chunks of ice ahead of them when stalking seals, to hide the blackness of their nose, but this is possibly an old wives' tale. In ice-free seas, when seals are absent, bears will kill beluga whales, or even dive to munch on kelp or shellfish.

If well fed and not in charge of cubs, polar bears will usually avoid attacking humans that do not appear to threaten them and do not have dogs that annoy them. (The barking of dogs will turn a normally placid and amiable bear into an aggressive one, to the point where, on many occasions, Inuit have found every dog in their chained dog-lines killed but not eaten. Presumably just to shut them up.) However, North Pole travellers end up a long way from a bear's normal coastal seal-killing grounds, so if they do cross the trail of a bear it is quite likely to be hungry and may well want to eat them. The Japanese explorer Naomi Uemura, who we had encountered at Resolute Bay at the beginning of his solo North Pole trip in 1978, was attacked inside his tent. He was lucky and escaped with his life, but his tent was torn to shreds. In 1990 two Norwegians, during a North Pole journey made at the time Mike Stroud and I were on the Soviet side of the pole, were forced to shoot a bear only a hundred and twenty miles from the pole. In 2000, only sixty miles from the pole, a bear attacked the flight engineer of a helicopter that had briefly landed on a floe. Trappers have had their arms bitten off, but have survived and many a hunter's lonely hut in the wilds has been aggressively smashed into by bears searching for food.

Park wardens inspecting the body of a bear which had, for no apparent reason, killed but not eaten a young woman in Glacier Park, found that the animal was riddled with trichina larvae. The wardens suggested that trichinosis might so madden a bear as to make it aggressive. Their high infestation by trichinosis is unfortunate and certainly not due to unhygienic habits. Like cats, they lick their paws clean after eating and avoid getting blubber on their fur. In the wild, they will often perch on the edge of a floe in order to defecate into the sea, rather than on to the ice.

Despite the many instances of fatal bear attacks, proof of their basic lack of aggression to humans surely lies in the experience of the town of Churchill, Manitoba on the west coast of Hudson Bay. It happens that ice often forms off Churchill earlier than elsewhere and generations of bears, knowing this, congregate there each fall to wait for the coming of the ice which will allow them to kill and eat seals. Whilst waiting they raid the municipal rubbish dump and wander around the town. Overfamiliar Churchill bears that smash windows and take up residence in schoolyards or shop entrances are discouraged and sometimes airlifted hundreds of miles away, but casualties are rare and most Churchillians welcome 'their' bears back each fall.

Compare this live-and-let-live situation with that of grizzly bears, which are naturally and automatically aggressive towards humans. Although California's state symbol is the grizzly, their bear population shrank from 150,000 in the late-nineteenth century to nil by 1925, due to mass extermination of grizzlies.

Even in the depths of the coldest winters, polar bears, when not hibernating, can travel far and wide using the drifting ice patterns between different parts of the Arctic Ocean. They keep warm thanks to being so well insulated, and they fail to show up at all on aerial heat-imaging photographs of the ice.

The insulation qualities of their fur is not, as is often believed, their main defence against the cold. Other more southerly-ranging bears, like the grizzly, have longer, more dense fur, but polar bears have a key layer of blubber, as much as three or four inches thick in places, which keeps them warm in or out of the water, and the nature of their fur coats means that they shed water easily and efficiently. Their ears are small and well supplied with blood vessels for efficient circulation, they are bodily big and bulky which helps with heat conservation, and they have a black skin under white fur, which makes for ideal solar heat convection. And with a stomach capacity for 150 pounds of high-energy seal blubber, their storage of energy reserves helps with the hibernation abilities which are so critical to winter survival.

Often, over the years, where I have noted the spoor of polar bears, they were alongside the equally clear prints of an Arctic fox. One ear-tagged Arctic fox was recorded as travelling on sea ice, over a five-month period, for fifteen hundred miles and surviving entirely on the leftover spoil of its adopted polar bear mentor.

Although polar bears in zoos, leading lives of luxury, can reach the age of forty, in the wild they normally die by the age of fifteen. Because, by the mid-1960s, bears were being shot in great numbers for their pelts, there were fears for their existence all over the Arctic. In 1967 international agreements began which led, in due course, to Russia and Norway banning all polar bear hunting, whilst Danish Greenland, Canada and American Alaska allowed only limited Inuit hunting. Bear populations gradually recovered and are now threatened by climate change, not by uncontrolled hunting. Global warming has caused Arctic sea ice to cover less and less of the polar bears' erstwhile territory. The US Geological Survey predicts that two-thirds of the world's polar bears will have gone by 2050.

I was, as always when camping on Arctic floes, happy to wake up after a night of no bear scares and no dubious noises outside the tent. Once the cooker was on, only its roar was audible. On my first morning solo on the edge of the pack ice, the moon was full but hidden at the time by the hills of Ward Hunt Island. So I pressed on with the lighter of my two sledges into the initial chaos of great broken ice blocks, often sinking up to my waist in soft snow traps between the blocks. Once the moon appeared, the icescape ahead of me stretched out beneath the starlit heavens, a fairyland I would love to have been able to paint. I have photos of such scenes taken over nearly forty years, and at home I enjoy just looking at them without feeling cold.

On my second day within the pack ice, I fell fifteen feet on to sharp-edged ice chunks whilst negotiating a huge slab. My sledge was torn along its belly, and although the glide performance of the runners seemed unaffected, the sledge was clearly no longer amphibious, since it would leak like a sieve. As I was still so near the old Ward Hunt hut which we had weatherproofed back in the mid-1980s, it was worth an extra day following my trail back to conduct a proper sledge repair.

By the time I returned to the ice edge, happy with my repair work, the full moon had begun to affect the floes, for the high tide was lifting and fracturing some and moving others apart. The resulting clouds of dark steam looked weird in the moonlight where newly open water contacted the far colder air. After eight hours of reasonable progress I had moved both sledges a mile through the worst rubble fields that I could remember. I would have stopped then, but I needed an old solid floe as it would offer less salty ice for drinking and, more importantly, a stronger refuge if the high tide caused major problems in this notorious fracture zone. I sucked squares of chocolate to ward off hypothermia and, becoming dangerously tired in a zone of moving black water moats, I decided that I would take my chances camping on any reasonably flat pan, however new the ice.

As things worked out I never had to take the risk because, crossing a temporary bridge made up of hundreds of small ice slabs, all about 12 inches thick and 2 feet square, my heavier sledge tilted suddenly and slid down one side of the bridge into the sea. I was jerked over by my harness and followed the sledge downwards, while desperately attempting to unfasten the harness quick-release tab. As one of my boots went under water, I managed both to release the harness and to grab a wedged slab to arrest my descent. The sledge was afloat, but only just, with several lumps of ice weighing it down.

I was already cold and I knew that my life depended on the speedy retrieval of two items – my cooker and the tent. Both were on the sledge which was sinking slowly under the weight of the ice slabs still sliding down off the bridge.

On my stomach and holding the anchored slab with one mitted hand, I fished around in the water with the other, for I was now as keen to get hold of the harness tow rope as I had recently been to get rid of it. Finding it only by taking my mitt off, I tried hauling the sledge in. At first it jammed, but after some jiggling it unsnagged and came free. I pulled hard and the sodden sledge wallowed to the surface. Once I had a firm position back on top of the treacherous bridge of slabs, I hauled the sledge, water cascading off its cover, inch by inch back to the surface and on to the ice.

The trouble then really began. I danced about like a madman. Both my mitts were back on and I used my 'cold hands revival technique' to restore life to the numb fingers. This involves a fast windmill motion with the fingers on the outside of the resulting centrifugal orbit. Usually my blood returns painfully to all my fingers: this time it did not. I took off the mitt and felt the dead hand. The fingers were ramrod stiff and ivory white. They might as well have been wooden. I knew that if I let my good hand go even partially numb, I would be unable to erect the tent and start the cooker, which I needed to do quickly for I was shivering in my thin hauling clothes.

I returned to the big sledge. The next few minutes were a nightmare. The zip of the sledge cover jammed. Precious time went by before I could free it and unpack the tent. By the time I had eased a tent pole into one of the four pole-sleeves, my teeth were chattering violently and my good hand was numb. I had to get the cooker going in minutes or it would be too late. I crawled into the partially erect tent, closed its door-zip and began a frustrating battle to start the cooker. I could not use the petrol lighter with my fingers, but I found some matches that I could hold in my teeth.

Starting an extremely cold petrol cooker involves careful priming so that just the right amount of fuel seeps into the pad below the fuel jet. The cold makes washers brittle and the priming plunger sticky. Using my teeth and a numb index finger, I finally worked the pump enough to squirt fuel on to the pad, but I was slow in shutting the valve, and when I applied the match a 3-foot flame reached to the roof. Luckily, I had had a custom-made flame lining installed, so the tent was undamaged. And the cooker was alight – one of the best moments of my life.

Slowly and painfully some life came back into the fingers of my good hand. An hour later, with my body warm again, I unlaced my wet boot. Only two toes had been affected. Soon they would exhibit big blood blisters and lose their nails, but they had escaped true frostbite. All around the tent cracking noises sounded above the steady roar of the cooker. I was in no doubt as to the fate of my bad hand. I had seen enough frostbite in others to realize that I was in serious trouble.

Human skin is designed to lose heat more efficiently than it gains it, which is very helpful in the tropics. We also have an inbuilt rescue function whereby frostbite to our most vulnerable parts, including fingers, toes and nose, is delayed by heat which rushes out from our body's core to help the threatened area. Providing this transference of core heat occurs in conditions where we can be kept warm, hypothermia can be avoided. But I was already core-cold and on the verge of hypothermia so, given another four minutes without the life-saving heat of my cooker, I would, I knew well, have ended my days beaten at last by the cold. As it was, I had to get to a hospital quickly to save some fingers from the surgeon's knife.

I hated to leave the warmth of the tent. Both hands were excruciatingly painful. I battered ice off the smaller sledge, unloaded it and hauled it back to the big sledge, where I reloaded it with bare necessities. I set out in great trepidation. Twice my earlier tracks had been cut by newly open leads, but luckily both needed only small diversions to detour the open water, and five hours later I was back on the ice shelf.

I erected the tent properly and spent three hours warming hands and feet over the cooker. I knew that I must try to avoid further damage to the frostbitten, but not dead, zones of my fingers, since the worst situation is one of freeze-thaw-refreeze to semi-damaged tissue. I drank hot tea and ate chocolate. I felt tired and dizzy, and the wind was showing signs of rising. I knew that I should not risk high wind-chill, and I must try to reach the solid shelter of the hut in conditions of good visibility.

The journey to the hut took for ever. Once I fell asleep on the move and woke in a trough of soft snow well away from my intended route. When I came to the hut I erected the tent on the floor, started the cooker and prepared the communications gear. I spoke to Morag in Resolute Bay. She promised to evacuate me the following day using a Twin Otter due to exchange weathermen at Eureka.

The fingers on my left hand grew great liquid blisters. The pain was bad so I raided my medical stores for drugs. The next day I found an airstrip near the hut and marked its ends with kerosene rags. When I heard the approaching ski plane, I lit the rags and an hour later I was on my way to Eureka.

Thirty-six hours after that I was at Ottawa General Hospital watching as a surgeon stripped skin and sliced blisters from my fingers. For the next two weeks I received daily treatment in a hyperbaric oxygen chamber. Back in England, I allowed the semi-damaged tissue to heal slowly in readiness for the truly dead-end knuckles of the thumb and each finger to be amputated. I took penicillin for four months to keep gangrene out of the open cracks, where the damaged but live flesh met the dead and blackened finger-ends. By the end of June I was able to saw the dead finger-ends off with a fretsaw. This helped the new stump areas heal in readiness for final surgery by an expert plastic surgeon.

Over twenty-six years of polar travel the frostbite odds had been narrowing. It could have been a great deal worse. As it was, my damaged fingers, for a while after the trauma, developed symptoms which resembled a common ailment known as Raynaud's disease, which affects one in twenty people, mostly women, who live in cold countries. Smoking can bring on the condition, as can repeated activities that damage nerves that serve blood vessels in the hands and feet, such as operating vibrating tools, or even long performances on pianos or typewriters or computer keyboards. Frostbite, or other local foot or hand injury, can cause Raynaud's.

Mild forms of the condition involve the narrowing of arteries which supply blood to the skin, and when this happens blood circulation to the extremities is limited. A Raynaud's event, or vasospasm, causes pain and a corpse-like look to the affected skin area. Even opening a refrigerator door can set this off. Severe forms of Raynaud's can cause disfigured fingers, gangrene and eventual amputation. My American brother-in-law, a doctor in Minnesota, developed Raynaud's and had to move south to warmer Georgia, such was the discomfort brought on by any cold temperatures, or even a cool breeze. I was lucky, for my fingers were, once I started full-time exercise again, to recover their previous excellent circulation performance.

On return from the Arctic I found myself heavily involved in a century-old controversy about the efficiency or otherwise of Captain Scott. His reputation had been impugned in the 1970s by a Cambridge-based writer with no polar experience, keen to make his name through the well-tried method of character assassination of a national icon. It worked well for him and his book was used as the basis for a so-called documentary film which is still shown all over the world as though it is historic reality rather than a collection of cleverly angled mistruths.

I spent two years reading over a hundred books about Scott and diaries by Scott's men. I started the research with an open mind, prepared to write my own highly critical views on how he did or did not deal with the obstacles and perils of travel in cold places. I ended up with the solid belief that for all-round achievements, especially scientific ones, he was the greatest polar explorer of all time.

Chapter Sixteen

> Thank God! there is always a Land of Beyond
> For us who are true to the trail;
> A vision to seek, a beckoning peak,
> A farness that never will fail
>
> ROBERT SERVICE, *FROM* 'THE LAND OF BEYOND' (1912)

In 2003 with Mike Stroud, I organized an attempt to complete a project, inspired by an American long-distance runner, that Mike had been planning for six years. It was to run a marathon on each of Earth's seven continents within seven days. British Airways agreed to fly us on an exceptionally tight schedule, using only existing jumbo jet schedules, with just enough time – an average of five hours – on each continent to complete a full marathon. Our sponsor, Land Rover, announced to the press:

> The team will run their first marathon in Antarctica and the 7-day clock will tick from the moment they start. A twin-engine plane will immediately fly them back to Santiago to run the South American marathon (Number 2). From there to Sydney, Singapore, London, Cairo and finally New York. But they will lose a whole day when they cross the international date line and will have to make this up by running two marathons within one 24-hour period – a morning run in London and

> another that night in Cairo. If they succeed, the two runners will have completed the seven runs in less than 7 × 24 hours and will see only six whole days in terms of sunrises and sunsets.

We had planned to start with Antarctica on one of the South Shetland islands but, at the last minute, the airstrip there was blocked, so we ran instead on the Falkland Islands, once the headquarters of what is now the British Antarctic Survey.

This Antarctic run was not exactly polar. The climate was balmy and I understood why inmates from the science bases in southern, or 'proper', Antarctica describe the bases of the north-protruding peninsula and the subantarctic islands, such as the Falklands, as the 'Banana Belt'. Army vehicles passed by every now and again, the drivers hooting and waving. Our progress was being reported on Falklands Radio. There were long climbs and the pebbly road was uneven. We passed by skull and crossbones signs warning of 21-year-old minefields beside the track. Three hours into the marathon we passed below Mount Tumbledown, site of fierce fighting during the 1982 conflict where British paratroops assaulted Argentinian infantry dug into its upper slopes.

The famous botanist, Sir Joseph Hooker, a meticulous man, described the flora of the Falklands under the geographical heading of *Flora Antarctica*. In dry areas we saw dwarf shrubs known as diddle-dee spread like heather with red berries, mixed with an overall dun-coloured grass, white plumed flower heads and patches of low pig vine. We also saw the occasional caracara hawk, often called Johnny Rook by local Falklanders, who are themselves known as Kelpers or Bennies. I had hoped to spot the beautiful Falklands kelp goose, but didn't. Running marathons on a tight schedule doesn't facilitate appreciation of the local fauna.

By the time we finished the seventh marathon, in New York, we were certainly tired but nothing like as exhausted as at the end of a long cold day's manhaul.

During the next year I lost my beloved wife Ginny to cancer, and within some eighteen months my mother and two of my three sisters also died.

I tried my hand at an Antarctic lecture cruise, setting out from Ushuaia at the southern tip of Tierra del Fuego and cruising the Antarctic coastline. A few years after the same ship sank whilst completing a similar lecture cruise. Years later, I was privileged to visit and land at Cape Horn in a small yacht skippered by the great yachtsman Sir Robin Knox-Johnston, which also left from Ushuaia. I easily get seasick so those two voyages cured me for ever of wanting to go back to sea.

After Ginny's death I looked for action that would, hopefully, at least lighten the darkness of my gloom. So when a running friend, Steven Seaton, the editor of *Runner's World* magazine, suggested that we run the North Pole Marathon for a charity, I agreed, and in the spring of 2004 I joined him in Svalbard, from where we were flown by helicopter to 89.5°N where the Russian ice base Barneo is manned by scientists every spring.

The Russians and Americans have used ice islands as floating bases since the middle of the twentieth century, but the first known such camp was that of Vilhjalmur Stefansson's 1913 expedition. Five of his men floated for six months on a solid floe not far north of the Alaskan coast. By way of terminology, an ice island will normally be at least thirty feet thick, whereas an ice floe is more likely to be but a third of that. Ice islands, like Barneo, are usually immune to easy fracturing by neighbouring floes and so can be safely used as active bases for much longer – 3,129 days in the case of one. Once they are caught in the Transpolar Drift and the East Greenland Current, these islands, just like the *Jeanette* and the *Fram*, drift out of the Arctic Ocean and a new science base will then need to be chosen for ongoing research work.

Since the Russians at Barneo had only two helicopters, each big enough to take eight passengers, there was a total of sixteen competitors in the marathon. Steven warned me that the others were mostly extremely capable marathon runners and that the two of us should expect to come last.

The race course involved going around a 5-mile trail over ice floes some five times. Thirty minutes after the start, Steven dropped back to adjust his snowshoes. In a while I caught up with a runner and began to think that I might not come last after all. The runner shouted to me, 'The Russians said we must wear goggles or risk sun-blindness. But they constantly mist up. What can I do?'

Because summer had not yet arrived and the sun was still quite low on the horizon, I knew that sun-blindness was not yet a danger and the Russians were being overcautious. But I thought to myself, 'Why tell him? This is a race!' So I shrugged politely as I passed him.

Over the next four hours I put my goggles down each time I passed another frustrated competitor trying to demist his. I came second! So at least one cold lesson I had learnt the hard way eventually paid dividends.

A more involved activity that I thought might jolt me out of my mood of despair and self-pity following Ginny's death was learning to climb. This would also enable me to raise funds for Marie Curie, the cancer charity I was involved with following their wonderful care for Ginny, and I felt would help to shake off the irrational vertigo from which I had suffered since a child. And, with luck, it would enable me to achieve a long-postponed attempt to become the first human to cross both ice caps and climb the highest mountain (postponed because of the vertigo).

A Swazi friend, Sibusiso Vilane, the first black man ever to climb Everest from Nepal, had asked me to join him when he attempted to be first from the Tibetan side. He advised me to learn how to climb through a mountain tour company called Jagged Globe, but their boss suggested that I might not be suitable as I was 'sixty, cardiac-challenged and missing some digits'. However, he said that if I went on two Jagged Globe training courses and got OK reports from the instructors, he would agree to enrol me on the Everest trip that he had arranged with Sibu.

The Alps went well, for it involved only trudging along snowy trails, but the second course, based from Quito in Ecuador, consisted of a dozen volcano climbs, each higher than the last. Cotopaxi was 19,000 feet above sea level, about the same height as Kilimanjaro. Two days later we climbed the nearby Chimborazo, which was over 20,000 feet above sea level.

These mountains were not cold. My guide Pepé stressed that rockfalls and electric lightning bolts were the main killers. He told us that neighbouring Colombia held the world record of 110 flashes per kilometre per year, compared with Italy at a mere 28 flashes per kilometre per year. The world annual toll from strikes was about 24,000 people dead, but ten times that number injured, many of whom then suffered all their lives from severe neurological troubles. Pepé warned us that the Quito volcanoes were especially vulnerable to strikes and we should be alert for warning signals in time to take cover. Such signals, which gave valuable seconds of time, included the raising of hair, skin tingle, sharp crackling noises, corona discharge and the vibration of any light metal objects.

'Get down on the ground.' Pepé ticked points off on his fingers. 'But not on moist places. Keep several metres between each person. Don't lie down, just squat with your feet together and with your head lowered, and cover your ears.'

Pepé had once found a well-known Norwegian climber on the Chimborazo crater-rim with a neat round burnhole drilled in the top of his head. His ice axe and crampons were mere molten metal, and the bolt's charge had passed down the frozen rope and killed his guide for good measure.

My Quito report was OK, so Jagged Globe accepted me for Everest with Sibu. I had trouble with a bout of angina on Kilimanjaro's rim a month later, but this disappeared on the way down. That same night two middle-aged South Africans died of heart attacks on Kili. None of these mountains was cold and none challenged my vertigo, for there were no visible big drops involved. I assumed that Everest would be both cold and vertiginous.

At a lecture I gave to the Chester branch of the Royal Geographical Society the previous summer I met one of their members, Louise Millington, and had since taken her out when she was not busy with the horse-transporting company that she had built up, based from her Cheshire home. She was thirty-six years old, full of life, mercurial, had a 10-year-old son, Alexander, and she jolted me out of my miserable state. We agreed to marry in March 2005 and honeymoon at the Everest Base Camp in Tibet.

One of the other climbers in the Sibu group was our doctor, an American who, on a previous Everest attempt, had suffered bad frostbite damage to his fingers and nose. 'It is usually one of three things that kills so many Everest climbers,' he told us. 'Too little oxygen, too cold, and bad weather.'

In the long, weather-dictated tent-bound hours in Base, our instructors, like others no doubt in all the other groups' tents, regaled us with Everest facts. Like the rest of the Himalayan mountain ranges, Everest was formed by the collision of two massive tectonic plates. The plate which carries the land, now known as India, broke away about 135 million years ago from the southern mega-continent of Gondwanaland and headed north until, bumping into the Asian plate, it collided with Tibet, causing the uplift of the highest mountains on Earth. The plate pressures still continue, and satellite measurements of Everest's height (29,035 feet or 8,850 metres) indicate that the summit grows at a rate of an inch a year.

Locals call Everest Chomolungma or Mother of Mountains, but back in the 1850s, when it was confirmed as the highest mountain in the world by the Trigonometric Survey of India, it was named Everest after the survey's superintendent. Once news got out that it was, indeed, the King of all Mountains, folk wanted to climb it.

People were well aware that the higher you climb the less oxygen is available, so in 1875 three French scientists ballooned to the height of Everest's summit. All three passed out and two died. Nonetheless, by the turn of the nineteenth century the British had started attempts to find an approach route on the Tibetan side. After thirty years and the death of Mallory, they began to think of an approach via Nepal, which in the 1950s eventually paid off.

As our doctor had stressed, a great many people have died on Everest and are still dying every year, due to the cold (since the temperature drops by 0.6°C for every 100 metres of climb) and the altitude (because the greater the height the lower the air pressure and the less oxygen there is to breathe). Nobody lives permanently above 17,500 feet, and those who have tried have not survived long. The Death Zone, our doctor explained, was anywhere above 21,000 feet and that was where the Advanced Base Camp, to which we would soon be heading, was situated. We would only stay there, he hoped, for as little time as was absolutely necessary, because whilst there our bodies would 'die a little every day'.

Once above 12,000 feet, he warned whilst fingering his frostbitten nose with a frostbitten finger, we would be vulnerable, however fit we felt, to high-altitude pulmonary oedema, a build-up of fluid in the lungs which is usually audible as a bubbling sound in the chest and can quickly drown victims in their own fluids. The victim may also bring up bloody sputum. Other symptoms of altitude sickness are that a climber becomes uncoordinated, disorientated, uncharacteristically irritable or irrational, and goes facially blue. Any of these are likely to indicate high-altitude cerebral oedema, which is a swelling of the brain, also caused by excess liquid in the body. The resulting pressure in the skull can cause paralysis, a stroke, or damaged eyesight.

In 1996, our guides told us, nine people had died alongside two of the most experienced group guides on Everest. The lesson learned from that tragedy was never to keep climbing beyond the moment when there is less than enough bottled oxygen for the return journey. If we were ever to run out of oxygen in the Death Zone, we were likely to join the ranks of the Everest dead.

The general opinion of the more experienced climbers in our group was that our Tibetan northern route was a bigger challenge than the Nepalese southern route. This was because our route involved more time spent higher than 8,400 metres, in the notorious Death Zone. The twin words 'altitude' and 'acclimatization' were on our group's lips much of the time. Sensible application of the latter, the old hands constantly assured us, would be our main way of defeating the potentially lethal effects of the former.

On the way up to Base Camp by Jeep, our group complained of lethargy, appetite loss and splitting headaches, so our doctor doled out Diamox pills, an altitude-sickness prevention drug which people say is also more effective than Viagra.

Our convoy slowly eased up into the main Himalayan range between India and Asia, the mightiest geographical feature on Earth's surface. It boasts more than a hundred peaks in excess of 24,000 feet (7,315 metres) above sea level, and includes all the famed fourteen 8,000ers, the trophy peaks over 8,000 metres (26,247 feet), whose summits are 'collected' by many dedicated high-altitude climbers, the first of whom was Reinhold Messner.

For hours we travelled on up over the high dusty plateau until we came to a couple of passes, the higher being the Lalung La at 16,810 feet (5,125 metres). The Tibetan Plateau stretches across south-west China, bounded by the deserts of the Tarim and Qaidam to the north and the Himalayan, Karakoram and Pamir mountain chains to the south and west. With an elevation of nearly five kilometres above sea level, this desolate, dry, windswept landscape is the world's highest plateau.

After crossing the Pang La pass at 16,800 feet above sea level, we reached the Rongbuk Monastery close to the original base camp used by the pioneering British expeditions of the 1920s. It was from here that Mallory and Irvine set out in 1924 never to return. Then we climbed sharply up a narrow valley, the Rongbuk Gorge, which widened quite suddenly to become a bleak, flat plain some five hundred metres wide between high hills, with Everest dead ahead. This plain, home to the modern Everest Base Camp, was dotted with the colourful tents of at least a dozen expedition groups and was swept by a bitter cold wind from the glaciers above. Everest herself, now only twelve miles away, rose impressively above us, black rock streaked with ice and crowned with snow.

Due largely to a Nepalese government clampdown on the number of climbers allowed annually on Everest, more and more groups and individuals were switching to our Tibetan approach. We learned that at least four hundred individuals would be hoping to climb the northern route over the next few weeks. Some years there was enough good weather to allow climbers to sneak briefly on to the summit, other years nobody made it at all, however great their skill and their strength. Most years people died trying. The current death rate was estimated at one in every ten attempts.

Louise and I shared a two-man tent, which was hardly a honeymoon suite. She suffered bad headaches, but stayed with me for a fortnight until our camp leader took our group away up to Advanced Base Camp, along with our gear on sixty-five yaks. She went back to Britain with a warning that she had dreamt that I must beware of frayed ropes.

An Irish friend of mine, one of the fittest men in Britain, met us on his way down from Advanced Base Camp. His eyesight had begun to bother him up there and his group leader had diagnosed tunnel vision. A doctor with an ophthalmoscope later discovered 'pools of blood' behind the retinas where blood vessels had burst. He was now due to head back to Ireland for treatment as soon as possible or, he had been warned, he would risk permanent eye damage and possible blindness.

I slept well on the first night at the first interim camp at 5,500 metres (18,045 feet) en route to Advanced Base. I had taken three hours to get there at a slow trudge with a light rucksack, and still had no headache, no sickness and no loss of appetite. Sibu kept telling me to drink more water, and I had done so, mostly to keep him happy, as I'm not normally a water drinker, despite knowing (and indeed preaching) all the standard dictums on the blessings to be had from H_2O.

Next morning our group moved on up the glacial valley, an ascent of 950 metres with shark-fin pinnacles of ice towering above each side of the trail, known as the Magic Highway. We crossed or skirted lakes of frozen meltwater, and great glaciers curved down from high valleys to join ours, but all, we knew, were shrinking. The main glacier had shrunk by over a hundred vertical feet in the past ten years alone. I kept up with the others without trouble, and after five hours we came to the tents of the second interim camp at 6,088 metres (about 20,000 feet).

I lay awake for a while listening to water dripping on to sleeping bags, the distant crackle of moving glacier ice and the muted rumble of some snoring neighbour. Then, with no warning at all and a nasty shock, I jerked up, gasping for air with a terrible sensation of suffocation. My heart beat wildly. The phenomenon passed as quickly as it came, and I felt drowsy again. Within minutes, or maybe mere seconds, I was again jumping up in a panic. Once more I felt as though I had been throttled. The instant the shock awoke me, my breathing reverted to normal, but as soon as I drowsed off again, the gasping for air routine was back. There was no way I could get any sleep.

Next day, after a sleepless, worried night, I learned from our doctor exactly what my problem was: an ailment known as Cheyne-Stokes periodic breathing, which occurs when the system that regulates breathing gets out of sync. The would-be sleeper responds involuntarily to a build-up in carbon dioxide by hyperventilating, which in turn leads to the breathing centre shutting off respiration. Carbon dioxide levels then increase and the unfortunate cycle repeats. A standard cure is for the victim to take Diamox tablets just before going to bed. Diamox blocks an enzyme in the kidneys and makes the blood acidic, which is interpreted by the brain as a signal to breathe more. However, with my breathing problem, I was already taking the maximum advised dose of two 250mg tablets daily. The only answer, our doctor advised, was to use oxygen whenever I needed to sleep at or above 20,000 feet.

The following day I shuffled up the steep trail to the Advanced Base Camp, where the tents of some four hundred climbers and their Sherpas were grouped hugger-mugger beside the ascent route. I was now at 6,460 metres (21,200 feet), higher than I had ever been. So far, I thanked God for small mercies, I appeared to have escaped retinal damage, severe headaches, heart pains, cerebral and pulmonary oedema, tensions with my fellow climbers, and even the hacking Khumbu cough that wracked many climbers even down at

Base Camp. Periodic breathing or Cheyne-Stokes syndrome would only affect me if I slept or dozed without oxygen, so my summit chances were still intact.

For two weeks our group, like most others, went up and down from Advanced Base Camp. Then, in the third week of May, truly acclimatized, we made our final trip upwards to await good summit-bid weather. I heard that several climbers had made attempts already, but bad weather had killed some and, from our tent, I watched others, aided by their Sherpas, limp down with frostbitten feet and hands.

It would turn out that only 60 of the 400 climbers who set out from the Tibetan Advanced Base Camp in 2005 actually reached the summit. This high failure rate was due to many causes. The weather was average to bad, but altitude sickness, diarrhoea and the Khumbu cough took their regular toll. The dry air at altitude can wreak havoc with even the toughest climber's prospects. Also known as high-altitude hack, the Khumbu cough can be bad enough to cause broken ribs.

One of the early British attempts to pioneer the northern route involved climber Howard Somervell in 1924. When a coughing fit wracked him just above the North Col, he found that his throat was obstructed. He could neither breathe nor call for help, so he sat down to die. Then in desperation, 'I pressed my chest with both hands, gave one last almighty push and the obstruction came up. Though the pain was intense, I was a new man,' he said afterwards. He had coughed up the desiccated mucous membrane of his throat.

The two main high-altitude sickness killers, cerebral and pulmonary oedema, are both caused by the body's reactions to lack of oxygen. Many people who travel from sea level to over 8,000 feet report symptoms ranging from headache to loss of appetite and nausea. Why? As the available oxygen falls, the body responds by increasing the blood flow to the brain, but it can overcompensate, whereupon fluid leaks from the blood vessels into the brain causing it to swell. The victim is then suffering cerebral oedema. Not surprisingly, the greater the elevation gain, the greater the swelling. The way to avoid falling victim is to ascend gradually, about a thousand feet a day over 8,000 feet, which gives the body time to acclimatize properly.

As the body tries to get as much oxygen from the air as it can, pulmonary oedema can result from the greatly increased blood flow through the lungs. It usually takes a few days to develop, and is exacerbated by overexertion. This is a serious condition which can kill in only a matter of hours and again is best avoided by gradual ascent. Treatment is by an immediate descent of several thousand feet and use of oxygen if available.

The body also responds to the lower oxygen levels by putting more red blood cells into circulation. Up to a point, this is a good thing. However, if it goes too far, the blood becomes thick and prone to clotting. Clots which get dislodged float around and can cause strokes, heart attacks and pulmonary embolisms. Due to my own cardiac state, my daily blood-thinning aspirin intake had been upped from 75mg to 350mg whilst I was at high altitude.

At the North Col camp the toilet arrangements were simple. You squatted as near as was safely possible to the edge of the ice precipice on the far side of the encampment. Slipping on the ice there would be a bad idea, for the resulting fall would be over a thousand feet. I spent a lot of time in the tent fiddling with my oxygen system in the knowledge that most deaths on the upper reaches of Everest are the result of oxygen shortage, and an efficient oxygen regulator is a key to survival.

Eventually our group set out from North Col camp. The sky was clear and the winds manageable, so we all made good time up the long steep snow ramps at quite a steep gradient to the next base. This 7,500-metre camp was much smaller than the previous one and the few dozen tents there were tattered, in some cases completely shredded.

Between 7,300 metres and 7,500 metres the wind had picked up and made life quite unpleasant. My oxygen mask kept needing adjustment, my frost-damaged feet spent a good deal of time complaining that my Kathmandu-purchased boots were too tight, and my frostbitten hand needed many halts to force blood back into the fingers during those stretches where I needed to keep the fixed rope on my left-hand side.

There are hundreds of knots and fixed points along the rope line, and you always use two slings and never unclip one until the other is attached to the rope beyond the obstacle. Many of the bodies lying along the rope line and below it are there because they slipped and fell when briefly unattached to the mountain or a rope. You can't add to the number of corpses who suffered that particular fate so long as you always use the two-sling system – and so long as the fixed rope does not break or come loose. The older ropes are often cut by falling rocks or chafed through by rubbing on sharp points.

The 7,500-metre camp was, in reality, a raggedy series of ledges: anywhere big enough for a tiny tent to be pitched with guy ropes tied mostly around rocks in lieu of tent pegs. The recent big winds had rendered many of the tents I passed mere skeletal tent-pole hoops attached to wildly fluttering bits of material. Every so often a couple of climbers would slowly descend. Many of them moved like zombies and were unrecognizable in their hooded, goggled sameness. One of them was our doctor, who had sensibly turned round, too sick to continue.

Between the camps at 7,500 metres and 7,900 metres the going became harder, with many slippery rocks and ice runnels to negotiate. A strong cold wind from one flank had the effect, I am not sure why, of blocking off my oxygen, at least partially, somewhere between the cylinder in my rucksack and my mask. This caused constant halts to turn away from the wind and breathe deeply. My hooded down jacket covered parts of the system to stop them freezing, but in order to reach the cylinder or to alter the flow setting, I needed to undo the jacket's main zip. Dribble from the mask often landed on the zip and froze it solid. Should my goggles mist up or move out of place, I again needed to unzip.

These sorts of clothing problems had often occurred on polar expeditions in far colder circumstances, but they had not involved the added complications of an oxygen system, or being attached to a mountainside, or feeling below par due to the altitude. In the Arctic most travel was at 3 or 4 feet above sea level, and in Antarctica we had suffered from altitude sickness at a mere 11,000 feet up. I kept checking that my system's pipes were not snagged, and the mask workings not frozen, but I never managed to discover why, every so often in strong winds, the oxygen stopped coming and I had to tear my mouth from the mask and try to gulp in air.

At 7,900 metres the camp was perched on tiny tilted ledges and felt, I thought, unpleasantly exposed. But I also enjoyed a new feeling of anticipation because the summit ridge, which had seemed so far away and so high as to be unobtainable for nearly seventy days, now for the first time looked within reasonable grasp. How many other hopeful folk had reached this point and likewise felt that they could make it, only to die within 48 hours? A good many. At least one out of every ten. The most famous were, of course, Mallory and Irvine in 1924.

In 1999 a group of top US climbers searched for Mallory and Irvine's bodies in the area around and above the 7,900-metre camp, especially in the snow basins beneath the steeper rock faces. Bodies dressed in brightly coloured Gore-Tex jackets were not hard to find. The climbers recorded: 'We found ourselves in a kind of collection zone for fallen climbers ... Just seeing these twisted, broken bodies was a pretty stark reminder of our own mortality.'

Then one of the Americans, Conrad Anker, spotted something different. He thought he had discovered the remains of Andrew Irvine: 'We were looking at a man who had been clinging to the mountain for seventy-five years. The clothing was blasted from most of his body, and his skin was bleached white. I felt like I was viewing a Greek or Roman marble statue.' Soon the five searchers were crouched around the body in awed silence.

> The body itself did the speaking. For here was a body unlike the others crumpled in crannies elsewhere on the terrace. This body was lying fully extended, face down and pointing uphill, frozen in a position of self-arrest, as if the fall had happened only

> moments earlier. The head and upper torso were frozen into the rubble that had gathered around them over the decades, but the arms, powerfully muscular still, extended above the head to strong hands that gripped the mountainside, flexed fingertips dug deep into the frozen gravel. The legs were extended downhill. One was broken and the other had been gently crossed over it for protection.

It was the body of George Mallory.

By the end of 2006, records showed that, in the 76 years since Mallory's death not far from my 7,900-metre tent, 2,062 climbers had reached the summit and 203 had died on the mountain. Since there were ten climbers in our two groups, I wondered if any would succumb to this Everest law of decimation. Five climbers had died on the mountain already during the past month, I knew, and maybe more, since there were a number of lone climbers as yet unaccounted for at Advanced Base Camp.

One of America's most famed modern-day climbers, David Breashears, described the act of climbing upwards on the route: 'Our bodies were dehydrated. Our fingers and toes went numb as precious oxygen was diverted to our brains, hearts and other vital organs. Climbing above 26,000 feet, even with bottled oxygen, is like running on a treadmill and breathing through a straw. Your body screams at you to turn around. Everything says: this is cold, this is impossible.'

The following year climber David Sharp, in a bad way some 1,300 feet below the summit, slowly deteriorated as climbers went by him on their way up and, later, back down. His legs, feet and fingers became frostbitten and dead, so he could no longer walk or use his hands. His oxygen gave out and he died, as some people do on this stretch of this mountain. When a climber near the summit of Mount Everest reaches a stage of exhaustion and oxygen starvation so severe that he can no longer move on his own initiative, he is typically left to die. It is simply impossible for one climber to descend such treacherous terrain carrying or dragging the inert body of another. The mountain is littered with the bodies of climbers who have simply sat down and died of exposure. Sibu nearly joined their ranks.

I came at last to the exposed series of ledges at 8,400 metres on which perched a few battered tents of the so-called Death Camp. We crawled into our tents tired but exhilarated. After seventy days we were nearly there. The tent was pitched on a slope. The Sherpas had done their best to find a flat spot, but there were none. I, with my own Sherpa, Boca Lama, and another tried to get ready for the night, unpacking our rucksacks and checking our oxygen systems without upsetting each other's space, all in a tiny two-man tent pitched on rocks and ice. Any item that escaped through the entry door was liable to slide, then fall for many thousands of feet to the snow terraces and glaciers below. Various dead bodies had been found in the tents here, including an Indian climber the previous week.

Sibu nearly died that day when his oxygen ran out, not far above the Death Camp, when he was on his way back down. We did not know this until the following morning when one of our Sherpas found him slouched beside the ropes an hour or two below the tents. A few days earlier, a Slovenian had died on the summit ridge, and a solo climber from Bhutan close by him ran out of oxygen and began to hallucinate due to hypoxia. He wandered by one of the old corpses near to the fixed rope, probably the one with green boots that most climbers remember, and thought he saw the corpse pointing at an object nearby. This turned out to be an orange oxygen cylinder, half-buried by snow. The Bhutani, to his joy, found that there was still oxygen in it, clipped it to his system and survived to tell his tale to everyone in Advanced Base Camp.

From the Death Camp, the final climb ascends and traverses a steep stretch of striated limestone know as the Yellow Band. At midnight, or thereabouts, the normal start time for final summit attempts, I struggled into my boots, pack and oxygen system, and with Boca Lama a few yards behind, grinning as usual, began the fairly steep climb up the fixed ropes with new batteries in my head torch. In seven or eight hours, on a fixed rope the whole way, I hoped to be on the summit of Everest.

We moved off into the night, pitch-black beyond the cone of our torchlight. There were slippery rocks, snow patches and a bewildering choice of upward-leading ropes, some frayed almost through, others brand new. In the torchlight it paid to take time. I found myself panting far more than on the previous climb, despite taking it slowly, but perhaps this was because of the gradient. I felt cold despite the exertion, and I felt dizzy, too. Something was wrong but nothing I could identify, so I kept going in a stop-start way, gasping for breath every few metres.

Then, some forty minutes after setting out, my world caved in. Somebody, it seemed, had clamped powerful arms around my chest and was squeezing the life out of me. And the surgical wire that held my ribs together felt as though it was tearing through my chest. My thoughts were simple. I am having another heart attack. I will be dead in minutes. No defibrillator on hand this time.

I remembered that Louise had pestered me to carry special pills with me – glyceryl trinitrate (GTN). You put one under your tongue, where it fizzes and causes your system to dilate in all the right places. I tore at my jacket pocket and, removing my mitts, crammed at least six tablets under my tongue before swallowing. I clung to the rope, hanging out over the great drop and waiting to die. My one glimpse of Boca Lama, who said nothing, was of his usual big grin as my torchlight lit up his features.

Five minutes later I was still alive. The tablets, I knew, could, if you are lucky, stave off a heart attack and give you time to get to a cardiac unit. They are not a means of avoiding an attack in order to allow you to continue climbing. This might not be my own end, but it was definitely the signal to descend to lower altitudes at once.

'I must go down quickly,' I told Boca Lama. He shook his head and the grin disappeared. It would, he explained, be too dangerous to descend until we could 'see our feet'. That meant dawn in five hours' time.

I knew my best hope of survival was to lose height rapidly. The tightness had gone from my chest, but the sharp discomfort around the stitch-wires was still there. I contemplated going on down without Boca Lama, but decided against it. Going up an icy, slippery, steep slope in the darkness is a lot safer than descending one. Statistically, the vast majority of accidents happen on the descent. The concentration of going up seems to disappear, to be replaced by a weary nonchalance. Nothing matters apart from a longing for warmth and comfort. Lost in these thoughts you become careless. The focus gone and the mind weary. It is all too easy to lose your footing or clip carelessly on to a rope. Three thousand metres of void waited directly below our tent.

Nine-times Everest climber, Ed Viesturs, has two favourite sayings: 'Just because you love the mountains doesn't mean the mountains love you' and 'Getting to the top is optional. Getting down is mandatory.' After four hours, enough light allowed us to continue the descent. The pain in my chest slowly faded. I felt both relieved and regretful.

Back at Advanced Base Camp, Duncan Chessell, who has led thirty-five Himalayan expeditions, said, 'For a sixty-year-old man to make it even this far is extraordinary. You would expect only 50 per cent of climbers to reach anywhere near this high, especially during this season.' I congratulated my fellow Jagged Globe climbers, especially Sibu, who was the first black person to climb Everest from both sides.

Within a day I was back down in Base Camp, and 48 hours after that I was checked out in Harley Street for new cardiac damage. None was evident, so it is likely that, on Everest and previously on Kilimanjaro, I had had mere angina warnings. It is impossible to know what would have happened if I had not heeded them or had not had the GTN tablets. I learnt later that, on the other side of the mountain a Scottish climber, 49-year-old Robert Milne, died of a heart attack on the same night and at the same height as I had my attack.

The tangible declared aim of my Everest attempt, all costs of which were sponsored by the generosity of Yorkshire businessman Paul Sykes, had been to raise £2 million for a Cardiac MRI Unit and Catheter Laboratory in the Great Ormond Street Hospital for

Children in London. The British Heart Foundation eventually raised the £2 million through the Ran Fiennes Healthy Hearts Appeal, despite my failure on the mountain, and I cut the ribbon to officially open the gleaming new clinic.

A couple of months later, Louise told me that she was pregnant and on Easter Day 2006 our daughter Elizabeth gave her first yell. A month later, at sixty-two years old, I changed my first nappy.

At no time during the 72 days on Everest had I noticed a beckoning void or, indeed, any alarming drop, only smooth white shoulders falling away below. Had anyone fallen down those slopes they would have surely died, like many before them, but my vertigo needs a visible void beneath my feet to activate it. Two of my goals when taking up Sibu's invitation to climb Everest had not been accomplished. I had failed to summit and I had failed to confront and banish my vertigo.

I remembered that, back on my Jagged Globe course, it had been suggested by one of the younger instructors, Kenton Cool, that anyone looking to challenge vertigo would be better off in the Alps rather than the Himalayas, since the Daddy of all Nasties was a mere three hours' drive from Geneva airport. This was the North Face (*Nordwand*) of the Eiger, also known to Germans as the *Mordwand* or Murder Wall due to the number of top international climbers who have died climbing it.

At some point I had tentatively approached Kenton to ask whether, if the Eiger was indeed a tougher challenge, exposure-wise, than Everest, he would be willing to guide me up it? And, if so, when? I knew that Kenton had climbed the North Wall of the Eiger with two friends and had taken three days and nights to do so. I also knew that he was held in huge respect by Britain's mountaineering community. He was thirty-three years old and supremely fit.

In response to my Eiger query, he was forthright. He would not even consider climbing the Eiger with me unless he first taught me how to climb to a standard where he was sure he would not be risking his own life. He suggested that to begin with I should read *The*

White Spider by Heinrich Harrer, the first man to climb the *Mordwand* back in 1938. Harrer summarized the climb thus:

> The North Wall of the Eiger remains one of the most perilous in the Alps, as every man who has ever joined battle with it knows. Other climbs ... may be technically more difficult, but nowhere else is there such appalling danger from the purely fortuitous hazards of avalanches, stone-falls and sudden deterioration of the weather as on the Eiger ... The North Face of the Eiger demands the uttermost of skill, stamina and courage, nor can it be climbed without the most exhaustive preparations ... The Eiger's Face is an irrefutable touchstone of a climber's stature as a mountaineer and as a man ... Anyone who makes headway on the North Face of the Eiger and survives there for several days has achieved and overcome so much – whatever mistakes he may have committed – that his performance is well above the comprehension of the average climber.

Jon Krakauer, a well-known US climber and author, wrote:

> The problem with climbing the North Face of the Eiger is that in addition to getting up 6,000 vertical feet of crumbling limestone and black ice, one must climb over some formidable mythology. The trickiest moves on any climb are the mental ones, the psychological gymnastics that keep terror in check ... The rockfall and avalanches that rain continuously down the Nordwand are legendary ... Needless to say, all this makes the Eiger North Face one of the most widely coveted climbs in the world.

From the point of view of a worthy vertigo-testing challenge involving plenty of ice and snow, the mountain seemed ideal and cheap to reach at weekends from Heathrow. So I went back to Kenton, and he agreed to have a go at teaching me how to climb on mixed rock and ice in the Alps.

For a charity, I asked Marie Curie Cancer Care if they would like to be involved again. They decided that, if an attempt on the Eiger was filmed and shown on the national news, they could raise between £1 million and £3 million. ITN agreed to record the project, and Paul Sykes once again sponsored my costs.

Kenton assured me that such an attempt would best be made in March, when winter temperatures should freeze loose rubble in place and minimize the likelihood of rockfalls.

'Which March?' I asked Kenton.

He smiled. 'That depends on when, if ever, you become sufficiently proficient for me not to consider you the lethal liability that you are right now.'

So month after month through 2006 I flew out to Geneva for five-day training sessions in the Alps, trying to imbibe a basic understanding of the principles of rope-work and how to use an ice axe (or two) in conjunction with crampon spikes in order to head in an upward direction on vertical ice sheets. Not just to help plod up slopes, as on Everest. One day we completed my first Grade Five waterfall, aptly named the *Cascade Difficile*. In November 2006 Kenton finally agreed that I could, if I continued my improvement, set a date of 1 March 2007 for the Eiger climb.

I got to know the mountains above Chamonix quite well through my training with Kenton. The town is possibly the greatest mecca in the world for mountaineers and is dominated by the great rounded summit of Mont Blanc. On average, one climber dies each and every day in and around Chamonix during the summer climbing season. Helicopters fly overhead on rescue missions, and sometimes come back with a body bag dangling beneath them.

Climbing guides who live in Chamonix and depend upon the Alpine snows for their livelihood, are worried, as is everyone in the winter sports industry, that the Alps are running out of snow. It is true that during Roman times the Alps were warmer even than they are today, but the current speed of warming is what worries French and Swiss scientists. They estimate that the Alps has lost half its glacier ice in the past century, and 20 per cent of that since the 1980s. Swiss glaciers have lost one-fifth of their surface area in just fifteen years. One side effect is an increased incidence of huge rockfalls and avalanches.

Kenton's long-time climbing partner, Ian Parnell, who had been with me for much of my failed Everest attempt, agreed to join us on the Eiger and he took over training me when Kenton was busy elsewhere. He kept Kenton up to date on my progress, and one of his reports included:

> Ran's hand, damaged by frostbite, of course proved a real hindrance, and at times his 'stumps' would prove completely ineffective at gripping the rock. I'm sure for Ran this was a real frustration, but he didn't let it show. The real big issue, however, was Ran's vertigo. Again, he would say very little and at times you could forget that he was battling a constant fear of heights, but when things got tricky and he became flustered, his vertigo would begin to spiral out of control.

In order to work on overcoming this, Kenton introduced me to a Scottish climbing instructor, Sandy Ogilvie, who took me one day to Swanage on the Dorset coast. Halfway across a sea-cliff route called the Traverse of the Gods, I lost a key hold and fell in a long pendulum swing, just missing the tide-free rocks below by a metre. I was left dangling free some twelve feet below the nearest point of the rock face. Soon afterwards Sandy took me to the Orkneys to climb the famous Old Man of Hoy. This sea stack was my first truly exposed climb, with a near 400-foot drop to the sea.

Amongst other lessons learnt, I realized that on such rock climbs there was the occasional key grip where my damaged finger ends could only gain an adequate hold – just – if they were in a state of maximum sensitivity which, when colder rather than warm, they were not. Thinking ahead to the Eiger, I knew that I could not afford to try such a climb one-handed, so, for the first time in all the long years of extreme polar projects, I bought a supply of hand-warmer packets to fit inside my mitts. Each little heatpack is shaped like a tea bag, 2 inches square, and contains a chemical mix which, once the paper container is torn open and the pack is exposed to air, slowly heats up to a touch better than body heat, and is meant to last for about six hours. Some I found were a lot better than others, but none worked well at high altitude because they got less oxygen, like me.

On 1 March 2007 I flew to Geneva with the family and drove a rental car to Grindelwald where we stayed at a family-run hotel, the Grand Regina, with a reputation among British tourists of being the best in all Switzerland. The owner, Hans Krebs, had kindly given us accommodation free of charge because he approved of and wanted to help our Marie Curie aims.

The hotel manager warned us of the consequences of the mountains not being as stable as they should normally be in midwinter. The rate of retreat of glaciers throughout the Alps, together with the thawing of the permafrost layer, had created temporary barrages of fallen rock, blocking high ravines and creating lakes. Increasingly torrential summer rains then burst the feeble dams of rubble, causing flash floods, mudslides and more loosened rock. The previous autumn the Eiger itself had suffered a major rockfall, a chunk bigger than two Empire State Buildings.

The March days slowly ticked by in Grindelwald. I began to find the bulk of the Eiger, looming over the hotel, a touch oppressive. I tried to keep busy, and I went for a daily two-hour run out of the village, along hilly lanes and up the glacial ravines. As I ran I heard the intermittent explosions of avalanches from the heights of the Alpine giants all around.

After six days of evil weather forecasts, I was padding about Grindelwald increasingly worried that we would never get a five-day clear period in March. Every time I looked out of the window or trudged through the village streets, I found myself looking up at that great black wall, the upper limits obscured in thick fog. One night I couldn't sleep and spotted a single pinprick of light high up on the bulk of the North Face. The very sight of it made my stomach muscles tighten as I imagined having to try to sleep anywhere on that hideous cliff.

In mid-March the weather forecast predicted five days of settled weather. Kenton and Ian arrived in Grindelwald with their ropes, and the ITN crew with their long-distance camera lenses. Ian wrote: 'For Ran, although he hid it well, Everest had been a failure. This time round we were to attempt the Eiger North Face, and while we didn't have the barrier of altitude, in my mind this was a much tougher challenge.'

We fixed on our crampons beneath a feature known as the First Pillar. Many climbers lose the route in this area, but Kenton seemed confident as he stared up at our first obstacle, some two thousand feet of mixed snow gulleys, loose scree, shiny ledges of smooth, compact limestone and temporarily lodged boulders. Few of the infamous Eiger tragedies had occurred on this first 2,000-foot climb, but the fallen detritus of many an Eiger incident lay all around us. I remembered, from one of the Eiger books, a photograph of climber Edi Rainer's body lying smashed in the scree of this catchment zone. And among these rubble-strewn lower reaches Chris Bonington, on his Eiger ascent, had passed by blood trails and a piece of flesh attached to some bone.

I knew that the world's top soloists, acrobats of the top league, could climb the *Mordwand* in hours, not days, without ropes and in their sticky-soled rock shoes as light as woollen socks. A single slip or false move would see them dead, crushed on the rock, but they survive on the confidence born of their expertise. The mere thought of climbing a single rock pitch unroped made me flinch.

In a few hours, with constant encouragement from Kenton and Ian, I had blundered my way up a thousand feet or more of the initial rubble slopes. Every few hours I tore open a new hand-warmer bag with my teeth and inserted the two tiny pouches into my mitts. They worked well, and whenever the sensitive stumps of my amputated fingers began to feel numb with cold, I positioned the hand-warmer pouch over their ends for a while.

I had never climbed on similar rock before: smooth like slate with almost nowhere to provide even the tiniest holding point for the tips of my ice axes and crampon spikes. At times I had to remove one or other of my mitts with my teeth and use my bare hand to clasp some rock bulge or slight surface imperfection in order to avoid a fall. This I hated to do, for my fingers, once cold, took forever to rewarm, even with my heat pouches.

At some point on a steep icy slope, to my considerable alarm and dismay, one of my boots skidded off a nub of protruding rock and my left crampon swung away from my boot. Although still attached by a strap, the crampon was useless. Luckily the same crampon had come loose once before, on a frozen waterfall while climbing with Kenton a month earlier. So I reined in my rising panic and, hanging from one axe and a tiny foothold, I managed, with much silent swearing, to reattach the crampon to the boot.

Ian recorded my ascent of the Difficult Crack through the eyes of a top-flight mountaineer who knew that I was facing my first big test on the North Face:

> Through Ran's two years of training for the route, he proved himself to be a competent and efficient ice and mixed climber, but steep rock tended to bring out his weaknesses. In particular, his ineffectual stumps for fingers on his left hand ... Ran's worst fear was that he might be forced to climb bare-handed. Luckily he had one big advantage. Whereas Kenton and I spent valuable time fretting and testing the security of the meagre hooks we'd uncovered, Ran, to put it bluntly, was clueless. His technique basically involved dragging his tools down the rock until they somehow snagged, then he would blindly pull for glory. His footwork on rock was similarly polished: a wild pedalling technique that for all its dry tooling naivety was surprisingly effective.

From the top of the Difficult Crack we could look immediately above us at an immense sheer wall, known as the Rote Fluh: smooth, red and infamous for its propensity to shower loose rockfalls on to the face below. From the crack we still had more than eight thousand feet of climbing, including traverses, on the North Face, much of which I knew would be a lot harder and more exposed than had been the 80-foot-high crack. Kenton had planned for us to bivouac the first night at a ledge known as the Swallow's Nest. Between the Difficult Crack and this refuge was the infamous Hinterstoisser Traverse, the key passage unlocking access to the centre of the wall.

In 1935 a couple of Germans, Sedlmayer and Mehringer, had climbed a record distance up the mountain, but at 3,300 metres they froze to death on a ledge. A year later Hinterstoisser and his companions, hoping to set a new record, if not to reach the summit, had come to the ledge of the frozen bodies which, with climbers' macabre humour, they named Death Bivouac, only to be themselves turned back by the weather and falling rocks. But fatally they had left no rope in place across their key traverse, and their desperate attempts to reverse their route over this slippery, vertical cliffside all failed. So they tried to rope down to reach a man-made porthole in the rock, behind which was a gallery for tourists on the train inside the mountain tunnel, but they never made it to this improbably safe haven. One fell and dropped free to the valley below, one was strangled by the rope and a third froze to death.

The first team to climb the North Face had used this same route, and the author of their story, Heinrich Harrer, wrote: 'The rocks across which we now had to traverse were almost vertical, plunging away beneath into thin air.' For 2,500 feet under my boots only the wind touched the plunging rock. My crampons skidded out of their tenuous holds. I gripped the black rope dangling from the rock as my feet scrabbled desperately to find a hold. Into my brain, unbidden, came the picture of my heavy body tearing Kenton off the cliff, and then the deadweight of us both pulling Ian away, and the rush of air as we cartwheeled through space. 'Will I scream?' was my main worry, strangely enough.

We reached the Swallow's Nest, a 4-foot-wide scab of frozen snow stuck to a little rock ledge. Answering the call of nature during the first day's climb was something I had successfully postponed, but the moment of truth arrived on the narrow ledge. There was a sharp breeze and I felt cold.

The world-famous climber Walter Bonatti, pioneer of some of the hardest cliffs in the Alps, wrote of his own Swallow's Nest visit in the 1960s: 'I was not the first man to tackle the Eigerwand alone. Two others had tried in recent years, but both had died in the attempt. The aura of fatality and blood that hangs over this killer mountain seemed painfully distinct to the eyes of a solo climber.'

When Joe Simpson and Ray Delaney bivouacked there seven years before us, two other climbers (Matthew Hayes from Hampshire and Phillip O'Sullivan from New Zealand) had fallen off, roped together, from an icy slope higher up and dropped past this ledge. Simpson wrote: 'I thought of their endless, frictionless fall, numbed in their last moments of consciousness by the full enormity of what was happening . . . I stared down thinking of them lying there tangled in their ropes, side by side . . . We didn't hear them go. They didn't scream.'

In the morning Ian warned me to be cautious with my boots and crampons. 'Put them on carefully. It's all too easy with cold hands trying to force a cold foot into a rigid boot to lose your grip and then, before you know it, a boot is gone – a long way. Then you are in serious trouble.'

From the Swallow's Nest we scaled the First Ice Field and a 300-foot-high, near-vertical gully of part-iced rock known as the Ice Hose. I definitely disliked this section which, as an amateur, I find difficult to describe. But I took some comfort from Harrer agreeing with me: 'There isn't a cranny anywhere for a reliable piton, and there aren't any natural holds. Moreover, the rock is scoured smooth by falling stones, breadcrumbed with snow, ice and rubble. It isn't an invitation to cheerful climbing, it offers no spur to one's courage; it simply threatens hard work and danger.'

More stones whistled by as I inched up the Hose but, although I found myself flinching and ducking, none made contact, and the next time I reached Kenton's belay position, he looked happy, clearly pleased that we had reached the Second Ice Field intact. This was the great white sheet easily identifiable from Grindelwald. At some point as we axed our way up it, Kenton saw an ice axe whistle by us on its way down the face. We never did identify its owner.

The next problem – rock not ice – was called the Flat Iron. In 1962 two British climbers, Brian Nally and Barry Brewster, were progressing below the buttress when Brewster was hit by a rock and injured. Chris Bonington and Don Whillans abandoned their own ascent in order to attempt a rescue, but the already unconscious Brewster was swept to his death by a rockfall before they could reach him.

Above the Flat Iron we came to Death Bivouac, a snow-clogged ledge long enough for the three of us to lie down head to toe. That night my right arm rested on the very edge of a 3,500-foot drop.

The Third Ice Field, a dizzy place, led to a 700-foot-high rock gash called The Ramp, graded by climbers as VI, 6 – a grade more difficult than I could climb without a number of falls when attempted during my British climbing outings.

Somewhere on the Ramp in 1961 an Austrian climber with a brilliant repertoire of ultra-severe Alpine ascents, the 22-year-old Adolf Mayr, came to grief attempting the first-ever solo ascent of the face. Down in Grindelwald queues of tourists waited their turn to gawp at 'Adi' through the hotel telescopes. Somewhere in the mid-section, at a spot named the Waterfall Chimney, he needed to traverse across wet rock. Watchers below saw him hack at a foothold with his axe. Then he stepped sideways, missed his footing and fell four thousand feet to his death.

The Ramp led to the Brittle Ledges, a tricky area of loose slate. My axes were no help, and eventually I had to remove my mitts and bury my bad hand deep into a vertical cleft to achieve the needed purchase. This move coincided with the failure of my last available hand-warmer pouch. Resupplies were unobtainable deep in my rucksack, and my hand soon grew numb with cold. This was bad timing because above the Brittle Ledges Ian led up a vertical wall of slate about ninety feet high.

Maybe I was too tired to think clearly, or perhaps my cold, numb left hand, incapable of gripping anything but my ice axe (and that thanks only to the crutch of its wrist loop), left me pretty much one-armed at the time. Whatever the reason, I worked harder and with greater desperation on that single 90-foot wall than on any previous part of the North Face.

Despite the brittle nature of the rock, the first few metres up from a little snow-covered ledge on to the Brittle Crack are really overhanging. The upper twelve feet involved an appallingly exposed traverse around a corner with space shouting at you from every direction. The tiny cracks and sparse piton placements available for my axes disappeared as I neared the top. All apparent handhold bulges were smooth and sloped downwards, and my bare fingers simply slid off them. My arms and my legs began to shake, my biceps to burn. Pure luck got me to the ice patch that capped the wall, into which I sank an axe with great relief and hauled myself up, a wreck, to the tiny snow ledge where a grinning Ian was belayed.

'This is it,' he said. 'We spend the night here. Lovely view.'

I lost a mitt off the ledge during the night, but I had a spare immediately available. The stumps of my left-hand fingers ached, but far less than all ten fingers had hurt on most polar trips.

On the morning of our fourth day on the face, I woke with a dry mouth and butterflies fluttering about in my stomach. Joe Simpson's professional description of the Traverse of the Gods was clear in my mind. 'For 400 feet the points of protection – weak, damaged pitons, battered into shattered downward-sloping cracks – are marginal to say the least. Most climbers would prefer not to weight such pitons statically, let alone fall onto them ... and the drop beneath the climber's feet is 5,000 feet of clear air.'

Ian wrote of the Traverse: 'It's dramatic, nervy climbing for experienced climbers, but for someone like Ran who suffers from vertigo, it can easily become a complete nightmare. The rock here is loose, covered in verglas in winter and frighteningly exposed. In fact, at one point your heels overhang the whole drop of the wall to the snows of Kleine Scheidegg below.'

I had a scary time on the Traverse and felt utterly drained while crawling up the White Spider, where I somehow managed to lose my windproof jacket, a bad item to lose at that height should the weather change. Above lay a thousand feet of intricate rock and ice gullies known as the Exit Cracks. I liked the sound of 'Exit'. The walls on both sides of the various grooves and chimneys of the cracks were smooth and often at 80°. One smooth-walled runnel all but stopped me.

Kenton pointed to a tiny ledge. 'Corti Bivouac,' he said, referring to an Italian climber who somehow survived to be rescued after his companion fell a hundred feet to a lower ledge, where he sat for five days until he died. His body dangled there for two years, ogled by telescope tourists down in Grindelwald.

The nightmare of the Exit Cracks ended with the welcome sight of a swathe of open sky, above which a steep wall of snow and ice led up to the summit ridge. This sharply angled snow wall was the reservoir, the source of the avalanches that sweep down the North Face. New, often wet, snow that settles here frequently fails to cohere firmly with the névé and ice beneath and sloughs away in lethal waves down the Exit Cracks, out over the Spider and beyond.

Ian led up this last steep climb, taking his time with care and caution. At 10 a.m. on the fifth day of the climb, and thanks entirely to the brilliance and patience of Kenton and Ian, we came to the Eiger summit. Although I realized that I had not rid myself of the curse of vertigo, my other aim, the Marie Curie fundraiser, raised £1.4 million. I had also learned that to be body-cold on a vertical climb involves a very different and more serious set of problems than on any polar journey. For a start, the best and most speedy warming-up exercise is to jump around and windmill your arms. This is not practical on a rock face.

After my Everest failure, one of the Jagged Globe instructors, Neil Short, had written to me with a suggestion: 'As you were so close I often wonder whether you are tempted to give it another go. Maybe you could go from the south side, with Kenton Cool, where you spend far less time above 5,300 metres.'

Marie Curie fundraisers were desperate for funds to train more nurses and Børge Ousland had still not summited Everest, so I was tempted. What decided me was a chance remark by Reinhold Messner, the world's greatest mountaineer, reported on Radio 4 as I sat in a traffic jam, to the effect that the tourist route on the Nepal side of Everest was in many ways easier than the Tibet climb. So I signed on with the group, Himalayan Guides Nepal, where Kenton Cool was a guide, and joined him at the Base Camp on the 'easy' side of the mountain.

Despite the excellent acclimatization schedule and coaching by Kenton (who has at the time of writing now summited an impressive eleven times), I again failed to get further than a couple of hours above the South Col camp (the equivalent of Tibet's Advanced Base Camp). I have hazy memories of that night, but do recall passing three death sites, one of a well-known Swiss climber who had died earlier that day, one of my Sherpa Tundu's father and one of Robert Milne who, three years earlier, had a heart attack the same night that I turned back in Tibet.

This was becoming annoying, especially since I had now twice been within six hours of the summit. In 2009 Marie Curie, having raised a further £1 million from my Nepal-side near miss, suggested that I try again. After contemplating my two failed climbs, I came to the conclusion that the altitude and the cold were having a greater effect on my performance once above the Death Zone than I had realized, and it was my innate competitive nature that had pushed me to stay ahead of others in my group, including Ian in Tibet and Kenton in Nepal, so as not to appear geriatric to them. I had, therefore, pushed myself too hard, and this had proved my undoing.

Once I had persuaded myself that this was sound reasoning, I went back to Marie Curie's bosses and made a deal. I would try one last time providing there was no publicity at all until after I summited. This they did not like because they raise far more funds with a long PR lead time when involved with any fundraising challenge. However, they knew that for me to be seen to fail a third time, even if I had no altitude-induced, possibly fatal, problem en route, would invite heavy media criticism of all parties involved. BBC Television News decided to film the attempt for the national news, which would greatly increase the fundraising ability of the project, and they, too, agreed to put no footage on air until I had summited.

Henry Todd, a well-known mountain group leader and the boss of Himalayan Guides Nepal, agreed that I could climb with Sherpa Tundu again, but this time without Kenton or other non-Sherpas. Since Tundu climbed with the strength and speed of a mountain goat, I knew there was no danger of my feeling in any way competitive.

So in March 2009, with a BBC TV team of three under veteran producer Mark Georgiou, we began the standard six weeks of acclimatization. The BBC cameraman was helicoptered out with altitude problems on the way up to Base Camp, but the other two took over and also trained Tundu to use a clever little camera for the higher zones which they could not reach.

As usual, the training involved going up and down the Khumbu Icefall, and the day after one such outing, an avalanche swept over part of the feature, knocking an Austrian group leader and his Sherpa into a crevasse. The Sherpa disappeared under a mass of ice rubble, but the Austrian somehow survived the ordeal of falling 45 feet and being wedged upside down in the crevasse until he was located by a rescue party and revived.

When the final night arrived, Tundu and I set out from the South Col camp and soon came to the steep snow slope where the year before we had passed the burial sites of his father and the other two men. In a few hours, under a vast starlit sky, we came to a sharp ridge line and to the South Summit which, I remembered, was the point my polar 'rival' Børge Ousland had reached in 2004 before turning back. This thought definitely boosted my resolve, which was just as well as I had begun to feel body-cold in a strangely different way to either the UK damp-cold or polar freezing-cold. I was later told that high-altitude mountaineering can result in a variant of standard frostbite which combines tissue freezing with hypoxia and general body dehydration.

Time seemed suspended as we toiled on and on along the summit ridge line, up the Hillary Step and, at last, to the small round patch of snow at the top. Since I was six inches taller than Tundu, I was at that moment the highest person on Earth. The view was one I will never forget. Far below us were clouds touched by moonlight and pierced here and there by the black peaks of great mountains. It was very cold. Tundu and I clasped each other, taking care not to disturb our face masks or the tubes to our oxygen cylinders.

'Now we go down,' Tundu shouted in my ear.

'First you film us for Mark,' I replied.

To help Marie Curie we needed to use the sat-phone at once so that they could maximize their fundraising. And we needed to film our arrival, which would enable the BBC to announce the success of the climb. Tundu nodded, unpacked the special camera and waved me into a 'summit pose'.

After a while fiddling with the camera controls, he shook his head at me. The camera would not work. He tried to explain, but all I could gather was that there was insufficient light. We must wait for sunrise. So we stayed and waited and I began to shiver violently. It seemed best to forget recording our arrival and to head down at once. But I could not make the sat-phone work either, for my fingers had gone dead.

In what seemed like an age, a Mexican climber from our climbing group arrived on the summit and, after looking at our BBC camera, shrugged and offered to take a photograph of the two of us, with which the BBC would have to make do.

Meanwhile, Kenton arrived with his clients and soon made my sat-phone work back to the *Today* programme in London. I was, they announced, the oldest Briton ever to scale the mountain and the first Old Age Pensioner to do so.

The Norwegian Erling Kagge had been first to reach both poles and climb Everest, but I was the first to achieve the crossing of both polar ice caps and summit the mountain. When Marie Curie closed their account on the fundraising results of my three mountain projects, my total raised was £6.3 million. Paul Sykes had sponsored all the costs of the climbs so there were no deductions from the total.

For a while after returning to Britain, I had problems with circulation in my feet and fingers, but within a few months they were back to normal. I decided to try no more journeys involving a combination of both extreme low temperatures and high altitude. It was enough to be cold with nowhere to fall, other than down a crevasse.

Afterword

Post-Everest

In 2007 Mike Stroud emailed me to suggest that we complete the first winter crossing of the Antarctic continent by manhauling supplies, just as we had in the summer of 1992. We discussed this and agreed that the extremely low temperatures involved would mean pre-positioning dumps of food and fuel along our intended route.

I went to the Polar Regions Unit of the Foreign Office in Whitehall to obtain the permit necessary for any non-governmental project in Antarctica. Their reply was that under no circumstances would anybody from any country receive a permit to travel in Antarctica during the polar winter, since there would be no available rescue facilities. Only if we could assure the Antarctic authorities that we were a hundred per cent self-sufficient and fully insured for the entire winter might we be allowed a permit.

For the next five years I put in place all that the rules required, including two 25-ton D6N Caterpillar vehicles, a ship's container modified into a caravan-on-skis for six people for a year and another for science research work. Fourteen bespoke fuel sledges were made to carry 200 tons of Jet A-1 fuel, and hundreds of sponsors donated specialist equipment.

Mike had to drop out due to hip trouble, but he continued his full involvement with the science programme. In north Sweden we selected two volunteer Caterpillar mechanics out of a group of applicants. Three British Antarctic Survey veterans joined the team, and our sponsor, Standard Chartered Bank, chartered an ice-strengthened ship from the South African government. The bank chose to sponsor the project since they were confident that they could use us to raise the sum of $5 million (which they would double) for their charity Seeing is Believing, which helps to prevent avoidable blindness worldwide.

Many schools signed on to our educational website and many scientific research bodies, including the European Space Agency, gave us research work to complete.

We called the project The Coldest Journey, and we set out from Crown Bay on Antarctica's Atlantic coastline in early 2013. I suffered frostbite and left the other five members of the ice team to carry on, knowing that this would not affect their mechanical abilities to continue, as I was only there to ski.

Some three hundred kilometres inland, a world record for winter travel in Antarctica, the vehicles ran into a lethal crevasse field at 10,000 feet above sea level and in 24-hour darkness. There they began their long winter vigil, conducting valuable research work in a volatile region, from which they will hope to escape with the return of daylight. By then their collected data will add considerably to man's knowledge of the intricate mechanisms that link ice sheet, ocean and atmosphere in the heart of Earth's great deep freeze. And they will truly know the meaning and the feeling of cold.

Appendix I

Climate change

This book is clearly not a scientific reference work and it does not carry any political clarion call about dire threats to humanity. However, it does describe cold events in general, and the interplay between cold and heat is what climate change is all about. What follows is not intended to be some subtle prophesy of doom, but just a few reasons why I think it would be good if things stay at least as cold as they currently are.

In the 1970s in the Arctic Ocean I designed our manhaul sledges so that, should any open-water canals impede progress, they would be waterproof. By the mid-1990s, with so much more open water about, my sledge design was based on that of a canoe. This is indicative of the overall melting of sea ice in the Arctic which was clearly noticeable to the human eye, not just to sensitive scientific measurements.

To be scientifically exact, the current annual rise in the world's sea level is around 3 millimetres, which does not sound alarming unless you happen to live on a low-lying island like those of the Maldives, which are already affected. It should, however, be a wake-up call for the one-third of the global population who live within 100 kilometres of a coastline, especially those in low-lying areas like New York, Miami and most of Holland.

There are two main ways by which the volume of water in the world's oceans may increase. First, land-based melting ice can pour into the sea and, second, if the water already in the oceans gets warmer, then the overall volume will increase, because warm water is less dense than cool water and, therefore, fills more space.

The world's supply of land-based ice is mostly grounded on the continent of Antarctica and on Greenland. At present, large areas of the Antarctic's ice cover, 4,200 metres thick in places, are melting and the huge floating ice shelves, which act as barriers to the flow from the inland ice sheets, are themselves melting from below and so are thinning; this reduces their effectiveness as barriers for the inland flow which causes sea-level rise. Southern Greenland is especially sensitive to temperature, which has been rising there since the 1980s and getting very close to 0°C. Continued warming is likely to result in increased sea levels because of the water expansion and the ice melt.

Observations of ice-sheet volume suggest that if all the land-based ice were to melt, our sea levels would eventually rise by some 70 metres worldwide. It is not surprising that Dutch architects are busy designing floating mobile homes.

Additional to the ongoing behaviour of the Antarctic and Greenland ice sheets (where 99 per cent of earth's glacier ice is stored), there is the matter of smaller mountain glaciers which are melting worldwide, and, combined, are currently causing more of the 3.2-millimetre annual sea-level rise than the ice sheets. If all the mountain glaciers and small ice caps, such as Iceland, were to melt, they would add about 40 centimetres to global sea rise. Between 2003 and 2009 the world's smaller glaciers (outside Antarctica and Greenland) lost 43 per cent of their ice when compared with the level in the 1960s.

The University of East Anglia, studying 50,000 living species, found that over half of their climatic range will be lost by 2080 if global warming is not quickly reduced. Chinese pandas, for instance, of which there are only some eight hundred in the wild in the world, depend for their continued existence on three species of bamboo which are slowly disappearing as the climate warms. Global fisheries around the world have been feeling the impact of climate change for the past four decades, with many species being forced to migrate to ever cooler, deeper waters.

The hole in the ozone layer is held responsible for much climate change and, although the protective ozone layer around the world as a whole decreased in the 1980s and 1990s by only 5 per cent, the really alarming reduction is over the South Pole. This is due to the polar vortex, a whirlpool of supercool air which forms at about –80°C in the stratosphere. The behaviour of the chemical chlorine within this vortex results in a localized ozone hole. Chlorine levels have risen over the last half-century, due to chlorofluorocarbons (CFCs) rising to the top of the stratosphere where ultraviolet sunlight acts on them to release the chlorine which destroys ozone.

Quite apart from the melting of ice sheets and glaciers, global warming is adversely affecting other cold-region environments, including snow cover and permafrost.

The under-snow world, or subnivium, is a seasonal micro-environment that serves as a refuge to a huge range of insects, animals and plants. This key shelter belt is at risk as, according to *Frontiers in Ecology and the*

Environment, some 3.2 million square kilometres of Northern Hemisphere snow cover during the critical months of March and April has disappeared. Permafrost is melting, due to rising temperatures in sub-Arctic regions, causing an accelerated release of greenhouse gases, including methane, into the atmosphere.

Forest fires in the Siberian forests, the most extensive forests in the world and vital to Earth's health, start earlier in warm years and have increased tenfold in the last twenty years.

Then there is the albedo factor. Albedo is the reflected solar radiation divided by the incoming solar radiation. Snow and ice have relatively high albedos and so tend to remain cooler than other surfaces exposed to short-wave radiation. Because most of Earth's snow and ice are in polar regions, these areas are expected to be the most affected by the snow/ice-surface albedo feedback effect. To put this simply: as a result of global warming, some snow or ice will melt and this will lower the relevant surface albedo which will, in turn, cause more solar radiation to be absorbed at the surface, which will then cause warmer conditions. In fact, the Arctic is one of the fastest-warming places on the planet.

The most serious impact humans are having on the environment is by causing the world to get warmer, mostly by emitting more and more carbon dioxide.

Because the climate's behaviour is exceptionally complex, any climate models that scientists and environmentalists put together have to take account of a great many unpredictables and interactions, including cloud behaviour, vegetation shifts, and many other variables. The more such processes are included in each new model, the more complete the picture, but also the greater the number of uncertainties that are highlighted. This, of course, helps the many naysayers waiting to pounce on any and all global warming predictions.

When Al Gore's controversial movie on the topic was released, the Professor of Meteorology at the Massachusetts Institute of Technology said: 'A general characteristic of Mr Gore's approach is to assiduously ignore the fact that the earth and its climate are dynamic. They are always changing, even without external forcing. To treat all change as something to fear is bad enough; to do so in order to exploit that fear is much worse.'

Many media meteorologists are also prone to downplay any connection between global warming and human causes. David Bernard used his position as Severe Weather Consultant for the CBS network and Chief Meteorologist for CBS Miami (a city vulnerable to rising sea levels) to describe climate change as a liberal plot to bring about 'global wealth redistribution'.

This sort of attitude may partly explain why polls on both sides of the Atlantic show a yawning gap between published scientific papers, which in most cases agree that human activities have an impact on climate change, and the general perception of over half the populace who, 2012 polls show, are either unaware that scientists overwhelmingly agree that Earth is warming because of humans or disagree with that position.

What is certain, whether humans are involved or not, is that global warming is a growing reality ... Cold, as we know it, is slowly but surely on the way out.

Appendix II

Individuals involved with the expeditions described in this book include:

1967 Norway
Peter Loyd, Simon Gault, Nick Holder, Don Hughes, Martin Grant-Peterkin, Vanda Allfrey

1970 Norway
Roger Chapman, Patrick Brook, Geoff Holder, Peter Booth, Brendan O'Brien, Bob Powell, Henrik Forss, David Murray-Wells, Vanda Allfrey, Rosemary Alhusen, Jane Moncreiff, Johnnie Muir, Gillie Kennard; George Greenfield (UK)

1976–8 Greenland/North Pole
Oliver Shepard, Charlie Burton, Ginny Fiennes, Geoff Newman, Mary Gibbs; Mike Wingate Gray (UK), Andrew Croft (UK), Peter Booth (UK)

1979–82 Transglobe
Oliver Shepard, Charlie Burton, Ginny Fiennes, Simon Grimes, Anton Bowring, Les Davis, Ken Cameron, Cyrus Balapoira, Howard Willson, Mark Williams, Dave Hicks, Dave Peck, Jill McNicol, Ed Pike, Paul Anderson, Terry Kenchington, Martin Weymouth, Annie Weymouth, Jim Young, Geoff Lee, Nigel Cox, Paul Clark, Admiral Otto Steiner, Mick Hart, Commander Ramsey, Nick Wade, Anthony Birkbeck, Giles Kershaw, Gerry Nicholson, Karl Z'berg, Chris McQuaid, Lesley Rickett, Laurence Howell, Edwyn Martin, John Parsloe, Peter Polley and others; Anthony Preston (UK), David Mason (UK), Janet Cox (UK), Sue Klugman (UK), Roger Tench (UK), Joan Cox (UK), Margaret Davidson (UK), Colin Eales (UK), Elizabeth Martin (UK), Sir Edmund Irving (UK), Sir Vivian Fuchs (UK), Mike Wingate Gray (UK), Andrew Croft (UK), George Greenfield (UK), Sir Alexander Durie (UK), Peter Martin (UK), Simon Gault (UK), Tommy Macpherson (UK), Peter Windeler (UK), Peter

Bowring (UK), Lord Hayter (UK), Dominic Harrod (UK), George Capon (UK), Anthony Macauley (UK), Tom Woodfield (UK), Sir Campbell Adamson (UK), Jim Peevey (UK), Eddie Hawkins (UK), Eddie Carey (UK), Peter Cook (UK), Trevor Davies (UK), Bill Hibbert (UK), Gordon Swain (UK), Captain Tom Pitt (UK), Alan Tritton (UK), Jack Willies (UK), Graham Standing (UK), Muriel Dunton (UK), Edward Doherty (UK), Bob Hampton (UK), Arthur Hogan-Fleming (UK), Dorothy Royle (UK), Annie Seymour (UK), Kevin and Sally Travers-Healy (UK), Jan Fraser (UK), Gay Preston (UK), Jane Morgan (UK)

1986–90 North Pole
Oliver Shepard, Mike Stroud, Laurence Howell, Paul Cleary, Beverly Johnson; Ginny Fiennes (UK), Alex Blake-Milton (UK), Andrew Croft (UK), George Greenfield (UK), Perry Mason (UK), Dmitry Shparo (UK), Steve Holland (UK)

1993–2000 Alaska, Arctic and Antarctica
Gordon Thomas, Dmitry Shparo, Laurence Howell, Morag Nicolls, David Fulker, Bill Baker, Graham Archer, Charles Whitaker, Granville Baylis, Steve Signal, 'Mac' Mackenney, Steve Holland, Mike Stroud, Oliver Shepard, Charlie Burton

2003 7×7×7 marathons
Mike Stroud

2005, 2008, 2009 Everest
Sherpa Tundu, Sibusiso Vilane, Kenton Cool, Ian Parnell

2007 Eiger North Face
Kenton Cool, Ian Parnell

2013 The Coldest Journey
Anton Bowring, Brian Newham, Ian Prickett, Spencer Smirl, Richmond Dykes, Rob Lambert

Appendix III

Outline history of Arctic exploration
compiled by P.M. Booth and R. Fiennes

The Arctic Ocean covers an area of 5 million square miles, and even in the depths of winter over 10 per cent of the Arctic Ocean is open water.

There follows a list of some of the known Arctic explorers. Apologies to all those, dead or alive, that we have unwittingly omitted.

BC 320	Pytheas, a Greek colonist from Massilia (Marseilles) is reported to have circumnavigated the British Isles and may have crossed the Arctic Circle
*c.*500 AD	According to legend, St Brendan sailed to North America from Ireland
870	Rabna Floki, a Viking from Norway, sailed west to Iceland
875	Ottar, another Viking, sailed to the Kola Peninsula and reached the White Sea. King Alfred the Great had Ottar's story translated into Anglo-Saxon
982	Erik the red (Erik Thorvaldsson) discovered Greenland, where he spent three years. He returned to Iceland and brought colonists back to Greenland in 986
*c.*1000	The Icelandic Sagas relate six tales of voyages to Vinland and Markland, which are probably the Newfoundland and Labrador areas of mainland America. One saga indicated that Bjarni Herjulfsson discovered America, another that Leif Eriksson did
1025	Gudleif Gudlaugsson is believed by some scholars to have landed on the coast of America after being blown off course
1059	Jon, a missionary, may have sailed to Vinland where he was murdered
1121	Bishop Erik Gnupsson left Greenland to search for Vinland.

	According to legend he spent a long time there before returning
1347	A ship from Greenland is known to have been on a routine voyage to Markland, probably to collect timber
*c.*1480–95	Bristol merchants are believed to have sent a number of ships to search for the 'Island of Brasil'. Some of the ships may have reached Canada
1497	John Cabot discovered the cod fishing grounds off Labrador and Newfoundland while searching for the Northwest Passage. European fishing fleets soon regularly fished the area
1498	John Cabot set off again to discover the Northwest Passage to Japan. He may have died in the attempt
1500	Gaspar Corte-Real, a Portuguese, sighted Greenland or Newfoundland
1501	Gaspar Corte-Real was lost after last being seen just north of Newfoundland while searching for the Northwest Passage. Miguel, his brother, suffered the same fate a year later
1504–6	French and Portuguese fishing fleets began fishing off Newfoundland
1508–9	Sebastian Cabot may have discovered Hudson Strait and Bay while searching for the Northwest Passage
1513	Vasco Nuñez de Balboa discovered the Pacific Ocean and claimed its seaboard from North to South Pole for Spain
1524–5	French and Spanish Northwest Passage expeditions reached Newfoundland
1527	Henry VIII sponsored two ships at the instigation of Robert Thorne for the first known attempt at the North Pole. The expedition failed
1527–8	John Rut may have reached 64°N before exploring the Labrador coast
1534–6	Two French expeditions explored the Gulf of St Lawrence and the St Lawrence River
*c.*1543	Jean Alfonse, a Frenchman, probably entered the Davis Strait
1553	Sir Hugh Willoughby and Richard Chancellor sailed in three ships to find the Northeast Passage. Willoughby and his crew died in the attempt, but he may have reached Novaya Zemlya. Chancellor eventually travelled overland from the White Sea to Moscow
1556	Steven Burrough reached the mouth of the Pechora River
1558	The Zeno Map was published
1569	Mercator published his map which possibly shows Ungava Bay

1576–8 Martin Frobisher sailed in three consecutive years to Baffin Island, mainly in search of gold. His ships brought back 1,200 tons of 'ore' but it proved to be worthless. He had sailed some way into Hudson Strait, which he called Mistakyn Strait

1580 Charles Jackman and Arthur Pet in the *George* and *William* were the first west Europeans to navigate in the Kara Sea

1584 A Dutchman, Oliver Burnel, tried to penetrate the Kara Sea but failed

1585–7 John Davis three times attempted to find a Northwest Passage to Cathay. He achieved a farthest north in Davis Strait of 72°12′N in the *Ellen*, a ship of 20 tons

1594–7 The Dutchman William Barents explored Spitsbergen and Novaya Zemlya. His surveying achievements were considerable. After wintering at Ice Haven, Novaya Zemlya in 1596–7, he and his crew successfully completed a remarkable voyage in small boats to Lapland some 1,600 miles away. Barents himself died near North Cape on 20 June 1597

1602 Captain George Weymouth sailed with letters for the Empress of Cathay in the *Discovery* and *Godspeed*. Unfortunately his crew mutinied in Davis Strait and he was forced to return. He claimed to have reached 69°N

1603 James Cunningham, an Englishman, rediscovered Greenland

1606 Captain John Knight sailed in the *Hopewell* to find the Northwest Passage. His ship was damaged off the coast of Labrador. Knight went ashore and was never seen again. He was probably killed by Eskimos

1607–8 Henry Hudson attempted to sail across the Arctic Ocean and achieved 80°23′N near Spitsbergen. He also landed on Novaya Zemlya

1610–11 Henry Hudson took the *Discovery* with a crew of 20 men and 2 boys in an attempt to find the Northwest Passage. After wintering in Hudson Bay, some of the crew mutinied and cast him adrift in an open boat to die. With him were his 7-year-old son and 7 men. The ship was brought back to England by Robert Bylot

1610–11 Jonas Poole sailed to Spitsbergen with the intention of sailing across the Arctic Ocean. His attempt degenerated into a fishing venture

1612–13 Captain Thomas Button took the *Discovery* and *Resolution* to Hudson Bay to find the Northwest Passage. After losing five men in a fight with Eskimos and more through hardship and cold during the winter at Fort Nelson, he returned in

1613. He decided that the passage existed (if at all) through Roe's Welcome Sound, which he entered to 65°N

1612 Captain James Hall was killed by Eskimos in Greenland. His death ended an expedition of which William Baffin was the pilot

1614 William Baffin visited Spitsbergen and may have seen Franz Josef Land

1614 William Gibbon in the *Discovery* was prevented from entering Hudson Strait by heavy ice

1615 The *Discovery* set off for the fourth time to find the Northwest Passage, commanded by Captain Robert Bylot (who had sailed with Hudson and Button), and with William Baffin as pilot. They reached Nottingham Island at the west end of Hudson Strait before returning

1616 Baffin and Bylot once more sailed in the *Discovery* with the aim of travelling up Davis Strait to 80°N, and then heading south-west until they reached Japan. They achieved 78°N and named Smith Sound, Jones Sound and Lancaster Sound, but did not enter the last two. Baffin's discoveries in Baffin Bay were later disbelieved and ignored for some two hundred years

1619–20 Jens Munk with two ships entered Hudson Bay and wintered near Churchill. Of the 65 men with him, only Munk and two others survived the winter and the voyage home

1620–35 Dutch fishing and whaling fleets occupied Spitsbergen and Jan Mayen Island in the Greenland Sea during the summer months. The fleets numbered about 300 ships manned by some 15,000 men

1625 William Hawkeridge in the *Lion's Whelp* spent some time in the north part of Hudson Bay, but accomplished nothing

1631 Luke Foxe in the 70-ton *Charles* sailed with a crew of 22 to Hudson Bay, meeting the *Henrietta Maria* by chance near James Bay. He later crossed the Arctic Circle in Foxe Basin before returning safely without loss

1631–2 Captain Thomas James in the *Henrietta Maria* spent the winter in James Bay, saving his ship by the drastic measure of deliberately sinking her in shallow water. Several men died from accident or scurvy before the remainder returned safely

1636–9 Elisha Busa explored the area of the Lena Delta (130°E) by land

1640 Postnik discovered the Indigirka River (150°E)

1644 A Russian trading post was established in the valley of the Kolyma River (160°E)

1646	Isai Ignatiev sailed east of the Kolyma River to trade in walrus ivory
1648	Dezhnev, Alexiev and Ankudinov sailed from Kolyma in seven ships and entered the Bering Strait from the north-west. Only Dezhnev and his crew survived after being shipwrecked on the coast of Kamchatka
1651–2	Jacques Buteux twice tried to reach Hudson Bay overland from the south to claim it for France. He was killed by Indians
1666	Wood and Flaws were shipwrecked on the coast of Novaya Zemlya
1670	The Hudson's Bay Company was formed. Thereafter temporary and later permanent trading posts were established at various places in the bay. Regular supply voyages from England took place. The area was the scene of constant and deadly conflict between the French and the English for many years, with some posts being captured and recaptured many times
1715–16	William Stewart of the Hudson's Bay Company walked inland from York Factory to an area between the Great Slave Lake and Lake Athabasca
1719–21	James Knight and 27 men in two ships attempted to sail to the Coppermine River through the Northwest Passage. They were never seen again. Forty years later two sunken ships and the remains of a house were found at Marble Island, 300 miles north of Churchill in Hudson Bay. Eskimos said that they had all died of hunger and disease
1721	Communications with the two large settlements in south-west Greenland lapsed. The Norsemen died out, suffering from malnutrition and rickets, some probably being killed by Eskimos. Eventually the region was recolonized for Denmark by the Norwegian missionary Hans Egede
1725–8	Vitus Bering, a Dane engaged by Czar Peter the Great, named St Lawrence Island in Bering Strait, but turned back at 67°18′N 170°W without sighting the American mainland
1728	Paars attempted and failed to cross Greenland's inland ice cap
1729	Henry Atkins of Boston sailed to Davis Strait while whaling
1731	Gvosdev commanded the first Russian expedition to cross the Bering Strait and reach Alaska
1733–42	The Great Northern Expedition of 570 men under Vitus Bering left St Petersburg and travelled overland for 3,000 miles eastwards. In 1740 Bering and Chirikov sailed from Petropavlovsk on the Kamchatka Peninsula. The former landed on Alaska

between Capes St Elias and St Hermogenes. Later his ship was wrecked on Bering Island, where Bering died of exhaustion and despair. Chirikov reached Cross Bay in Alaska, where he landed some men. They were never seen again

1741 Captain Christopher Middleton attempted to find the Northwest Passage in the north-west of Hudson Bay. He discovered Wager Inlet or Bay

1746 William Moor explored Wager Bay in the belief that it might be the Northwest Passage

1749 William Coats explored the east coast of Hudson Bay

1751 Dalager attempted and failed to cross Greenland's inland ice cap

1751 Captain MacCallum of the Greenland Fishery reached 83½°N

1755 An Act of Parliament offered a £5,000 reward to the first ship to sail within one degree of the North Pole

1761 William Christopher in the *Churchill* sailed 90 miles up the Chesterfield Inlet. The following year he returned and confirmed that the inlet did not contain the Northwest Passage

1767 Synd landed at Cape Prince of Wales, Alaska, while searching for the Northwest Passage

1770–2 Samuel Hearne and an Indian guide walked from Churchill to the mouth of the Coppermine River, a round trip of about 1,300 miles. He was probably the first white man to stand on the northern shore of Canada

1773 Captain J.C. Phipps MP sailed in the *Racehorse* and *Carcass* with the intention of reaching the North Pole. He was stopped by ice at 80°42′N near Spitsbergen. One of the crew on this journey was 14-year-old Horatio Nelson

1777 Walter Young in the *Lyon* achieved 72°42′N in Baffin Bay

1778 Captain James Cook in the *Resolution* attempted the Northeast Passage from the Pacific, but was stopped by ice at Icy Cape (70°41′N). He did, though, ascertain that Russia and the North American continent were separated

1788 Joseph Billings, an Englishman, who had served under Cook, worked for Catherine the Great of Russia to map the North Cape. He failed to complete his work

1789 Alexander Mackenzie with a dozen Indians and people of mixed race canoed down the Mackenzie River from the Great Slave Lake to its mouth in the Beaufort Sea

1791–5 George Vancouver in the *Discovery* and William Broughton in the *Chatham* explored the coast of Alaska. There was much Spanish activity in this area at this time

1806 William Scoresby, a British whaling captain, achieved 81°30′N 19°E north of Spitsbergen

1809 Hedenstrom, Sannikov and Koshevin explored the New Siberian Islands which had been discovered by hunters in the previous few years. It was confirmed that the soil of Lyakov Island contained mammoth bone

1809 John Clarke may have reached the mouth of the Mackenzie River

1810 Sanniko, a Russian trader, discovered two new Siberian Arctic Islands

1816 Otto von Kotzebue reached Cape Krusenstern (67°N) in Alaska

1817 Two British whalers under Captain Muirhead crossed the north end of Baffin Bay at an alleged latitude of 77°N

1817 William Scoresby Jnr surveyed Jan Mayen Island

1818 Commander David Buchan and Lieutenant John Franklin in the *Dorothea* and *Trent* attempted to sail to the North Pole past Spitsbergen, but were forced to give up when storms and ice damaged the ships. They achieved 80°17′N

1818 An Act of Parliament was passed offering rewards of £20,000 for the discovery of the Northwest Passage

1818 Commander John Ross and Lieutenant William Edward Parry in the *Isabella* and *Alexander* attempted to discover the Northwest Passage. After finding Smith Sound blocked with ice and passing by Jones Sound, Ross entered Lancaster Sound. He believed this sound to be blocked off by mountains and so returned. He was later criticized for this decision

1819–20 Parry, in the *Hecla* and *Griper*, penetrated Lancaster Sound, passed Cornwallis Island, and achieved 110°W on 6 September 1819 in Viscount Melville Sound, thus winning a bounty of £5,000 offered by Order in Council. They spent the winter on Melville Island and crossed it on foot, using pikes and blankets as tents. The expedition was remarkable for its high morale, excellent health and good discipline. It achieved a furthest west of 113°48′W

1819–22 Franklin canoed and walked 5,550 miles with, amongst others, Hood, Back and Dr Richardson, and several Canadian voyageurs. His route was Hudson Bay–Lake Winnipeg–Pine Island Land–Lake Athabasca–Great Slave Lake–mouth of Coppermine River–Kent Peninsula–Bathurst Inlet–Coppermine River–Great Slave Lake. They suffered terrible hardships and several men died. At the end they were reduced to eating lichen, deerskins and any bones they could find. Franklin's work was helped largely by the journeys of Hearne and Mackenzie and by other explorers, including Back, Hood, Richardson, Hepburn, Kendall, Simpson and Rae

1820–3 Lieutenant Ferdinand von Wrangel, a Russian, surveyed the Siberian coast. During his travels he completed one epic 1,530-mile journey with his dog teams in 78 days. He was subsequently governor of Russian America, now Alaska

1821–3 In yet another attempt to find the Northwest Passage through Hudson Strait, Commander Parry in the *Hecla* and *Fury* determined that Repulse Bay was landlocked and explored the Melville Peninsula. He named the Fury and Hecla Strait and spent a second winter at Igloolik. Ice prevented him from passing through the strait so he returned home in October 1823

1822 The William Scoresbys (father and son) discovered Scoresby Sound and charted part of the east coast of Greenland. In the following year they published a highly informative book

1823 Captains Claverin and Sabine in the *Griper* explored and surveyed the north-east coast of Greenland

1824–5 Parry in the *Hecla* and *Fury* attempted to find the Northwest Passage through Prince Regent Inlet. After wintering on the Brodeur Peninsula, both ships were damaged by storm and ice. *Fury* was abandoned and the *Hecla* returned home

1824 Commander Lyon failed to reach Repulse Bay after the *Griper* was nearly sunk by storms in Bay of God's Mercy and Roe's Welcome Sound

1825–7 Franklin, Richardson, Back, Dease and others travelled down the Mackenzie River to its mouth in small specially built boats. In spite of ice in the Beaufort Sea, Franklin and Back sailed west for 174 miles to 148°52′W before returning. He discovered Herschel Island, Camden Bay and Prudhoe Bay. Meanwhile Richardson and Kendall travelled east for 900 miles to the mouth of the Coppermine River, and then walked to the Great Slave Lake, where both parties joined up again at Fort Franklin. More than 1,000 miles of the north Canadian shoreline had been surveyed

1825–8 Captain F.W. Beechey in the *Blossom* sailed through the Bering Strait to Icy Cape. He sent his mate Elson to Barrow Point in the hope of meeting Franklin, who was expected from the east; no sign was seen. They were one year and 156 miles apart

1827 Parry in the *Hecla* reached Treurenberg Bay, Spitsbergen. From there, dragging sledge boats, he set out for the North

Pole. Although they travelled over 900 miles over the ice, drifts and currents caused them only to reach a point 172 miles north of the ship, at 82°45′N

1829–33 Captain John Ross, largely financed by a gin distiller called Felix Booth, took a 150-ton paddle steamer (the *Victory*) to Prince Regent Inlet, where he removed the engine which had proved unreliable. Over the next two years he explored the Boothia Peninsula on foot, raised the Union Flag at the North Magnetic Pole, and his nephew James C. Ross discovered King William Island. He was eventually forced to abandon the *Victory* and after much hardship was rescued in Lancaster Sound by his old ship the *Isabella*

1833 Commander George Back explored and mapped the Great Fish River (now called the Back River). His map of the river remained in use until 1948

1836–7 While commanding the *Terror*, Back entered the Foxe Channel but was beset with ice

1837–9 Thomas Simpson and Peter Dease of the Hudson's Bay Company travelled down the Mackenzie River to the Beaufort Sea where they turned west and reached Barrow Point. Moving east they travelled over Rae Strait without realizing it (the strait was iced over), and mapped the south coasts of Victoria Island and King William Island. The intense strain of the work told on Simpson who, at thirty-one years of age, suddenly became distraught, shot two of his companions and probably himself

1839 John Bell of the Hudson's Bay Company explored the Peel and Rat rivers

1840 John Bell established Fort McPherson (as it was later known) on the Peel River

1845–8 Sir John Franklin, aged fifty-nine, and Captain Francis Crozier sailed in the *Terror* and *Erebus* to find the Northwest Passage. After wintering at Beechey Island, both ships were beset with ice off King William Island and were finally abandoned in Victoria Sound. Although they had provisions for three years, all 139 men perished in the ships or during the march south to the area of the mouth of the Back River. Some forty expeditions were sent to find them over the next ten years

1847–8 Sir John Richardson, John Rae and John Bell searched between the Mackenzie River and the Coppermine River for Franklin, but without success. John Rae had previously carried out surveys in the area of the Rae Isthmus

1848 Thomas Lee, in a whaler (the *Prince of Wales)*, sailed 150 miles into Jones Sound

1848–9 Sir James Ross and Edward Joseph Bird in the *Investigator* and *Enterprise* sailed to Lancaster Sound in search of Franklin. They were beset by ice in Barrow Strait but made four sledge journeys in that area and along the shores of Somerset Island, and were on one journey nearer to solving the Franklin mystery than any search party until 1857

1848–52 Captain T.E.L. Moore in the *Plover* searched for Franklin from the west, reaching Barrow Point in boats

1849 John Gravill in a British whaler entered Jones Sound. He carried out the first reported landing on the south of Ellesmere Island

1849 Henry Kellett in the *Herald* discovered Herald Island near Wrangel Island in the East Siberian Sea

1849 The Royal Thames Yacht Club schooner *Nancy Dawson* commanded by Robert Sheddon assisted the *Plover* in the search for Franklin from Alaska

1849–50 James Saunders in the *North Star* eventually reached Prince Regent Inlet while attempting to resupply Sir James Clark Ross's search party and look for Franklin in Smith and Jones sounds

1850 Charles Forsyth and William Snow in the *Prince Albert* were sponsored by Lady Franklin to look for her husband. They were prevented by ice from going beyond Fury Beach, but then entered Wellington Channel where they found news of Franklin's winter quarters at Beechey Island

1850–2 Captain Horatio Austin, who had previously been with Parry, spent two winters in the area of Barrow Strait, in an attempt to locate Franklin. There he met Captain William Penny, the well-known whaling skipper. Austin's search parties sledged nearly 7,000 miles before returning home in 1852

1850–5 Captain Richard Collinson and Captain Robert McClure in the *Enterprise* and *Investigator* were ordered to conduct a search from the Pacific and Bering Strait. Collinson's voyage was the more remarkable since he sailed eastwards through the Northwest Passage and nearly reached King William Island. After four winters in the Arctic, he arrived home in 1855. Meanwhile McClure had to abandon his ship in 1853 on the north coast of Banks Island.

1852–5 Four ships were sent back to the Arctic the same summer under Sir Edward Belcher, a man with no Arctic experience. Captain Henry Kellett (*Resolute*) and Captain Leopold

McClintock (*Intrepid*) wintered at Melville Island and found a report about the position of McClure's ship (*Investigator*) 160 miles away. Next year McClintock, who had previously wintered with James Ross and also with Austin, was in the field for 105 days discovering Prince Patrick Island and travelling 1,408 miles, the greatest distance covered by men hauling their own sledges. Lieutenant Frederick Meecham did a journey of 1,336 miles in only 70 days

Leaving the *North Star* at Beechey Island as a base, Belcher wintered in Northumberland Sound in the *Assistance* and *Pioneer*. After a further winter in Wellington Channel, Belcher found that he was unable to reach Lancaster Sound. He abandoned his two ships and made his way to the *North Star*. There he joined up with the crews of the *Intrepid*, *Resolute* and *Investigator*, which had all been abandoned. When the supply ships *Phoenix* and *Talbot* arrived, these two ships and the *North Star* carried all the crews back to England, where Belcher was court-martialled and only narrowly acquitted

(The *Resolute* was later found drifting undamaged in the Davis Strait by an American whaling captain, Buddington, in the *George Herz* in September 1855. The US government bought her, re-equipped her and gave the ship as a gift to the Admiralty)

1852 In another expedition sponsored by Lady Franklin, Edward Inglefield achieved a farthest north of 78°23′N in Smith Sound. The *Isabel* later entered Jones Sound before sailing to Beechey Island through Lancaster Sound and then searching the east coast of Baffin Island

1853–5 An American, Elisha Kane, sailed in the *Advance* through Baffin Bay and became iced in at Rensselaer Island on the west coast of Greenland. He achieved 80°35′N with sledge and boat parties and explored the Kane Basin before abandoning his ship and escaping by boat and on foot to Godhavn

1853 Seeman carried out hydrographical work in the Bering Strait

1854 Dr John Rae of the Hudson's Bay Company reported that, during a survey journey to the west coast of Boothia Peninsula from the Coppermine River, he had been told by Eskimos that they had seen about thirty white men dragging a boat southwards over the ice and that several bodies had later been found nearby.

When the Crimean War broke out, the Government declined to make any further search

1855 James Anderson and James Stewart of the Hudson's Bay Company approached Montreal Island from the mainland by way of Back River and found relics of Franklin's expedition

1855 Lieutenant John Rodgers reached 72°05′N 174°37′W

1857–9 Lady Franklin now engaged McClintock to command the *Fox*, a steam yacht of 177 tons. During his second winter, McClintock discovered a record left in 1848 on King William Island by Captain Francis Crozier who, after Franklin's death, had abandoned the two ships (*Terror* and *Erebus*) and was leading 105 survivors southwards.

Relics of all sorts were later found, as well as two skeletons in a 28-foot boat. This boat was estimated to weigh 700–800 pounds and the sledge 650 pounds. Now, thirteen years after Franklin had left England, McClintock and other experienced Arctic travellers had lightened and considerably improved travel equipment. Such progress was, regrettably, soon forgotten

1860–1 Isaac Hayes led an American expedition in the *United States* with the intention of sailing to the North Pole via Smith Sound (many people still believing that the Arctic Ocean was free of ice). When his ship became iced in at Foulke Fjord in north-west Greenland, he sledged across to Ellesmere Island and claimed a farthest north of 81°35′N, but this was later disputed. He probably achieved 80°14′N at Cape Joseph Goode

1861 Torrell and Nordenskjöld explored Hinlopen Strait by boat, reaching a farthest north of 80°42′N at Phipps Island and discovering Prince Oscar Land and the two islands Charles XII and Drabanten off Spitsbergen

1863 Captain Elling Carlsen followed Barents' route round Novaya Zemlya's northern point and found his hut, of 300 years before, undisturbed. He circumnavigated Spitsbergen for the first time

1867 Whymper attempted, but failed, to cross the Greenland ice cap

1868 Captain Von Otter commanded the *Sofia* with A.E. Nordenskjöld as scientific adviser and achieved a farthest north of 81°42′N 17°30′E

1868 Koldeway led the first German North Polar Expedition in the *Germania*, which was prevented from reaching East Greenland. A latitude of 81°05′N was reached

1869–70 The *Germania* and *Hansa* under the command of Koldeway once more tried to reach the North Pole. The *Germania* only completed some local but useful discoveries on East

Greenland. The *Hansa* was crushed by ice and her crew escaped after a 201-day and 600-mile drift on an ice floe

1871 Lieutenant Carl Weyprecht in the *Isbjörn* attempted the Northeast Passage

1871–3 Charles Hall led a United States polar expedition in the *Polaris*. After passing through Smith Sound, *Polaris* was stopped by ice at 82°11′N. While wintering at Thank God Harbour in Polaris Bay, Hall died in mysterious and suspicious circumstances, possibly from arsenic poisoning. On the return journey a party became separated from the ship on an ice floe. These men were finally rescued off the coast of Labrador after drifting for 1,300 miles on the pack ice for over five months. The *Polaris* was abandoned in Foulke Fjord and the remaining crew were picked up by a whaler from their boats

1871 A.E. Nordenskjöld reached Phipps Island (Spitsbergen) by sledge from Mussel Bay where the *Polhem* had established winter quarters

1872–4 Lieutenant Carl Weyprecht and Lieutenant Julius Payer were beset by ice in the *Tegetthof* within sight of Novaya Zemlya. After a year's drift, they discovered and explored the Franz Josef archipelago. Payer reached Cape Fligely (81°51′N) by sledge, the most northerly land in the Old World

1873 D.L. Braine and Commander James Greer searched Smith Sound for Hall and the *Polaris*

1875 Allen Young in the *Pandora* attempted the Northwest Passage. After sailing down Peel Channel, he was forced to abandon the attempt by heavy ice in Franklin Strait

1875–6 George Nares and Henry Stephenson in the *Alert* and *Discovery* tried to reach the North Pole by way of Smith Sound. The latter ship wintered on the north side of Lady Franklin Bay on Ellesmere Island. The *Alert* continued through Robeson Channel to winter quarters at Floeberg Beach (82°28′N). From there Albert Markham and Alfred Parr sledged to 83°20′N. Meanwhile Pelham Aldrich travelled west along the north coast of Ellesmere Island, reaching Yelverton Bay. He established Capes Aldrich and Columbia as the northernmost points of Ellesmere Island at a latitude of 83°06′N. The expedition suffered greatly from scurvy. One man died from the *Alert*, and two from *Discovery*

1875 Nordenskjöld in the *Proven* commanded by Kjellman reached the mouth of the Yenisei River in the Kara Sea (80°E). He repeated the voyage in the following year

1878–9 A.E. Nordenskjöld navigated the Northeast Passage from west to east in the *Vega* in an expedition largely sponsored by the Swedish government. As always he carried out extensive scientific work

1878–80 Frederick Schwatka led an American expedition to search for relics of Franklin's expedition in King William Island

1879–80 John Spicer in the American whaler *Era* discovered the Spicer Islands in Foxe Basin. His discovery was not confirmed until 1946

1879–82 Commander de Long (USN) and G.W. Melville went through the Bering Strait hoping to winter on Wrangel Island, which they believed to be continental. The *Jeanette* was beset by pack ice and drifted for two years in the Siberian Ocean before being crushed and sunk at 77°36′N 155°E near Herald Island. Henrietta and Jeanette islands were discovered by them. After many hardships Melville and 9 men reached safety in the mouth of the Lena. Two of de Long's party survived, de Long and 11 others dying at Bulun, where Melville found their bodies in 1882

1880 Leigh Smith in the English yacht *Eira* explored the westerly part of Franz Josef Land, discovering many islands. He made valuable marine and botanical collections

1881–2 Leigh Smith once more explored Franz Josef Land. When the *Eira* sank, he was forced to spend a winter there before escaping to Novaya Zemlya

1881–4 Captain Richard Pike commanded the *Proteus* which took an American expedition under Adolphus Greely to Lady Franklin Bay, Ellesmere Island. The *Proteus* returned leaving Greely and 24 men, who built Fort Conger at Discovery Harbour. They stayed there for two years, exploring Ellesmere Island by sledge. When relief expeditions failed to reach them, they sailed by boat south to Cape Sabine where they wintered. By the time Schley's relief expedition rescued them, many men had died of starvation and scurvy, one had killed himself, and one had been executed for persistently stealing food. One of his sledge forays under Lieutenant J.B. Lockwood had achieved a northerly record of 83°24′N

1882–3 First International Circumpolar Year. This was the idea of Karl Weyprecht, confirmed by the International Polar Congress in Hamburg in 1879 by twelve countries. Some seven hundred men were involved at the 12 research sites set up around the Arctic to carry out scientific studies. Greely's ill-fated expedition was part of the project

1882–3 Leonard Stejneger, an American, explored an area in the Bering Strait

1883–6 Lieutenants Garde and Holm of the Royal Danish Navy surveyed the coast of south-east Greenland to continue the work of Lieutenant Graah in 1829. From this time, the Danes sent many expeditions to Greenland

1888 Fridtjof Nansen completed the pioneer crossing of Greenland's ice cap, from Umivik Bay to Godthaab

1888 Joe Tuckfield, an American whaling captain, confirmed that there were many whales in the area of Herschel Island. From that time whalers sailed east of Point Barrow and used Herschel Island as a winter base

1888–9 Lord Lonsdale became the first recorded tourist on Banks Island when he made a six-day excursion from the Mackenzie Delta to Cape Kellett while on a private expedition

1890 Warburton Pike accompanied by James Mackinlay of the Hudson's Bay Company explored the Back River area, the former for sporting reasons. They were the third group of Europeans ever to do so, the first and second being Back (1833–5) and Anderson and Stewart (1855)

1891–2 Robert E. Peary sledged from Inglefield Gulf on the west of Greenland to Navy Cliff in the north

1893–5 Peary crossed the Greenland ice cap again from Whale Sound to Independence Fjord

1893–6 Nansen and Sverdrup intended to use pack-ice drift to reach the North Pole in the specially constructed *Fram*. After becoming beset north-west of the New Siberian Islands, they drifted for 35 months, achieving a highest north of 85°57′N 100°E. Sverdrup eventually extracted the *Fram* from the ice west of Spitsbergen. Meanwhile Nansen and Lieutenant Johansen attempted to reach the Pole over the ice. They turned south 228 miles from their objective at 86°12′N 100°E. After many hardships and dangers they were rescued by chance in the Franz Josef archipelago

1894–7 Frederick Jackson, an English sportsman, charted much of Franz Josef Land. It was he who came across Nansen and Johansen and rescued them

1897 Salomon Andrée, a Swede, tried to balloon to the North Pole from Danes Island, Spitsbergen. Although it was known that he covered 295 miles, he disappeared. In 1930 the bodies of Andrée and his companions were found on White Island, where they had walked after abandoning the balloon on the ice. Photographs found with the bodies were successfully developed

1898–1902 Peary made his first serious attempt at the North Pole through Smith Sound in the *Windward*. Leaving the ship at Cape D'Urville he sledged to Fort Conger, proved that Bache 'Island' was in fact a peninsula, and returned to the *Windward* after suffering many hardships. He lost eight toes through frostbite. In later years he determined Greenland's northernmost point, which he called Cape Morris K. Jessup (83°39'N). In 1902 he set off northwards from Cape Hecla and reached a farthest north of 84°17'N

1898–1902 Otto Sverdrup in the *Fram* explored the area of Hayes Fjord (meeting Peary) and then Jones Sound. Sledging parties discovered Axel Heiberg Island and Amund Ringnes Island in the Sverdrup Islands group. They also reached Beechey Island in the south-west corner of Devon Island

1900–1 Prince Luigi Amadeo, Duke of Abruzzi, led a North Pole expedition which sailed to Franz Josef Land in the *Stella Polare*. Captain Umberto Cagni started with sledges from Teplitz Bay and achieved 86°34'N 65°20'E, which was 22 miles further north than Nansen had managed. Hampered by the ice drift, the party only just reached Harley Island and safety. Three men were lost during the expedition

1901 Zeigler reached a record (for a ship at that time) 82°04'N in the *America*

1903–6 Roald Amundsen in the *Gjöa* became the first man to navigate the Northwest Passage. His route was Lancaster Sound–Barrow Strait–Peel Sound–Rae Strait–Queen Maud Gulf–Coronation Gulf–Amundsen Gulf

1903 The Canadian North-West Mounted Police (NWMP) established a post at Herschel Island to control the behaviour of the American whalers there. It remained until 1964

1904 Canadian geologist R.P. Low claimed Ellesmere Island for Canada while doing a topographical survey in his ship *Neptune*

1905–6 The persistent Peary took the *Roosevelt* to Grant Land (Ellesmere Island). From there he set out for the North Pole with a large force of Eskimos and dogs. Bad weather and ice conditions prevented him from succeeding, but he achieved a record 87°06'N 70°W

1905–7 Alfred Harrison led a private British expedition which surveyed Herschel Island and visited Banks Island.

1906–7 Vilhjalmur Stefansson (who had Icelandic origins) took part in an expedition organised by Ernest de Koven Leffingwell. He studied the Eskimos in the Mackenzie Delta and Jones Islands

1906–7 Joseph-Elzear Bernier patrolled the islands in the District of Franklin in the *Arctic*. His aim was to take possession of all the islands for Canada. In 1907 Senator Pascal Poirier introduced the Resolution of possession of all lands and islands between the Canadian land mass and the North Pole. This became known as the sector theory. It was endorsed by Bernier and by Czarist Russia. Otto Sverdrup, whose own expedition had claimed part of the archipelago for his homeland, was disappointed by the $67,000 given him in exchange for the 'expropriation' of all his claims. The 1875 Nares travels were largely used, by way of priority of discovery, as a basis for British, therefore later Canadian, sovereignty claims

1906–8 Ludwig Mylius-Erichsen led a Danish expedition to north-east Greenland which carried out the first survey of this unknown area. He, Lieutenant Hagen and Jorgen Bronlund died of starvation largely due to inaccuracies in Peary's 1894 map. A second survey party of Lieutenant J.P. Koch, Aage Bertelsen and Tobias Gabrielsen survived and, during the following spring, discovered Bronlund's body, his diary and a bottle containing Hagen's vital sketch-charts

1907–9 Dr Frederick A. Cook claimed to have reached the North Pole on 21 April 1908, having set out from Axel Heiberg Island. This was disbelieved by many at the time, and is still in dispute. Whatever is the truth, Cook spent 14 months away from civilization in the Arctic regions, which was a considerable achievement of endurance

1908–9 Bernier continued his task of establishing sovereignty over the islands. He also found and recovered many relics of Parry's and Kellett's expeditions

1908–9 Peary claimed to have reached the North Pole on 6 April 1909, having set out from the *Roosevelt* which was in winter quarters at Cape Sheridan, Ellesmere Island. Ross Marvin drowned in a lead while returning with a support party. Peary's claim has been doubted by some because of the speed of his return. He travelled 485 miles as the crow flies in 16 days, an average of 30.3 miles a day at the very least

1908–12 Stefansson in a joint expedition with Rudolph Anderson studied Eskimos along the north coast of Canada and found the 'Blond Eskimos' of Victoria Island

1909–12 Ejnar Mikkelsen and Iver Iversen explored the north-east coast of Greenland and found messages from Mylius-Erichsen as well as two food depots, but failed to find his diaries. They learnt too that Peary's 'Peary Channel' to the west coast did not exist, and this led to a terrible journey back to base, where the two exhausted men arrived after the ship had departed. They existed there for a year before being rescued

1912 Three expeditions prospected Baffin Island for gold, but like Martin Frobisher 350 years earlier, did not have any success

1912 Knud Rasmussen crossed Greenland from Inglefield Gulf to Denmark Fjord, having set out from Thule. He took with him Peter Freuchen and two Eskimos. During the journey he charted and surveyed the 1,200 miles they travelled in a largely unknown region of Greenland. The information he gathered confirmed that Peary's outline of north-east Greenland was wrong

1912–14 Two Russian expeditions under Sedov and Broussilov ended in disaster while attempting to reach the North Pole. Sedov died in Franz Josef Land and the expedition returned. Broussilov's *St Anna* drifted north in the pack ice of the Kara Sea to 82°55′N (a drift of 1,540 miles in 18 months). Only two members of the crew survived

1913 J.P. Koch made the longest traverse of the Greenland ice with ponies, travelling from east to west from Denmark Harbour to Upernavik

1913–17 Donald MacMillan, an American, set out to find 'Crocker Land' which Peary claimed to have sighted north of Axel Heiberg Island. After reaching 82°30′N 108°22′W, he realized that the land did not exist, and returned

1913–18 The Canadian Arctic Expedition under Stefansson was split into a Southern Party which was to carry out scientific work in Coronation Gulf, and a Northern Party which was to explore in the *Karluk*. In the event the *Karluk* became ice-bound in the Beaufort Sea where she drifted for 3½ months before sinking. Two months later the crew reached Wrangel Island after the loss of eight men in the moving pack ice. Twelve survivors were eventually saved as a result of a heroic 600-mile journey to the Bering Strait in 17 days by the ship's mate Captain Robert Bartlett and one Eskimo. Meanwhile Stefansson, who had left the ship in order to hunt for game, carried out independent sledge journeys exploring the eastern seaboard of the Beaufort Sea, crossing Banks Island and visiting the Sverdrup and Parry Islands. The Southern Party successfully carried out its work

1915 W.E. Ekblaw discovered Tanquary Fjord in Ellesmere Island. It was next visited in 1961 by Geoffrey Hattersley-Smith of the Canadian Defence Research Board

1915 The Russian Admiral Vilkitski navigated the Northeast Passage east to west and carried out much hydrographical work in the Siberian Sea

1917 Knud Rasmussen, Thorild Wulff and Lauge Koch (a nephew of J.P. Koch) formed the Second Thule Expedition which explored the north-west of Greenland from North Star Bay. Wulff and an Eskimo died from hunger and exhaustion

1920–3 Dr Lauge Koch led the Danish Bicentenary Jubilee Expedition to north-west Greenland to continue mapping the coastline

1921–4 Rasmussen, on his famous Fifth Thule Expedition, spent 3½ years with a number of Greenland Eskimos and Danish scientists studying the Eskimos of Arctic Canada. In one year he traversed the entire Northwest Passage by dog sledge, a distance that had taken Franklin, Back, Richardson, Rae and others 25 years to complete

1921–4 George Binney was responsible for organizing the first of three Oxford Expeditions, which successfully carried out considerable work in the Arctic between the two World Wars. After a botanical and biological programme in 1921 in Spitsbergen, he led expeditions to North East Land in 1923 and 1924, using wireless for the first time and latterly a seaplane, the *Athene*

1923 Lieutenant Mittelholzer, a Swiss pilot, made several short flights in the area of Spitsbergen

1924 Amundsen and Riiser-Larson flew as far as 87°34′N and just managed to return to land

1925 Amundsen and Lincoln Ellsworth tried to fly to the North Pole from Spitsbergen in two Dornier flying boats. Six men flew in all. They reached 87°43′N, where they were forced to land through engine trouble and one flying boat was abandoned. They spent twenty-five days making a runway on the ice for the other flying boat, which then successfully took off and all returned safely

1926 Commander R.E. Byrd and Floyd Bennett flew from Spitsbergen, supposedly to the North Pole and back, in 15 hours on 9 May

1926 Sixteen people (including Amundsen, Ellsworth, Malmgren and the pilot Umberto Nobile) flew in an Italian dirigible, the *Norge*, over the North Pole, where they dropped American, Italian and Norwegian flags. They departed from Spitsbergen in the *Norge* on 11 May and landed at Teller, Alaska on 14 May after a flight of 3,300 miles

1926 Hubert Wilkins and Carl B. Eielsen explored considerable areas of the Beaufort Sea by a single-engine aeroplane from Point Barrow

1926 James Wordie, tutor of St John's College, Cambridge, who had previously been chief scientist on Shackleton's 1914–17 *Endurance* expedition to Antarctica, was on his fifth Arctic expedition mapping the area around Clavering Island in east Greenland. In 1929 the nearby Peterman Peak, the highest mountain then known within the Arctic Circle, was climbed. A cruise to Baffin Bay in 1934 was handicapped by difficult ice conditions, but in 1937 he successfully carried out his cosmic ray investigations, the excavation of Eskimo house sites and the survey of coastlines in north-east Baffin Island. One of Wordie's great achievements was to train men such as Sir Vivian Fuchs to carry on the work in polar regions which he had inspired

1926–31 An American Greenland Expedition under Professor William H. Hobbs lasted from 1926 to 1931

1927 Twenty-year-old H.G. (Gino) Watkins led an expedition to Edge Island, Spitsbergen

1927 Wilkins and Eielsen again flew from Point Barrow but were forced down by engine trouble many miles to the north-west of the point. After drifting on ice and walking, they safely made land

1928 General Umberto Nobile, Dr Finn Malmgren and 16 others flew over the North Pole in the airship *Italia*, which unfortunately crashed on the return journey to Spitsbergen. Half the party died or were missing presumed dead when the survivors were finally rescued. The German Captain Lundborg rescued Nobile, who was subsequently disgraced in Italy and went to Russia. A further tragedy was the loss of Amundsen in a rescue aeroplane

1930 Dr H.K.E. Krüger led the German Arctic expedition from north Greenland across Ellesmere Island to Lands Lokk, after which they were never seen again

1930–1 Gino Watkins led the British Arctic Air Route Expedition, which had the aim of mapping and surveying southern Greenland and studying the meteorology there, with an eye to an eventual air route between England and Canada. A meteorological station was established on the ice cap which Augustine Courtauld manned by himself from 3 December 1930 to 5 May 1931. He was rescued by Gino Watkins minutes after the fuel for his Primus stove ran out

1930–1 The German Greenland Expedition under Professor Alfred

	Wegener had one party working in West Greenland, one in the east at Scoresby Sound and a station on the ice cap. Wegener died returning from the ice cap station
1930–2	Ushakov, a Russian, mapped the islands of the unexplored Northern Land north-east of Cape Chelyuskin
1931	Hubert Wilkins attempted to cross the Arctic Ocean in an American submarine, the *Nautilus*
1932–3	The Second International Circumpolar Year manned 45 permanent research stations in the Arctic, Antarctica and to a lesser extent in the temperate and tropical zones. Fourteen nations participated
1932–3	Unable to raise sufficient funds to cross the Antarctic continent, Gino Watkins returned to East Greenland with Riley, Rymill and Chapman. On 20 August Watkins went out hunting in his kayak and was never seen again
1933	Alexander Glen led an 18-man summer expedition from Oxford to Spitsbergen to carry out a scientific programme
1933–4	Lieutenant Martin Lindsay, who had been a member of Watkins's first expedition to east Greenland, Andrew Croft and Lieutenant Daniel Godfrey RE successfully surveyed the then unknown mountains between Scoresby Sound and Mount Forel, including the highest peak within the Arctic Circle. They approached the area from the west coast of Greenland and carried out the longest self-supporting dog-sledge journey ever achieved of 1,080 miles
1933–8	Tom Manning had spent much of his life surveying and doing research in the Canadian Arctic. After two years in the district around Hudson Bay, he returned to England to organize an expedition to Southampton Island. Rowley, Baird and Bray accompanied him there, but returned in 1937, leaving him alone. They returned in 1938, when Bray was drowned. Manning, his wife Jackie, Rowley and Baird have had a great impact and influence on the opening up and development of Arctic Canada since the end of the Second World War
1934–5	An Oxford expedition, organized by Edward Shackleton, and under the leadership of Dr Noel Humphreys, was based at Etah in north-west Greenland. The six members became too dependent upon Eskimos, who were short of dog food, and the exploration of Ellesmere Island had to be curtailed
1935–6	A ten-man scientific expedition from Oxford, led by Glen with Andrew Croft as his second in command, carried out a comprehensive programme in North East Land. Two ice-cap

stations were created and manned, and a very detailed survey was made of the whole island, about the size of Wales. An intensive ten-month study of the ionosphere proved to be of considerable value in the development of radar. Croft and Whatman crossed Spitsbergen to Klaas Billen Bay

1937–8 A survey of the east coast of Ellesmere Island, to the south of Bache Peninsula, was undertaken by John Wright and Richard Hamilton, both of whom had previously been with Glen. Meanwhile the leader, David Haig-Thomas, sledged to Amund Ringnes Island

1937–8 Ivan Papanin and other scientists landed at the North Pole by ski plane in May 1937. There they began a well-organized drift on a large ice floe down to the east coast of Greenland, and were finally evacuated by an icebreaker in February 1938 near latitude 70°N

1937 Chkalov and Gromov, Russian pilots, flew over the North Pole non-stop from Moscow to North America

1940–4 Sub-Inspector Henry Larsen of the Royal Canadian Mounted Police (RCMP), commanding the 80-ton schooner *St Roch*, navigated through the Northwest Passage in 1940–2, following Amundsen's route but in the reverse direction, from west to east. In 1944 he sailed through Lancaster and Melville sounds, thence southwards through Prince of Wales Strait to Vancouver, completing a classic voyage in 86 days

1946 The end of the Second World War sparked off tremendous enthusiasm and initiative in opening up the Arctic regions. The Canadian Army and Air Force set the pace by carrying out a highly successful 3,000-mile journey by snow machine, called Exercise Musk-Ox, from Hudson Bay to Victoria Island and thence southward via Coppermine, Great Bear Lake and through the sub-Arctic to Grande Prairie, Alberta. The exercise was commanded by Baird, who had previously been in the Arctic with Manning, and Croft was the British representative. Many expeditions of all nationalities have worked and explored the Arctic regions. Most British ones have tended to be small, scientific specialized expeditions, often supported to some degree by the Royal Geographical Society and the Scott Polar Research Institute

1948–57 A series of scientific expeditions were led by Paul-Emile Victor on the Greenland ice cap

1952–4 Commander John Simpson RN with Hamilton as chief scientist led a Joint Services Expedition to Queen Louise Land, Greenland. Twenty-one scientists and servicemen carried out

	geological, glaciological and geomorphological work and established a weather station. At one stage Sunderland flying boats of the RAF were used to establish a temporary base on an ice-free lake 200 miles inland
1953–72	Dr Geoffrey Hattersley-Smith and a team of between 8 and 20 men carried out geological and other scientific research at Tanquary Fjord, Ellesmere Island, every summer throughout this period
1954	Scandinavian Airline Systems started regular commercial flights over the Arctic Ocean
1958	The nuclear-powered US submarine *Nautilus* crossed from the Pacific to the Atlantic Ocean without surfacing, passing over the North Pole on 3 August and crossing the Arctic Ocean in 96 hours
1959	The *Skate*, another nuclear-powered US submarine, surfaced at the North Pole on 17 March by breaking through the ice
1959–61	Victor led further French expeditions to Greenland
1960	The nuclear-powered US submarine *Seadragon* sailed the Northwest Passage from east to west
1963	Bjorn Staib, a Scandinavian, reached 86°N and escaped by 'boarding' an American floating ice station. Several such stations had been established
1965	A Scottish expedition consisting of Dr Hugh and Myrtle Simpson, Roger Tufft and Bill Wallace crossed the Greenland ice cap ski-hauling sledges
1967	Ralph Plaisted, an American, attempted to reach the North Pole by skidoo from north Ellesmere Island. He was evacuated at 83°36′N
1968	Ralph Plaisted successfully reached the North Pole on 19 April, having left from Ward Hunt Island on skidoos, with a team of four men
1968	Dr Hugh and Myrtle Simpson manhauled their sledge to 84°42′N on 26 March, north of Ward Hunt Island
1968–9	Wally Herbert, Major Ken Hedges RAMC, Allan Gill and Dr Roy (Fritz) Koerner of the British Trans-Arctic Expedition crossed the Polar ice cap using dogs, the first to do so. They left Point Barrow, Alaska on 21 February 1968, reached the North Pole on 5 April 1969 and landed on one of the Seven Islands, just to the north of North East Land on 29 May 1969. They had covered 3,720 miles in 476 days
1970	Count Monzino, an Italian millionaire and sportsman, reached the North Pole on 19 May 1970. His five-man team was supported by 13 Eskimos and 150 huskies

1971	The Anglo-Danish Trans-Greenland Expedition made the longest manhauling traverse over the ice cap under the leadership of D. Fordham and J. Andersen
1974–6	Naomi Uemura, Japanese, made a 7,450-mile solo journey with dogs from Greenland to Alaska
1977	Wally Herbert and Allan Gill attempted to circumnavigate Greenland by dog sledge and open boat
1977	The Russian nuclear-powered ship *Arktika* reached the North Pole from the Laptev Sea on 19 August 1977
1978	Naomi Uemura reached the North Pole alone from Cape Columbia, Canada
1978	A Japanese ten-man expedition led by Kaneshige Ikeda sledged to the North Pole
1979	Dmitry Shparo (Russian) led six skiers to the North Pole having departed from Henrietta Land. He was the first to reach the North Pole from Eurasia
1979–82	Transglobe Expedition – first circumpolar surface journey round Earth
1986	Will Steger reached the North Pole with dog teams and no air support
1986	Jean-Louis Etienne reached the North Pole solo
1988	Dmitry Shparo completed the first crossing of Arctic Ocean from Eurasia to North America
1989	Dmitry Shparo and his son crossed the Bering Strait on foot
1994	Børge Ousland completed the first unsupported journey to the North Pole
2000	David Hempleman-Adams made the first hot-air balloon flight to within one degree of latitude of the North Pole (1926 flight by Nobile was in a dirigible)
2001	Børge Ousland made the first solo crossing of the Arctic Ocean
2003	Rupert (Pen) Hadow made the first solo unsupported journey to the North Pole from North America
2005	Tom Avery's group make a dog journey to the North Pole in an attempt to recreate Peary's 1909 journey
2007	Belgians Alain Hubert and Dixie Dansercoer completed the first and only Arctic Ocean crossing from Cape Arkticheskiy in Siberia to Greenland

Appendix IV

Outline history of Antarctic exploration
compiled by P.M. Booth and R. Fiennes

There follows a list of some of the known Antarctic explorers. Apologies to all those, dead or alive, that we have unwittingly omitted.

650 AD	According to the legends of Polynesian Rarotonga, their chief Ui-te-Rangiora set out in the war canoe *Te-Iui-O-Atea* and headed south until the ocean was covered with 'white powder and great white rocks rose high into the sky'. The ancient Greeks named the constellation of stars above the North Pole *arctos* (bear). Later they dubbed the South Pole region as 'opposite the bear' or *anti-arctos*. Aristotle deduced that Earth was a sphere and that the northern land mass of Eurasia must be balanced by some then-unknown southern continent, *Antarktikos*. For over a thousand years religions branded as heresy such geographical theories not based on theology
1519–22	An expedition led by Ferdinand Magellan circumnavigated the world, confirming that it was round, in 1520
1570	Ortelius published a map called *Theatrum Orbis Terrarum* which showed an Antarctic continent: *'Terra australis non dum cognita'*
1578	Sir Francis Drake passed through the Magellan Straits. For two centuries it was thought that Terra del Fuego was part of a huge polar land mass
1642	Abel Tasman discovered Tasmania
1675	A British expedition under Antonio de la Roche may have discovered South Georgia
1699	The astronomer Edmond Halley was sent south by the Admiralty to seek for 'South unknown lands' and conduct a

survey of magnetic variation. He penetrated almost as far as South Georgia

1722 The colourful Frenchman, Yves Joseph de Kerguelen-Tremarec, in the *Fortune*, discovered the Kerguelen Islands south of 49°. He returned with tales of a paradise and was sent out a second time. Co-travellers on the latter journey put the lie to his storytelling and he was imprisoned. In that same year the Dutchman Jacob Roggeveen managed to reach almost to 65°S and reported the presence at that record southing of many birds, indicating nearby land

1738–9 Captain Jean-François-Charles Bouvet de Lozier sailed in the *Aigle* and *Marie* to annex Terra Australis (the South Land) for France. He discovered Bouvet Island (54°S in the South Atlantic) on 1 January 1739

1762 The ship *Aurora* reported discovering the Aurora Islands (53°S 38′W), now known as Shag Rocks

1768–71 Lieutenant James Cook, RN, in the *Endeavour* circumnavigated the world. One of his tasks was to find Terra Australis before the French. He did not do so, but he did establish that the land, if it existed at all, must be south of latitude 40°S

1771–2 Yves Joseph de Kerguelen-Tremarec in the *Fortune* discovered Kerguelen Island (49°S 70°E) on 12 February 1772, but thought it was part of the polar land mass

1771–2 Marion-Dufresne in the *Mascarin* discovered the Prince Edward Islands (13 January 1772) and the Crozet Islands (23 January 1772)

1772–5 Commander James Cook in the *Resolution* and Captain Tobias Furneaux in the *Adventure* attempted to find Bouvet 'Land' but failed to do so because its position had been incorrectly reported. Cook then sailed south and became the first European to cross the Antarctic Circle. In 1774 he achieved a latitude of 71°10′S before being stopped by pack ice. By 1775 he had circumnavigated the polar continent in high southern latitude and crossed the Antarctic Circle four times. On occasions he was within a day's sail of land, but never saw it. He took possession of South Georgia for King George III (17 January 1775) and discovered the South Sandwich Islands (30 January 1775). He ended his southern travels uncertain as to the existence of a southern continent

1776–80 James Cook in *Resolution* and Charles Clerke in the *Discovery* visited and named Prince Edward Islands, and visited Kerguelen Island

1778 British sealers started to use South Georgia as a base for their operations, followed by the Americans three years later. From this time sealers and whalers worked in the Southern Ocean regularly, visiting Kerguelen Island, Crozet Island and rediscovering Bouvet Island in 1808. This activity increased and in 1820 over 35 sealing and whaling expeditions took place, mainly British and American. Stocks of fur seals were soon exhausted

1810 An Australian sealing expedition in the *Perseverance* discovered Macquarie Island on 11 July

1819–20 William Smith, an Englishman, was blown off course in the *Williams* and discovered South Shetland Islands on 18 February. Returning later in the year, he landed and took possession of the islands on 16 October. The *Williams* returned once more to investigate the discovery with Edward Bransfield as master under the instructions of Captain Shirreff RN. On 30 January 1820, Bransfield landed on the north-western coast of Graham Land. He was probably the first man to land on the Antarctic continent

1819–21 Tsar Alexander I sent Captain Thaddeus von Bellingshausen and Captain M.P. Lazarev in the *Vostok* and *Mirny* to find the continent. Bellingshausen circumnavigated the world to the south of latitude 60°S and six times crossed the Antarctic Circle. He probably sighted land twice, but did not realize it; the first occasion was on 28 January 1820 (two days before Bransfield landed on Graham Land) when he probably saw Kronprinsesse Märtha Kyst (Princess Martha Coast). Thus it is likely that Bellingshausen is the discoverer of the Antarctic continent. He also discovered Peter I Island and Alexander I Island in January 1821

1820 The American sealer Nathaniel B. Palmer in the *Hero* saw the peaks of Graham Land at Palmer's Coast on 16 November 1820. There was also an ambitious British sealing voyage under Robert Fildes in the *Cora*

1820–1 Eleven men from the sealer the *Lord Melville* land on King George Island, in the South Shetland group, and spend the winter there

1821 The American sealer John Davis landed on the Antarctic peninsula

1821–2 The British sealer George Powell in the *Dove* and Nathaniel B. Palmer in the *James Monroe* discovered and charted South Orkney Islands on 6 December 1821

1822–3 Benjamin Morrell, an American sealer, in the *Wasp*, probably reached 70°14'S in the Weddell Sea. He also made the first recorded landing on Bouvet Island

1822–4 James Weddell, British, achieved 74°15'S 34°16'W (in the Weddell Sea) in the *Jane*

1828–31 Henry Foster in the *Chanticleer* charted Deception Island and made pendulum and magnetic observations. He also charted part of the Palmer Coast

1829–31 The first American government-sponsored exploring expedition led by Benjamin Pendleton in the *Seraph* visited South Shetland Islands in 1830. The *Seraph* reached 101°W south of 60°S

1830–2 John Biscoe, British, in the *Tula* and Avery in the *Lively* circumnavigated the continent, reached 69°S 10°43'E, discovered Enderby Land on 28 February 1831, Adelaide Island on 15 February 1832, and the northern Biscoe Islands. On 21 February 1832 he discovered land (an extension of Bransfield's and Palmer's discoveries) which he called Graham Land

1833–4 A British expedition under Captain Peter Kemp in the *Magnet* discovered Heard Island on 27 November 1833 and Kemp Land on 26 December of the same year

1837–40 The Frenchmen Jules Dumont d'Urville and C.H. Jacquinot in the *Astrolabe* and *Zelée* discovered Adélie Land on 22 January 1840, claiming it for France. They then discovered Clarie Coast (now Wilkes Coast) a few hours after Charles Wilkes, on 31 January 1840

1838–9 John Balleny, British, in the *Eliza Scott* and H. Freeman in the *Sabrina* discovered Balleny Islands on 9 February 1839 and saw land east of the Sabrina Coast. The first recorded woman to cross the Antarctic Circle was lost on board the *Sabrina*, which was owned by the Enderby brothers who were British oil merchants and paid for many British polar ventures over the years. The name and nationality of the lost woman is not known

1838–42 Lieutenant Charles Wilkes led the United States Exploring Expedition of five unsuitable and badly equipped ships. The coast of Wilkes Land (first sighted in December 1839) was charted, although some of Wilkes's work was later found to be erroneous. Nevertheless his contribution was considerable, and he was the first to recognize the land as a continent. William Walker in the 96-ton *Flying Fish* sailed to 70°S 105°W before being stopped by ice. Cadwaladar Ringgold in the *Porpoise* achieved 68°S 95°44'W

1839–43 James C. Ross in the *Erebus* and Francis R.M. Crozier in the *Terror* circumnavigated the continent and entered the Ross Sea. After discovering and charting the coast of Victoria Land and landing at Franklin and Possession Islands, they discovered Ross Island and the Ross Ice Barrier (or Ross Ice Shelf). Mount Erebus, an active volcano, was named by the expedition. They had achieved a furthest south of 78°10'S 161°27'W

1844–5 T.E.L. Moore in the *Pagoda* reached 67°50'S 39°41'E while carrying out an important magnetic survey

1872–6 George S. Nares, with British naval officers Wyville and Thompson, took the first steamship, the *Challenger*, to 66°40'S 78°22'E. They carried out important oceanographical ice researches and scientific observations at various southern islands

1873–4 The German sealer Dallman, in the *Grönland*, first charted Bismarck Strait

1874 American, British and German expeditions observed the Transit of Venus in December 1874 on Kerguelen Island

1882 The first International Geophysical Year (IGY). In the early nineteenth century Alexander von Humboldt persuaded the British and the Russians to set up a worldwide network of geomagnetic monitoring stations. Scientists Gauss, Maury and Weyprecht inspired further international cooperation, starting with IGY 1882. The next IGY was 1932–3, followed by 1957

1892–3 Members of a British whaling reconnaissance expedition carried out scientific work in the Joinville Islands and Trinity Peninsula

1892–3 A French expedition under Commandant Lieutard in the *Eure* reasserted sovereignty of Kerguelen Island and carried out hydrographic surveys

1892–3 The Norwegian whaler Carl Anton Larsen in the *Jason* discovered Foyne Coast and reached 64°40'S 56°30'W in the Weddell Sea. He also collected fossils on Seymour Island. The Scotsmen William Bruce and W. Burn Murdoch in the *Balaena* and *Active* discovered Active Sound

1893–4 C.A. Larsen discovered King Oscar II Land and Robertson Island. He reached 68°10'S in the Weddell Sea

1894–5 Norwegians Henrik J. Bull and Leonard Kristensen in the *Antarctic* reached Coulan Island (74°S). Lichens were discovered by Carsten Borchgrevink (a schoolmaster who had shipped as an AB) on Possession Island and Cape Adare. The latter was the first landing on Victoria Land (14 January 1895)

1897–9 Adrien de Gerlache, a Belgian, accompanied by Amundsen,

Dr Frederick Cook and others, found the Gerlache Strait between Graham Land and the Palmer Archipelago (which he named). The *Belgica* was beset and drifted with the ice for twelve months, the first exploring vessel to winter in the Antarctic. (Dr Frederick Cook was later the first claimant for reaching the North Pole)

1898–1900 The Norwegian Borchgrevink led a British expedition which explored the coast of Victoria Land. Borchgrevink and ten men wintered at Cape Adare, the first men to do so intentionally in the Antarctic. The *Southern Cross* reached 78°21′S, where it was stopped by the Ross Ice Shelf (which had retreated south over the years). Borchgrevink and Colbeck travelled over the ice to 78°50′S. Zoological, geological, meteorological and magnetic work was carried out. Dogs were used on the continent for the first time

1901–3 Professor Erich von Drygalski led a German expedition in the *Gauss* which discovered and mapped Kaiser Wilhelm II Land, exploring it by sledge. Drygalski once used penguin oil to stoke the ship's furnace when it ran out of fuel. In 1902 von Drygalski and his crew on the *Gauss* became trapped between the floes and, although stuck in the ice for a year, they undertook a valuable programme of scientific research

1901–4 The British National Antarctic Expedition, led by Commander Robert Falcon Scott RN, sailed to McMurdo Sound in the *Discovery*. Members of the expedition included Ernest Shackleton, Albert Armitage and Dr Edward Wilson. After wintering at the Sound they discovered King Edward VII Land. Scott, Shackleton and Wilson attempted to reach the South Pole, but were forced to turn back having achieved 82°17′S on 30 December 1902. They suffered from hunger, scurvy and exhaustion, only reaching safety with difficulty. W. Colbeck in the relief ship *Morning* discovered Scott Island. A balloon was used in Antarctica for the first time

1901–4 Otto Nordenskjöld and C.A. Larsen wintered on Snow Hill Island (east of Graham Land) with the Swedish South Polar Expedition. The first major sledge journey in Antarctica was made along the Larsen Ice Shelf to 66°S. The *Antarctic* was crushed and sunk by pack ice while trying to relieve them. All members were safely rescued by the Argentine vessel *Uruguay*

1902–4 Dr W.S. Bruce led a Scottish National Expedition in the *Scotia*, discovering the Caird Coast and carrying out the first oceanographic survey of the Weddell Sea

1903–5 Dr Jean-Baptiste Charcot wintered at Booth Island (off west Graham Land) in the *Français*. He discovered and charted Loubet Coast, and mapped parts of the Palmer Archipelago

1903–7 The Norwegian Captain Carl Larsen in the *Fortuna* established the first whaling station on South Georgia

1907–9 Ernest Shackleton led the British Antarctic Expedition in the *Nimrod* which wintered at Cape Royds, Ross Island. Shackleton, Armitage, Dr Eric Marshall and Frank Wild travelled south over the Ross Ice Shelf before crossing the Transantarctic Mountains (where they lost all their ponies). Hampered by very low temperatures (–70°F) and storms, they reached 88°23′S 163°E, which is 97 miles short of the South Pole. Professor David and Douglas Mawson reached the South Magnetic Pole and took possession of Victoria Land on 16 January 1909. Shackleton claimed the South Polar Plateau for King Edward VII on 9 January 1909

1908–10 Jean-Baptiste Charcot wintered at Petermann Island (Biscoe Islands) in the *Pourquoi Pas*, mapping new regions of the Graham Land coast and carrying out scientific work

1909 Douglas Mawson and Professor David were the first to reach the South Magnetic Pole

1910–12 A German expedition under Wilhelm Filchner in the *Deutschland* discovered Luitpold Coast and the Filchner Ice Shelf, and was beset in pack ice for nine months. The scientific measurements that they took showed that there were four alternating ocean layers in the Atlantic, transporting warmer and colder water south and north respectively, with the Weddell Sea playing a central role. While crossing the Southern Ocean around South Georgia, Wilhelm Brennecke, oceanographer on the *Deutschland*, had also noted that there was a sudden drop in the saltiness of the surface water flowing north. He did not realize it, but he had just discovered the Antarctic Convergence. At around 50°S, it is probably the most reliable boundary for defining the start of the Antarctic region and the distinctive cold, frigid waters to the south. All the key elements of the Atlantic Ocean circulation system had been found

1910–12 After establishing a base at the Bay of Whales, Roald Amundsen and five men reached the South Pole on 14 December 1911, using dogs and sledges. They spent three days in the area before returning safely

1910–12 Captain R.F. Scott RN in the *Terra Nova* wintered at McMurdo Sound. After depots had been laid, Scott and 11 men climbed the Beardmore Glacier. There, 300 miles short of the Pole, four men of the support party were sent back. About two weeks later the three remaining men of the support party turned back, leaving Scott, Captain L.E.G. Oates, Dr Edward Wilson, PO Edgar Evans and Lieutenant 'Birdie' Bowers to continue manhauling their sledges south. They reached the Pole on 17 January 1912, just over a month after Amundsen. Bitterly disappointed, Scott and his men marched back, gradually weakening from starvation and scurvy. Evans died first from exhaustion, then Oates walked out of the tent never to be seen again. Scott, Wilson and Bowers were trapped in their tent by a blizzard 11 miles from the next depot, where they died of hunger, cold and exhaustion. Their bodies and diaries were found by a search party in October on the Ross Ice Shelf

1911–12 Lieutenant Choku Shirase, Japanese, landed at the Bay of Whales and sledged to 80°05′S 156°27′W in King Edward VII Land

1911–14 Douglas Mawson led the Australasian Antarctic Expedition which discovered King George V Land, Queen Mary Land and the Shackleton Ice Shelf. Adélie Land was explored, as was the area of the South Magnetic Pole

1914–17 The *Endurance* became beset in the Weddell Sea while carrying the British Imperial Trans-Antarctic Expedition led by Sir Ernest Shackleton. The ship sank after a 700-mile drift. With strenuous efforts, Shackleton took his party to Elephant Island in the ship's boats. Leaving 22 of his men there, Shackleton and five men sailed in the 22-foot 6-inch boat *James Caird* to seek help. Through Shackleton's leadership and F.A. Worsley's brilliant navigation they safely reached the west coast of South Georgia. Shackleton, Worsley and T. Crean walked across the island to the whaling station at Grytviken. The main party was finally rescued by the Chilean vessel *Yelcho*

1914–17 Captain A.E. MacIntosh took the *Aurora* into the Ross Sea with the intention of linking up with Shackleton in the *Endurance*. A storm tore the *Aurora* from her moorings, stranding ten men on the ice. The ship was beset for nine months, and during the drift Oates Land was discovered. Of the ten men stranded on Ross Island, only seven were still alive when rescued by Captain John Davis in the *Aurora* in January 1917

1921–2 While en route for the Enderby Land area in the *Quest*, Shackleton died on 5 January 1922 at South Georgia. The expedition continued under Frank Wild, but failed to find any new land

1925–39 Neil Mackintosh (British), with the Discovery Investigations expeditions, conducted a series of marine investigations in Antarctic waters

1927 A Norwegian expedition managed to land on Bouvet Island, the world's most isolated island, 1,000 miles from anywhere

1928–9 The Australian aviator Hubert Wilkins, with American pilot Carl Eielson, pioneered air reconnaissance in Antarctica and was the first man to introduce the aeroplane and aerial photography to the Antarctic. He twice attempted to fly across the continent from the Weddell Sea to the Ross Sea, but failed. From aerial photographs he came to the erroneous conclusion that Graham Land was an archipelago

1928–30 Rear Admiral Richard E. Byrd USN (*City of New York*) took a biplane as part of a well-equipped expedition to Antarctica and made the first flight over the South Pole from his base in Little America I on the Ross Ice Shelf on 29 November 1929. He also explored by air King Edward VII Land and Byrd Land

1929–30 Sir Hubert Wilkins continued his aerial reconnaissance of Graham Land, unfortunately confirming the earlier erroneous discoveries. At the same time the Norwegian Lars Christensen (the *Norvegia*) with air reconnaissance made extensive discoveries in Queen Maud Land

1928–37 The five Norwegian (Christensen) Antarctic expeditions explored various areas, notably Enderby Land and Dronning Maud Land

1929–31 A joint British, Australian and New Zealand expedition under the command of Sir Douglas Mawson explored the area between Enderby Land and Wilhelm II Land, adding Princess Elizabeth and MacRobertson Lands to the map

1933–4 Lincoln Ellsworth, an American, attempted to fly across the Continent. His plane was wrecked on sea ice in the Bay of Whales

1933–5 Admiral Byrd returned to the Ross Ice Shelf. He established the largest base in the Antarctic up to that time, and became the first man to winter solo in Antarctica. He carried out extensive aerial exploration and successfully used tracked vehicles on the ice. From his aerial photographs it was shown that Graham Land is a peninsula

1934–5 Lincoln Ellsworth was prevented by bad weather from flying from Graham Land to the Ross Sea

1934–7 John Rymill and the British Graham Land Expedition wintered in the *Penola* in successive years at the Argentine Islands and Debenham Islands. They sledged to 72°S in King

George VI Sound, proving the channels reported by Wilkins in 1928–9 to be non-existent

1935–7 The Norwegian Mrs Mikkelson in the *Thorshavn* became the first woman to set foot on the continent

1935–9 Lincoln Ellsworth, piloted by H. Hollick-Kenyon, successfully flew across the continent from Dundee Island to the Bay of Whales in November 1935. He named Ellsworth Land and landed four times during the crossing. He continued aerial exploration in 1938–9

1938–9 The German explorer/airman, Alfred Ritscher, led an expedition which photographed some 350,000 square kilometres of Dronning Maud Land, and claimed part of it for Germany. On board the *Schwabenland* he carried two 10-ton Wal seaplanes. Initially their activities were kept quiet, but in March 1939 he announced having discovered and surveyed 135,000 square miles of Antarctica, and swastika markers were airdropped on to a series of points delineating territory which might, after the war, be claimed by Germany. No such claims were, in fact, ever advanced

1939–41 Admiral Byrd of the United States established two bases on the Ross Ice Shelf. Much useful exploration and scientific work was carried out. The expected permanent occupation was not effected because Congress did not provide funds in 1941

1943–5 John Marr and Andrew Taylor in the *Fitzroy*, the *William Scoresby* and the *Eagle*, led British government expeditions (Operation Tabarin) to establish science bases

1945 The Falkland Islands Dependencies Survey (forerunner of the British Antarctic Survey) was established by Edward Bingham and Kenneth Pierce-Butler (the *Fitzroy*, the *Trepassey*, the *John Biscoe* and the *William Scoresby*) to carry out scientific work in that part of Antarctica claimed by the British. Work has been continuous at many different bases until the present day

1946–7 Admiral Byrd led a vast American expedition involving some 4,800 men to Byrd Land. The aim of Operation Highjump was to test equipment in polar conditions: ice-breakers, helicopters, aircraft, radar and tracked vehicles (Weazels) were all taken and used. Although the expedition was short in duration, many aerial photographs were taken, but there was little ground control

1947–8 The United States sent two ice-breakers with helicopters (*Burton Island* and *Port of Beaumont*) to establish ground control points so that photographs taken during Operation Highjump could be used for mapping

1947–8 Commander Finn Ronne USN led a privately financed expedition. He based himself and his party of 21 men and 2 women (one of whom was his wife) at Stonington Island off the west coast of Graham Lane. Ronne explored large areas of the continent by air, photographing some 450,000 square miles for the first time (but with little or no ground control). His party was assisted by and assisted a British exploratory party also wintering at Stonington Island

1947+ After the Second World War various nations, including Argentina, Chile, United Kingdom, France, Australia, USA, USSR, South Africa, New Zealand, Japan, Belgium and Norway set up permanent bases in Antarctica. All claimant nations agreed to free access during the International Geophysical Year 1957–8. With the signing of the Antarctic Treaty in 1961 all territorial claims were placed in abeyance. Under the Treaty only work of a scientific nature can be carried out and all military activity is restricted to support for the scientists

1949–52 A Norwegian-British-Swedish Expedition led by the Norwegian Captain John Giaever carried out scientific work in Queen Maud Land, making the first seismic traverse on the inland ice sheet

1955–8 The Soviet Comprehensive Antarctic Expedition established bases on the Knox Coast (Mirny), at the magnetic pole (Vostok), and at the Pole of Inaccessibility (Sovetskaya) (82°06′S 54°58′E) as part of the International Geophysical Year effort. The two inland bases were established by using motorized sledges

1955–8 As their part of the IGY, New Zealand, Australia, South Africa and Britain funded the Commonwealth Trans-Antarctic Expedition led by Dr Vivian Fuchs (the *Theron* and the *Magga Dan*). Dr Fuchs and Sir Edmund Hillary led separate groups to the South Pole from opposite coasts and then met at the Pole. Dr Fuchs completed the first land traverse of Antarctica (using the Shackleton resupply plan of two separate expeditions).

Sir Edmund Hillary led a New Zealand team which laid supply depots from Scott Base on the Ross Ice Shelf and reached the South Pole on 3 January 1958

Dr Vivian Fuchs led a party from Shackleton Base on the Weddell Sea via South Ice Base to the South Pole, which he reached on 20 January 1958. Two days later both the Fuchs and Hillary groups left for Scott Base which they reached on 2 March 1958. The Fuchs group had completed a journey of

2,180 miles in 99 days. Seismic ice depth soundings and gravity measurements were made throughout the journey. Much geological and glaciological work was accomplished

After the 1957 IGY innumerable localized expeditions by government scientists of many nations have taken place, some highly ambitious and some on an annual basis. Many have been fine examples of cooperation between two or more countries. In addition, a handful of private expeditions have managed to raise the considerable sums needed to visit and operate in Antarctica

1956–7 During Operation Deep Freeze I, the Americans established bases on Ross Island (McMurdo Station) and at Kainan Bay. An airstrip was built on the Ross Ice Shelf. On 31 October 1956 Admiral George Dufek (Operation Deep Freeze II commander) landed at the South Pole where, by February 1957, the Scott–Amundsen Base had been established. Other coastal stations were placed, and Byrd Station was established using tractors from Little America. Under Paul Siple the first team wintered at the South Pole

1957–8 International Geophysical Year. Twelve nations established 55 stations on the Antarctic continent and its surrounding islands. Scientific work of many kinds was carried out, work which is still being continued today. The year was remarkable for the spirit of international cooperation which it engendered amongst those taking part. The USSR established Vostok Base

1959 The Antarctic Treaty was initialled by twelve nations

1961 The Antarctic Treaty was signed, being due for review in 1991

1979–81 Transglobe Expedition's Antarctic crossing by Fiennes, Burton and Shepard. They were the first to cross from coast to coast as a single team (not as a pincer, 2-team project). 'The staggering achievement of linking up trans-polar expeditions, north and south, into a journey encircling the earth was proposed by Charles de Brosses, an eighteenth-century French geographer, but it had to wait until the idea was revived by Lady Virginia Fiennes and her husband, the authorities having ridiculed it, decided to prove that it could be done' (Quoted from *The Explorations of Antarctica: The Last Unspoilt Continent* by Professor G.E. Fogg and David Smith)

1985–6 Robert Swan, Roger Mear and Gareth Wood manhauled to the South Pole from Ross Island, covering a distance of 828.3 miles without aerial resupply. Their ship (the *Southern Quest*) sank off Ross Island

1986–7 Norway's Monica Kristensen (the *Aurora*) led an air-supplied attempt with dog teams to reach the South Pole by Amundsen's route and then return to the Bay of Whales. Severe snow conditions forced the teams to turn back only 273.4 miles short of the Pole

1989 Metz and Murden on skidoos were the first women overland to the South Pole

1989–90 A little-known journey by four Norwegian skiers using dog teams and air support crossed Antarctica. Two of this team were airlifted out at the Pole

1989–90 A six-man international team led by Will Steger (USA) and Jean-Louis Etienne (France) used dog teams, air and (USSR) tractor resupply to cross the longest span of Antarctica (4,007.8 miles) via the South Pole

1989–90 The South Tyrolean Reinhold Messner and the German Arved Fuchs crossed the Antarctic continent by manhaul and were resupplied by air

1992–3 The Norwegian Erling Kagge manhauled solo and unsupported to the South Pole

1992–3 The American Ann Bancroft led the American Women's Expedition which manhauled (womanhauled) with air resupply to the South Pole

1992–3 The Pentland South Pole Expedition achieved the first unsupported crossing of the Antarctic continent by Fiennes and Stroud

1994 Norwegian Liv Arnesen was the first woman to ski solo to the South Pole

1996 The Norwegian Børge Ousland completed the first unsupported solo crossing of Antarctica (with expert use of wind power)

1997–8 Belgians Alain Hubert and Dixie Dansercoer set a record for the longest distance covered in one day (271 kilometres) when crossing from Crown Bay to McMurdo

The Antarctic Treaty

To date the continent of Antarctica remains about the only territory which has not been fought over. This happy status is due mostly to the continent's remoteness, but as technology has increasingly trivialized the word 'remote', so it has become more important for all interested countries to reach a formal agreement as to what is and is not mutually acceptable behaviour 'down south'. The 1961 treaty is still accepted by all relevant signatories and is treated as 'indefinite'.

Glossary of Selected Snow and Ice Terms

Temperature conversion: Although Celsius can be converted to a rough approximation of Fahrenheit by multiplying by two and then adding 32, a more exact conversion is degrees Fahrenheit = (degrees Celsius × 9/5) + 32. Similarly, Fahrenheit can be converted to a rough approximation of Celsius by subtracting 32 and then dividing by two, but a more exact conversion is degrees Celsius = (degrees Fahrenheit – 32) × 5/9

ablation	All processes by which snow, ice or water in any form is lost from a glacier, floating ice or snow cover. These include melting, evaporation, calving, wind erosion and avalanches. Also used to express the quantity lost by these processes
bergschrund	The fissure which separates downwards moving glacier ice from the bordering rock wall and any ice apron attached to it. When there is no apron it is called a *randkluft*
calving	The breaking away of a mass of ice from a floating glacier, ice front or iceberg
cirque glacier	A glacier which occupies a separate rounded recess which it has formed on a mountainside
close pack ice	Composed of floes mostly in contact. Ice cover 7/10ths to 9/10ths
fast ice	Sea ice which remains fast along the coast, where it is attached to the shore, to an ice wall, to an ice front, or over shoals, or between grounded icebergs. Fast ice may extend a few metres or several hundred kilometres from the shore. Fast ice may be more than one year old. When its surface level becomes higher than about two metres above sea level, it is called an ice shelf
finnesko	Boots made entirely of soft fur. Often lined with sennegrass, an Arctic plant that absorbs moisture well

first-year ice	Floating ice of not more than one-year's growth developing from young ice. Thickness from 30 centimetres to 2 metres. Characteristically level where undisturbed by pressure, but where ridges occur they are rough and sharply angular
frazil ice	Fine spicules or plates of ice in suspension in water
frost smoke	Fog-like clouds, due to the contact of cold air with relatively warm water, which appear over newly formed leads, or leeward of the ice edge, and which may persist while new ice is forming
grease ice	A later stage of freezing than frazil ice, when the spicules and plates of ice have coagulated to form a thick soupy layer on the surface of the water. Grease ice reflects little light, giving the sea a matt appearance
growler	A piece of ice almost awash, but often invisible to a ship's pilot until too late
hail	Precipitation of small balls or pieces of ice (hailstones) with a diameter ranging from 5 to 50 millimetres, or sometimes more, falling either separately or agglomerated into irregular lumps. When the diameter is less than about 5 millimetres, the balls are called ice pellets
hoosh	Stew, usually made from pemmican and melted snow; a primary food on the sledging trail
hummock	A mound or hillock of broken floating ice forced up by pressure. May be fresh or weathered. A corresponding projection may also occur on the underside of the ice canopy and is called a bummock
ice blink	White glare on the underside of clouds, indicating the presence of pack ice or an ice sheet which may be beyond the range of vision
icefall	Similar to a waterfall, but frozen. A steep fall or flow of ice, sometimes from great heights
ice fog	A suspension of numerous minute ice crystals in the air, reducing visibility at the earth's surface. The crystals often glitter in the sunshine. Ice fog produces optical phenomena such as luminous pillars and small haloes
icefoot	Fringe of ice at shoreline, common in Antarctica
ice rind	A brittle, shiny crust of floating ice, formed on a quiet surface by direct freezing or from grease ice, usually in water of low salinity. Thickness less than 5 centimetres. Easily broken by wind or swell, commonly breaking in rectangular pieces

ice rise	A mass of ice resting on rock and surrounded either by an ice shelf, or partly by an ice shelf and partly by sea. No rock is exposed and there may be none above sea level. Ice rises often have a dome-shaped surface. The largest known is about a hundred kilometres across
ice shelf	Where glaciers meet a coastline they can continue to flow out over the sea for many miles to form floating or grounded ice piers, known as ice shelves or floating glacier tongues. This happens when the seaward flow rate is greater than the speed at which the action of the sea can undermine and shear off the advancing ice front.
katabatic	Type of wind in which air flows down a slope
miles	Also called nautical miles. Unit of distance equal to 1/100th of a (geographic)degree of latitude, about 15 per cent longer than the common (statute) mile
miles (statute)	Unit of distance on land equal to 5,280 feet or 1,760 yards
multi-year ice	Sea ice two summers or more old
névé	Granular type of snow, compacted into glacial ice
nilas	A thin elastic crust of floating ice, easily bending on waves and swell and rafting under pressure. It has a matt surface and is up to 10 centimetres thick. When under about 5 centimetres in thickness it is very dark in colour; when more than 5 centimetres, rather lighter
pemmican	Mixture of precooked dried meat and lard used as a mainstay of the diet on the polar sledging trail (*see* hoosh)
polynya	Area of open water in an otherwise ice-covered sea, often caused by the strong flow of warm winds
powder snow	A thin, dry snow surface which is composed of loose, fresh ice crystals
pressure ice	A general term for floating ice which has been squeezed together and in places forced upwards, when it can also be described as rafted ice, hummocked ice or ridge
pulk	A light fibreglass manhaul sledge
rafted ice	A form of pressure ice in which one floe overrides another
ridging	Pressure process by which floating ice becomes forced up in ridges

rime	A deposit of ice composed of grains more or less separated by trapped air, sometimes adorned with crystalline branches, produced by the rapid freezing of supercooled and very small water droplets
rotten ice	Floating ice which has become honeycombed in the course of melting, and which is in an advanced state of disintegration
sastrugi	Sharp, irregular ridges formed on a snow surface by wind erosion and deposition. The ridges are parallel to the direction of the prevailing wind
sea ice	Layer of ice on the surface of the sea that breaks up at least annually
second-year ice	Sea ice which has not melted in the first summer of its existence. By the end of the second winter it attains a thickness of 2 metres and more. It stands higher out of the water than first-year ice. Summer melting has somewhat smoothed and rounded the hummocks, while accentuation of minor relief by differential melting may have caused others to develop. Bare patches and puddles are usually greenish-blue
shuga	An accumulation of spongy white ice lumps, a few centimetres across, formed from grease ice or slush and floating on the sea's surface
snotsicle	A thread of frozen mucus, suspended from the nose of the owner
snow-blindness	Impairment of vision resulting from exposure to snow glare, and causing intense pain
snow bridge	Snow that has filled the gap in a crevasse. Often strong enough to support weight, allowing passage across the gap
verglas	A thin sheet of see-through ice as though painted on to rock
water sky	Dark streaks on the underside of clouds, indicating the presence of open water or broad leads in the floating ice

(Note: Words such as glacier that are defined and discussed in the text are omitted from this Glossary)

Picture Acknowledgements

The author and publishers would like to thank the following copyright-holders for permission to reproduce images in this book:

© Mary Evans Picture Library: 2
© Corbis: 3, 4, 5, 6, 7, 8
© Bryn Campbell/*Observer*: 14
© Simon Grimes: 16, 25, 36
© Mike Hoover: 17
© John Cleare: 26
© Mike Stroud: 29, 30
© Ian Parnell: 39

All other images are drawn from the author's own collection.

The author and publishers have made all reasonable efforts to contact copyright-holders for permission, and apologise for any omissions or errors in the form of credits given. Corrections may be made for future printings.

Index